FOOD EXPERTS
ACROSS THE COUNTRY AGREE:
THIS IS THE BEST
NATURAL FOODS COOKBOOK...

"A delicious surprise!"
Atlanta Journal

"Full of all kinds of recipes, from those
loved by health food fadists...
to just wholesome dishes!"
Chicago Tribune

"Most impressive!"
Minneapolis Tribune

"Good recipes abound... well-edited
and easy to follow."
Newsday

"The best and certainly the most complete!"
Baltimore Sun

"A treasury of domestic and foreign dishes
that should close the culinary gap!"
Cincinnati Enquirer

"Marvelous recipes for using natural foods."
House & Garden

The New York Times Natural Foods Cookbook

Jean Hewitt

AVON
PUBLISHERS OF BARD, CAMELOT, DISCUS AND FLARE BOOKS

Design: Nicole de Jurevev/Words Pictures & Such
Editorial Coordination: Leslie J. Elliott Associates
Associate Editor: Elizabeth Phelan

Assistant Designer: Estelle Walpin
Researcher & general assistant: Janet Doeden

The type face is Palatino and Palatino Semibold.

AVON BOOKS
A division of
The Hearst Corporation
959 Eighth Avenue
New York, New York 10019

First Avon Printing, November, 1972.

AVON TRADEMARK REG. U.S. PAT. OFF. AND
FOREIGN COUNTRIES, REGISTERED TRADEMARK—
MARCA REGISTRADA, HECHO EN CHICAGO, U.S.A.

Printed in the U.S.A.

WFH 23 22 21 20 19 18

This book is dedicated to
the thousands of people across the country
who believe in, and practice,
the natural way of eating for good health—
and especially to those who
contributed recipes to this collection.

TABLE OF CONTENTS

INTRODUCTION

Following the entry for each chapter are the names of the recipes and their contributors as they appear in the chapter except in cases where the same contributor offered more than one recipe; recipes not listed were submitted anonymously or are from the author's files.

J. Koppes, West Salem, Ohio; Lentil Soup I, **Amy Leos, Cambridge, Mass.**; Lentil Soup II, **Virginia Samet, Natural Life Styles, New Paltz, N.Y.**; Black Bean Soup, **Mrs. Don A. McQueen, Big Sur, Calif.**; Bay Borscht, **David Lytton, Sonoma Natural Foods, Sebastopol, Calif.**; Cauliflower Soup, **Deborah Ballon, West Hempstead, N.Y.**; Celery Chowder, Potato Chowder, **Grandma Jenny Doeden, Honey Creek, Wis.**; Egg and Lemon Soup with Fiddleheads, **Mary Ann Taylor, Boston, Mass.**; Fresh Pea Soup, **The Leopard, New York, N.Y.**; Fruit Bat Soup, **Hera Ware Owen, "Eating in the South Seas," Koror, Caroline Islands**; Garlic Soup, **Mrs. Milton V. Wilker, Hasbrouck Heights, N.J.**; Spring Soup, **Patricia Ullberg, Sunderland, Md.**; Black Mushroom Soup, Cold Cucumber Soup I, Homemade Chicken Broth, **Diana Gorenstein, Princeton, N.J.**; Potato Soup, Connecticut Garden Gazpacho, **Nancy Siegler, Rowayton, Conn.**; Sweet Potato Soup, **Marnie Potash, West Orange, N.J.**; Brown Potato Soup, **Lela Klinger, Lima, Ohio**; Danish Green Tomato Soup, **Jane S. Lehac, Woodstock, N.Y.**; Cold Cucumber Soup II, **P. Smith, New York, N.Y.**; Cold Cucumber Soup III, **Barbara D. Slack, Medfield, Mass.**; Best Barley Soup, **Victor Boff Health Foods, New York, N.Y.**; Zucchini Soup, **Myrle M. Burk, Waterloo, Iowa**; Blender Vegetable Cream Soup, **Sondra Wachtfogel, Kings Park, N.Y.**; Vegetable Bean Soup, **Esther Goedel, New York, N.Y.**; Vegetable Soup Italian Style, **Ellen Yanch, Manhasset, N.Y.**; Wine and Clove Soup, **Stefania Scoggins, Chatsworth, Calif.**; Blender Tomato-Avocado Soup, **Ann Wigmore, Hippocrates Health Institute, Boston, Mass.**; Yogurt Gazpacho, **Zen Hashery, Serendipity III, New York, N.Y.**; Amazing Fruit Soup, **Irene Borger, Old Bennington, Vt.**; Musart's Fruit Soup, **Musart Spiral Foods, New York, N.Y.**; Rose Hips Soup, **Mrs. Charles A. Hallett, New York, N.Y.**; Bone Marrow Gruel, **Malcolm "Tink" Taylor, "Commentary on Conservation," Holderness, N.H.**; Macrobiotic Super Soup with Buckwheat Dumplings, **Andy Roman, New College, Sarasota, Fla.**

4 FISH 56

Clam Pie, **Marie Foster, Harwich, Mass.**; Baked Flounder Roll-Ups, **Hannah Bostwick, N.J.**; Camp Fish Stew, **Durward L. Allen, Dept. of Forestry & Conservation, Purdue Univ., Lafayette, Ind.**; Fish in Tomato Sauce, **Miriam Desylva, Mount Vernon, Ohio**; Salmon Loaf, **Mrs. A. Wright, Broadalbin, N.Y.**; Salmon Steaks with Scallions, **Ursula Larizza, New York, N.Y.**; Flower of Shrimp, **Jane McCallum, New York, N.Y.**; Shrimp with Vegetables, **Janet McClelland, New York, N.Y.**; Skewered Shrimp with Rice, **Esther Goedel, New York, N.Y.**; Shrimp with Yogurt, **Laurie Kleinberg, South Pasadena, Calif.**; Namasu, **Patsy T. Mink, Member of Congress, Hawaii**; Baked Trout, **Philip Roos, Boulder, Colo.**

5 MEAT & POULTRY 66

Pocket of Gold, **Edith Marks, New York, N.Y.**; Musart Strip Beef, Musart Sprouted Beef Loaf, **Musart Spiral Foods, New York, N.Y.**; Organic Chuck Roast, **Mrs. Melvin E. Corders, Organic Farms and Mission, Henning, Minn.**; Buttermilk Roast, **Else L. Sappington, Fort Worth, Tex.**; Marinated Flank Steak, **Jane Margulies, New York, N.Y.**; Hamburgers Plus, **Phyllis Title, Plainview, N.Y.**; Middle-Eastern Beef, Caraway Chicken Livers, **Robert Hannon, Greenwich, Conn.**; Health-ful Chop Suey, **Veda Brenneman, New Castle, Ind.**; Cracked Wheat Casserole, **Mrs. Daniel Abbott, East Concord, N.H.**;

Plantation Casserole, **Warren L. Vincent, Hempstead, Tex.**; Soy Chili, **Judith Zoll, Princeton, N.J.**; Swedish-Style Meatballs with Caper Sauce, **H. A. Insinger, St. Charles, Mo.**; Six-Layer Dinner, Hunter's Loaf, **Mrs. R. Glenn Doeden, Honey Creek, Wis.**; Beef 'n Wheat Meatballs, Chicken Tandoori, **Mother Nature's, Scarsdale, N.Y.**; Potato Meat Loaf, **Mabel Burkholder, Fleetwood, Pa.**; Meat Loaf, **Mrs. Samuel Kalmer, Stamford, Conn.**; Rice-Stuffed Meat Loaf, **Mrs. George H. Hanson, Idaho Falls, Idaho**; Soy Meat Loaf, **E. A. Dietrich, Dietrich's Organic Farm, Genoa, Ohio**; Sunflower Meat Loaf, **Natural Sales Co., Pittsburgh, Pa.**; Veal Casserole, **Marnie Potash, West Orange, N.J.**; Honey of a Lamb, **Hannah Bostwick, N.J.**; Lamb Loaf, **Elsa A. Weich, Germantown, N.Y.**; Pork and Vegetable Skillet Supper, **Mrs. William Bennett, Oregon, Wis.**; Whole Wheat Scrapple, **Grandma Jenny Doeden, Honey Creek, Wis.**; Peachy Liver for Liver Haters, **Eve Kaufman, Natural Life Styles, New Paltz, N.Y.**; Liver 'n Onions, **Patrice Fisher, Valley Stream, N.Y.**; Kidneys on Toast, **Pauline Werner, Pittsburgh, Pa.**; Sautéed Liver Balls, **Grace Perryman, West Islip, N.Y.**; Freezer Liver, **Dorothy P. Angel, Park Ridge, Ill.**; Tripe Stew, **Mrs. Joseph Gnocchi, Monroe, N.Y.**; Sesame Baked Chicken, **Sarah Jackson, The Healthway, Westport, Conn.**; Chicken with Yogurt, **Natural Life Styles, New Paltz, N.Y.**; Honeyed Chicken, **Evelyn Leibu, New York, N.Y.**; Chicken and Egg Casserole, **Margaret B. White, Monterey, Mass.**; Chicken Carrie, **Rose Schaffer, West Orange, N.J.**; Hot Chicken Salad, **Mrs. Leon Morris, Connellsville, Pa.**; Luscious Chicken Livers, **Ursula Larizza, New York, N.Y.**; Chicken Livers with Sour Cream, **Jill A. Miller, Natick, Mass.**; Giblet Sauté, **Isabel Gordon, Green's Farms, Conn.**

6 VEGETARIAN MAIN DISHES   100

Eggplant Steaks, **Brownie's Creative Cookery, New York, N.Y.**; Eggplant and Cheese Casserole, **Mrs. Irving Troemel, Ridgewood, N.J.**; Peas Roast, **Organic Foods Co-op, Berkeley, Calif.**; Zucchini-Cheese Casserole, **Diana Gorenstein, Princeton, N.J.**; Zucchini Frittata, **Constance Weikart, Grabill, Ind.**; Winter Casserole, **Leonard's Eco-Farms, Westport, Conn.**; Carrot Loaf, **Mrs. C. W. Lynn, Foods for Life, Orlando, Fla.**; Avocado Burgers, **Gary Doore, Ecology Action, San Diego State, San Diego, Calif.**; Lima Bean Loaf, Sunflower Seed Loaf, **Mrs. Andrew J. Koppes, West Salem, Ohio**; Barley Lentil Kasha, **Irene Williams, East Brunswick, N.J.**; Lentil-Millet Patties with Tomato Sauce, Red and Sweet Curry, **Judy Taylor, New York, N.Y.**; Lentil Stew, Soy Burgers, **Shoshana Margolin, New York, N.Y.**; Lentil and Barley Stew, **Maudallen Sandford, Azle, Tex.**; Cajun's Delight, **Warren L. Vincent, Hempstead, Tex.**; Vegetarian Sausages, **Hannah Stafford, Haddon Heights, N.J.**; Soybean and Nut Loaf, **Ted and Roberta Gill, None Such Diner, Yucaipa, Calif.**; Soybean and Vegetable Casserole, **Tobi Rosenstein, Santa Monica Co-op, Los Angeles, Calif.**; Pressure-Cooked Soybeans, **Mother Nature's, Scarsdale, N.Y.**; Baked Soybeans I, **Linda Becker, New York, N.Y.**; Baked Soybeans II, **Mrs. Robert Fatzingero, Coopersburg, Pa.**; Soy-Rice Burgers, **Carol Kort, Cambridge, Mass.**; Soybean Patties, **Fred A. Cagle, Jr., Dept. of Botany, Univ. of Minn., Minneapolis, Minn.**; Broiled Soy Cakes, **Helen McCutcheon, Lakeland, Fla.**; Millet-Stuffed Peppers, Farinata, **Anna Pardini, Big Indian, N.Y.**; Millet Stew, **Susan Hillyard, Scarsdale, N.Y.**; Millet 'n Vegetables, Millet Casserole I, Buckwheat and Peanut Casserole, Wild Rice and Buckwheat Loaf, **A. Scheresky, Glen Ewen, Saskatchewan, Canada**; Millet Soufflé, Millet Casserole II, **M. M. Machlowitz, Glenside, Pa.**; Vegetable Rice Casserole, **Judith Muschel, New York, N.Y.**; Brown Rice Oriental Style, **Mrs. A. L. Wernick, Orange, Conn.**;

Buckwheat Groats Loaf, **Avis Hall, East Hampton, N.Y.**; Buckwheat-Stuffed Cabbage Rolls, **Mrs. A. Balaban, New York, N.Y.**; Wheat Loaf, **Charles A. Geoffrion, Bloomington, Ind.**; Wheat Germ Loaf, **Mrs. Samuel Kalmer, Stamford, Conn.**; Wheat and Nut Loaf, **Mrs. Hal Campbell, The Diet Shop, Oklahoma City, Okla.**; Nut Casserole, **Ann McVeigh**; Nut Loaf, **Deon Kaner, San Rafael, Calif.**; Eggs Grinnell, **Bev Post, Franklin, N.J.**; Egg Foo Yong, **Lillian E. Stutz, R. N., Wheaton, Md.**

7 VEGETABLES   130

Jerusalem Artichokes, **Vita-Green Farms, Vista, Calif.**; Asparagus Casserole, Basil Carrots, **Mrs. Constance Weikart, Grabill, Ind.**; Spanish Green Beans, **Nova Messler, Tulsa, Okla.**; Pickled Beets, **Frances Kolbe, Maryland, N.Y.**; Sweet and Sour Cabbage, **S. J. Leiter, Boston Univ., Boston, Mass.**; Rice-Stuffed Cabbage Rolls, **A. Scheresky, Glen Ewen, Saskatchewan, Canada**; Toasted Carrots, **Esther Goedel, New York, N.Y.**; Carrot Casserole, **Oscar Muller, Long Beach, N.Y.**; Fruited Carrots, **Mrs. Leon Leffer, New York, N.Y.**; Minted Cauliflower, **Ursula Larizza, New York, N.Y.**; Chick-Peas, **Red Owl Health Foods, Westfield, Mass.**; Chick-Pea Sauce, **Leonard's Eco-Farms, Westport, Conn.**; Bollos de Mazorca, **Bertha Giraldo, New York, N.Y.**; Eggplant Parmigiana, **Mrs. Richard B. Gould, New York, N.Y.**; Eggplant and Squash, **Mrs. Russell Smith, Nanticoke, Pa.**; Eggplant Croquettes, **Reva Rudley, Matawan, N.J.**; Eggplant Casserole, **Edward Schadler, St. Joseph, Mich.**; Eggplant Hush Puppies, **Claire Gunter, Orange, Tex.**; Letcho, **Shoshana Margolin, New York, N.Y.**; Baked Eggplant, **Organic Foods Co-op, Berkeley, Calif.**; Eggplant Provencale, **Alys Monitto, New York, N.Y.**; Spring Greens Puree, Pokeweed au Gratin, **Bev Post, Franklin, N.J.**; Beet Greens, **Edith Ilsley, Asbury, N.J.**; Dandelion Greens I, **Dorothy Warner, Stewartstown, Pa.**; Dandelion Greens II, Pokeberry or Poke Salet, **Durward L. Allen, Department of Forestry and Conservation, Purdue Univ., Lafayette, Ind.**; Comfrey Greens, **June Salander, Rutland, Vt.**; Radish and Spinach Greens, **Mrs. Milton V. Wilker, Hasbrouck Heights, N.J.**; Brown Rice and Spinach Casserole, **Jane S. Lehac, Woodstock, N.Y.**; Green Sauce and Noodles, **Lydia Stonier, New York, N.Y.**; Leeks, **H. A. Insinger, St. Charles, Mo.**; Leek and Vegetable Stew, **Else L. Sappington, Fort Worth, Tex.**; Sweet and Sour Lentils, **Lynne Lederman, Great Neck, N.Y.**; Okra Stew, **Jeanette G. Smith, New Rochelle, N.Y.**; Stewed Okra, **Elsa A. Weich, Germantown, N.Y.**; Parsnip Pie, **The Good Earth, Fairfax, Calif.**; Peas and Onions, **Mary Ann Taylor, Boston, Mass.**; New Potatoes, **James Moran, New York, N.Y.**; Tzimmes Deluxe, **Frances Alper, New York, N.Y.**; Curried Soybeans, **Ellen Sheinfeld, New York, N.Y.**; Soybean Pistou, **Mrs. Vukasin Asanovic, New York, N.Y.**; Soybeans with Tomato Sauce, **Marilyn Machlowitz, Princeton, N.J.**; Soybean Cheese or Curd, **Mrs. C. W. Lynn, Foods for Life, Orlando, Fla.**; Squash Blossoms, **Monastery of our Lady of the Rosary, Summit, N.J.**; Fried Green Tomatoes, **Mrs. Leon Leffer, New York, N.Y.**; Basic Tomato Sauce, **Irvin L. Peterson, Nebraska Wesleyan Univ., Lincoln, Neb.**; Baked Honeyed Turnip, **Margaret Simko, New York, N.Y.**; Vegetable Mélange, **Gloria Cox, New York, N.Y.**; Vegetables and Rice, **Jeanne Calmann, New York, N.Y.**

8 SALADS   164

Special Dinner Salad, **Jacquelyn Cornforth, Portsmouth, R.I.**; Springtime Salad, **Mrs. A.**

Wright, Broadalbin, N.Y.; The Hearty Salad Bowl, Thousand Island Dressing, **W. Marvin Lundy, Lone Pine Farm, Inglefield, Ind.**; Grated Salad, **Jimmie Elmer, New York, N.Y.**; Salad Niçoise London Style, **Mrs. Michael Lewis, London, U.K.**; Full Meal Salad, **James Moran, New York, N.Y.**; August Salad, **Leona Train Rienow, Hollyhock Hollow Farm, Selkirk, N.Y.**; Green Bean Salad I, **Alys Monitto, New York, N.Y.**; Green Bean Salad II, Slaw with Vinegar Dressing, **Reva Rudley, Matawan, N.J.**; Dandelion Salad, Carrot Salad I, **Mrs. Jerome Whitney, Shelton, Conn.**; Romaine and Radish Salad, **Willa Swiller, Philadelphia, Pa.**; Cuke Salad, **Esther Goedel, New York, N.Y.**; Mediterranean Cucumber Salad, **Jane Margulies, New York, N.Y.**; Marinated Zucchini, Hard Bread Salad, Marinated Broccoli Salad, **Rose Marie Williams, Gardiner, N.Y.**; Corn Salad, **Mrs. E. J. Eysink, Sully, Iowa;** Fruited Cabbage Salad, Tossed Salad, Homemade Tahini, Sesame Dressing, **Leonard's Eco-Farms, Westport, Conn.**; Shredded Cabbage Salad, **Rosemarie West, The Honey Shop, Richmond, Va.**; Sauerkraut Salad, Watercress with Cream Cheese, Apple-Lemon Salad, **Hildegard Jürgens, Rye, N.Y.**; Carrot Salad II, **Iva Bremer, Toledo, Ohio;** Littlechew, Peanut Dressing, **Ann Wigmore, Hippocrates Health Institute, Boston, Mass.**; Raw Beet Salad, **Mrs. Roy Wilkins, Newberg, Ore.**; Cabbage Slaw with Cashew Dressing, **Mrs. Lester Koontz, Mansfield, Ohio;** Texas Cole Slaw, **Mrs. F. O. Teten, Liberty, Tex.**; Eggplant Salad, **Vegetarian Hotel, Woodridge, N.Y.**; Pickled Beet Salad, **Stanley Fine, New York, N.Y.**; Chick-Pea Platter, **Sarah Jackson, The Healthway, Westport, Conn.**; Sweet Potato Salad, **L. M. Zell, Key to Health Food Shop, Bellefontaine, Ohio;** Tabooley, **The Diet Shop, Oklahoma City, Okla.**; Blueberry Rice Salad, **Irma Wineland, Mansfield, Ohio;** Sandrahene Salad, **Sandra Potholm, Brunswick, Me.**; Tropical Sun Salad, **Anastasia Duval, St. Thomas, V.I.**; Olympian Salad, **Selma Endicter;** Melon Salad, **Eve Kaufman, Natural Life Styles, New Paltz, N.Y.**; Fresh Orange Salad, **Ursula Larizza, New York, N.Y.**; Apple-Banana Salad, **Mrs. H. G. Chamberlain, Highland Orchard, New Concord, Ohio;** Apple Slaw, **Mrs. Andrew J. Koppes, West Salem, Ohio;** Homemade Mayonnaise, **Margaret Margulies, East Meadow, N.Y.**; Eggless Mayonnaise, **Lillian E. Stutz, R.N., Wheaton, Md.**; Thick Mayonnaise, **Louise Gelsthorpe, Bloomington, Ill.**; Avocado Dressing, **Johanna Kent Braith, Musart Spiral Foods, New York, N.Y.**; Avocado-Tofu Dressing, Basic Tofu Dressing, **Alan Talbott, Wholly Foods, Berkeley, Calif.**; Caesar Salad Dressing, **B. Polow, Morristown, N.J.**; Cheese and Tomato Dressing, **Susan Claire Baver, Musart Spiral Foods, New York, N.Y.**; French Dressing, **Mrs. Daniel Abbott, East Concord, N.H.**; Fruit and Oil Dressing, **Bertha McLaughlin, Mansfield, Ohio;** Fruit Salad Dressing, **Mrs. G. C. Brenzel, New Smyrna Beach, Fla.**; Russian Dressing, **Peg Cronin Rapp, West Hurley, N.Y.**; Honey Cream Dressing for Fruits, **Marilyn N. Tajar, Naugatuck, Conn.**; Salad Dressings I and II, **Susan Hillyard, Scarsdale, N.Y.**; Salad Dressing III, **Phyllis Title, Plainview, N.Y.**; Green Dressing, **Sondra Wachtfogel, Kings Park, N.Y.**; Herb Dressing, **Mother Nature's, Scarsdale, N.Y.**; Perfect Dressing, **Max Huberman, Natural Health Foods, Youngstown, Ohio;** Yarrow Vinegar, **Bev Post, Franklin, N.J.**

9 SPROUTS 194

Hiziki and Rice, **Virginia Samet, Natural Life Styles, New Paltz, N.Y.**; Chicken Chow Mein, **Ann Uibelhoer, West Orange, N.J.**; Green Revolution Breakfast, **Mildred J. Loomis, School of Living, Freeland, Md.**; Lucerne Salad, **Red Owl Health Foods, Westfield, Mass.**; Sprouted Chick-Pea Salad, **Frederic Sadtler, Fort Washington, Pa.**; Bean Sprout Salad,

Elsa A. Weich, Germantown, N.Y.; Red Cabbage and Sprouts, **Isabelle and Bob, Natural Life Styles, New Paltz, N.Y.;** Sprout and Hazelnut Salad, **Mother Nature's, Scarsdale, N.Y.;** Sprouted Tabooley Salad, **Mrs. Lawrence Burrell, Fairview, Okla.;** Sprouted Wheat Balls, **El Molino Mills, Alhambra, Calif.;** Broiled Sprouted Wheat Patties, **Irene Williams, East Brunswick, N.J.**

10 GRAINS & CEREALS   204

Nut-Apple Breakfast, **Little Silver Conservation Commission, Little Silver, N.J.;** Breakfast Nutriment, **Diana Jacoby, Northport, N.Y.;** Simple Breakfast, **Kathleen Chicanot, New York, N.Y.;** Honey-Oats Cereal, **Tobie Happersberger, Sacramento, Calif.;** New England Mix, **Verne Thomas, Hancock, N.H.;** Heavenly Munch, **Nancy McKain, Boston, Mass.;** Ready-to-Eat Cereal, **Wendy Culin, White Plains, N.Y.;** Pecan Crunch, **Mrs. Kenneth Bebb, Wichita Falls, Tex.;** Puffed Brown Rice, **Leonard's Eco-Farms, Westport, Conn.;** Applicious, **Helen K. Nearing, Harborside, Me.;** Island Breakfast Cereal, **Marian Nihlen, Plymouth, Montserrat, W. I.;** Uncooked High Energy Cereal, **Siga Loggie, New York, N.Y.;** Corn Meal Mush, **E. A. Dietrich, Dietrich's Organic Farm, Genoa, Ohio;** Pistachio-Raisin Brunch Loaf, **Pauline H. Wright, Washington, D.C.;** Corn Meal Mush and Soy Grits, **El Molino Mills, Alhambra, Calif.;** Millet with Cheese, Millet Cereal, **Red Owl Health Foods, Westfield, Mass.;** Millet Pilaf, **Patricia Ullberg, Sunderland, Md.;** Millet Breakfast Cereal, **A. Scheresky, Glen Ewen, Saskatchewan, Canada;** Four Grain Homemade Cereal, **Mrs. C. W. Lynn, Foods for Life, Orlando, Fla.;** Breakfast Rice, **Mrs. E. J. Eysink, Sully, Iowa;** Barley Pilaf, **Irene Williams, East Brunswick, N.J.;** Garden State Couscous, **Tudi Bertin, Edison, N.J.;** Jerry's Rice, **Mary Ann Taylor, Boston, Mass.;** Green Rice, **Margaret W. Squire, Meriden, Conn.;** Glory Rice, **Doris Pickering, Van Nuys, Calif.;** Fruit and Rice, **Patricia Benham, Darien, Conn.;** Brown Rice with Chicken, **Sue Bailey, Natural Life Styles, New Paltz, N.Y.**

11 BREADS   220

Brown Rice and Whole Wheat Muffins, Three Grain Muffins, **Mrs. Andrew J. Koppes, West Salem, Ohio;** Bran Muffins, **Cynthia Hedstrom, New York, N.Y.;** Corn Muffins, **Stanley Fine, New York, N.Y.;** Wheat Germ Muffins, **Mrs. G. Euery, Rushndale, Mass.;** Buckwheat-Corn Muffins, Barley Flour Drop Biscuits, **M. M. Machlowitz, Glenside, Pa.;** Whole Wheat Muffins, **Mrs. Daniel Abbott, East Concord, N.H.;** Sunflower Muffins, **Red Bank Health Foods, Red Bank, N.J.;** Peanut Butter-Apricot Muffins, **Charlotte Scripture, New York, N.Y.;** Blueberry Muffins, **North Country School, Lake Placid, N.Y.;** Banana Oatmeal Muffins, **Lillian E. Stutz, R.N., Wheaton, Md.;** Yogurt Muffins, **Diana Gorenstein, Princeton, N.J.;** Whole Wheat Popovers, **Patricia Ullberg, Sunderland, Md.;** Wheat Germ Wafers, **Christiane Forbringer, Gillette, N.J.;** Quick Health Bread, **Zola Nelson, Tulsa, Okla.;** Corn Bread, **Arrowhead Mills, Deaf Smith County, Tex.;** Spoon Bread, **Mrs. Ray Sacher, Roosevelt, N.Y.;** Logan Bread, **Malcolm "Tink" Taylor, "Commentary on Conservation," Holderness, N.H.;** Honey Date Loaf, Crusty White Bread, **Grace Perryman, West Islip, N.Y.;** Fruity and Nutty Tea Loaf, **Marilyn N. Tajar, Naugatuck, Conn.;** Nut Butter Loaf, **Joanna Dejesu, New York, N.Y.;** Fat-Free Date Bran Bread, Leonard's Special Bread, **Leonard's Eco-Farms, Westport, Conn.;** Orange-Nut

Bread, Bettie's Whole Wheat Bread, **Bettie Mustard, Delaware Valley Committee for Protection of the Environment, Moorestown, N.J.;** Whole Wheat Banana Bread, **Barbara D. Slack, Medfield, Mass.;** Pumpkin Bread, **Merry Knowlton, Princeton, N.J.;** Steamed Date-Nut Loaf, **Leslie Brin, New York, N.Y.;** Parker House Rolls, Perfect Pecan Rolls, **Victor Boff Health Foods, New York, N.Y.;** Honey Whole Wheat Rolls, Corn and Molasses Bread, Mixed Whole Grain Bread, Cracked Rye Bread, **Heidi Wortzel's Cooking School, Newton Centre, Mass.;** Hamburger Rolls, Whole Wheat Coffeecake Dough, Breadsticks, Whole Wheat English Muffins, **Abbie Page and Saundra Altman, West Lafayette, Ind.;** Currant Buns, **Virginia Samet, Natural Life Styles, New Paltz, N.Y.;** Bagels, **Jane E. Eidler, Searingtown, N.Y.;** Caraway Puffs, Oatmeal-Dill Bread, **Mrs. E. J. Eysink, Sully, Iowa;** Pizza Dough, **Mrs. Richard Osterbick, Richard's Natural Food Farm, Eagle, Mich.;** Sugarless Doughnuts, **Anna Pardini, Big Indian, N.Y.;** Yeast-Raised Whole Wheat Doughnuts, **A. Scheresky, Glen Ewen, Saskatchewan, Canada;** Whole Wheat Sour Dough Onion Bread, **Victor L. Richman, New York, N.Y.;** Oatmeal Muffins, **Jean H. Ballon, West Hempstead, N.Y.;** Unleavened Bread, **Ellen Glazer, Cambridge, Mass.;** Steamed Yeast Bread, Blueberry Bread, Bread-Perfect Every Time, **Lynne Lederman, Great Neck, N.Y.;** Soya-Carob Bread, **Walnut Acres, Penns Creek, Pa.;** Yeast-Raised Corn Bread, **John McMahan, Clifford, Ind.;** Barbara's Basic Refrigerator Bread, **Barbara Boodman, Lexington, Mass.;** Golden Braids, **Nan Isaacson, Malverne, N.Y.;** Health Loaf, **Nancy Swearer, Swarthmore, Pa.;** Health Bread, **Patricia P. Hart, Fairfield, Conn.;** Six Loaves to Feed a Family of Five for a Week, **Joann Seaver, Philadelphia, Pa.;** Mixed-Grain Bread, **Amy Leos, Cambridge, Mass.;** Three Wheat Bread, **Susan Zolla, New York, N.Y.;** Half and Half Bread, **Sandra Horsted, Waunakee, Wis.;** Delicious Oatmeal Bread, **Racine Rockwood, South Weymouth, Mass.;** Old Country Pumpernickel, **Peg Cronin Rapp, West Hurley, N.Y.;** Berkeley Rye Bread, **Juanita Neilands, Dept. of Biochemistry, Univ. of Calif., Berkeley, Calif.;** Graham-Rye Bread, **Mrs. Donald Teel, Lansing, Mich.;** Cracked Wheat Bread, **Sandra Postal, Ardsley, N.Y.;** One-Bowl Wheat Germ Bread, **Stefania Scoggins, Chatsworth, Calif.;** Annmarie's Best Bread, **Annmarie Colbin, New York, N.Y.;** High Protein Whole Wheat Bread, **Mrs. William H. Tate, New York, N.Y.;** Sprouted Whole Wheat Bread, **El Molino Mills, Alhambra, Calif.;** Organic Whole Wheat Bread, **Sara Hafner, Amherst, Mass.;** No-Knead Quick Whole Wheat Bread, **Mrs. George H. Hanson, Idaho Falls, Idaho, and Denise Mercedes Feliu, Committee on Poetry, Cherry Valley, N.Y.;** Spoon-Stirred Whole Wheat Bread, **Tobie Happersberger, Sacramento, Calif.;** Hearty Bread, **Jill A. Miller, Natick, Mass.**

12 PANCAKES, WAFFLES & PASTA 294

Old-Fashioned Buckwheat Hot Cakes, **Taylor's Natural Foods, Fort Worth, Tex.;** Delicious Nutritious Pancakes, **Mary Cerulli, North Caldwell, N.J.;** Oatmeal Griddlecakes, **Lillian E. Stutz, R.N., Wheaton, Md.;** Easy Wheat Pancakes, **Mrs. Daniel Abbott, East Concord, N.H.;** Raised Wheat Pancakes, **Sylvia White, New York, N.Y.;** Buckwheat Pancakes, **Kathleen Bernstein, New York, N.Y.;** Barley Flour Pancakes, **M. M. Machlowitz, Glenside, Pa.;** Great Speckled Pancakes, **Frances Chastain, Lexington, Mass.;** Wheat Germ Pancakes, French Toast, **Mrs. Peter Seldin, Croton-on-Hudson, N.Y.;** Cashew Whole-Grain Pancakes, **Mrs. Richard Osterbick, Richard's Natural Food Farm, Eagle, Mich.;** Cottage Cheese Pancakes I, **Lynne Lederman, Great Neck, N.Y.;** Cottage Cheese Pancakes II, **Sylvia Levy, New York, N.Y.;** Goat Cheese Pancakes, **Francis**

13 YOGURT   310

14 DESSERTS   314

Old Millmont, Pa.; Apple-Oat Crisp, **Else L. Sappington, Fort Worth, Tex.;** Banana Sweet Potato Pudding, **Reva Rudley, Matawan, N.J.;** Cranberry Crunch, **Grazing Fields Bogs, Buzzards Bay, Mass.;** Cottage Cheese Berry Soufflé, **Margaret B. White, Monterey, Mass.;** Whole Wheat Berry Pudding, **Irene Williams, East Brunswick, N.J.;** Bread Pudding with Orange, **Mrs. M. Dean, Wyckoff, N.J.;** Plantation Pudding, Baked Brown Rice with Dates, Gingerbread I, Apple Oatmeal Cookies, Homemade Graham Crackers, **Mrs. Andrew J. Koppes, West Salem, Ohio;** Indian Pudding, **Mrs. William Indoe, New York, N.Y.;** Old-Fashioned Tapioca Cream, **San Rafael Health Foods, San Rafael, Calif.;** Currant and Rice Pudding, **Karen Frisher, Huntington Station, N.Y.;** Sweet Pellao, **Tracy Seaver, Storrs, Conn.;** Baked Rice Pudding, **Kathleen Bernstein, New York, N.Y.;** Pineapple-Noodle Pudding, **Marnie Potash, West Orange, N.J.;** Velvet Pudding, **Mrs. Marge Renhult, Northboro, Mass.;** Oil Pastry, **Leta C. Crafts, Lisbon Falls, Me.;** Wheat Germ Pie Crust, **Jo Stallard, Galisteo, N.M.;** Apple-Carrot Pie, **Andy Roman, New College, Sarasota, Fla.;** Five-Minute Raw Blueberry Pie, **Shoshana Margolin, New York, N.Y.;** Golden Pineapple Pie, **Mrs. Christ B. Miller, Bird-in-Hand, Pa.;** Yogurt Cheese Pie, **L. M. Zell, Key to Health Food Shop, Bellefontaine, Ohio;** Rhubarb Cream Pie, **Mrs. Donald Golightly, Wadena, Minn.;** Pie-ettes, **Mrs. D. Rossi, New York, N.Y.;** Pumpkin Pie, **Leona Hicks, Portland, Ore.;** Raw Apple Cake, **Mrs. Lawrence Burrell, Fairview, Okla.;** Whole Wheat Apple Cake, **Jane Margulies, New York, N.Y.;** Apple Wheat Germ Coffeecake, **Mrs. Vukasin Asanovic, New York, N.Y.;** Applesauce-Oatmeal Cake, Molasses Drops, Tahini Cookies, **Mrs. A. Wright, Broadalbin, N.Y.;** Unleavened Health Nut-Honey Cake, **Ruth Kaplowitz, Parsippany-Troy Hills, N.J.;** Pumpkin Cake, **Grace Slyboom, West Chester, Pa.;** Mayonnaise Raisin Cake, **Joyce Middlebrook, Dobbins, Calif.;** Strawberry Shortcake, **Barbara Lungren, Northridge, Calif.;** Carrot Cake, **Mrs. Gerald Carp, New York, N.Y.;** Wonderful Old-Fashioned Gingerbread, Carob or Carob-Raisin Chip Cookies, **Irene Borger, Old Bennington, Vt.;** Date and Nut Cake, Dutch Butter Cookies, **Mrs. E. J. Eysink, Sully, Iowa;** Raw Fruit "Cake", **Katherine Evans, Canton, Ohio;** Quick Upside-Down Cake, Raisin Cookies, **Mrs. William Bennett, Oregon, Wis.;** Mock Cheesecake, Carrot Cookies, **Beatrice Castiglia, Pelham, N.Y.;** Organic Cheesecake, **Mrs. Amedeo Nazzaro, Newfoundland, N.J.;** Whole Wheat Spongecake, **Mrs. Alfred Schuh, Buchanan, Mich.;** Sunshine Cake, Carob Nut Brownies, **M. M. Machlowitz, Glenside, Pa.;** Whole Wheat Poundcake, **Francine Berkowitz, Washington, D.C.;** Fig Filling, Uncooked Honey Frosting, **Mrs. W. A. Webber, Dayton, Ohio;** Easy Bar Cookies, **B. Polow, Morristown, N.J.;** Apricot Bar Cookies, Nut Squares, **Tobi Rosenstein, Santa Monica Co-op, Los Angeles, Calif.;** Jelly Cakes, **Ellen Jaffe, Natural Life Styles, New Paltz, N.Y.;** Peanut Butter and Banana Bars, **Carol Stephenson, Weston, Mass.;** Scotcher Shortbread, **Isabel Gordon, Green's Farms, Conn.;** Sesame Strips, **Brownie's Creative Cookery, New York, N.Y.;** Carob Brownies, **Barbara D. Slack, Medfield, Mass.;** Carob and Honey Brownies, **Victor Boff Health Foods, New York, N.Y.;** Wheat Germ Squares, Applesauce Cookies, Cashew Coconut Cookies, Coconut Shortcake, **Lillian E. Stutz, R.N., Wheaton, Md.;** Mollie Cookies, **Billy R. Dillard;** Apple Cookies, **Susan Eisen;** Carob Chip Cookies, **Marjorie Fisher, Evanston, Ill.;** Honey Cookies, **Health Food Centers, Columbus, Ohio;** Oatmeal Drop Cookies, Raisin-Nut Oat Cookies, **Mrs. Leon Berkowitz, Tenafly, N.J.;** Honey-Sesame Bites, **Rosemarie West, The Honey Shop, Richmond, Va.;** Sorghum-Date Cookies, **Zola Nelson, Tulsa, Okla.;** Sunflower Seed Cookies, **Sally Sacks, Stamford, Conn.;** Whole Wheat Fruit Cookies, **Sondra Wachtfogel, Kings Park, N.Y.;** Wheat Germ Snicker-Doodles, **Miriam Boss, Albany, N.Y.;** Chestnut Cream-Filled Cookies, **Marie Foster, Harwich, Mass.;** Ginger

Cookies, **Hildegard Hilton, Storrs, Conn.;** Italian Sesame Cookies, **Adeline Buljeta, New York, N.Y.;** Nutballs, **Deborah Ballon, West Hempstead, N.Y.**

INTRODUCTION

Around the turn of the century, before the advent of large-scale mechanized farming and modern food production methods, people took the special pleasures of fresh, natural and unrefined foods for granted. Most lived on the land in rural areas or cultivated backyard gardens in towns. Today, people are rediscovering the textures, tastes and nutritional benefits of the natural, fresh foods that Grandmother knew.

In Grandmother's day, fresh home-grown fruits and vegetables gave seasonal flavor and food value to soups, stews and desserts and were lovingly canned or turned into jams, jellies and pickles for year-round enjoyment. The cookie jar was always filled with homemade oatmeal and raisin cookies made with honey from the hives in the hollow and eggs from chickens scratching in the yard. At least once a week the fragrance of bread baking filled the house as loaves of cracked wheat, raisin-pumpernickel and seeded rye were lined up to cool. Chemical fertilizers, pesticide sprays and dusts were almost unknown, and farm animals were allowed to roam and develop without man's interference. When a neighbor slaughtered a hog or cow, there were always special tidbits to buy—nothing was wasted. There might be tripe for a stew, a hog's head for head cheese, ground pork scraps for sausage or beef liver to make Grandpa's favorite dish. Sacks and barrels at the general store were filled with unrefined and unprocessed ingredients that had a short shelf-life but lots of flavor.

Grandmother's day may be gone forever, but this book should make it easier than ever before to recapture the old-fashioned goodness and flavor, in easy-to-follow recipes, of her style of cooking. The more than 700 recipes, collected from across the country, are for good-tasting dishes calling for basic, fresh, unrefined and non-highly-processed ingredients: natural foods.

The recipes specify whole grains rather than refined, bleached and enriched products; brown rice in preference to white rice; honey and molasses instead of sugar. Unhydrogenated vegetable oils, lard and butter are favored over solid vegetable shortenings. And the natural flavors of the fresh produce and grains are enhanced by moderate use of herbs, sea salt, vegetable- and seaweed-based seasonings and some spices.

In choosing meat and poultry recipes, emphasis was placed on extending economy cuts of meat by the addition of vegetables, wheat germ, nuts, seeds and eggs, and on full use of those much-neglected storehouses of nutrients, the organ meats: liver, kidneys, brains, sweetbreads, and so on. Since many Americans consume animal protein beyond recognized needs, the vegetarian main dishes are suggested as occasional alternates to meat dishes and as fresh ideas for established vegetarians.

A special advantage to this book is that many ingredients used in the recipes were unknown to our grandmothers. They have been used and appreciated for centuries in other cultures, and are now available to us. The Chinese mastered the glories of soybeans, bean curd and fermented bean pastes in cooking; Indians and other Far-Eastern peoples have used millet; seaweeds are standard in the traditional Japanese diet.

These and other ingredients such as alfalfa sprouts, wheat germ, yogurt and sunflower seed kernels, all once associated with faddists, are now being welcomed with enthusiasm by thousands of people for their flavor, texture and nutrient value when they are incorporated into a balanced diet. This book tells how to prepare them (see *Yogurt*) or even grow them (see *Sprouts*), and how to use them in delectable combinations.

The ingredients for the recipes are available in supermarkets, in health food stores, at farm stands, by mail order, in the country meadow or even in your own back yard. An Ingredient Chart in the back of the book gives sources for the purchase of, and information on, the more unusual foods called for in the recipes. But the key to flavor and food value lies in freshness, and it behooves the cook to search for the outlet that offers the freshest produce and has the fastest turnover of staples and dairy products.

Above all, the dishes made from these recipes can furnish a varied, well-balanced diet based on the four main groups: fruits and vegetables; dairy products; meat, fish and other protein sources; grains and cereals. The emphasis is on the flavor potential and nutritional value of the ingredients, and not on any specific benefits that may be attributed to them. No claims are made here for natural and organic eating as miracle cures for any disease or condition. Many people follow specialized, and generally restricted, eating patterns because of humanitarian, philosophical, religious or cultist beliefs. Others seeking special foods include ecologically-minded citizens who favor organic growing methods as a result of their concern about the ravages of man on our environment.

The goal of this book is to help *all* individuals and families eat better and enjoy it more, and to make every mouthful of food taste good and contribute nutrients needed for good health. This book also challenges the reader to know exactly what he is eating by preparing dishes from basic ingredients.

Those already committed to a natural food regime will find new ideas, new combinations of ingredients and new ways to serve interesting, good-tasting meals in these recipes. The majority of the recipes were contributed by dedicated followers of the natural foods and organic gardening movements and represent years of home-testing in kitchens across the country. Wherever possible the actual instructions provided by the contributor have been given, although the ingredient references have been made uniform throughout so that the reader will not worry that "soybean flour" in one recipe is different from the "soy flour" of another. If this book does not contain *your* favorite natural foods recipe, I would be grateful if you would share it with me.

Below are details about some aspects of natural food cultivation, consumption and cookery which have been of great interest to many of us raised on processed, refined foods for whom Grandmother's fresh bread is but a dim memory. There are also hints for coping with the transition period for those who wish to switch to a natural foods regime.

Organic Gardening and Organic Meats. Many people acknowledge that organically grown foods taste better; whether because they are harvested at the peak of their development and marketed immediately or because of special organic growing methods has never been settled (for the non-devotee). But there is certainly less likelihood of pesticide residues being present. Regrettably, there is no official well-publicized proof that all organically grown produce—that is, grown without chemical fertilizers, sprays or dusts—is nutritionally superior. It is hoped that extensive testing and analyses will be carried out before long by a respected independent laboratory or government agency to determine whether there are nutritional pluses to organically grown foods in addition to their proven advantages.

The benefits of restoring the soil with humus, compost and natural wastes, all part of organic growing, are praised both by ecologists and agriculturists. Water run-off is reduced, soil structure and aeration are improved, and there is greater development of desirable soil organisms. Though the number of organic gardeners and farmers is growing, the demand for such foods far outstrips current supply so that prices are high for the non-gardener. Worse, there is again a lack of formal standards and some difficulty in determining whether foods sold as "organic" are the real thing.

Organically raised cattle and poultry are not subjected to injections of growth-promoting and disease-resistant drugs, and are allowed to roam freely on land that has been neither chemically fertilized nor sprayed with pesticides. The animals feed only on organically raised food. Hence supplies of organic meat are limited, prices are high and the meat fibers tend to be tough, although more flavorful, it is claimed, than their commercially raised counterparts.

Revolutionary Diets Then and Now. Some historians see an analogy between the "age of reform" of the 1840's with its peace, women's rights, and popular health movements and the current revolt against established customs.

Sylvester Graham, a reformer whose name is synonymous with whole wheat flour, advocated temperance, vegetarianism with whole grains, and strict personal hygiene. His followers preached that candy led directly to the grave.

During the same era, Fruitlands and Brook Farm were among the many experiments in communal living. Fruitlands, based on non-dairy vegetarianism, was operated by Amos Bronson Alcott (the father of Louisa May) in Massachusetts; he referred to it as "Love Colony." Journals published in London during the late 1800's promoted vegetarianism, with water as the only acceptable beverage, and labeled the practice of overeating a sin. There were restaurants and shops specializing in lentils, peas, beans and oatmeal porridge.

Today there are lacto-vegetarians, or those whose diets include dairy products; ovo-lacto vegetarians, whose diets include eggs and dairy products, and non-dairy fruitarians. Other groups are devoted to raw or low-heat cooked foods, yoga and macrobiotic regimes. Seventh Day Adventists, who are mostly ovo-lacto vegetarians, maintain average to excellent nutritional standards, but some fruitarians have been reported to suffer from diet deficiencies.

In the macrobiotic diet, nutritional balance takes second or third place to (1) the balance between *yin*, equated with acidity and expansion, and *yang* connected with alkalinity and contraction, and (2) the need for love while cooking. The Zen macrobiotic diet, which has no direct connection with Zen Buddhism, is the most potentially dangerous with its ultimate goal of a diet consisting exclusively of unpolished rice.

The Bibliography at the back of this book suggests sources for more information on these tangential movements, but a listing does not constitute an endorsement. Anyone following a restricted diet should be examined by a physician who may suggest that a dietitian prepare a detailed ingested-foods profile analysis and calculation of nutrients supplied.

Switching to Natural Foods. Preparing dishes from scratch helps you to know *exactly* what you are eating. When basic ingredients are used it is simple to determine if a new eating pattern provides all the essential nutrients, in quantities generally recommended, within the calorie level suggested for each individual. No two people have exactly the same nutritional needs.

It isn't always easy to switch from a highly-processed-food diet to meals prepared only from natural foods. For instance, nuts, seeds, fresh and dried fruits and unsweetened cultured or frozen milk-based desserts would be the only desserts in a model regime. This is hard to take for the cultivated sweet tooth, and is the reason for including cake, pie, cookie and hot bread recipes.

But these recipes for baked desserts are made with whole grains, nuts and a minimum of sugar. Even after the transition period, unleavened heavy-textured breads favored by some purists may not be palatable to many people and so this book includes recipes calling for baking powder, baking soda and unbleached white flour. Less sweetening is used than in regular recipes and wherever practical, it is in the form of honey or molasses. Raw sugar has been said to offer little more in nutritional benefits than refined white sugar, so amounts are held to a minimum.

A casual glance in the average shopping cart at a supermarket reveals quantities of low- or non-nutritive snacks and beverages, and highly-processed convenience foods of uncertain nutritive values. Obesity is one of the most serious medical problems in the country, perhaps not unconnected to these so-called "empty-calorie" foods that tend to displace the basic nutritious foods in the diet which are needed to maintain proper weight levels and health.

This book has recipes for good-tasting snacks, beverages, cookies and candies that can woo young and old away from the soda-sundae-and-snack-chip syndrome and provide a positive contribution to nutrition needs. There are recipes for simple sandwich fillings that, in combination with whole grain naturally fortified breads, can put good nutrition and flavor into the lunch box and picnic hamper.

There are suggestions for preparing baby foods from scratch that can wean mother and child from prepared products. Fresh vegetables, fruits, poultry and meats, simply cooked, don't need flavor enhancers, or even sugar and salt, to tempt a child's appetite and nourish him adequately.

Convenience foods are touted as time-savers, and purchasers pay dearly for the built-in maid service, but the extra amount of time it takes to fix a dish from scratch is worthwhile when it gives a better-tasting, more nourishing, and often cheaper product. The recipes in this book can prove it.

—JEAN HEWITT

1
APPETIZERS

Natural food devotees eschew alcoholic beverages but down Tiger's milk flips, celery cocktails and green eye-openers with gusto. The appetizers in this chapter can bridge the gap between both groups and provide tasty morsels of good nutrition.

POTTED CHEDDAR

1 tablespoon butter
¼ pound grated Cheddar cheese
⅛ teaspoon cayenne pepper
Sea salt to taste
1 egg yolk
¼ cup heavy cream

1. Melt the butter in a small saucepan. Add cheese, cayenne and salt and heat over low flame until cheese is melted.

2. Beat egg yolk and cream together and slowly stir into cheese mixture. Cook over low heat, stirring constantly, until very thick and smooth. Pour into a small jar, cool, cover and refrigerate.

Yield: About one cup cheese spread.

LIPTAUER CHEESE

¼ cup goat cottage or semi-soft cheese
¼ cup soy or safflower margarine
1 teaspoon capers
1 teaspoon paprika
½ teaspoon anchovy paste
½ teaspoon caraway seeds
1 tablespoon finely chopped onion or chives
Sea salt and freshly ground black pepper to taste
Small squares thinly sliced homemade whole wheat bread

Using a wooden spoon, cream the cheese and margarine together. Stir in remaining ingredients except the bread. Wrap in wax paper and refrigerate overnight. Serve thinly sliced, on the bread squares.

Yield: About one-half cup.

SOY CHEESE APPETIZER

1 cup soy cheese (tofu or bean curd, see page 158)
¼ cup chopped green pepper
1 tablespoon finely chopped scallion
Sea salt to taste
2 tablespoons homemade mayonnaise (see page 186)

Mix all ingredients together and serve as a spread or dip or on lettuce leaves.

Yield: Four servings.

ALMOND-ERICS

1 pound blanched almonds
1 tablespoon melted butter
Sea salt to taste
½ teaspoon cayenne pepper, or to taste
¼ cup tamari (soy sauce)

1. Toss the almonds with the butter and toast over low heat, in a heavy skillet, until golden. Add salt, cayenne and tamari and continue cooking, stirring often, until nuts are fairly dry.

2. Allow to cool, then store in an airtight jar in the refrigerator.

Yield: Six servings.

Note: Walnuts can be done the same way but substitute curry powder for cayenne.

BEAN CURD APPETIZER

1 cup soy cheese (tofu or bean curd, see page 158)
1 tablespoon tamari (soy sauce)
1 teaspoon sesame oil
2 tablespoons chopped cilantro or parsley
1 scallion, chopped
Freshly ground black pepper to taste

1. Slice the cheese and arrange on a small plate or dish.

2. Combine the tamari and oil and pour over the cheese. Sprinkle with the cilantro or parsley, the scallion and pepper. Chill.

Yield: Four servings.

SESAME SEED SPREAD

1 cup cottage cheese
⅓ cup toasted sesame seeds
1 tablespoon chopped parsley
1 teaspoon lemon juice
Grated fresh horseradish to taste
2 tablespoons finely diced green pepper
2 tablespoons finely diced sweet red pepper
Sea salt to taste
Whole wheat crackers

Combine all the ingredients except the crackers and mix well. Chill. Serve with crackers.

Yield: Six servings.

GUACAMOLE

1 ripe avocado, peeled, pitted and mashed roughly with a fork
2 tomatoes, skinned and diced
1 small onion, finely chopped
Finely chopped fresh hot green chili pepper to taste
Lemon juice or lime juice to taste
Sea salt to taste
Celery stick dippers

Combine all ingredients except celery dippers. Serve at once, with celery dippers.
Yield: Six servings.

AVOCADO APPETIZERS

2 cups chicken broth (see page 52)
1 to 1½ teaspoons unflavored gelatin, approximately
Beet juice
3 small avocados
Lemon juice
⅓ cup yogurt (see page 311)
Lobster coral or red caviar
Crushed ice
6 lemon wedges

1. If the broth is already slightly jellied, use the smaller amount of gelatin. In some instances a homemade chicken broth will not require the addition of any extra jelling material. Soften the gelatin in the broth if it is liquid, or only partly jelled. Heat, stirring, until gelatin dissolves. Color faintly pink with beet juice. Pour into an oiled shallow dish. Chill.

2. Halve the avocados, remove pits and brush exposed surfaces with lemon juice. Chop jellied chicken broth and pile into cavities.

3. Top with yogurt and then coral or caviar. Set halves in ice and serve with lemon wedges.
Yield: Six servings.

MOCK HERRING APPETIZER

2 onions, cut crosswise in ½-inch-thick slices and separated into rings
2 ribs celery, cut in 1-inch pieces
1 medium-size eggplant, peeled and cut into long strips about 1-inch thick
Vegetable salt to taste
1 teaspoon whole cloves
1 bay leaf, crumbled
1 teaspoon brown sugar
1 tablespoon lemon juice
1 cup yogurt (see page 311) or sour cream
Pumpernickel bread slices

1. Place the onion rings and celery in a colander over boiling water and steam, covered, five minutes.

2. Add eggplant sticks and steam until they are tender but not mushy. Turn vegetables into a bowl and cool.

3. Combine the salt, cloves, bay leaf, brown sugar, lemon juice and yogurt or sour cream. Stir into cooled vegetables. Chill well. Serve on pumpernickel bread.

Yield: Six servings.

MOCK SALMON APPETIZER

2 hard-cooked eggs
1 small onion
2 cups cooked drained fresh peas
3 carrots, grated
2 tablespoons oil
Vegetable salt to taste
¼ cup unblanched almonds, finely ground in Moulinex grinder
2 tablespoons wheat germ
2 tablespoons chopped parsley
6 to 8 Boston lettuce cups

1. Grind the eggs, onion and peas through the coarse blade of a meat grinder.

2. Stir in the carrots, oil, salt, almonds, wheat germ and parsley. Mix well and chill. Serve in Boston lettuce cups.

Yield: Six to eight servings.

GOUGÈRE PUFFS

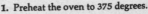

1 cup hot water
½ cup butter
¼ teaspoon sea salt
¼ teaspoon raw sugar
1 cup unbleached white flour or organic whole wheat flour
4 large eggs
⅔ cup grated Swiss or Gruyère cheese
1 teaspoon dry mustard
Few grains cayenne pepper

1. Preheat the oven to 375 degrees.

2. In a small saucepan, combine the water, butter, salt and sugar. Heat until butter is melted and mixture boiling. Stir in the flour all at once, stirring vigorously with a wooden spoon.

3. Continue stirring over medium heat until mixture leaves the sides of the pan clean.

4. Remove from the heat and beat in the eggs, one at a time, very well. Stir in all but three tablespoons of the cheese, the mustard and cayenne. Drop by teaspoonfuls onto an oiled baking sheet, sprinkle with remaining cheese and bake 35 to 40 minutes or until well puffed and golden.

5. Turn off the oven heat and let puffs remain in oven three minutes longer. Serve hot.

Yield: About three dozen puffs.

Note: The contributor uses only organic ingredients and serves the puffs plain. If desired, the puffs can be filled with cheese, ham or clam mixture.

PINEAPPLE DIP

1 cup low fat cottage cheese
1 tablespoon lemon juice
3 tablespoons finely chopped fresh
  or preserved drained ginger
1 tablespoon honey
1 medium-size ripe pineapple,
  peeled, cored and cut into chunks

1. Place cottage cheese and lemon juice in electric blender and blend until smooth.

2. Add ginger and honey and place in a serving bowl. Spear pineapple cubes with toothpicks and set in the dip or arrange around the bowl of dip.

Yield: Six servings.

RAW (ORGANIC) VEGETABLES WITH CURRY DIP

½ cup homemade mayonnaise
  (see page 186)
½ cup sour cream or yogurt
  (see page 311)
1 teaspoon curry powder
½ teaspoon turmeric
¼ teaspoon chili powder
¼ teaspoon ginger
¼ teaspoon paprika
Few grains cayenne pepper
Sea salt to taste
Cauliflowerets
Carrot sticks
Green pepper strips
Whole green beans
Scallions
Radishes
Turnip sticks
Celery dippers
Cucumber sticks

1. Mix together the mayonnaise, sour cream or yogurt, curry, turmeric, chili powder, ginger, paprika, cayenne and salt. Refrigerate for at least one hour.

2. Place bowl of curry dip in center of large tray and arrange the crisp, raw vegetables around in an attractive design.

Yield: Twelve servings.

YOGURT DIP

6 walnut halves
1 clove garlic
1 tablespoon olive oil
1 cup yogurt (see page 311)
¼ cup very finely diced peeled
  cucumber
½ teaspoon lemon juice or vinegar
Whole grain crackers

1. Place walnuts, garlic and oil in an electric blender and blend to a paste. This can also be done in a mortar and pestle.

2. Stir into the yogurt with cucumber and lemon juice or vinegar. Chill and serve with crackers as dippers.

Yield: Four servings.

FALAFEL

2 cups cooked dried chick-peas
  or 1 can (1 pound 4 ounces)
  chick-peas, drained and rinsed
⅓ cup water
1 slice firm whole wheat bread,
  crusts removed
1 tablespoon unbleached white
  flour
½ teaspoon baking soda
3 cloves garlic, finely chopped
1 egg, lightly beaten
2 tablespoons chopped parsley
¾ teaspoon sea salt
¼ teaspoon freshly ground black
  pepper (optional)
¼ teaspoon ground cumin
½ teaspoon turmeric
¼ teaspoon basil
¼ teaspoon marjoram
1 tablespoon tahini
  (sesame paste) or olive oil
Cayenne pepper to taste
Flour for coating
Fat or oil for deep-frying

1. Grind the chick-peas through the coarse blade of a meat grinder.

2. Add the remaining ingredients except for the flour for coating and the fat. Mix well. The mixture will be soft.

3. Form the mixture into one-inch balls, coat with flour and fry, in a basket, four or five at a time, in the fat or oil heated to 365 degrees. The balls rise to the surface and are light brown when cooked. This takes about two minutes. Drain on paper towels.

Yield: About twenty falafel.

SOYBEAN DIP

1 cup cooked cold soybeans
   (see page 157)
1½ tablespoons chopped onion
2 tablespoons tomato paste
2 tablespoons chopped Greek
   olives
¼ cup toasted sesame seeds
2 tablespoons chopped parsley
Sea salt to taste
Whole wheat crackers

Mash the beans with a fork and stir in remaining ingredients except the crackers. Mix and chill well. Serve with crackers.

Yield: Six servings.

CHICK-PEA DIP

1 can (1 pound 4 ounces)
   chick-peas, drained
3 tablespoons tahini (sesame
   paste)
½ cup lemon juice
1 tablespoon olive oil
3 cloves garlic, finely chopped
Raw vegetable dippers and
   Middle-Eastern flat bread

With a fork, mash the chick-peas, tahini, lemon juice, olive oil and garlic together to make a thick, coarse paste. Serve with the vegetable dippers and bread.

Yield: Ten servings.

FRESH CLAM DIP

½ cup chopped fresh raw or
   steamed clams, drained
½ cup cottage cheese
2 tablespoons chopped chives
1 teaspoon lemon juice
Sea salt and freshly ground
   black pepper to taste

Combine all ingredients and mix well. Serve with raw vegetables or homemade whole wheat crackers.

Yield: Six servings.

HERBED STUFFED EGGS

6 hard-cooked eggs, shelled and
halved lengthwise
¼ cup yogurt (see page 311)
¼ cup sesame seeds, ground in
Moulinex grinder
1 tablespoon chopped parsley
¼ teaspoon marjoram
Sea salt or kelp to taste
Toasted sesame seeds

1. Remove the yolks from the egg halves
and mash in a bowl. Stir in the yogurt,
ground seeds, parsley, marjoram and salt
or kelp.

2. Pile mixture back into whites and
garnish with toasted sesame seeds.

Yield: Six servings.

SUNNY EGGS

6 hard-cooked eggs, peeled and
sliced lengthwise
3 tablespoons homemade
mayonnaise (see page 186)
1 tablespoon cider vinegar
¼ teaspoon kelp
½ teaspoon dry mustard
Few grains cayenne pepper
3 tablespoons sunflower seed
meal
1 tablespoon grated onion or
chopped chives
Sea salt to taste
¼ cup alfalfa sprouts
(see page 195)
Sunflower seed kernels

1. Remove the yolks of the eggs to a bowl
and mash well.

2. Add mayonnaise, vinegar, kelp, mustard,
cayenne, sunflower seed meal, onion or
chives and salt. Mix well.

3. Spoon yolk mixture back into whites.
Garnish with sprouts and several sunflower
kernels stuck into each egg half.

Yield: Six servings.

EGGPLANT AND PINE NUT APPETIZER SPREAD

1 medium-size eggplant
¾ cup olive oil, approximately
10 cherry tomatoes
1 clove garlic, finely chopped
2 tablespoons finely chopped onion
½ cup pine nuts
Sea salt and freshly ground black pepper to taste
¼ cup finely chopped parsley
Lemon wedges
Sesame seeded whole wheat or pumpernickel bread slices

1. Trim off and discard end slices of eggplant and cut eggplant into one-quarter-inch-thick slices.

2. Heat some of the oil in a heavy skillet and cook eggplant in it until golden brown on both sides, adding more oil as necessary. Drain browned slices on paper towels. Chop eggplant and place in a bowl.

3. Chop tomatoes and add to bowl. Add garlic, onion, and pine nuts. Season with sea salt and pepper. Chill. Serve sprinkled with chopped parsley, with lemon wedges and bread.

Yield: Six servings.

CHEESE PARTY DIP

½ pound shredded Cheddar cheese
1½ cups skinned chopped ripe tomatoes
1 tablespoon chopped hot green chili pepper
Carrot sticks
Scallions
Cauliflowerets
Zucchini sticks
Cucumber sticks

1. Place cheese and tomatoes in a small saucepan and heat gently until cheese is melted. Add chili pepper. Transfer to serving dish over candle warmer.

2. Serve with raw vegetable dippers.

Yield: Six servings.

PEGGY'S PÂTÉ

1 egg, washed
1 cup spring water, approximately
½ rib celery, diced
1 medium-size carrot, diced
1 small onion, diced
1 tablespoon whole hulled millet
Sea salt to taste
Kelp to taste
1/16 teaspoon saffron
¾ pound chicken livers
1 tablespoon chopped parsley
¼ teaspoon freshly ground black pepper
⅛ teaspoon curry powder
2 tablespoons oil
¼ cup wheat germ
½ teaspoon onion juice
1 tablespoon chopped chives (optional)
Parsley sprigs and radish roses
Whole wheat toast rounds or whole wheat crackers

1. Place egg in a small saucepan and cover with spring water. Bring to a boil and simmer 12 minutes. Remove egg, reserve water, and cool egg under cold water. Peel.

2. To the water left in the saucepan, add the celery, carrot, onion and millet. Bring to a boil. Add sea salt, kelp and saffron. Cook until vegetables are barely tender, adding more water if necessary.

3. Add chicken livers and cook only until livers are firm, about three minutes. Remove livers and set aside.

4. With a slotted spoon, lift vegetables and millet into an electric blender. Add parsley, pepper, curry powder and enough of the cooking water to blend mixture to a smooth paste.

5. Pass livers and peeled egg through medium blade of a food chopper. Mix with blended mixture, oil, wheat germ, onion juice and chives and chill well. Pack into an oiled bowl and chill well.

6. Unmold onto a cold plate and garnish with parsley sprigs and radish roses and serve with rounds of whole wheat toast or whole wheat crackers.

Yield: Eight servings.

Note: The contributor uses organic livers and fertile eggs.

INDIVIDUAL ONION TARTS

Pastry:
- ½ cup butter, room temperature
- 3 ounces cream cheese, at room temperature
- 2 tablespoons heavy cream
- 1¼ cups unbleached white flour
- ½ teaspoon sea salt

Filling:
- 3 tablespoons butter
- 6 large onions, finely chopped
- ½ cup finely shredded Swiss cheese
- 1½ cups heavy goat's or cow's cream
- 3 eggs, lightly beaten
- Sea salt to taste
- ⅛ teaspoon nutmeg
- ⅓ cup freshly grated Parmesan cheese

1. To prepare pastry, cream together the butter and cream cheese until smooth and creamy. Beat in the cream. Work in the flour and salt to make a dough.

2. Wrap in wax paper and chill several hours or overnight.

3. Preheat the oven to 425 degrees.

4. To prepare filling, heat the butter and sauté the onions in it very slowly until transparent and golden.

5. Roll out the pastry on a lightly floured board to ⅛-inch thickness and cut into rounds to fit bite-size muffin tins. Fit rounds into tins.

6. Divide the onions among the lined tins. Sprinkle with the Swiss cheese. Combine the cream, eggs, salt and nutmeg and spoon over the Swiss cheese and onion.

7. Sprinkle with Parmesan cheese and bake eight minutes. Reduce oven heat to 350 degrees and bake 15 minutes longer or until tarts are set and lightly browned on top. Serve warm.

Yield: About two and one-half dozen tarts.

Note: If desired, natural cheeses, organically grown onions and fertile eggs can be used.

SPINACH TART

Pastry:
- 1 cup stoneground whole wheat flour
- ¼ teaspoon sea salt
- ½ cup butter
- ¼ to ½ cup ice water

Filling:
- 2 cups shredded fresh spinach leaves
- 2 tablespoons finely chopped onion
- ¼ teaspoon rosemary, crushed
- 1 cup sliced mushrooms
- 3 tablespoons sweet butter
- 1 tablespoon whole wheat flour
- 1 cup grated Swiss cheese
- 1½ cups heavy cream
- 4 eggs, lightly beaten
- ½ teaspoon sea salt
- ¼ teaspoon freshly ground black pepper
- Few grains cayenne pepper
- ⅛ teaspoon nutmeg
- ¼ teaspoon raw sugar

1. To prepare pastry, place the flour and salt in a bowl. Cut in the butter until well blended. Add ice water, one tablespoon at a time, working water in until mixture feels wet and almost slimy. (Whole grain flours absorb moisture more slowly than regular bleached flours.) Roll into a ball and chill 30 minutes.

2. Preheat the oven to 325 degrees.

3. Roll the chilled dough to one-quarter-inch thickness, between sheets of wax paper, making a circle that will fit a 10-inch pie plate.

4. Peel the paper off one side and press dough into an oiled 10-inch pie plate. Carefully peel off top layer of paper. Bake five minutes.

5. Meanwhile, to make the filling, place spinach, onion and rosemary in a saucepan and cook, covered until wilted. Drain. Place in an electric blender. Blend until smooth, using a tablespoon or two of the cooking liquid if necessary.

6. Increase oven heat to 400 degrees.

7. Sauté the mushrooms briefly in the sweet butter. Sprinkle with flour and cook, stirring, one minute.

8. Place mushroom mixture in bottom of partially cooked pie shell. Top with spinach puree and sprinkle with cheese.

9. Beat cream and eggs together and add salt. pepper, cayenne, nutmeg and sugar. Pour over the mixture in pie shell.

10. Bake 15 minutes. Reduce oven heat to 325 degrees and bake about 30 minutes longer or until puffed, browned and set. Cool slightly before cutting. Serve warm.

Yield: Eight to ten servings.

2
BEVERAGES

Devout followers of natural food regimes do not drink wine, liquors, soda beverages or artificially-flavored drinks. The beverages in this chapter fit in with the book's aim to provide good-tasting and nutritious alternates for foods with little or no food value. The recipes will provide refreshing drinks for all occasions and most can be made without an expensive electric juicer. The combinations of raw vegetable and fruit juices are almost limitless if one does own one of the machines.

GOLDEN APRICOT SHAKE

1½ cups apricot nectar, make
    from fresh apricots when
    possible
1 cup milk
1 teaspoon lemon juice
2 cups frozen homemade eggnog
    or vanilla ice cream

Put all ingredients in an electric blender and
blend until smooth.

Yield: Four servings.

APRICOT APPETIZER

2 cups unsweetened apricot
    nectar
½ cup brewer's yeast
⅛ teaspoon mace
1 sprig mint

Combine all the ingredients in an electric
blender and blend until smooth.

Yield: Four to six servings.

BANANA-MILK DRINK

3 tablespoons carob powder or
    1 egg
1 tablespoon non-fat dry milk
    solids
2 tablespoons honey
½ teaspoon smooth raw peanut
    butter
½ ripe banana
4 cups milk

1. In an electric blender, place the carob
powder or egg, the milk solids, honey,
peanut butter, banana and one cup of the
milk.

2. Blend until smooth. Add remaining milk
and blend. Serve hot or cold.

Yield: Four servings.

LEMONADE SYRUP

Grated rind of 6 lemons
(or limes)
Juice of 12 lemons (or limes)
2 quarts boiling water
2¼ cups raw sugar or
brown sugar
Cold water
Ice cubes

1. Combine the rind and juice and let stand overnight.

2. Pour the boiling water over the sugar, stir to dissolve, bring to a boil and boil five minutes. Cool.

3. Combine syrup with lemon juice mixture.

4. To serve, dilute lemonade syrup with equal parts cold water.

Serve over ice.

Yield: Two and one-half quarts syrup or five quarts lemonade.

ORANGE STRAWBERRY WAKE-UP

1 cup orange juice
1 cup fresh strawberries
1 egg
½ cup non-instant dry milk solids
½ cup water

Put all ingredients in an electric blender and blend until smooth.

Yield: Four servings.

STRAWBERRY COOLER

1 pint fresh strawberries
½ cup raw sugar or honey
2 cups homemade vanilla ice
cream
2 quarts ice cold goat's milk

1. Place the strawberries and sugar or honey in an electric blender and blend until smooth.

2. Add the ice cream and one cup of the goat's milk and blend again.

3. Combine blender mixture with remaining goat's milk.

Yield: Eight to ten servings.

MID-MORNING PICKUP

½ cup unsweetened prune juice
½ cup fresh apple juice
1 teaspoon nut butter
1 teaspoon yogurt (see page 311)
1 teaspoon sesame oil

Blend all ingredients in an electric blender.
Yield: One serving.

WATERMELON JUICE

Force ripe watermelon through a
very fine conical strainer

Cantaloupe juice can be made the same
way. According to the contributor, this
juice is a particularly appealing,
mild-tasting, hot weather beverage for a
small infant.

PINEAPPLE-COCONUT DRINK

½ cup coconut milk
½ cup unsweetened pineapple
juice
1 teaspoon wheat germ
1 tablespoon yogurt (see page 311)

Combine all ingredients in an electric
blender and blend until smooth.
Yield: One serving.

FRUITED MILK SHAKE

1 cup milk
6 ice cubes, crushed
1 tablespoon honey
¾ cup diced mixed fresh fruits
  such as apples, strawberries,
  blueberries, pears, peaches and
  apricots

Place all ingredients in an electric blender and blend 30 seconds.

Yield: Two servings.

EASY BLENDER LUNCH

1 banana
1 apple, cored
1 pear, cored
½ to ¾ cup orange juice
2 tablespoons raisins

Place all ingredients in an electric blender and blend until smooth. Pour into a bowl and eat with a spoon, or drink from a glass.

Yield: One to two servings.

RUSSIAN FRUIT TEA

A cup, ¾'s full, hot, brewed
  regular or herb tea
Raw sugar or honey to taste
1 apple, quartered, cored and
  finely diced

1. Sweeten the tea with sugar or honey and add the apple.

2. Let stand several minutes then eat the apple pieces with a spoon and drink the tea.

Yield: One serving.

Note: Other fruits, such as pears, peaches, oranges and grapes can be substituted for the apple.

OUR OWN HEALTH DRINK

1 cup water
1 carrot, diced
2 tablespoons chopped dates
2 tablespoons sesame seeds
2 tablespoons wheat germ

Put all ingredients in an electric blender and blend until smooth.

Yield: Two servings.

SESAME SEED MILK

½ cup sesame seeds
1½ cups water

Put seeds and water in an electric blender and blend at high speed for 45 seconds. Strain through double thickness of cheesecloth.

Yield: One serving.

NUT AND SEED MILK

¼ cup sunflower seed kernels
¾ cup cashews or blanched almonds
3 cups cold water
2 tablespoons honey
Sea salt to taste
½ teaspoon soy milk powder

1. Place kernels, nuts and one cup of the water in an electric blender and let soak 15 minutes. Blend until smooth.

2. Add remaining ingredients, including remaining water, and blend until well mixed. Serve very cold.

Yield: Three servings.

CARROT-MILK DRINK

½ cup carrot juice
½ cup soy milk or cow's milk
¼ cup chopped almonds
2 teaspoons wheat germ

Blend all ingredients until smooth in electric blender.

Yield: Two servings.

CARROT-PINEAPPLE APPETIZER

2 cups unsweetened pineapple juice
½ cup diced raw carrot
1 tablespoon lemon juice
1 tablespoon brewer's yeast
⅛ teaspoon basil

Put all ingredients in an electric blender and blend until smooth.

Yield: Four to six servings.

COMFREY COCKTAIL

2 to 3 cups young tender comfrey leaves, washed, drained and chopped
¼ cup celery leaves, chopped
1 small onion, chopped
2 tablespoons chopped fresh basil
½ cup shredded escarole
1 apple, cored, chopped
3 to 4 mint leaves, chopped
Tomato juice or fresh apple cider
Sea salt and honey to taste

1. In a bowl, mix together the comfrey, celery leaves, onion, basil, escarole, apple and mint leaves.

2. Place one-half cup of the greens mixture in an electric blender with one-quarter cup tomato juice or apple cider and blend briefly. Pour into a pitcher and repeat with remaining mixture and more juice.

3. Add enough extra juice to give a drinkable consistency to the blended mixture. Season with salt and sweeten with honey.

Yield: About one and one-half quarts.

WILD GREENS PUNCH DE LUXE

½ gallon boiling water
1½ quarts plus 1 cup shredded
    wild, edible greens from
    among the following:
    comfrey, dandelion, lamb's
    quarters, nettles, wild
    strawberry leaves, lemon
    geranium, watercress,
    rose petals, squash blossoms,
    chickweed, purslane or
    nasturtium flowers
1 strip orange rind
1 strip lemon rind
Honey to taste
1 can (6 ounces) frozen orange
    juice concentrate
½ cup lemon juice
Unsweetened pineapple juice
    or fresh apple juice

1. Pour the boiling water over one and one-half quarts of shredded mixed wild greens, orange rind and lemon rind, bring to a boil and simmer 20 minutes. Strain mixture and sweeten with honey while hot. Cool.

2. Add orange juice concentrate and lemon juice and make up to one gallon with pineapple juice or apple juice.

3. Place one cup of punch in an electric blender with the remaining cup of shredded greens. Blend well, strain, add to punch and chill.

Yield: One gallon.

GOLDEN TOMATO JUICE

½ peck (4 quarts) yellow plum
    tomatoes, washed
3 onions, chopped
1 cup chopped parsley
1 cup chopped celery
3 teaspoons sea salt

1. Place tomatoes, onions, parsley, celery and salt in a large kettle. Bring to a boil and simmer until tomatoes are soft.

2. Press through a Foley food mill. Heat to boiling and pour into clean, sterilized canning jars. Process in a water bath for 15 minutes. Tighten covers, let cool and store in a cool dark place.

Yield: About three quarts.

Note: The contributor uses her own organically grown tomatoes and vegetables. Red plum tomatoes can be substituted for yellow.

TOMATO-SAUERKRAUT DRINK

½ cup tomato juice
½ cup sauerkraut juice
1 teaspoon chopped parsley
2 teaspoons brewer's yeast

Blend all ingredients in an electric blender.
Yield: One serving.

VEGETABLE DRINK

½ cup tomato juice
¼ cup celery juice
¼ cup carrot juice
¼ bunch watercress, chopped
1 teaspoon chopped parsley
1 teaspoon lemon juice
2 teaspoons brewer's yeast

Blend all ingredients in an electric blender.
Yield: Two servings.

HEALTH COCKTAIL

1 quart skinned ripe tomatoes
1 large sprig parsley
1 teaspoon finely chopped scallion
2 tablespoons chopped inner-rib
  celery leaves
1 teaspoon sea salt

1. Put the tomatoes in an electric blender,
one at a time, and blend until smooth after
each addition.
2. Add remaining ingredients; blend until
smooth. Serve very cold.
Yield: About three cups.

TAHN

1 cup yogurt (see page 311)
3 cups ice water
Ice cubes

Combine yogurt and water in an electric
blender and blend one minute. Pour over
ice cubes.
Yield: Four servings.

DAHI

1 quart yogurt (see page 311)
Juice of 12 limes
½ to 1 cup raw sugar or honey,
    approximately
Spring water

1. Place yogurt, lime juice and sugar to taste in an electric blender and blend until sugar has dissolved.

2. Pour into a gallon jug or container and fill with ice cold spring water.

Yield: Sixteen servings.

HELEN'S EYE-OPENER

1 envelope unflavored gelatin
1 tablespoon Tang
1 tablespoon blackstrap molasses
1 tablespoon brewer's yeast
⅓ cup Tiger's milk
1 cup wheat germ
Cold water

1. In a pitcher, combine all the ingredients except the water. Mix well.

2. Stir in enough water to make a beverage-like consistency. Pour into a glass and drink at once.

Yield: One serving.

LIVER COCKTAIL

2 ounces raw calves' liver
1 carrot, quartered
Sea salt to taste
Water

Place the liver, carrot and salt in an electric blender and blend until smooth. Blend in enough water to make the mixture drinking consistency.

Yield: One serving.

3
SOUPS

A homemade soup has always been superior to any dried, canned or frozen product, and almost any of Grandmother's recipes for soups will still produce a hearty, good-tasting and nutritious luncheon or dinner mainstay.

In the recipes that follow, emphasis is on unusual recipes that are not found in standard texts but that combine honest, fresh ingredients in appetizing combinations.

A good homemade broth, whether based on poultry, meat or vegetables, is still the secret to many good-tasting soups made from scratch, and recipes for such broths are included. Vegetable cooking water contains valuable nutrients and can be the basis for vegetable broths to be used in vegetable soups, supplemented where necessary with vegetable extracts, bouillon cubes, powders and salts.

Try one of these recipes and your family or guests will urge you to make more of "those different kinds of soups" in which you control all of the ingredients.

AVOCADO SOUP

1 large ripe avocado, peeled
    and pitted
2 cups nut milk or seed milk
    (see page 25)
½ teaspoon kelp or dulse
    (seaweed)
¼ teaspoon oregano
⅛ teaspoon summer savory
Yogurt (see page 311)

1. With a stainless steel or wooden spoon, mash the avocado, or blend to a puree in an electric blender. Gradually beat or blend in the milk.

2. Add the kelp or dulse, the oregano and savory. Pour into a saucepan and heat until just below the simmer point. Do not boil or the avocado will taste bitter.

3. Serve, topped with yogurt, in heated bowls.

Yield: Four servings.

THICK BEAN SOUP

1 cup dried soybeans, picked
    over and washed
1 cup whole barley, washed
¾ cup cracked wheat (bulghur)
Water
Sea salt
1 clove garlic
1 onion, chopped
1 bay leaf
Vegetable broth powder
1 cup mixed split peas and lentils
2 cups shredded kale, spinach
    or escarole
Tamari (soy sauce) to taste

1. Place soybeans, barley and cracked wheat in a large bowl. Cover well with cold water and let soak several hours or overnight.

2. Place soybeans, barley and wheat with soaking liquid in a large kettle. Add water to give a depth of two inches above the soybeans. Add salt, garlic, onion and bay leaf. Bring to a boil, partly cover and simmer until soybeans are barely tender, about two hours.

3. Add the vegetable seasoning, split peas and lentils and continue to cook until everything is tender. Add water as necessary.

4. Add the greens and tamari and cook until greens are wilted.

Yield: Twelve to sixteen servings.

CORN MEAL SOUP

¼ cup stoneground corn meal
½ cup cold water
1 quart boiling chicken broth or beef broth (see pages 52, 53)

Mix the corn meal with the water and gradually stir into the boiling broth. Simmer, stirring, 15 minutes.

Yield: Four servings.

Note: Oatmeal can be substituted for the corn meal if preferred.

LENTIL SOUP I

1½ cups lentils, picked over and washed
Cold water
1 tablespoon butter
2 tablespoons sesame oil or soy oil
3 cloves garlic, finely chopped
2 small onions, chopped
1 large rib celery, chopped
¼ cup chopped celery leaves
2 carrots, thickly sliced
⅓ cup raw brown rice
2 tablespoons chopped parsley
Freshly ground black pepper to taste (optional)
1 tablespoon sea salt
3 tablespoons brewer's yeast
1½ tablespoons miso (soybean paste) or to taste

1. Place the lentils in a bowl and cover with cold water. Let soak while preparing other vegetables.

2. In a heavy kettle, heat the butter and oil and add garlic, onions, celery, celery leaves, carrots, rice and parsley. Cook, stirring, for five minutes over medium heat.

3. When the onions have wilted, drain the lentils and add to the kettle. Add one and one-half quarts fresh water, the pepper, salt and brewer's yeast.

4. Bring to a boil, cover and simmer until vegetables are tender and liquid begins to have a brownish color, about one and one-half hours.

5. Remove one-half cup of the broth and mix with the miso until smooth.
Return to the kettle. Cook 20 minutes longer.

Yield: Six servings.

Note: Barley or millet can be used in place of the rice, and two cups of shredded dark green leafy vegetables, such as kale, spinach and escarole, can be added with the miso mixture.

LENTIL SOUP II

1½ tablespoons oil
1½ cups chopped onions
  2 cups dried lentils, picked over and washed
  2 quarts cold water, approximately
  2 small potatoes, scrubbed and cooked in boiling salted water
  1 large carrot, grated
  1 tablespoon chopped fresh basil
  2 cups fresh or canned tomato juice
Sea salt to taste (optional)
¾ cup shredded spinach
½ cup dry white wine (optional)
  Grated hard goat's cheese
  Sprigs fresh basil

1. Heat the oil in a heavy kettle and sauté the onion in it until transparent. Add the lentils and water. Bring to a boil, cover and simmer over low heat until lentils are tender, about two hours. Watch the water level and replenish as necessary to keep lentils covered.

2. Peel and dice potatoes and add to cooked lentils.

3. Add carrot, basil, tomato juice, salt and spinach to kettle and cook until spinach wilts and turns dark green, about four minutes after mixture returns to the boil. Stir in the wine. Serve with grated hard goat's cheese. Garnish soup with basil sprigs.

Yield: Ten servings.

BLACK BEAN SOUP

  3 tablespoons oil
  1 onion, finely chopped
  1 rib celery with leaves, chopped
1½ cups black beans, picked over and washed
  6 cups vegetable broth (see chapter introduction), chicken broth or beef broth (see pages 52, 53)
½ teaspoon sea salt
  Freshly ground black pepper to taste
  3 tablespoons brewer's yeast
  2 tablespoons whole wheat flour
  1 tablespoon celery seeds
½ cup lemon juice
  Dry sherry to taste (optional)
  Lemon slices
  1 hard-cooked egg, chopped

1. Heat the oil in a heavy kettle and sauté the onion and celery in it until tender. Add beans and broth. Bring to a boil, cover and simmer three hours or until beans are tender.

2. Puree in an electric blender, in batches, with the salt, pepper, brewer's yeast, flour and celery seeds.

3. Return pureed soup to the kettle and reheat, stirring, until mixture thickens slightly. Stir in the lemon juice and sherry. If the consistency is too thick, it can be adjusted with more broth, or water. Serve in bowls, topped with lemon slices and chopped egg.

Yield: Six to eight servings.

SPLIT PEA SOUP

2 cups split green peas,
  picked over and washed
2½ cups cold water
2 smoked pork hocks or
  1 ham bone
2 teaspoons sea salt
2 ribs celery with leaves,
  roughly chopped
½ white turnip, sliced
1 onion, sliced
1 large carrot, quartered
1 bay leaf
¼ teaspoon chervil
½ teaspoon savory

1. Place the split peas in a kettle with the remaining ingredients. Bring to a boil, cover and simmer for one and one-half to two hours or until the split peas are tender.

2. Remove hocks. Discard bone, skin and gristle. Dice meat and place in a clean saucepan.

3. Pass soup through a food mill or electric blender and add to ham pieces. Reheat and check seasonings.

Yield: Eight servings.

MEDLEY SOUP

2 slices (about 1½ pounds)
  beef shin or shank with
  the bone in
2 or 3 beef bones or veal bones
10 cups water
¼ cup yellow split peas, washed
¼ cup whole barley, washed
¼ cup green split peas or lentils,
  washed
¼ cup lentils, washed
1½ tablespoons salt
2 carrots, quartered
1 onion, sliced
1 white turnip, sliced
2 sprigs parsley
2 bay leaves, crumbled
½ teaspoon thyme
¼ cup chopped parsley

1. Place the beef and bones in the bottom of a heavy, deep kettle. Add the water and bring to a boil. Boil 10 minutes, removing the scum as it forms.

2. Add the yellow split peas, barley, green split peas, lentils, salt, carrots, onion, turnip, parsley sprigs, bay leaves and thyme.

3. Bring to a boil again, cover and simmer two hours or until meat and barley are very tender.

4. Remove bones and discard. Remove shin and dice meat. Discard shin bones and return meat to kettle.

5. Garnish soup with chopped parsley before serving.

Yield: Six to eight servings.

BAY BORSCHT

2 tablespoons oil
3 large onions, chopped
3 beets, peeled and grated
2 beets, peeled and cubed
1 carrot, chopped
2 potatoes, peeled and cubed
1 medium-size head red cabbage, shredded
2 quarts vegetable broth (see chapter introduction) or beef broth (see page 53)
2 cups chopped skinned fresh or canned tomatoes
½ teaspoon dill seeds, freshly ground
2 bay leaves, crumbled
1 tablespoon soy flour
3 tablespoons brewer's yeast
1 teaspoon sea salt, or to taste
Sour cream or yogurt (see page 311)

1. Heat the oil in a large kettle and sauté the onions, beets, carrot, potatoes and cabbage, stirring occasionally, for 15 minutes.

2. Add broth, cover and simmer until vegetables are crisp-tender.

3. Combine tomatoes, dill seeds, bay leaves, soy flour, brewer's yeast and salt and add to kettle. Cook 10 minutes. Serve topped with sour cream or yogurt.

Yield: Six to eight servings.

CAULIFLOWER SOUP

1 medium-size head cauliflower, broken into flowerets and steamed until tender over boiling water
3 tablespoons butter
2 onion slices
1 teaspoon vegetable broth powder
2 cups milk, scalded
1 quart boiling spring water
1 teaspoon vegetable salt
1 egg yolk, lightly beaten
2 tablespoons grated Swiss or Gruyère cheese

1. Drain the cooked cauliflower and pass through a food mill or blend until smooth in an electric blender.

2. Heat the butter and sauté the onion in it until tender. Add vegetable broth powder. Stir milk and water into pureed cauliflower and combine with onion mixture. Add vegetable salt. Cook five minutes; strain.

3. Add a little of the hot liquid to the egg yolk, return to bulk of mixture in pan and stir in the cheese.

Yield: Six servings.

BRUSSELS SPROUT SOUP

10 ounces Brussels sprouts
3 tablespoons oil
1 small onion, finely chopped
Sea salt to taste
⅓ cup water, chicken broth (see page 52) or vegetable broth (see chapter introduction)
2 tablespoons whole wheat flour
2 cups milk
2 cups chicken broth (see page 52) or vegetable broth (see chapter introduction)
⅛ teaspoon nutmeg

1. Remove and discard the outside leaves of the sprouts. Wash sprouts well. Drain and pat dry. Cut in half through the stem.

2. Heat the oil in a saucepan and add sprouts, onion and salt. Sauté gently until sprouts turn darker green, about five minutes.

3. Add the water, bring to a boil, cover and simmer 10 minutes or until sprouts are barely tender. Evaporate any liquid remaining by removing cover and heating.

4. Sprinkle with the flour and cook, stirring, one minute.

5. Heat the milk and broth to boiling and stir into the sprout mixture. Add nutmeg and salt. Bring to a boil, stirring.

Yield: Four servings.

CELERY CHOWDER

1 quart chopped celery, preferably the outer ribs with their leaves
2 cups boiling water
1 large potato, grated
2 tablespoons butter
1 tablespoon unbleached white flour
1 quart milk, scalded
Sea salt to taste
⅛ teaspoon nutmeg
2 hard-cooked eggs, chopped

1. Drop the celery into the boiling water. Add the potato and let simmer until celery is crisp-tender and potato is cooked.

2. Meanwhile, combine the butter and flour in a saucepan. Gradually beat in the milk, bring to a boil and stir until mixture thickens slightly. Add salt and nutmeg and stir into celery mixture.

3. Add the eggs, check seasoning and simmer, stirring continuously, until mixture is smooth and slightly thickened. Serve immediately.

Yield: Six to eight servings.

EGG AND LEMON SOUP WITH FIDDLEHEADS

1½ cups washed fresh
fiddlehead greens (see note)
8 cups boiling homemade
chicken broth (see page 52)
4 eggs, beaten until frothy
½ cup lemon juice

1. Place the fiddlehead greens in a saucepan and add one cup of the broth. Cover and simmer five minutes.

2. Meanwhile, beat the eggs while gradually adding the lemon juice. Add a cup or so of the remaining hot broth to the egg-lemon mixture, mixing well. Return to bulk of broth in saucepan.

3. Heat, stirring, until mixture just thickens, but do not allow to boil. Drain the fiddleheads and add to the soup.

Yield: Six servings.

Note: Fiddlehead greens are the tightly curled tips of the fronds of the common fern when they first emerge from the ground in the spring. Uncurled mature ferns are poisonous. Frozen fiddlehead greens are available in some areas.

FRESH PEA SOUP

2 pounds organically grown
peas (about 2 cups)
Boiling spring water
Sea salt to taste
1 tablespoon chopped fresh mint
1 scallion, finely chopped
1½ cups goat's or cow's heavy
cream
Whole wheat bread croutons or
chopped chives

1. Place the peas in a saucepan with boiling water to extend one-half inch above peas. Add salt, mint and scallion. Cover and cook until peas are tender, about 10 minutes.

2. Put the peas and cooking liquid into an electric blender and blend until smooth. Add cream and blend briefly.

3. The soup can be reheated and served hot, garnished with the croutons, or cooled and chilled and served cold, garnished with the chives.

Yield: Four servings.

FRUIT BAT SOUP

(This soup is offered on the off-chance that a reader may find himself in Micronesia, specifically the Caroline Islands, where this is a natural, native delicacy.)

3 fruit bats, well washed but neither skinned nor eviscerated
Water
1 tablespoon finely sliced fresh ginger
1 large onion, quartered
Sea salt to taste
Chopped scallions
Soy sauce and/or coconut cream

1. Place the bats in a large kettle and add water to cover, the ginger, onion and salt. Bring to a boil and boil 40 minutes. Strain broth into a second kettle.

2. Take bats, skin them and discard skin. Remove meat from the bones and return meat, including any of the viscera fancied, to the broth. Heat.

3. Serve liberally sprinkled with scallions and further seasoned with soy sauce and/or coconut cream.

Yield: Four servings.

GARLIC SOUP

2 large heads fresh garlic
Boiling water
2 quarts cold water
2 tablespoons sea salt
Freshly ground black pepper to taste
2 whole cloves
¼ teaspoon sage
¼ teaspoon thyme
4 sprigs parsley
2 tablespoons oil
3 egg yolks
¼ cup butter, melted
6 to 8 slices stale whole wheat Italian bread, buttered
½ cup grated Swiss or Gruyère cheese

1. Separate the heads of garlic into cloves. Pour boiling water to cover over all. Drain. Slip the skins off the garlic cloves and place in a kettle with the water, salt, pepper, cloves, sage, thyme, parsley and oil.

2. Bring to a boil and simmer 30 minutes.

3. Beat the egg yolks until thick and gradually beat in the butter. Strain the soup and add very slowly, while beating vigorously, to the egg yolk mixture. Reheat but do not boil.

4. Place a slice of the bread in the bottom of an individual bowl. Sprinkle with cheese and pour the soup over all.

Yield: Six to eight servings.

Note: This soup does not have an outrageously strong garlic flavor as one might suppose.

SPRING SOUP

1 pound tender young peas
½ cup water
3 tablespoons sweet butter
½ cup chopped shallots or white part of leeks
1 small head oak leaf, Bibb or Boston lettuce, washed and drained
3 cups milk, scalded
3 vegetable broth cubes
½ teaspoon vegetable salt
¼ teaspoon white pepper
1 cup heavy cream

1. Shell the peas and cook in the water until barely tender. Puree and return to the pan.

2. Heat the butter and sauté the shallots in it until tender. Place lettuce and milk in an electric blender and blend until smooth; add to pea puree.

3. Season with broth cubes, vegetable salt and pepper. Add shallots and cream and heat to serving temperature but do not allow to boil.

Yield: Four servings.

Note: The contributor says that this is delicious if fresh, organically grown vegetables, raw milk and raw cream are used. Otherwise, it is rather ordinary, although still a good soup.

MUSHROOM AND BARLEY SOUP

1 cup whole barley, washed
2 quarts boiling homemade vegetable broth (see chapter introduction), chicken broth or beef broth (see pages 52, 53)
2 sprigs parsley
2 ribs celery with leaves, diced
1 onion, finely chopped
1 carrot, sliced
Sea salt to taste
1 pound mushrooms, sliced if large
Tamari (soy sauce) to taste

1. Combine the barley, broth, parsley, celery and onion in a large kettle. Bring to a boil, cover and simmer until the barley is tender, about one and one-half hours.

2. Add remaining ingredients and cook until carrot is tender.

Yield: Eight servings.

BLACK MUSHROOM SOUP

¼ cup dried black mushrooms (available in Italian and Oriental markets)
Warm water
1 quart homemade chicken broth (see page 52)
2 tablespoons oil
1 clove garlic, chopped
1 tablespoon grated fresh gingerroot (available fresh or canned in Oriental markets)
2 tablespoons tamari (soy sauce)
½ cup sliced bamboo shoots
½ cup sliced scallions

1. Place the dried mushrooms in a small bowl. Cover with warm water and let soak 15 minutes. Drain and slice mushrooms.

2. Place the chicken broth in a large saucepan and heat to boiling. Meanwhile, heat the oil in a small skillet and sauté the garlic and mushrooms in it three minutes.

3. Add mushroom mixture to broth along with ginger, soy sauce, bamboo shoots and scallions. Cover and simmer two hours.

Yield: Four servings.

POTATO SOUP

2 cups boiling vegetable broth (see chapter introduction), chicken broth or beef broth (see pages 52, 53)
4 small potatoes, peeled and cubed
1 teaspoon dill seeds, ground in a mortar and pestle
1 onion, finely chopped
1 leek, chopped
Sea salt to taste
1 tablespoon soy flour
1 tablespoon brewer's yeast
1½ cups milk
2 tablespoons chopped parsley or chives

1. Place the broth in a saucepan and add the potatoes, dill seeds, onion, leek and salt. Bring to a boil, cover and simmer until the potatoes are tender, about 15 minutes.

2. Puree the mixture in a food mill or in an electric blender. Mix the soy flour and brewer's yeast together and gradually blend in the milk.

3. Combine the pureed potato mixture and milk mixture in a saucepan and reheat. Serve garnished with parsley or chives.

Yield: Four servings.

POTATO CHOWDER

6 slices lean bacon, diced
3 tablespoons chopped onion
2 cups water
1 teaspoon sea salt
5 medium-size potatoes, peeled and diced
1 cup carrots, finely diced
1 cup shredded spinach
4 cups milk, scalded

1. Fry the bacon bits in a heavy skillet until crisp. Add onion and sauté until tender. Add water, salt, potatoes and carrots. Bring to a boil, cover and simmer until vegetables are tender, about 15 minutes.

2. Add the spinach and cook until it is just limp and dark green, about three minutes. Add the milk and bring mixture to just below the simmer point. Do not boil. Serve immediately.

Yield: Six servings.

SWEET POTATO SOUP

1 quart peeled sweet potatoes cut into chunks
3 cups thickly sliced leeks or onions
3 carrots, cut into chunks
3 ribs celery, sliced into large chunks
2 quarts water
Sea salt to taste
Freshly ground pepper to taste (optional)
1 tablespoon soy margarine
¼ cup goat's or cow's milk
2 tablespoons toasted sesame seeds
1 tablespoon caraway seeds
2 teaspoons chopped fresh tarragon or ½ teaspoon dried tarragon

1. Place the sweet potatoes, leeks, carrots, celery and water in a large kettle. Add salt and pepper. Bring to a boil, cover and simmer 40 minutes. The soup will be lumpy.

2. With a slotted spoon, remove half of the carrots and celery and some firmer potato chunks and reserve.

3. Puree the remainder of the soup in a food mill or an electric blender until smooth. Return to the kettle and add the reserved vegetables, the margarine, milk, sesame seeds, caraway seeds and tarragon. Reheat; check seasonings. Serve immediately.

Yield: Eight servings.

BROWN POTATO SOUP

6 medium-size potatoes, peeled
and diced
1 medium-size onion, diced
Water
2½ cups skinned chopped fresh
or canned tomatoes
4 tablespoons unbleached
white flour
1 tablespoon bacon drippings
Sea salt and freshly ground
pepper to taste

1. Place potatoes and onion in a saucepan
and add water to cover. Bring to a boil and
simmer 15 minutes. Add tomatoes and
simmer five minutes longer.

2. Meanwhile, place flour and bacon
drippings in a small, heavy skillet and heat
slowly, stirring constantly, until flour
browns. (Do not allow to burn or it will be
bitter.) Stir into simmering vegetable
mixture.

3. Season with salt and pepper. If mixture
is too thick, add more water.

Yield: Six servings.

SUNFLOWER SEED SOUP

2 tablespoons butter
¾ cup shredded carrot
1 onion, finely chopped
¼ cup water
3 medium-size tomatoes, skinned
and blended in an electric
blender until smooth
1 cup chicken broth or beef broth
(see pages 52, 53)
1 teaspoon dill seeds, crushed to
powder in a mortar and pestle
1 tablespoon honey
¼ cup sunflower seed flour
Yogurt (see page 311)
1 scallion, finely chopped
½ ripe avocado, sliced

1. Heat the butter in a saucepan and sauté
the carrot and onion in it over low heat
about three minutes. Add water, cover
and cook until vegetables are barely tender.

2. Add vegetable mixture including the
liquid to the tomato mixture in the blender
and blend until smooth.

3. Pour mixture back into the saucepan
and add the broth, dill, honey and
sunflower seed flour. Reheat to below
simmer point, stirring constantly. Serve
garnished with yogurt, chopped scallion
and avocado slices.

Yield: Four servings.

SUNFLOWER BROTH

2 tablespoons oil
1 medium-size onion, finely
  chopped, or 4 scallions,
  chopped
2 cups sunflower seed kernels
1 teaspoon sea salt
1½ quarts boiling vegetable broth
  (see chapter introduction),
  chicken broth or beef broth
  (see pages 52, 53)
1 teaspoon summer savory
1 cup shredded spinach or
  romaine (optional)

1. Heat the oil in a heavy saucepan. Sauté the onion or scallions in it until tender but not browned. Add the sunflower seed kernels, salt and broth.

2. Bring to a boil, cover and simmer gently 40 minutes or until kernels are tender. Add the savory and spinach or romaine. Boil two minutes. Alternately, the soup can be blended in an electric blender and the spinach omitted if a creamed texture is preferred.

Yield: Six servings.

DANISH GREEN TOMATO SOUP

¼ cup butter
2 onions, sliced
8 green tomatoes, washed and
  cut into chunks
1 cup chicken broth or beef
  broth (see pages 52, 53)
1 tablespoon arrowroot
1 cup milk
Sea salt to taste
Freshly ground black pepper
  to taste (optional)
1 teaspoon sugar
Sour cream or yogurt
  (see page 311)
Chopped chives or dill weed

1. Melt the butter in a heavy skillet and sauté the onions and green tomatoes in it until soft but not brown. Puree in an electric blender or in a food mill. Add the broth.

2. Blend the arrowroot with the milk and add to tomato mixture. Bring to a boil, stirring until mixture thickens. Season with salt, pepper and sugar.

3. Serve topped with sour cream or yogurt and chives or dill. Alternately, the soup may be cooled and chilled to serve cold.

Yield: Six servings.

COLD CUCUMBER SOUP I

2 large cucumbers, peeled, halved lengthwise, seeded and finely chopped
1 quart boiling chicken broth (see page 52)
3 tablespoons butter
1 onion, finely chopped
¼ pound mushrooms, sliced
Sea salt to taste
Freshly ground black pepper to taste (optional)
1 cup light cream
2 tablespoons chopped chives

1. Add the cucumbers to the boiling chicken broth, cover and simmer 10 minutes.

2. Heat the butter in a small skillet and sauté the onion in it until tender. Add mushrooms and cook three minutes longer. Add to the broth mixture.

3. Season to taste with salt and pepper. Cook three minutes. Cool and chill.

4. Just before serving, stir in the cream. Serve sprinkled with chives.

Yield: Four servings.

COLD CUCUMBER SOUP II

¼ cup whole barley, washed
1 large onion, chopped
¼ cup snipped fresh dill weed
2 cups boiling water
2 large cucumbers, peeled, halved lengthwise, seeded and cut into one-inch pieces
1 bunch watercress, washed and chopped
2 tablespoons lemon juice
1 cup yogurt (see page 311)
Chopped chives or parsley

1. Add the barley, onion and dill weed to the boiling water, cover and simmer until barley is tender, about one hour.

2. Add cucumbers and watercress and cook 10 minutes. Cool. Puree in an electric blender, or force through a food mill. Stir in the lemon juice and yogurt. Chill. Serve garnished with chives or parsley.

Yield: Four servings.

COLD CUCUMBER SOUP III

2 tablespoons butter
½ onion, finely chopped
1 clove garlic, finely chopped
3 large cucumbers, peeled, halved
  lengthwise, seeded and chopped
3 tablespoons unbleached white
  flour
2 cups homemade chicken broth
  (see page 52)
1 teaspoon sea salt
¾ cup sour cream or yogurt
  (see page 311)
1 tablespoon snipped fresh dill
  weed
1 teaspoon grated lemon rind
⅛ teaspoon mace

1. Heat the butter in a heavy skillet and sauté the onion, garlic and cucumbers in it until onion is tender, about 10 minutes.

2. Sprinkle with the flour; stir well. Gradually stir in the broth. Add the salt and bring to a boil. Cover and simmer until cucumber is tender. Cool. Puree the mixture, in batches, through an electric blender or a food mill. Stir in the sour cream or yogurt, the dill, lemon rind and mace. Chill several hours.

Yield: Four to six servings.

BEST BARLEY SOUP

¼ cup whole barley, washed
6 cups boiling vegetable broth
  (see chapter introduction) or
  beef broth (see page 53)
1 cup sliced carrots
½ cup diced celery
¼ cup chopped onions
2 cups skinned chopped
  tomatoes
1 cup fresh peas
Sea salt to taste
½ cup chopped parsley

1. Place barley and broth in a heavy kettle, cover and simmer until barley is tender, about one hour. Add remaining ingredients, except the parsley, and cook, covered, until vegetables are barely tender.

2. Add the parsley but do not cook any further.

Yield: Six servings.

ZUCCHINI SOUP

1 pound zucchini (3 to 4 small),
  washed and sliced
1 cup homemade chicken broth
  or beef broth (see pages 52, 53)
Sea salt to taste
⅛ teaspoon basil
⅛ teaspoon thyme
⅛ teaspoon marjoram
2 cups milk
Whipped cottage cheese or
  yogurt (see page 311)

1. Place the zucchini, broth and salt in a
saucepan and bring to a boil. Cover and
simmer gently until tender. Cool.

2. Add the basil, thyme and marjoram
and puree in an electric blender or in a food
mill. Stir in the milk and heat, but do not
boil. Serve topped with cottage cheese
or yogurt.

Yield: Four servings.

VEGETABLE SOUP

6 cups boiling water, tomato
  juice (see page 27) or
  vegetable broth (see chapter
  introduction)
3 tablespoons rolled oats or ½
  cup whole wheat berries,
  coarsely ground
1 tablespoon rice polishings
2 cups chopped skinned
  tomatoes
1 bay leaf
Sea salt to taste
2 tablespoons sesame oil or
  safflower oil
1½ cups shredded cabbage
1½ cups chopped celery
½ cup sliced green beans
½ cup fresh peas
½ teaspoon marjoram
2 tablespoons chopped parsley
½ cup cooked brown rice
  (see page 217) or
  uncooked whole wheat
  noodles (see page 309)
1 cup shredded escarole

1. Combine the boiling water, juice or
broth in a kettle with the oats or whole
wheat berries and the rice polishings and
cook until thickened.

2. Add remaining ingredients, except the
escarole, and cook, covered, until
vegetables and noodles are tender, about
15 minutes.

3. Add escarole and cook three minutes
longer.

Yield: Six servings.

BLENDER VEGETABLE CREAM SOUP

1 quart milk
½ cup cooked parsnips
½ cup cooked peas
½ cup diced celery
½ cup cooked carrots
½ cup raw corn kernels
¼ cup whole wheat flour
Sea salt to taste
1 sprig parsley
1 sprig fresh dill
Toasted soybeans

1. Place all the ingredients except the soybeans in an electric blender and blend until smooth. Pour into a saucepan and heat, stirring, until mixture comes to a boil and thickens.

2. Serve sprinkled with soybeans as garnish.

Yield: Four servings.

Note: Other combinations of cooked, and raw, vegetables can be used.

VEGETABLE-SOY SOUP

1½ cups cooked soybeans (or 15½-ounce can, drained) (see page 157)
¼ cup water
2 tablespoons oil
2 onions, chopped
1 clove garlic, chopped
2 ribs celery, diced
1 green pepper, seeded and diced
2 carrots, scrubbed, or scraped, and diced
2 cups skinned chopped fresh or canned tomatoes
1 quart homemade chicken broth (see page 52) or water
½ teaspoon thyme
2 tablespoons chopped parsley
1 teaspoon sea salt, or to taste

1. Place three-quarters cup of the soybeans in an electric blender with the water and blend until smooth.

2. Heat the oil in a kettle and sauté the onions and garlic in it until tender.

3. Add celery, green pepper and carrots and cook five minutes longer, stirring occasionally.

4. Add tomatoes, broth, thyme, parsley, salt and blended beans, bring to a boil, cover and simmer gently until vegetables are crisp-tender.

5. Add remaining whole beans and reheat.

Yield: Six servings.

VEGETABLE BEAN SOUP

3 pounds meaty beef bones
(shin, shank)
5 cups water
2½ teaspoons vegetable salt
¾ cup navy or pea beans
3 cups warm water
2 tablespoons whole barley
½ cup sliced onions
½ cup diced celery
1 cup sliced carrots
1 cup sliced leeks

1. Place beef bones and five cups water in a large kettle with one and one-half teaspoons of the vegetable salt. Bring to a boil, cover and simmer three hours, skimming as necessary. Strain broth and return to kettle. Remove meat from bones and reserve; discard bones.

2. Soak the beans in the warm water two hours.

3. Pour beans and water into a saucepan and simmer, covered, 30 minutes. Add barley and remaining vegetable salt and simmer 30 minutes longer.

4. Add beans to broth. Add remaining ingredients, including reserved meat, and simmer until vegetables are crisp-tender, about 15 minutes.

Yield: Four to six servings.

VEGETABLE SOUP ITALIAN STYLE

3 tablespoons olive oil
1 medium-size onion, chopped
1 clove garlic, finely chopped
1 quart homemade chicken broth
or beef broth (see pages 52, 53)
2 large plum tomatoes, skinned
and chopped
⅓ cup raw brown rice
Sea salt to taste
1 medium-size zucchini,
washed and sliced
1 medium-size potato, peeled
and cubed
Freshly grated Parmesan or
Romano cheese

1. Heat the oil in a kettle and sauté the onion and garlic in it until tender but not browned. Add the broth, tomatoes, rice and salt. Bring to a boil, cover and simmer 20 minutes.

2. Add the zucchini and potato and cook 20 minutes longer or until rice is tender. Serve with grated cheese.

Yield: Four servings.

WINE AND CLOVE SOUP

6 cups water
2 cups dry white wine
6 whole cloves
½ frying chicken (2½ to 3
pounds), washed and cut
into small serving pieces
Sea salt to taste (optional)
4 tomatoes, diced
1 cup fresh peas
1 cup sliced green beans
½ cup diced celery
4 artichoke hearts, quartered
(optional)
4 large potatoes, peeled
and diced
Yogurt (see page 311)

1. Place water, wine, cloves and chicken
in a large pot. Bring to a boil and simmer
30 minutes. Add salt, tomatoes, peas,
beans, celery and artichokes. Cook 15
minutes.

2. Add potatoes and cook until they are
tender.

3. Serve with a spoonful of yogurt on top
of each serving.

Yield: Six to eight servings.

CONNECTICUT GARDEN GAZPACHO

3 tomatoes, skinned and seeded
1 clove garlic
1 green pepper, seeded and
quartered
1 carrot, sliced
1 onion, quartered
½ cup lemon juice
1 cucumber, peeled and cubed
2 tablespoons chopped chives
2 large sprigs parsley
¼ cup chopped fresh basil
1½ teaspoons chopped fresh
chervil
¼ cup olive oil
Sea salt to taste
3 cups chilled chicken broth (see
page 52) or vegetable broth
(see chapter introduction)
Whole wheat bread croutons or
sunflower seed kernels

Blend half of all the ingredients, except
the croutons or sunflower seed kernels, in
an electric blender until smooth. Repeat
with other half of ingredients. Combine
halves and chill well. Garnish with whole
wheat bread croutons or sunflower seed
kernels.

Yield: Four servings.

BLENDER TOMATO-AVOCADO SOUP

3 cups tomato juice
(see page 27)
1 tomato, skinned
1 small onion, quartered
½ green pepper, diced
¼ cup almond butter
Vegetable salt to taste
1 ripe avocado, peeled, pitted and
sliced
1 tablespoon lemon juice
½ teaspoon kelp

Combine all the ingredients in an electric blender and blend until smooth. Chill and serve cold or lukewarm.

Yield: Four servings.

YOGURT GAZPACHO

4 tomatoes, skinned and coarsely
chopped
1 tablespoon chopped hot green
seeded chilies, fresh or canned,
or to taste
1 onion, finely chopped
¼ cup chopped parsley
Sea salt to taste
3 cups yogurt (see page 311)
Radish or cucumber slices
Watercress sprigs

1. Combine the tomatoes, chilies, onion, parsley and salt. Chill in the refrigerator at least two hours.

2. Stir in the yogurt. Garnish each serving with radish or cucumber slices and a sprig of watercress.

Yield: Four servings.

AMAZING FRUIT SOUP

½ pound mixed dried fruits
   (pitted prunes, apricots,
   raisins, pears, peaches, apples)
2½ quarts water
2 pounds mixed fresh fruits
   (cubed or sliced peaches,
   apricots, pears, plums, apples;
   whole strawberries,
   blueberries, blackberries)
¼ cup lemon juice
Honey to taste
Yogurt (see page 311)

1. Combine the dried fruits and water in a large saucepan. Bring to a boil and simmer over low heat until tender, about 30 minutes.

2. Add the fresh fruits, except berries, and cook five minutes. Add berries and cook five minutes longer. Remove from the heat and add the lemon juice. Sweeten with honey. Cool and chill well.

3. Serve very cold, or hot, with a dollop of yogurt.

Yield: Six to eight servings.

Note: The contributor suggests, "For those who have not given up alcohol add a swig of gin to the chilled soup before serving. Starts dinner parties off with a bang."

MUSART'S FRUIT SOUP

2 quarts plus ½ cup
   spring water
½ pound dried apricots
1 cup raisins
½ pound pitted prunes
2 cinnamon sticks, each
   broken into three pieces
1 cup unsweetened pineapple
   juice
1 cup currant or berry juice
3 tablespoons arrowroot

1. Place two quarts of water in a large bowl. Add the apricots, raisins and prunes and let soak overnight.

2. Next day, place mixture of fruits and water in a large kettle and bring to a boil. Add the cinnamon sticks, cover and simmer until the fruits are tender. Add the pineapple juice and currant or berry juice.

3. Mix the arrowroot with the remaining water until smooth. Stir into the soup and heat, stirring, until mixture thickens. Cool and serve just above room temperature or chill and serve in chilled bowls.

Yield: Eight servings.

HOMEMADE CHICKEN BROTH

1½ quarts boiling water
　Backs, wings and necks of
　　two or three chickens
1 onion, quartered
1 carrot, quartered
2 ribs celery with leaves, diced
1 teaspoon sea salt
4 peppercorns
2 bay leaves
2 sprigs parsley

To the boiling water in a large saucepan, add remaining ingredients, cover and let simmer two hours. Strain. Concentrate by boiling if necessary for richer flavor.

Yield: About one quart.

ROSE HIPS SOUP

2 cups (½ pound) dried rose
　hips (see note)
Water
½ cup raw sugar, or honey to
　taste
1½ tablespoons arrowroot
Whipped cream
Slivered almonds

1. Crush or grind the rose hips and place in a saucepan with one and one-half quarts water. Bring to a boil, cover and simmer 45 minutes, stirring occasionally.

2. Strain through a fine sieve. Measure liquid and return to the saucepan. Add enough water to make liquid up to one and one-half quarts. Add sugar or honey.

3. Mix arrowroot with small amount of water and add to rose hips liquid. Heat, stirring, until mixture thickens.

4. Cover and chill. Serve cold with garnish of whipped cream and slivered almonds.

Yield: Six servings.

Note: Dried rose hips, also called nypon, are available at Swedish delicatessens such as Nyborg & Nelson, 937 Second Avenue, New York, N.Y.

　Rose hips soup may be served as a dessert, too.

HOMEMADE BEEF BROTH

4 pounds shin or shank
  of beef, cut in slices
3 pounds soup bones
2 pounds beef flanken,
  skirt or chuck, cut up
Water
1 large onion
2 carrots, quartered
2 ribs celery with leaves,
  quartered
2 bay leaves
2 sprigs parsley
1½ tablespoons sea salt
1 leek, halved

1. Place shin, bones and beef in a large
kettle. Add cold water to cover (about three
quarts). Bring to a boil and boil 10 minutes,
skimming off surface scum as it forms.

2. Add the remaining ingredients, cover
and simmer four hours. Strain through a
fine strainer. Remove meat from bones and
return to broth or use in casserole dish.
Taste strained broth and if not strong
enough, concentrate by boiling rapidly,
uncovered.

Yield: About three quarts.

SoBa (BUCKWHEAT NOODLES IN SOUP)

1 8-ounce package buckwheat
  noodles (available in some
  health food stores)
Boiling water
Cold water
1 tablespoon oil
1 bunch scallions, finely chopped
1 3-inch piece kombu (seaweed,
  available in Oriental markets
  and health food stores)
Sea salt to taste

1. Add the noodles to two quarts boiling
water and when water comes to the boil
again, add one cup cold water. Repeat this
three times. Remove kettle from the stove
and let stand 10 minutes. Drain noodles,
rinse with cold water and reserve.

2. Meanwhile, heat the oil in a small
saucepan and sauté the scallions in it until
tender. Add three cups cold water and the
kombu. Cover and simmer over low heat
15 minutes. Season with salt.

3. Pour boiling water over the reserved
noodles to reheat them. Drain. Arrange
noodles in four bowls and pour the scallion
soup mixture over all.

Yield: Four servings.

BONE MARROW GRUEL

6 to 8 pounds heavy beef shank
marrow bones, cut into short
pieces (avoid knuckle joints
or sections)
Cold water
4 onions
Sea salt to taste
2 cups diced celery
1½ cups sliced carrots
Freshly ground black pepper
to taste (optional)
¼ teaspoon thyme
⅛ teaspoon summer savory

1. Scrape the marrow from two or three bones and set aside.

2. Place remaining bones in a large kettle and barely cover with cold water. Chop two of the onions and add along with the salt, celery and carrots.

3. Bring mixture up to simmer point very slowly; do not let boil. Set pot over flame-tamer or low heat so that mixture is just below simmer point; leave 12 to 16 hours. Add water if level goes too low. Remove from heat and let stand overnight to cool well.

4. Thinly slice the remaining onions and brown in the reserved marrow. Add marrow from cooled bones, using enough cooking liquid to make marrow pour out.

5. Season the mixture with salt, pepper, thyme and savory. This can be eaten on bread or with potatoes or returned to the strained broth or soup from the bones. If the soup is to be served separately, it should be strained, chilled and the fat removed from the surface. Serve the soup hot or cold. It will be a jelly when cold.

Yield: Four servings marrow and soup.

MACROBIOTIC SUPER SOUP WITH BUCKWHEAT DUMPLINGS

2 tablespoons hiziki (seaweed, optional)
4 cups water, approximately
2 tablespoons oil
1 medium-size onion, chopped
1 medium-size carrot, diced
3 radishes, sliced
1 medium-size apple, cored and diced
½ cup almonds
2 tablespoons raisins
¼ cup buckwheat flour
Sea salt
Boiling water
½ cup chopped kale, spinach or watercress
2 teaspoons miso (soybean paste)
1 teaspoon brewer's yeast
1 teaspoon soy flour
2 tablespoons chopped parsley
2 tablespoons toasted sesame seeds
¼ cup wheat germ

1. Soak the hiziki in the water for five minutes. Drain and reserve both the seaweed and the liquid.

2. Heat the oil in a heavy saucepan and sauté the onion, carrot and radishes in it over low heat until barely tender. Add the apple and soaked seaweed. Add nuts and raisins; stir well with chopsticks.

3. Combine the buckwheat, one-sixteenth teaspoon salt and enough of the reserved soaking liquid or water to make a soft smooth dough that can be formed into a cigar shape. Cut the roll into half-inch circles and drop into boiling water. Cook, covered, three minutes, or until done. Drain and add to the vegetable mixture. Add the kale.

4. Cook until greens become limp and dark colored, about one minute.

5. Meanwhile, dissolve the miso, brewer's yeast and soy flour in the remainder of the reserved soaking liquid. Stir into the vegetable mixture and reheat but do not boil.

6. Season with salt to taste and garnish each serving with parsley, sesame seeds and wheat germ.

Yield: Four servings.

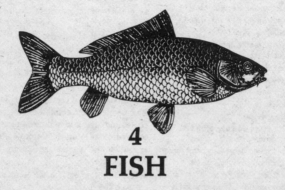

4
FISH

In spite of the mercury scare, fish and shellfish still have an important part to play in a varied, well-balanced diet. The recipes here suggest combinations of ingredients to be used with fish, and ways of preparing it, that make it appealing and extra nourishing. Although freshness is the key to good flavor and maximum nutritive value for all ingredients, it is especially important for fish.

CLAM PIE

Pastry:
2 cups whole wheat flour
1 cup unbleached white flour
½ teaspoon sea salt
¼ cup sesame oil or safflower oil
Ice water

Filling:
1½ cups clam juice
3 cups diced potatoes
1 carrot, diced
1 large onion, finely chopped
2 cups finely chopped clams
⅛ teaspoon freshly ground
    black pepper
Kelp to taste
¼ cup unbleached white flour
½ cup light cream

1. To prepare pastry, place the whole wheat flour, unbleached white flour and salt in a bowl. Add oil and work in with the fingers.

2. Add ice water a teaspoon at a time until dough clings together. Wrap in wax paper and chill.

3. To prepare filling, place clam juice, potatoes, carrot and onion in a saucepan and bring to a boil. Cover and simmer until vegetables are barely tender, about 12 minutes.

4. Add clams, pepper and kelp. Mix the flour with the cream and stir into the clam mixture. Bring to a boil, stirring until mixture thickens. Cool.

5. Preheat the oven to 400 degrees.

6. Divide the pastry dough in half and roll out one half between sheets of wax paper to fit a deep 10-inch pie plate or casserole. Pour in cooled clam mixture. Roll out remaining dough between sheets of wax paper and use to cover pie. Seal edges; make a steam hole.

7. Bake 10 minutes, reduce oven heat to 350 degrees and bake until pastry is done, about 30 minutes longer.

Yield: Six servings.

BAKED FLOUNDER ROLL-UPS

½ cup cooked shredded kale,
  spinach, Swiss chard or wild
  greens, well drained
1 egg, lightly beaten
¼ cup wheat germ
⅛ teaspoon nutmeg
 Sea salt to taste
1 clove garlic, finely chopped
4 large flounder or sole fillets
4 thick slices tomato
 Oil

1. Preheat the oven to 350 degrees.
2. In a bowl, mix together the cooked greens, egg, wheat germ, nutmeg, salt and garlic.
3. Spread over the fillets and roll up as for a jellyroll. Secure with toothpicks and set, rolled side up, in a buttered baking dish. Top each fillet with a slice of tomato. Brush with oil and bake 20 minutes or until fish flakes easily.

Yield: Four servings.

BAKED FISH

½ cup chopped scallions
1 green pepper, seeded and diced
1 carrot, finely diced
1 tomato, skinned and chopped
 Sea salt and freshly ground black
  pepper to taste
1 tablespoon snipped fresh dill
  weed
2 halibut or cod steaks (each
  ¾ inch thick)
1 teaspoon lemon juice
¼ cup water
3 tablespoons butter
1 cup yogurt (see page 311)

1. Preheat the oven to 350 degrees.
2. Combine the scallions, green pepper, carrot, tomato, salt, black pepper and dill. Place half the mixture in the bottom of an oiled baking dish.
3. Place fish on top, season with salt and pepper and sprinkle with lemon juice. Cover with remaining vegetable mixture. Pour the water over all. Dot with the butter. Cover tightly and bake 25 minutes or until fish flakes easily.
4. Spread yogurt over the top of dish and return to oven just long enough to warm yogurt, about four minutes.

Yield: Two servings.

CAMP FISH STEW

3 freshwater fish such as perch,
  bass, pike (each 2 to 3 pounds)
Water
8 slices bacon, diced
1 large onion, chopped
3 large potatoes, diced
Sea salt to taste
1 cup evaporated milk

1. Split the uncleaned fish down the back and remove large meaty slab from head to tail from each side of the backbone. Lay each slab skin side down and slide a thin boning knife along the inner surface of the skin, neatly removing the clean fillet.

2. Place the fillets in a large heavy skillet, add one-half cup water, cover tightly and steam five minutes. Drain off liquid and reserve. Cool fish and cut into two-inch pieces.

3. Discard fish innards and skin and put heads, backbones, fins, etc., in a saucepan. Add the reserved fish liquid plus enough extra water to cover. Cover and simmer until heads fall apart.

4. Strain the stock through two thicknesses of muslin and reserve.

5. In a kettle, render the bacon bits. Pour off all but three tablespoons of the fat. Add the onion to the kettle and cook until transparent.

6. Measure the reserved fish stock and, if necessary, make up to eight cups with water. Add with potatoes and salt to the kettle. Bring to a boil, cover and simmer until potatoes are tender, about 20 minutes. Add fish; reheat. Add milk and reheat but do not allow to boil.

Yield: Six servings.

FISH IN TOMATO SAUCE

2 tablespoons olive oil
1 onion, finely chopped
1 clove garlic, finely chopped
1½ cups skinned chopped ripe
  tomatoes
1 tablespoon chopped parsley
Sea salt or kelp to taste
1 fresh hot chili pepper, seeded
  and chopped
¼ teaspoon oregano
1 pound boneless firm white fish
  such as cod, halibut or striped
  bass

1. Heat the oil in a saucepan and sauté the onion and garlic in it until transparent and tender but not browned.

2. Add the tomatoes, parsley, salt or kelp, the chili pepper and oregano. Bring to a boil and simmer 20 minutes.

3. Cut the fish into two-inch squares and add to the sauce. Cover and simmer eight minutes or until fish flakes easily.

Yield: Four servings.

SALMON LOAF

1 can (1 pound) salmon
1 rib celery, chopped
1 small onion, chopped
1 tablespoon chopped parsley
1 tablespoon wheat germ
1 tablespoon bone meal
1 tablespoon brewer's yeast
1 egg, lightly beaten
1 cup milk

1. Preheat the oven to 350 degrees.

2. Empty can of salmon into an oiled casserole and flake with a fork. Add celery, onion, parsley, wheat germ, bone meal and yeast.

3. Mix together the egg and milk and stir into the salmon mixture. Set in a pan of boiling water and bake until set, about one hour.

Yield: Four servings.

SALMON STEAKS WITH SCALLIONS

1 bunch scallions
2 tablespoons olive oil
2 salmon steaks (¾ inch to 1 inch thick)
Sea salt and freshly ground black pepper to taste
1 teaspoon chopped fresh basil leaves
1 tablespoon wine vinegar
1½ cups cooked brown rice (see page 217)
Lemon juice to taste

1. Trim scallions and wash well. Dry and cut lengthwise into quarters and then crosswise into two-inch lengths.

2. Heat the oil in a heavy skillet, add scallions and cook over medium heat until they are golden, turning with a spatula as they cook.

3. Place salmon steaks on top of scallions. Season with salt and pepper, sprinkle with basil and add vinegar. Cover and steam four minutes, moving salmon steaks with spatula twice but not turning.

4. Uncover and sauté steaks several minutes to reduce pan juices. Lower heat, cover and cook about two minutes longer or until fish flakes easily.

5. Remove salmon and scallions to a warm platter. Add rice to skillet and quickly stir-fry in pan juices. Sprinkle with lemon juice and serve with fish.

Yield: Two servings.

BAKED SHRIMP

⅓ cup oil
2 tablespoons finely chopped shallot or scallion
1 clove garlic, finely chopped
2 tablespoons chopped parsley
1 teaspoon savory
3 tablespoons lemon juice
1 cup dried whole wheat bread crumbs
2 tablespoons freshly grated Parmesan cheese
2 pounds cooked, shelled and deveined shrimp
¼ cup dry white wine or clam broth

1. Preheat the oven to 350 degrees.

2. Heat the oil and sauté the shallot or scallion and the garlic in it until tender but not browned. Add parsley, savory, lemon juice, crumbs and cheese.

3. Arrange shrimp in a buttered baking dish and sprinkle the bread crumb mixture over. Pour the wine or clam juice over. Bake 10 to 15 minutes or until heated through.

Yield: Four to six servings.

FLOWER OF SHRIMP

1 pound shrimp
Sea salt
2 cups plus 3 tablespoons water
3 tablespoons oil
2 medium-size onions, cut in eighths
½ medium-size head cauliflower, broken into flowerets
1½ tablespoons arrowroot
¼ cup soy sauce
4 cups hot cooked brown rice (see page 217)

1. Shell the shrimp, reserving shells. Devein shrimp and sprinkle with salt. Set aside. Place shells and two cups water in a saucepan, bring to a boil, cover and boil 15 minutes. Strain stock and discard shells.

2. Heat the oil in a skillet and sauté the onions and cauliflower in it four minutes. Add strained shrimp stock, cover and simmer until vegetables are crisp-tender, about two minutes.

3. Add the shrimp and cook, covered, until shrimp turn pink, about five minutes. Dissolve arrowroot in remaining water and add to skillet with soy sauce. Stir until mixture thickens. Serve over rice.

Yield: Six servings.

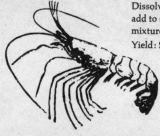

SHRIMP WITH VEGETABLES

3 tablespoons oil
1 pound shrimp, shelled and deveined
½ medium-size onion, finely chopped
¾ cup Italian green peppers cut in 1-inch squares
½ cup sliced celery
1½ cups sliced Chinese cabbage, white part only
1½ teaspoons miso (soybean paste)
⅓ cup water
½ teaspoon raw sugar
2 teaspoons parsley
Sea salt and freshly ground black pepper to taste
2 cups mung bean sprouts (see page 195)
1 cup snow peas
Cooked brown rice (see page 217)
Blanched almonds

1. Heat the oil in a wok or heavy skillet. Add the shrimp and cook, stirring, until they turn pink. Remove from skillet and keep warm.

2. Add onion, green peppers, celery and cabbage to the skillet and cook five minutes, stirring constantly. Mix the miso with the water and add with sugar, parsley, salt and black pepper.

3. Cover and cook over low heat eight minutes.

4. Stir in the shrimp. Place bean sprouts on top; do not stir in. Place snow peas on top of sprouts and do not stir. Cover and simmer two minutes.

5. Serve over brown rice, sprinkled with almonds.

Yield: Four servings.

SHRIMP AND SPROUTS

3 tablespoons butter
1 pound shelled deveined shrimp
1 cup sliced mushrooms
1 cup clam juice
1 tablespoon tamari (soy sauce)
1 cup mung bean or soybean sprouts (see page 195)
½ cup sliced water chestnuts
2 teaspoons arrowroot
2 tablespoons water

1. Heat the butter in a heavy skillet. Add the shrimp and cook, stirring, until they turn pink. Add mushrooms and cook two minutes longer.

2. Stir in the clam juice and tamari and bring to a boil. Add bean sprouts and water chestnuts and cook two minutes.

3. Mix the arrowroot with the water and stir into skillet. Stir until mixture thickens.

Yield: Four servings.

SKEWERED SHRIMP WITH RICE

1½ to 2 pounds large shrimp
   (about 20)
¼ cup oil
¼ cup lime juice
 2 tablespoons soy sauce
 2 tablespoons butter
¼ cup chopped onion
 1 cup sliced mushrooms
 2 tablespoons chopped parsley
 4 cups hot cooked brown rice
   (see page 217)
 3 limes, sliced

1. Wash the shrimp. Cut the shell down the back of each and devein but leave shell intact. Combine the oil, lime juice and soy sauce in a bowl and add the shrimp. Marinate in the refrigerator 30 to 60 minutes.

2. Meanwhile, heat the butter in a small skillet and sauté the onion in it until transparent. Add mushrooms and cook three minutes longer. Stir in the parsley and add onion mixture to the rice. Keep warm.

3. Thread the shrimp onto four individual skewers, alternating with lime slices. Broil under a preheated broiler or over hot coals, about three minutes each side, brushing with marinade when skewers are turned. Serve on top of rice mixture.

Yield: Four servings.

SHRIMP WITH YOGURT

 3 tablespoons butter
 2 tablespoons finely chopped
   onion
1½ pounds shelled deveined
   shrimp
⅓ cup finely chopped parsley
¼ teaspoon caraway seeds,
   lightly crushed
¼ clove garlic, finely chopped
½ cup dry white wine or clam
   juice
 Kelp to taste
½ cup yogurt (see page 311)

1. Heat the butter in a skillet and sauté the onion in it until transparent. Add the shrimp and cook, stirring, until shrimp turn pink.

2. Add parsley, caraway seeds, garlic, wine or clam juice and kelp. Bring to a boil, cover and simmer two minutes. Remove from the heat and stir in the yogurt.

Yield: Four servings.

NAMASU

2 cucumbers
Sea salt
½ cup tiny cooked, shelled and
    deveined shrimp
2 or 3 one-foot-long thin strips
    of wakame (Japanese seaweed)
Water
1 tablespoon raw sugar
¼ cup Japanese rice vinegar

1. Cut cucumbers in half lengthwise. Peel and remove seeds. Slice cucumbers thinly and sprinkle with salt. Set aside 10 minutes.

2. Rinse cucumbers and squeeze out excess water. Add shrimp to cucumbers.

3. Soak the wakame in water to cover for five minutes. Cut or tear soft portion of wakame from the core into one-inch lengths.

4. Combine cucumbers, shrimp and wakame. Mix together sugar, one-half teaspoon salt and the vinegar. Pour over cucumber mixture and chill in refrigerator an hour or longer.

Yield: Two servings.

BAKED TROUT

1 trout (11 to 14 inches)
1 lemon, cut into eighths
1 boletus edulis (wild mushroom
    found in Rocky Mountain region
    in summer below timber line),
    sliced, or ¼ cup sliced
    mushrooms
Salt and freshly ground black
    pepper to taste

1. Clean the trout. Place four lemon wedges and the mushroom slices in the cavity. Season inside and outside of fish with salt and pepper.

2. Wrap in heavy-duty aluminum foil and set directly in white-hot coals of a charcoal fire that has been allowed to burn down.

3. Cook, turning often, 10 minutes, or until fish flakes easily. (Trout can be cooked on a grill over hot coals but will take longer to cook.) Serve with extra lemon wedges.

Yield: Two servings.

5
MEAT & POULTRY

The meat and poultry recipes in this chapter are offered as economical,
good-tasting and nutritious alternates to the more conventional
roasts, pot roasts and stews found in most regular cookbooks.
There are some old standbys included, but trying a new way of fixing
liver or giblets, or preparing veal hearts or sweetbreads for the first time,
will provide variety in your diet.
Hopefully, it will encourage further experiments with the organ meats
that have never attained the measure of distinction in American
kitchens they hold in European cuisines.

POCKET OF GOLD

4 slices bacon
1 cup chopped onions
1 large clove garlic, finely
 chopped
½ cup sliced mushrooms
¼ green pepper, chopped
3 sprigs parsley, chopped
3 sprigs fresh dill, chopped
8 peppercorns, crushed
Sea salt to taste
1 cup Italian-style plum tomatoes
 or skinned chopped fresh
 tomatoes
½ cup wheat germ
1 (3-pound) first-cut brisket
 of beef
Freshly ground black pepper to
 taste
Unbleached white flour
2 tablespoons oil or butter
3 large onions, chopped
½ cup dry red wine or beef broth
 (see page 53), approximately
2 tablespoons black bean paste
 (available in Oriental food
 stores)

1. Chop three bacon slices and mix with one cup chopped onions, the garlic, mushrooms, green pepper, parsley, dill, peppercorns and salt. Mix well.

2. Add one-half cup tomatoes and the wheat germ.

3. Form a pocket in the brisket by cutting into the meat horizontally, making the pocket as large as possible, but taking care not to cut through to the edges.

4. Fill the pocket with the wheat germ mixture and sew together or secure with toothpicks. Rub the outside of the meat with salt and pepper and sprinkle lightly with flour.

5. Preheat the oven to 300 degrees.

6. In a heavy casserole or a Dutch oven, render the last slice of bacon. Add the oil or butter and the three chopped onions and sauté until tender. Add meat and brown on both sides.

7. Combine remaining tomatoes, one-half cup wine or broth and the black bean paste. Pour over meat and bring to a boil. Cover and bake two hours or until meat is tender; turn after one hour and check to see that sauce has not evaporated. If necessary, add more wine or broth.

8. To serve, slice from top to bottom carefully so that stuffing stays in place.

Yield: Six servings.

MUSART STRIP BEEF

3 tablespoons safflower oil
2 cups thin strips sirloin beef tips
Sea salt and freshly ground black
    pepper to taste
¼ teaspoon basil
¼ teaspoon thyme
¼ teaspoon chervil
¼ teaspoon summer savory
1 cup sliced cauliflowerets
1 cup sliced broccoli flowerets
½ cup sliced mushrooms
½ cup alfalfa seed sprouts (see
    page 195)
1 cup mung bean sprouts (see
    page 195)
1 cup chopped watercress
½ cup shredded carrot
1 cup chopped or shredded
    cabbage
1 cup spinach leaves, shredded
¾ cup water
1 teaspoon arrowroot
1 tablespoon tamari (soy sauce)
Cooked brown rice (see page 217)

1. In a wok or a heavy skillet, heat the oil. Add the beef and stir-fry until browned. Add salt, pepper, basil, thyme, chervil and savory.

2. With wok or skillet over fairly high heat, add the cauliflowerets, broccoli, mushrooms, alfalfa seed sprouts, mung bean sprouts, watercress, carrot, cabbage and spinach. Season with salt and pepper and add one-half cup of the water. Cover and cook about three minutes.

3. Remove from the heat. Mix the arrowroot with the tamari and remaining water. Pour over vegetables. Return to the heat and cook, stirring, until mixture thickens and clears.

4. Serve with brown rice.

Yield: Four to six servings.

ORGANIC CHUCK ROAST

1 boneless chuck roast
    (3 to 4 pounds), aged
Sea salt and freshly ground black
    pepper to taste

1. Preheat the oven to 325 degrees.

2. Season the beef with salt and pepper and place in a casserole or roasting pan. Cover tightly and bake one hour per pound of meat.

Yield: Six to eight servings.

Note: The contributor raises organic beef and ages it naturally.

BUTTERMILK ROAST

1 bottom beef round or fresh
   boned pork shoulder
   (3 to 4 pounds)
Vegetable salt
2 tablespoons oil
2 cups buttermilk
1 cup water
2 tablespoons apple cider vinegar
1 large onion, sliced
½ bay leaf
3 peppercorns, crushed
6 carrots, quartered
2 large potatoes, quartered
6 small white onions

1. Sprinkle the meat with the salt and rub
it in. Heat the oil in a heavy casserole or a
Dutch oven, add the meat and brown on
all sides. Remove any excess fat or oil.

2. Add the buttermilk, water, vinegar,
onion, bay leaf and peppercorns. Bring to
a boil. Cover and let simmer very slowly
until meat is tender, about two and
one-half hours.

3. Add carrots, potatoes and onions.
Season with vegetable salt to taste and
cook, covered, 20 minutes or until
vegetables are cooked. Serve gravy,
thickened with flour if desired, separately.

Yield: Six to eight servings.

MARINATED FLANK STEAK

2 pounds flank steak (the
   contributor buys organic
   flank steak)
½ cup soy sauce
2 tablespoons honey
2 tablespoons lemon juice
1 teaspoon ground ginger
3 cloves garlic, finely chopped

1. Trim the fat from the steak and score
it deeply with diagonal slashes. Place in a
shallow ceramic or glass dish.

2. Combine remaining ingredients and
pour over steak. Allow to marinate at room
temperature four to six hours, turning
every two hours.

3. Drain the steak and broil over a charcoal
fire or under a preheated broiler to
desired degree of doneness, turning once,
about five minutes on each side.

Yield: Four servings.

HAMBURGER AND BEANS

3 cups (1 pound) small dried red
   beans or kidney beans
6 cups water
2 bay leaves
1 onion, studded with 3 cloves
2 pounds ground beef chuck
½ pound pork sausage meat
3 large onions, chopped
2 cloves garlic, finely chopped
3 cups homemade tomato sauce
   (see page 161) or canned
   Italian-style tomatoes
1 tablespoon chili powder
2 small hot chili peppers, seeded
   and chopped
¾ teaspoon curry powder
1 tablespoon powdered cumin
1 tablespoon sea salt

1. Wash and pick over the beans and place in a kettle with six cups water. Let soak several hours or overnight.

2. Bring the beans and soaking water to a boil. Add the bay leaves and onion studded with cloves. Cover and simmer until beans are barely tender, about 25 minutes.

3. Meanwhile, put the beef, sausage meat, chopped onions and garlic in a large skillet and cook, stirring often, until all pinkness has gone from the meats.

4. Add meat mixture to cooked beans and stir in remaining ingredients. Simmer gently one hour. Cool; chill. Remove surface fat. Reheat very slowly.

Yield: Twelve servings.

HAMBURGERS PLUS

1½ pounds ground beef round
2 egg yolks
¾ cup coarsely chopped peanuts
1 large onion, finely chopped
2 tablespoons butter
½ teaspoon dry mustard
½ cup homemade catchup or
   tomato sauce (see page 161)
½ cup whole wheat bread crumbs
¾ cup mung bean sprouts
   (see page 195)
2 cloves garlic, finely chopped
Sea salt and freshly ground black
   pepper to taste
Wheat germ
Soy oil for frying

1. Mix together the meat, egg yolks and peanuts.

2. Sauté the onion in the butter until wilted. Add to meat mixture. Stir in mustard, catchup or tomato sauce, the bread crumbs, mung bean sprouts, garlic, salt and pepper.

3. Form into hamburger patties and coat with wheat germ. Heat enough oil in a heavy skillet to barely cover the bottom. Add the patties and fry until browned and done.

Yield: Six to eight servings.

MIDDLE-EASTERN BEEF

1 pound lean ground beef round
1 tablespoon safflower oil (optional)
¼ cup raisins, chopped
⅛ teaspoon sea salt
Freshly ground black pepper to taste
1 small onion, finely chopped
⅓ cup watercress leaves (no stems)
⅓ cup wheat germ
1 cup yogurt (see page 311)
Chilled Russian-style tea

1. Place the beef in a skillet, along with the oil if beef is extremely lean, and cook, stirring, until all pinkness has gone. Pour off all liquid and discard.

2. Add raisins, salt and pepper and cook, stirring, until meat is slightly browned. Cool.

3. Combine onion, watercress leaves, wheat germ and yogurt in a bowl and add cooled beef mixture. Chill thoroughly. Serve with glasses of chilled extra-strong Russian-style tea.

Yield: Four servings.

HEALTH-FUL CHOP SUEY

3 tablespoons oil
3 medium-size onions, chopped
4 large ribs celery, sliced diagonally
¾ pound beef sandwich steaks, cut into one-inch strips
1 quart mung bean sprouts (see page 195)
Water or chicken broth (see page 52)
2 tablespoons blackstrap or unsulphured molasses
⅓ cup soy sauce
3 tablespoons cornstarch
2 tablespoons cold water
½ cup sliced mushrooms
½ cup sliced water chestnuts
Cooked brown rice (see page 217)

1. Heat the oil in a skillet and sauté the onions in it until tender. Add the celery and cook two minutes longer. Add beef strips and cook over high heat two minutes.

2. Add mung bean sprouts and enough water or broth to barely cover. Bring to a boil and simmer, covered, 15 minutes.

3. Combine molasses, soy sauce, cornstarch and water. Stir into bean sprout mixture. Stir until mixture thickens. Cook five minutes.

4. Add mushrooms and water chestnuts. Reheat and serve over brown rice.

Yield: Four servings.

CRACKED WHEAT CASSEROLE

1 pound ground beef chuck
½ onion, finely chopped
¾ cup boiling water
1 cup cracked wheat (bulghur)
2 cups skinned chopped fresh tomatoes or canned tomatoes
2 tablespoons tomato paste
1 teaspoon sea salt
½ teaspoon thyme
¼ teaspoon marjoram
¼ teaspoon summer savory

1. Preheat the oven to 325 degrees.

2. Place the meat and onion in a skillet and heat, stirring, until meat is browned.

3. Pour water over wheat and add to meat mixture. Add remaining ingredients and mix well. Turn into an oiled 1½-quart casserole, cover and bake one hour.

Yield: Four to six servings.

PLANTATION CASSEROLE

3 tablespoons oil
¾ cup chopped onions
¾ cup chopped celery
¾ cup chopped green pepper
3 cloves garlic, finely chopped
3 medium-size hot chili peppers, seeded and chopped
½ pound ground beef round
1 tablespoon butter
1 tablespoon whole wheat flour
1 teaspoon curry powder
½ cup beef broth (see page 53)
½ cup milk
Sea salt to taste
2 cups homemade tomato sauce (see page 161)
4 cups cooked brown rice (see page 217)
¾ cup coarsely chopped pecans
1 cup shredded Cheddar cheese

1. Preheat the oven to 375 degrees.

2. Heat the oil in a heavy skillet and sauté the onions in it until tender.

3. Add celery, green pepper, garlic, hot peppers and ground beef. Cook, stirring, until beef loses its pink color.

4. In a small saucepan, melt the butter and blend in the flour and curry powder. Gradually add the broth and milk and bring mixture to a boil, stirring. Add salt and continue cooking until mixture thickens.

5. Add curry sauce, tomato sauce, brown rice, pecans and half of the cheese to the vegetable mixture. Mix well and season with salt. Pour mixture into an oiled casserole, sprinkle with remaining cheese and bake until casserole is bubbly hot and the cheese on top has melted, about 25 minutes.

Yield: Six to eight servings.

SOY CHILI

- 3 tablespoons butter
- 1 medium-size onion, finely chopped
- 1 small green pepper, seeded and finely chopped
- 1½ pounds ground beef round
- 2 tablespoons chili powder, or to taste
- 1 teaspoon sea salt
- 1 can (2 pounds 14 ounces) tomatoes
- 2 cups cooked soybeans (see page 157)
- 1 cup homemade tomato sauce (see page 161)

1. Heat the butter in a heavy skillet and sauté the onion in it until tender. Add green pepper and beef and cook slowly until no pink color is left in the meat.

2. Increase the heat and brown the meat. Add remaining ingredients. Cover and cook over low heat for an hour. Cool and refrigerate overnight. Reheat slowly.

Yield: Six servings.

MEATBALLS

- 1 pound ground beef round or chuck
- ¼ cup soy grits
- ½ cup beef broth (see page 53)
- ½ cup finely chopped onion
- 5 tablespoons oil
- 1 thick slice whole wheat or rye bread
- ¾ cup soy milk
- ¾ teaspoon sea salt
- ⅛ teaspoon nutmeg
- 1 egg, lightly beaten
- ¼ cup wheat germ
- Whole wheat flour
- 3 cups tomato sauce (see page 161)
- Brown rice (see page 217) or artichoke noodles

1. Break up the meat, using the fingers, and place meat in a bowl. Soak the soy grits in the broth.

2. Sauté the onion in two tablespoons of the oil until tender but not browned. Add to meat with soaked soy grits.

3. Soak the bread in the milk three minutes. Add to meat mixture. Add the salt, nutmeg, egg and wheat germ. Mix well. Shape into one-inch balls; roll in whole wheat flour.

4. Heat remaining oil in a skillet and brown the meat balls in it on all sides. Heat the tomato sauce in a saucepan and add the meatballs. Simmer 15 minutes. Serve with brown rice or artichoke noodles.

Yield: Four servings.

SWEDISH-STYLE MEATBALLS WITH CAPER SAUCE

1 pound ground beef round
¾ cup wheat germ
¼ cup chopped onion
1 egg, lightly beaten
1 teaspoon sea salt
Freshly ground black pepper to taste
1½ tablespoons soy sauce or Worcestershire sauce
1¼ cups milk
2 tablespoons oil
2 tablespoons unbleached white flour
1 cup light cream
2 tablespoons drained capers

1. Combine the meat, wheat germ, onion, egg, salt, pepper, soy sauce and three-quarters cup of the milk in a bowl. Mix well.

2. Shape the mixture into 36 balls. Heat the oil in a heavy skillet and brown the balls, a few at a time, in the oil. Drain on paper towels and keep warm.

3. When all balls are browned, sprinkle the flour into the skillet and cook, stirring, one minute.

4. Stir in remaining milk and the cream. Bring to a boil, stirring, and cook two minutes. Add the capers and meatballs. Simmer 10 minutes.

Yield: Four to six servings.

SIX-LAYER DINNER

2 cups finely chopped or shredded carrots
1 green pepper, seeded and chopped
Sea salt and freshly ground black pepper to taste
2 cups sliced raw potatoes
½ cup raw brown rice
1 cup sliced onions
1½ pounds ground beef round
⅓ cup wheat germ
1 quart tomato juice, preferably homemade (see page 27)

1. Preheat the oven to 325 degrees.

2. Combine carrots and green pepper.

3. Seasoning each layer with salt and black pepper, place the potatoes in the bottom of a well-buttered casserole, sprinkle with the rice and then cover, in layers, with the onions, beef, carrots and green pepper and wheat germ.

4. Pour the tomato juice over all. Cover tightly and bake two and one-half hours.

Yield: Six to eight servings.

BEEF 'N WHEAT MEATBALLS

1 cup whole wheat berries
1½ cups beef broth (see page 53)
5 tablespoons sesame oil
1 onion, grated
2 teaspoons chopped parsley
2 pounds ground beef round
1 teaspoon soy flour
1 tablespoon brewer's yeast
1½ teaspoons vegetable salt
½ teaspoon basil
3 tablespoons whole wheat
   bread crumbs
1 egg, lightly beaten
2 tablespoons whole wheat flour
Water, if necessary
Sea salt to taste

1. Combine whole wheat berries and broth in a small saucepan and bring barely to a boil. Allow to soak overnight in the refrigerator.

2. Heat two tablespoons of the oil in a skillet and sauté the onion in it until tender. Add the parsley. Drain and add the wheat berries, reserving soaking liquid until later.

3. To the skillet, add soy flour, brewer's yeast, vegetable salt, basil, bread crumbs and egg. Mix well and form into bite-size balls. Chill several hours.

4. Heat remaining oil in a heavy skillet and brown the meat balls in it on all sides. Drain on paper towels and keep warm.

5. Sprinkle flour into skillet. Measure reserved soaking liquid and if necessary make up to one cup with water. Stir liquid into the skillet and bring to a boil, stirring constantly until mixture thickens.

6. Season with sea salt and pour over meatballs.

Yield: Eight servings.

POTATO MEAT LOAF

2 pounds ground beef round
1 cup tomato juice (see page 27)
1 onion, finely chopped
2 cups finely shredded raw potatoes
1 tablespoon chopped parsley
1 carrot, shredded
2 eggs, lightly beaten
1 teaspoon vegetable salt

1. Preheat the oven to 375 degrees.

2. Mix all the ingredients together and pack into an oiled 9-by-5-by-3-inch loaf pan. Bake one hour or until done.

Yield: Six to eight servings.

MEAT LOAF

2 eggs
½ teaspoon sea salt
1 teaspoon bone meal
2 tablespoons brewer's yeast
1 cup sunflower seed meal
½ cup chopped onion
¼ teaspoon freshly ground
   black pepper
1 teaspoon dolomite
½ teaspoon sage
1 teaspoon kelp
½ cup shredded carrots
1 pound ground beef round
2 parsnips, thinly sliced
2 hard-cooked eggs

1. Preheat the oven to 300 degrees.

2. Put the uncooked eggs, salt, bone meal, yeast, sunflower seed meal, onion, pepper, dolomite, sage and kelp in an electric blender and blend until smooth.

3. Put the carrots and beef in a bowl. Pour egg mixture over. Mix well.

4. Make a layer of parsnip slices in the bottom of a well-buttered 8½-by-4½-by-2½-inch loaf pan. Top with half the meat mixture. Place the hard-cooked eggs in the middle of the meat and press down so that they are half submerged in the meat layer.

5. Top with remaining meat mixture and bake one hour or until done.

Yield: Six servings.

MEAT LOAF PLUS

1 pound ground beef round
1 onion, finely chopped
1 clove garlic, finely chopped
½ cup finely chopped celery
2 carrots, grated
1 tablespoon chopped parsley
¼ cup pumpkin seeds, finely
   chopped or pulverized in
   an electric blender
½ cup soy grits
1 cup milk
1½ teaspoons salt
1 egg, lightly beaten
½ teaspoon sage

1. Preheat the oven to 325 degrees.

2. In a large bowl, combine the beef, onion, garlic, celery, carrots, parsley and pumpkin seeds.

3. Soak the grits in the milk for two minutes. Add to meat mixture with salt, egg and sage. Mix well and pack into an oiled 9-by-5-by-3-inch loaf pan. Bake one hour.

Yield: Six servings.

RICE-STUFFED MEAT LOAF

Filling:
1¼ cups beef broth (see page 53)
⅓ cup raw brown rice
2 tablespoons butter
¼ cup chopped onion
¼ cup chopped celery
2 tablespoons chopped parsley
2 tablespoons wheat germ
1 egg, lightly beaten
½ teaspoon sage
Sea salt and freshly ground
   black pepper to taste

Loaf:
2 eggs, well beaten
½ cup milk
¼ cup dried bread crumbs
2 tablespoons wheat germ
¼ cup chopped onion
½ teaspoon thyme
1 teaspoon sea salt
Freshly ground black pepper
   to taste
1 pound ground beef round
½ pound ground beef heart

Topping:
⅓ cup homemade tomato sauce
   (see page 161)
1 teaspoon dry mustard
3 tablespoons brown sugar
¼ teaspoon nutmeg

1. For the filling, place the broth and rice in a small saucepan. Bring to a boil, cover and simmer slowly until liquid has been absorbed, about 30 minutes.

2. Meanwhile, melt the butter and sauté the onion in it until tender. Add the celery and cook one minute longer.

3. Combine rice, onion mixture and remaining filling ingredients and set aside.

4. Preheat the oven to 350 degrees.

5. For the loaf, combine the eggs, milk, bread crumbs, wheat germ, onion, thyme, salt and pepper. Mix well.

6. Add the egg-and-milk mixture to the ground beef and heart. Mix lightly.

7. Pat half the meat mixture into a buttered casserole or 9-by-5-by-3-inch loaf pan. Top with the rice mixture. Cover with remaining meat mixture.

8. For the topping, mix all ingredients together and pour over the loaf or casserole. Bake 50 minutes or until done.

Yield: Six to eight servings.

HUNTER'S LOAF

2 tablespoons plus 1¾ teaspoons sea salt
1 gallon boiling water
1 medium-size head cabbage, cored and leaves pulled apart
1½ cups drained pitted ripe olives
1½ pounds ground beef round
¼ cup finely chopped onion
1 egg, lightly beaten
¼ teaspoon freshly ground black pepper
½ cup soft whole wheat bread crumbs
¼ cup milk
½ teaspoon caraway seeds
¼ teaspoon thyme
1 tablespoon butter
1 tablespoon unbleached white flour
Beef broth (see page 53)
⅓ cup dry white wine or beef broth

1. Add two tablespoons salt to the boiling water and plunge the cabbage leaves into the water. Cook eight minutes or until the leaves have wilted. Drain.

2. Preheat the oven to 350 degrees.

3. Reserve one-quarter cup olives whole and chop remainder. Combine chopped olives, the beef, onion, egg, remaining salt, the pepper, bread crumbs, milk, seeds and thyme. Mix well.

4. Line a well-buttered 9-by-5-by-3-inch loaf pan with cabbage leaves. Cover with half the meat mixture. Arrange another layer of cabbage leaves over the meat and top with remaining meat and then cabbage leaves.

5. Cover loosely with aluminum foil, place on a baking sheet and bake one and one-quarter hours. Remove foil. Place wire cooling rack over loaf and drain off liquid from loaf into a measuring cup. Reserve.

6. Turn loaf onto a warm serving platter and keep warm while preparing sauce.

7. Melt the butter; blend in the flour. Make up the reserved liquid to three-quarters cup with beef broth and stir in the butter-flour mixture. Stir in the wine or extra broth and bring to a boil, stirring until mixture thickens. Stir in the reserved whole olives. Serve sauce separately.

Yield: Six servings.

MUSART SPROUTED BEEF LOAF

Loaf:
1 pound ground beef round
2 eggs, lightly beaten
½ cup finely chopped onion
¼ cup spring water
1 teaspoon sea salt
1 cup mung bean sprouts (see page 195)
1 cup sprouted grain bread crumbs (see page 286)

Sauce:
2 tablespoons chopped onion
1 clove garlic, finely ground
4 tablespoons soy margarine
2 tablespoons unbleached white flour
1 cup goat's milk
1 tablespoon tamari (soy sauce)
¼ pound mushrooms, sliced
¼ teaspoon chervil
Sea salt to taste
Brown rice (see page 217)

1. Preheat the oven to 350 degrees.

2. To prepare loaf, combine the beef, eggs, onion, water, salt, mung bean sprouts and crumbs. Mix well.

3. Pack the meat mixture into an oiled 8½-by-4½-by-2½-inch loaf pan. Bake 40 minutes.

4. Meanwhile, for the sauce, sauté the onion and garlic in two tablespoons of the margarine. Sprinkle over and stir in the flour. Gradually blend in the milk and bring to a boil, stirring.

5. When mixture thickens, add the tamari. Sauté the mushrooms in the remaining margarine and add to the sauce with the chervil and salt.

6. Serve the loaf with brown rice and the mushroom sauce.

Yield: Six servings.

Note: The contributor uses organic beef.

SOY MEAT LOAF

½ cup green soybeans
Water
1 pound ground beef round
  or chuck
3 ribs celery, chopped
1 large onion, chopped
4 tomatoes, skinned and chopped
1 teaspoon sea salt

1. Pick over and wash the soybeans.
Cover with water and let soak overnight.

2. Blend the soybeans in batches in an
electric blender, using soaking liquid as
necessary, until thoroughly chopped.

3. Preheat the oven to 350 degrees.

4. Combine the chopped soybeans with
beef, celery, onion, tomatoes and salt and
pack into an oiled 8½-by-4½-by-2½-inch
loaf pan. Bake one hour.

Yield: Six servings.

SUNFLOWER MEAT LOAF

1½ pounds ground beef round
1 tablespoon soy sauce
1 cup sunflower seed meal
1 egg, lightly beaten
2 tablespoons grated onion
1 teaspoon sea salt
½ cup non-fat dry milk solids
½ cup milk
1 tablespoon tomato paste
1½ cups hot homemade tomato
  sauce (see page 161)

1. Preheat the oven to 350 degrees.

2. Combine all the ingredients except the
tomato sauce and pack into an oiled 8½-
by-4½-by-2½-inch loaf pan.

3. Bake one hour. Serve with tomato sauce.

Yield: Six servings.

STUFFED BEEF ROLL

Stuffing:
- ⅓ cup butter
- ¼ cup finely chopped onion
- ¼ cup finely chopped celery
- ¼ cup shredded carrot
- ⅓ cup sliced mushrooms
- ¼ cup finely chopped green pepper
- 1 cup whole wheat bread crumbs
- ¼ cup wheat germ
- ¼ teaspoon sea salt
- Freshly ground black pepper to taste
- ½ teaspoon sage
- 1 egg, lightly beaten

Beef roll:
- 1½ pounds ground beef round
- 1 cup whole wheat bread cubes
- ¾ cup milk
- ¼ cup wheat germ
- 1 egg, lightly beaten
- 1 teaspoon prepared mustard
- 1½ teaspoons sea salt
- ¼ teaspoon freshly ground black pepper
- 1 cup homemade tomato sauce (see page 161)

1. To prepare stuffing, melt the butter in a skillet and sauté onion in it until wilted. Add the celery, carrot, mushrooms and green pepper and cook three minutes longer. Remove skillet from the stove.

2. Add remaining stuffing ingredients and mix well.

3. Preheat the oven to 350 degrees.

4. In a large bowl, combine the ingredients for the beef roll except for the tomato sauce. Mix lightly. Turn the mixture out onto wax paper and spread into a rectangle about 12 by 8 inches.

5. Spread the stuffing over the ground beef mixture. Roll up jellyroll fashion starting with a short end and using the paper to guide the rolling. Place in a shallow baking dish and bake 50 minutes.

6. Serve topped with hot tomato sauce.

Yield: Six servings.

VEAL CASSEROLE

⅓ cup whole wheat flour
Sea salt and freshly ground
    black pepper to taste
2½ pounds boneless veal shoulder
    cut into 2-inch squares and
    pounded
¼ cup butter
1 pound mushrooms, sliced
1 pound fresh water chestnuts,
    washed, peeled and sliced, or 2
    cans (5 ounces each) drained
    and sliced water chestnuts
2 cups veal or chicken broth (see
    page 52)
2 tablespoons tamari (soy sauce)
1 tablespoon miso (soybean
    paste)
¼ cup sherry (optional)
Brown rice (see page 217)

1. Preheat the oven to 350 degrees.

2. Season the flour with salt and pepper and use to coat the veal. Reserve one tablespoon leftover flour mixture.

3. Heat two tablespoons butter in a heavy skillet, add the veal and brown on all sides. Remove to a warm casserole.

4. Add remaining butter to the skillet and sauté the mushrooms and water chestnuts in it two to three minutes.

5. Gradually add one and one-half cups of the broth to the soy sauce and bean paste in a small bowl. When well blended, add to mushroom mixture in the skillet. Cover and cook five minutes.

6. Mix reserved flour with remaining broth and stir into skillet. Cook, stirring, until mixture thickens slightly; season with salt and pepper. Add sherry and pour over meat in the casserole. Cover tightly and bake 35 minutes or until meat is tender. Serve over brown rice.

Yield: Eight servings.

HONEY OF A LAMB

1 shoulder of lamb (5 to 6
  pounds)
1 cup honey
1 clove garlic, finely chopped
½ teaspoon kelp
½ teaspoon cayenne pepper

1. Place the lamb on broiler rack and broil
under broiler preheated to 350 to 400
degrees, turning meat often until it is half
done. Alternately, meat can be roasted
in 325-degree oven.

2. Combine remaining ingredients and
brush over both sides of the meat and
continue to broil, basting every 10 minutes,
until meat is tender, a total of about one
and one-quarter hours. Serve any leftover
basting sauce separately.

Yield: Four servings.

LAMB LOAF

2 tablespoons butter
1 tablespoon chopped onion
1 tablespoon chopped green
  pepper
½ pound mushrooms, sliced
¼ cup chopped parsley
1½ pounds ground lamb shoulder
½ teaspoon rosemary, crushed
1 cup milk
¼ cup wheat germ
½ cup whole wheat bread crumbs
  Sea salt and freshly ground
  black pepper to taste
1½ cups homemade tomato sauce
  (see page 161)

1. Preheat the oven to 350 degrees.

2. Heat the butter in a heavy skillet and
sauté the onion, green pepper and
mushrooms until tender, about five
minutes.

3. Place the parsley, lamb, rosemary, milk,
wheat germ and bread crumbs in a large
bowl and add the cooked onion mixture.
Season with salt and pepper and mix
lightly.

4. Form the mixture into a loaf shape,
place in an oiled baking dish and pour
over the sauce. Bake 50 minutes, basting
frequently with the sauce.

Yield: Six servings.

CHICK-PEAS AND BULGHUR

2 cups dried chick-peas
Water
¾ pound boned lamb shoulder
  cut into cubes
Sea salt and freshly ground black
  pepper to taste
1 onion, finely chopped
2 tablespoons butter
1 cup bulghur
1 tablespoon chopped fresh
  mint leaves or ½ teaspoon
  dried mint
Yogurt (see page 311)

1. Pick over and wash the chick-peas. Cover with water and let soak overnight. Drain chick-peas and reserve liquid.

2. Next day, place lamb in a saucepan and add chick-pea soaking water and enough extra water if needed to barely cover meat. Season with salt and pepper and add onion. Bring to a boil, cover and simmer 30 minutes.

3. Add chick-peas and cook 40 minutes longer or until chick-peas are tender. Heat the butter in a skillet and brown the bulghur in it slowly. Add to the lamb mixture and cook 25 minutes or until bulghur is tender. Add mint, check seasoning and serve topped with yogurt. Yield: Six servings.

PORK AND VEGETABLE SKILLET SUPPER

1 pound finely diced lean pork
2 tablespoons oil
½ cup 1-inch pieces green beans
½ cup fresh peas
½ cup diced carrot
½ cup diagonally sliced celery
1 tablespoon soy sauce
  Sea salt and freshly ground
  black pepper to taste
¾ cup chicken broth (see page 52)
⅓ cup cooked soybeans
  (see page 157)

1. Sauté the pork in the oil until well browned and almost completely cooked. Practically no pink will remain in the middle of the pieces of pork when they are almost cooked.

2. Add the green beans, peas, carrots, celery, soy sauce, salt and pepper and cook quickly three minutes while stirring. Add the broth. Cover and cook about eight minutes or until vegetables are crisp-tender.

3. Stir in the soybeans and heat. Yield: Four servings.

WHOLE WHEAT SCRAPPLE

2 pounds pork neck bones or
  fresh pork hocks, cut up
1½ quarts water
1 onion, studded with 2 whole
  cloves
Sea salt to taste
4 peppercorns, crushed
1½ cups uncooked whole wheat
  cereal or corn meal
½ teaspoon sage
⅛ teaspoon mace
Bacon drippings for frying

1. Place the pork in a kettle with the water. Bring to a boil and skim off the scum. Add the onion studded with the cloves, the salt and peppercorns. Cover and simmer gently two hours or until meat falls off bones.

2. Strain off the broth and measure one quart, adding water if necessary. Remove meat from bones, discard bones and chop meat finely.

3. Heat the broth to boiling and while stirring gradually pour in the whole wheat cereal or corn meal. Cook, stirring, 15 minutes.

4. Add chopped meat, sage, mace and salt to cereal or corn meal mixture. Pour into an oiled 9-by-5-by-3-inch loaf pan and allow to cool.

5. To serve, heat bacon drippings in a heavy skillet and fry thick slices of the scrapple until browned on both sides.

Yield: Six servings.

PEACHY LIVER FOR LIVER HATERS

1½ pounds calves' or beef liver,
  trimmed, washed and sliced
  thinly
Wheat germ
2 tablespoons soy oil or
  safflower oil
2 tablespoons chopped onion
2 tablespoons tomato paste
2 fresh ripe peaches, sliced

1. Dredge the liver slices in the wheat germ. Heat the oil in a heavy skillet and brown the liver slices quickly on both sides, about five minutes.

2. Add onion and tomato paste and simmer three to five minutes longer. Add the peach slices and heat until they are warmed through.

Yield: Six servings.

LIVER LOAF

2 tablespoons bacon drippings
1 pound beef liver, skinned, trimmed and sliced
½ pound pork sausage meat
1½ cups whole wheat bread crumbs
2 tablespoons chopped onion
1 teaspoon soy sauce
1 tablespoon lemon juice
1 teaspoon sea salt
¼ teaspoon freshly ground black pepper
1 teaspoon celery salt
2 eggs, lightly beaten
½ cup beef broth (see page 53)
4 slices lean bacon

1. Preheat the oven to 350 degrees.

2. Heat the bacon drippings in a heavy skillet. Add the liver slices and brown them in the drippings. Put liver and the sausage meat through the medium blade of a meat grinder.

3. Add remaining ingredients except the bacon. Pack into a 9-by-5-by-3-inch loaf pan, top with bacon and bake 45 minutes or until done.

Yield: Four servings.

LIVER 'N ONIONS

1 pound beef liver, trimmed and thinly sliced
Wheat germ
Sea salt to taste
2 tablespoons soy oil
1 large sweet Spanish onion, thinly sliced crosswise and separated into rings
4 slices lean bacon
1 cup dry white wine or chicken broth (see page 52)

1. Preheat the oven to 350 degrees.

2. Dredge the liver slices in wheat germ mixed with salt.

3. Heat the oil in a heavy skillet and brown liver quickly in it on both sides. Transfer to a shallow baking dish. Top with onion rings and bacon.

4. Pour in the wine or broth and bake, uncovered, 20 minutes or until liver is tender and bacon cooked.

Yield: Four servings.

CALVES' BRAINS WITH SCRAMBLED EGGS

1 pound calves' brains
1 quart water
1 tablespoon vinegar
1¾ teaspoons sea salt
6 eggs, lightly beaten
½ cup milk
¼ teaspoon freshly ground
    black pepper
3 tablespoons butter

1. Wash the brains and place in a saucepan with the water, vinegar and one teaspoon of the salt. Bring to a boil, cover and simmer 20 minutes. Drain.

2. Remove the membranes from the brains and separate brains into small pieces.

3. Mix the eggs, milk, remaining salt and the pepper together. Heat the butter in a skillet and add the brains. Brown on all sides. Add the egg mixture and cook, stirring until egg mixture sets.

Yield: Four servings.

BRAISED VEAL HEARTS

2 veal hearts, veins and arteries
    removed and hearts well washed
2 tablespoons butter
½ cup chopped onion
1 clove garlic
1 carrot, quartered
1 bay leaf
2 ribs celery, cut up
Sea salt and freshly ground black
    pepper to taste
2 cups chicken broth,
    approximately (see page 52)

1. Slice hearts across the grain into one-half-inch slices.

2. Melt the butter in a heavy saucepan and sauté the heart slices in it until browned on all sides.

3. Add the onion, garlic, carrot, bay leaf, celery, salt and pepper and cook five minutes, stirring occasionally. Add two cups broth, bring to a boil, cover tightly and simmer gently until heart slices are tender, about one hour. Add more broth if necessary during the cooking.

Yield: Four servings.

STUFFED VEAL HEARTS

2 veal hearts, cut in half, veins
and arteries removed and
hearts well washed
3 tablespoons oil
1 tablespoon chopped onion
1 clove garlic, finely chopped
½ cup chopped mushrooms
1 tablespoon chopped parsley
1 cup soft whole wheat bread
crumbs
Sea salt and freshly ground
black pepper to taste
¼ teaspoon thyme
1 egg yolk
2 cups diced carrots
2 cups diced celery
1 onion, chopped
2 cups chicken broth (see page 52)
4 slices bacon

1. Trim off any excess fat from hearts.

2. Heat the oil and sauté one
tablespoon chopped onion and the garlic
in it until tender. Add mushrooms and
cook quickly three minutes. Remove pan
from the heat and add parsley, bread
crumbs, salt, pepper, thyme and egg yolk.

3. Preheat the oven to 325 degrees.

4. Stuff the cavities of the veal hearts with
the mushroom mixture and tie together.

5. Place the carrots, celery, onion and
broth in a casserole that is just big enough
to take the hearts side by side. Bring to a
boil, place stuffed hearts on top of
vegetables and broth and lay slices of
bacon over the top of the hearts.

6. Cover casserole tightly and bake two
hours or until hearts are tender.

Yield: Four servings.

KIDNEYS ON TOAST

2 lambs' or calves' kidneys,
skinned, cored and cut into
slices
Whole wheat flour or unbleached
white flour
Sea salt and freshly ground
black pepper to taste
¼ cup butter
1 cup sliced mushrooms
½ cup beef broth or chicken broth
(see pages 52, 53)
4 slices hot buttered whole
wheat toast
2 tablespoons chopped parsley

1. Dredge the slices of kidney in flour
seasoned with salt and pepper. Heat the
butter in a heavy skillet and brown the
kidney pieces quickly in it on all sides.

2. Add the mushrooms and cook, stirring,
two minutes. Sprinkle with one tablespoon
of the seasoned flour mixture; stir to blend.

3. Gradually stir in the broth and bring to
a boil, stirring. Simmer two to three
minutes or until the kidneys are tender (do
not overcook). Serve over toast, sprinkled
with parsley.

Yield: Four servings.

SAUTÉED LIVER BALLS

1 pound beef liver
1 onion
6 soda crackers or whole wheat crackers
1 teaspoon sea salt
5 drops Tabasco sauce or ⅛ teaspoon cayenne pepper
2 tablespoons evaporated milk
2 eggs, lightly beaten
2 tablespoons chopped parsley
3 tablespoons bacon drippings

1. Wash the liver and trim off gristle and skin. Put the liver, onion and crackers through the coarse blade of a meat grinder.

2. Add salt, Tabasco or cayenne, the milk and eggs. Mix well.

3. Form into bite-size balls; roll in chopped parsley. Heat the bacon drippings in a heavy skillet and fry the balls in it until browned on all sides.

Yield: Four servings.

Note: The contributor says if the family is against liver on principle, never admit that the balls are anything but plain meatballs.

FREEZER LIVER

3 pounds beef liver, or 2 whole livers, skinned, tubes removed and liver thinly sliced
½ cup whole wheat flour
½ cup soy flour
½ cup wheat germ
2 teaspoons sea salt
1 teaspoon tarragon, crushed rosemary or thyme (optional)
Olive oil

1. Rinse and drain liver pieces and dry on paper towels.

2. Mix together the flours, wheat germ, salt and herb if used.

3. Dip the liver slices in the dry mixture.

4. To cook, heat olive oil to a depth of one-quarter inch in a heavy skillet and fry as many pieces of liver as needed quickly until well browned, turning often.

5. Spread extra liver on a baking sheet, or heavy-duty aluminum foil, so that the pieces do not touch, and freeze. Store in a plastic bag, tightly closed, and remove pieces as required. They can be fried frozen or allowed to thaw first.

Yield: Ten servings.

SWEETBREAD KEBABS

1½ pounds sweetbreads
Water
1 tablespoon vinegar
1 teaspoon sea salt
½ cup oil
½ cup wine vinegar
1 teaspoon tamari (soy sauce)
2 tablespoons finely chopped onion
⅛ teaspoon freshly ground black pepper
¼ teaspoon thyme
¼ teaspoon marjoram
8 slices bacon, each cut into three pieces
2 green peppers, seeded and cut into 1-inch squares

1. Wash the sweetbreads very well and place in a saucepan with water to cover. Add one tablespoon vinegar and the salt, bring to a boil, cover and simmer 20 minutes. Drain sweetbreads and plunge into ice water to cool and become firm.

2. When the sweetbreads are cool, place on a board, cover with a towel and place a weight on top. Let stand 20 minutes. This makes sweetbreads firm rather than spongy.

3. Remove membranes and break sweetbreads into about 24 pieces.

4. Combine the oil, wine vinegar, tamari, onion, pepper, thyme and marjoram in a bowl. Add the sweetbreads and marinate in the refrigerator two to three hours. Stir occasionally.

5. Wrap a piece of bacon around each piece of sweetbread and alternate with squares of pepper on six individual skewers.

6. Place on a broiler rack and broil two to three inches from the heat. Broil seven to 10 minutes, turn, brush with marinade and broil about three minutes longer or until bacon is cooked.

Yield: Six servings.

HEAD CHEESE

1 hog's head, quartered with ears,
 brains, eyes, snout and most of
 excess fat removed, well washed
Water
1 hog's heart
1 hog's liver
Sea salt and freshly ground black
 pepper to taste
1 tablespoon sage, or to taste
Corn meal

1. Place the head pieces in a large kettle and cover with cold water. Bring to a boil and boil rapidly 10 minutes while removing the scum from the surface. Cover, reduce heat and simmer until meat falls from the bones, about three hours.

2. In a separate pan, place the heart and liver, cover with water, bring to a boil, cover and simmer until tender, about one hour. Drain and put the meat through the medium blade of a meat grinder.

3. Remove head meat from the bones. Discard bones and put the meat through the meat grinder. Measure broth head was cooked in and reserve. Combine ground head meat with liver and heart meat and season with salt, pepper and sage.

4. Return the meat to the broth that the head was cooked in and bring to a boil. Gradually stir in corn meal (one and one-half cups for every quart of broth), until mixture thickens to a mush. Cook two minutes. Pour into roasting or loaf pans and let cool. Chill well.

5. The head cheese can be sliced and fried in bacon drippings or sliced thinly for sandwich fillings or cold cuts.

Yield: About sixteen servings.

TRIPE STEW

3 pounds honeycomb tripe
5 tablespoons sea salt
Water
3 tablespoons bacon drippings
1 cup chopped onions
½ teaspoon rosemary, crushed
2 tablespoons chopped parsley
1 teaspoon basil
⅛ teaspoon cayenne pepper
½ teaspoon freshly ground black pepper
1 teaspoon raw sugar (optional)
1 cup diced carrots
½ cup diced celery
½ cup small lima beans
Boiled potatoes

1. Wash the tripe very well, rinsing under running water several times. Cut into one-half-inch slivers. Place in a bowl and add three tablespoons of the salt and water to cover. Let soak 30 minutes, drain and rinse well.

2. Heat the bacon drippings in a large kettle and sauté the onions in it until tender. Add tripe, water to cover, rosemary, parsley, basil, cayenne, black pepper, sugar and remaining salt.

3. Bring to a boil, cover and simmer gently two and one-half to three hours, or until tripe is tender. Add carrots, celery and lima beans during last 25 minutes of cooking.

4. Serve stew over boiled potatoes in soup plates.

Yield: Eight servings.

CHICKEN WITH FRUIT

¼ cup butter
2 frying chickens (each 2½ pounds), cut into serving pieces
1 onion, sliced
¼ pound mushrooms, sliced
1¼ cups chicken broth (see page 52)
3 tablespoons lemon juice
1 teaspoon sea salt
¼ teaspoon ground cloves
¼ teaspoon allspice
⅓ cup unsulphured molasses
4 teaspoons arrowroot
2 tablespoons cold water
1 cup cubed fresh pineapple
4 green-tipped bananas halved lengthwise and then crosswise

1. Heat the butter in a heavy skillet, add the chicken pieces and brown on all sides. Add onion and mushrooms and cook five minutes longer.

2. Add broth, juice, salt, cloves, allspice and molasses. Cover and simmer 30 minutes or until chicken is tender.

3. Blend the arrowroot with the cold water and stir into the skillet. Stir until mixture thickens. Add pineapple and banana pieces. Heat through but do not boil.

Yield: Eight servings.

CHICKEN TANDOORI

1 cup yogurt (see page 311)
3 tablespoons lime juice
1½ teaspoons grated fresh gingerroot
1½ teaspoons ground coriander
1 teaspoon ground cumin
½ teaspoon ground anise seeds
½ teaspoon cayenne pepper
1 clove garlic, finely chopped
1 chicken (2½ to 3 pounds), cut into serving pieces
⅓ cup melted butter
Lime wedges

1. Combine all ingredients except the chicken, butter and lime wedges and mix well. Set the chicken in a bowl and pour the yogurt mixture over all. Marinate in the refrigerator 24 hours, turning often.

2. Preheat the oven to 375 degrees.

3. Place the chicken pieces on a rack in a shallow roasting pan and bake 45 to 60 minutes, or until done, basting three times with the melted butter during the cooking.

4. Serve with lime wedges.

Yield: Four servings.

SESAME BAKED CHICKEN

1 egg, lightly beaten
½ cup milk
½ cup whole wheat flour
1 tablespoon baking powder
1 tablespoon sea salt
2 tablespoons sweet paprika
2 tablespoons sesame seeds
1 frying chicken (2½ to 3 pounds), cut into serving pieces
½ cup melted butter

1. Preheat the oven to 350 degrees.

2. Beat the egg and milk together. Combine the flour, baking powder, salt, paprika and sesame seeds in a paper bag.

3. Dip the chicken pieces in the egg mixture and then shake in the paper bag. Place the chicken pieces skin side up in a baking dish so that they do not touch each other. Pour melted butter over and bake until done, about one hour.

Yield: Three to four servings.

CHICKEN WITH YOGURT

1 tablespoon butter
1 tablespoon safflower oil
1 frying chicken (3 to 3½ pounds), cut into serving pieces
⅛ teaspoon cayenne pepper
½ cup chicken broth (see page 52) or water
½ cup dry white wine or chicken broth (see page 52)
2 tablespoons chopped chives
Sea salt to taste
1 tablespoon unbleached white flour
½ cup yogurt (see page 311)

1. Heat the butter and oil in a heavy skillet and fry the chicken pieces in it, a few at a time, until golden brown. Return all chicken to the skillet.

2. Add cayenne, cover skillet and cook over moderate heat 10 minutes, turning chicken once.

3. Add broth or water and wine or more broth. Sprinkle with chives and salt, cover and cook over low heat for 20 minutes or until chicken is done. Remove chicken to a warm platter.

4. Remove surface fat from broth. Mix flour and yogurt and add to skillet. Cook until thickened but do not boil. Pour over chicken.

Yield: Four servings.

HONEYED CHICKEN

2 frying chickens (each 2½ to
   3 pounds), cut into serving
   pieces
1 cup honey, approximately
1½ cups wheat germ
1 tablespoon chopped parsley
½ teaspoon thyme
½ teaspoon basil
Sea salt and freshly ground
   black pepper to taste
Soy oil

1. Dip each piece of chicken in the honey
to give a thin coating all over. Mix together
the wheat germ, parsley, thyme, basil, salt
and pepper.

2. Coat honeyed chicken with wheat germ
mixture.

3. Add soy oil to depth of one-half to
three-quarters inch in a heavy skillet and
heat. Add chicken pieces so that they make
a single layer. Cook over medium to low
heat until browned, turning several times.

4. Cover skillet and cook until chicken is
done, about 10 minutes.

Yield · Six servings.

CHICKEN AND EGG CASSEROLE

1½ slices whole wheat bread,
   crumbled
½ cup milk
3 cups finely diced cooked
   chicken
1 teaspoon grated onion
½ teaspoon sea salt
⅛ teaspoon freshly ground
   black pepper
1 tablespoon chopped parsley
2 tablespoons oil or melted
   butter
3 eggs, separated

1. Preheat the oven to 350 degrees.

2. Soak the bread in the milk. Add chicken,
onion, salt, pepper, parsley and oil or
butter. Beat the egg yolks well and add.

3. Beat the egg whites until stiff but not
dry and fold into chicken mixture. Pour
into an oiled soufflé dish or casserole and
set in a pan of boiling water. Bake until
set, about 30 minutes.

Yield · Four servings.

CHICKEN CARRIE

3 tablespoons melted chicken fat
1 large Bermuda onion, thinly sliced
3 green peppers, seeded and cut lengthwise into strips
1 teaspoon sea salt
¼ teaspoon freshly ground black pepper
2 large Idaho potatoes, peeled and thinly sliced
2 whole chicken breasts
¼ cup chicken broth (see page 52) or water

1. Heat the chicken fat in a heavy skillet. Add the onion, green peppers, salt and pepper and cook over low heat until onion is transparent.

2. Place potatoes on top of ingredients in skillet and then place chicken breasts on top of potatoes. Pour in broth or water. Cover and simmer gently until chicken and potatoes are cooked, about 20 to 25 minutes.

Yield: Two servings.

HOT CHICKEN SALAD

4 whole chicken breasts
1 cup chicken broth (see page 52)
1 small onion
½ bay leaf
¼ cup chopped celery leaves
Sea salt and freshly ground black pepper to taste
2 tablespoons grated onion
½ cup diced celery
2 tablespoons chopped parsley
3 hard-cooked eggs, sliced or chopped
⅔ cup homemade mayonnaise (see page 186)
½ cup wheat germ

1. Place chicken breasts, broth, onion, bay leaf, celery leaves, salt and pepper in a skillet. Bring to a boil, cover and simmer until tender, about 15 minutes. Cool in the broth.

2. Preheat the oven to 350 degrees.

3. Remove chicken meat from bones and skin; dice meat finely. Strain and reserve broth. Mix chicken with onion, celery, parsley, eggs, salt and pepper.

4. Remove surface fat from broth and use a tablespoon or two of broth to thin down mayonnaise.

5. Add thinned mayonnaise to chicken mixture and pour into an oiled casserole. Top with wheat germ and bake 30 minutes or until bubbly hot and lightly browned.

Yield: Six servings.

CARAWAY CHICKEN LIVERS

1 pound chicken livers, rinsed
  and each cut into two pieces
Whole wheat flour
Sea salt and freshly ground
  black pepper
3 tablespoons butter
1 teaspoon caraway seeds,
  lightly bruised
⅓ cup Madeira wine or chicken
  broth (see page 52)

1. Dredge the livers in flour seasoned with salt and pepper.

2. Heat the butter in a heavy skillet and sauté the caraway seeds in it over gentle heat two minutes. Turn up the heat and add the livers.

3. Sauté the livers until well browned on all sides but still pink in the middle. Slowly pour the wine or broth over and simmer two minutes.

Yield: Four servings.

LUSCIOUS CHICKEN LIVERS

1 pound chicken livers
1 tablespoon dry mustard
1 tablespoon curry powder
1 tablespoon ground ginger
1 tablespoon garlic powder
1 tablespoon sea salt
3 tablespoons olive oil
1 cup frozen peas
3 tablespoons chopped parsley
Brown rice (see page 217)

1. Place the livers in a colander and rinse with cold water. Drain. Cut each liver in half.

2. Mix together the mustard, curry, ginger, garlic powder and salt. Heat the oil in a heavy skillet, add the dry spice mixture and stir in the oil for 15 seconds.

3. Add livers and sauté, turning frequently until browned, about 10 minutes. Add peas, cover and cook until they thaw, uncover and simmer three minutes or until peas are tender. Sprinkle with parsley. Serve over brown rice.

Yield: Four servings.

CHICKEN LIVERS WITH SOUR CREAM

2 tablespoons butter
2 medium-size onions, cut into eighths
1 pound chicken livers, trimmed
1 teaspoon sea salt
1/8 teaspoon freshly ground black pepper
1/4 teaspoon thyme
1/2 cup sour cream or yogurt (see page 311)

1. Heat the butter in a heavy skillet and sauté the onions in it until tender. Push onions to one side of pan and add livers. Brown quickly over high heat, turning frequently, a few at a time if pan is not large enough for a single layer. Cook over medium heat until livers are pink just in the middle. Do not overcook.

2. Add salt, pepper and thyme.

3. Add sour cream or yogurt and reheat but do not boil.

Yield: Four servings.

GIBLET SAUTÉ

1 pound chicken giblets (hearts, gizzards, livers, wing tips and necks), trimmed and cut into bite-size pieces (reserve trimmings)
1/4 cup oil
Sea salt
1/2 teaspoon freshly ground black pepper
1/2 teaspoon thyme
1/4 cup dry white wine or chicken broth (see page 52)
3 1/2 cups water
1 cup raw brown rice
1 clove garlic, finely chopped
1/4 cup chopped parsley

1. Brown the trimmed giblets in the oil in a heavy skillet.

2. Add one teaspoon salt, the pepper, thyme and wine or broth. Cover tightly and simmer one hour.

3. Meanwhile, place trimmings and water in a saucepan, bring to a boil, cover and simmer 30 minutes. Drain, reserving the broth. Discard trimmings or give to the dog.

4. Put the broth in a saucepan with the rice and salt to taste. Cover and simmer 40 minutes or until rice is tender.

5. Add garlic and parsley to cooked giblets and keep warm until rice is cooked. Make a bed of rice on a warm platter and top with the giblet mixture.

Yield: Four servings.

CHICKEN GIBLET STEW

¾ pound chicken gizzards
¼ pound chicken hearts
2 cups chicken broth
(see page 52) or water
1 onion, chopped
1 bay leaf, crumbled
Sea salt and freshly ground
black pepper to taste
1 pound chicken livers, cut into
bite-size pieces
¼ cup whole wheat flour
1 tablespoon butter
¼ cup oil
1 clove garlic, finely chopped
¼ pound mushrooms, sliced
1 cup diced celery
1 cup diced carrots
½ teaspoon basil
½ teaspoon marjoram
½ teaspoon thyme
Cooked homemade whole wheat
noodles (see page 308)

1. Wash the gizzards and hearts very well and place in a saucepan with the broth or water, the onion, bay leaf, salt and pepper. Bring to a boil, cover and simmer until tender, about 45 minutes.

2. Remove the gizzards and hearts, chop finely and reserve. Reserve the broth.

3. Coat the liver pieces with the flour seasoned with salt and pepper. (Reserve any remaining seasoned flour.) Heat the butter and two tablespoons of the oil in a heavy skillet.

4. Fry the livers quickly in the skillet until browned on all sides. Remove and reserve. Add the remaining oil, the garlic and mushrooms to the skillet and cook two minutes. Add celery and carrots and cook three minutes, stirring occasionally.

5. Add reserved broth and chopped gizzards and hearts, bring to a boil, cover and simmer until vegetables are barely tender, about 12 minutes.

6. Add reserved liver pieces, any remaining seasoned flour, the basil, marjoram, thyme, salt and pepper.

7. Heat, stirring, until mixture thickens slightly. Cook three minutes longer. Serve over homemade noodles.

Yield: Four servings.

Note: Any combination of gizzards, hearts, wings and necks may be used in the broth but all skin and bone should be discarded before dicing.

6
VEGETARIAN MAIN DISHES

This is not a vegetarian cookbook, but the author recognizes the many
diversified groups who do adhere to this regime of eating for
humanitarian, philosophical, health or religious reasons. Also, studies have
suggested that many Americans, especially those in the middle-income
and upper-income brackets, consume an excess of animal protein.
These vegetarian main dishes are offered as occasional substitutes for
animal and fish protein and to lend variety, economy and new eating
experiences to family dining.
Balancing an all-vegetable diet—with or without dairy products—based on
nuts, seeds, peas, beans, whole grains and such requires thought,
planning and expert dietary knowledge to ensure that adequate amounts
of essential amino acids and other nutrients will appear in the diet.
This is particularly true for children, pregnant women and others with
special needs. A completely new regime of eating should
not be undertaken lightly.

EGGPLANT STEAKS

2 large eggplants, peeled and
   sliced lengthwise into ½-inch
   slices
1 cup unbleached white flour
4 eggs, lightly beaten
2 cups cold water
1 teaspoon sea salt
1 teaspoon thyme
2 cups whole wheat bread crumbs
1 cup wheat germ
½ cup sesame seeds
½ cup soy oil, approximately
Tomato sauce (see page 161)

1. Dredge the eggplant slices in flour.
Set aside.

2. Combine the eggs, water, salt and
thyme. Mix together the bread crumbs,
wheat germ and sesame seeds.

3. Dip floured eggplant into the egg
mixture and then into crumb mixture.

4. Heat the oil in a heavy skillet and fry
the eggplant slices in it until golden and
tender. Drain on paper towels. Serve
with tomato sauce.

Yield: Six servings.

EGGPLANT AND CHEESE CASSEROLE

1 medium-size eggplant, peeled
   and cubed
Boiling water
Milk
2 slices whole wheat bread
2 eggs, beaten
1 cup grated Cheddar cheese

1. Preheat the oven to 350 degrees.

2. Put the eggplant in a saucepan with
water to cover, cover and simmer until
tender, about 15 minutes. Drain and mash
eggplant.

3. Meanwhile, pour milk over bread to
cover. Let soak five minutes. Squeeze
excess milk from bread. Pull apart and add
to eggplant; mix.

4. Add eggs and cheese and mix. Pour into
an oiled casserole and bake one hour, or
until set and lightly browned on top.

Yield: Six servings.

ZUCCHINI-CHEESE CASSEROLE

2 pounds zucchini, cut into
½-inch slices
½ cup boiling water
2 eggs, lightly beaten
1 pound cottage cheese
1 cup cooked brown rice (see
page 217)
1 onion, finely chopped
Sea salt to taste
½ teaspoon marjoram
1 tablespoon chopped chives
½ cup grated Parmesan cheese

1. Place zucchini and boiling water in a
saucepan, cover and boil five minutes.
Drain and use liquid in soup.

2. Preheat the oven to 350 degrees.

3. Combine the eggs, cottage cheese, rice,
onion, salt, marjoram and chives. Place half
the zucchini in the bottom of a buttered
casserole, top with half the rice mixture,
then repeat layers.

4. Sprinkle with the Parmesan cheese and
bake 45 minutes.

Yield: Three servings.

ZUCCHINI FRITTATA

2 tablespoons oil
5 finger-length, small zucchini,
cut in ¼-inch-thick slices
5 eggs, lightly beaten
1 tablespoon chopped parsley
¼ teaspoon thyme
3½ tablespoons grated Parmesan
cheese
Sea salt to taste
Freshly ground black pepper to
taste (optional)

1. Heat the oil in a medium-size omelet
pan, add the zucchini and cook until lightly
browned on all sides.

2. Combine the eggs, parsley, thyme, two
tablespoons cheese, the salt and pepper.

3. Pour egg mixture over zucchini and
cook over medium heat until mixture
almost sets, shaking pan occasionally.

4. Sprinkle with remaining cheese and run
under preheated broiler to brown lightly.

Yield: Two servings.

Note: The contributor grows vegetables
and herbs organically.

VEGETARIAN CUTLETS

2 small raw beets, peeled
1 carrot
2 onions
2 eggs, well beaten
2 tablespoons oil
½ cup sunflower seed kernels, finely ground
½ teaspoon caraway seeds
½ cup wheat germ
½ teaspoon vegetable salt

1. Grind the beets, carrot and onions through the finest blade of a meat grinder. Strain off excess liquid (use in soup).

2. Combine vegetables with remaining ingredients and mix well. If mixture is too wet to form into patties, add more wheat germ. Chill 30 minutes. Shape into patties.

3. Fry the patties in a lightly oiled skillet until browned; turn to brown the other side.

Yield: Four servings.

WINTER CASSEROLE

4 carrots, grated
3 onions, finely chopped
4 ribs celery, diced
1 green pepper, seeded and chopped
1 cup shredded escarole
½ cup crushed pignoli (pine nuts)
1 cup whole wheat bread crumbs
3 eggs, well beaten
4 cups cooked brown rice (see page 217)
3 tablespoons toasted sesame seeds
Sea salt to taste
Sauce (recipe below)

Sauce:
½ cup butter
2 tablespoons lemon juice
3 tablespoons chopped parsley
2 tablespoons chopped fresh basil leaves

1. Preheat the oven to 350 degrees.

2. Place the carrots, onions, celery and green pepper in a colander over boiling water. Cover and steam until barely tender. Add escarole and steam three minutes longer.

3. Mix steamed vegetable mixture with pignoli, bread crumbs, eggs, rice, sesame seeds and salt and turn into an oiled casserole. Cover and bake 30 minutes.

4. Just before serving, pour the sauce over casserole.

Yield: Eight servings.

Combine all ingredients in a small saucepan and heat.

Yield: About one and one-quarter cups.

PEAS AND BARLEY CASSEROLE

2 tablespoons oil
1 onion, finely chopped
½ cup yellow split peas, washed and drained
2½ cups boiling chicken broth (see page 52)
¼ cup soy grits
½ cup whole barley, washed and drained
2 tablespoons chopped parsley
3 tablespoons fresh snipped dill weed
Sea salt to taste
¼ pound mushrooms, sliced

1. Heat the oil in a heavy saucepan and sauté the onion in it until tender. Add the split peas and cook three minutes.

2. Meanwhile, add one-half cup broth to grits and set aside.

3. Add barley to saucepan and cook two minutes, stirring occasionally. Add remaining broth, soaked grits, the parsley, dill and salt. Bring to a boil and simmer, covered, until liquid has been absorbed and barley is tender, about 55 minutes. Add mushrooms and cook five minutes longer.

Yield: Four servings.

PEAS ROAST

1 pound dried green split peas
1 medium-size onion
Water
Sea salt to taste
½ teaspoon marjoram
2 eggs, lightly beaten
Tomato sauce (see page 161)

1. Pick over and wash the split peas and place in a saucepan with the onion and water to cover. Bring to a boil, cover and cook gently until tender, about 30 minutes.

2. Preheat the oven to 350 degrees.

3. Drain off excess water (use in soup) and pass the peas and onion through a food mill or sieve. Season with salt and marjoram.

4. Beat in the eggs and pour mixture into an oiled 9-by-5-by-3-inch loaf pan. Bake 30 minutes or until loaf is set. Serve with tomato sauce.

Yield: Six servings.

DILLED CARROT CUTLETS

2 cups cooked and drained
  soybeans (see page 157)
1 large carrot, grated
½ teaspoon sea salt
¼ cup finely chopped cashews
2 tablespoons snipped fresh
  dill weed
1 egg, lightly beaten
⅓ cup wheat germ
¼ cup oil

1. Mash the soybeans with a potato masher until smooth. Stir in carrot, salt, cashews and dill.

2. Shape the mixture into cutlet shapes. Dip into the egg and coat with the wheat germ.

3. Heat the oil in a skillet. Add the cutlets and fry quickly until lightly browned on both sides. Drain on paper towels.

Yield: Six servings.

CHICK-PEA LOAF

3 cups cooked dried or drained
  canned chick-peas or garbanzos
1 cup chopped celery
¼ cup finely chopped onion
1 cup whole wheat bread crumbs
⅓ cup tomato sauce
  (see page 161)
1 tablespoon soy sauce
2 tablespoons soy flour
1 cup ground nuts (walnuts,
  almonds, pecans)
1 teaspoon sage
2 tablespoons oil
2 tablespoons chopped parsley
2 eggs, lightly beaten
Sea salt to taste

1. Preheat the oven to 375 degrees.

2. Mash the chick-peas and put in a large bowl. Add remaining ingredients and mix well. Turn into a well-oiled 9-by-5-by-3-inch loaf pan and bake 30 minutes or until set.

Yield: Six servings.

CARROT CASSEROLE

2½ cups finely diced carrots
1 small onion, finely chopped
½ cup water
Sea salt to taste
1 tablespoon raw sugar or honey
¼ cup soy grits
2 tablespoons snipped fresh
dill weed
¼ cup sunflower seed kernels
1 egg, lightly beaten
¼ cup sliced blanched almonds

1. Place carrots, onion, water and salt in a saucepan. Bring to a boil, cover and simmer until carrots are barely tender, about 20 minutes.

2. Preheat the oven to 350 degrees.

3. Stir sugar, soy grits, dill weed, sunflower seed kernels and egg into cooked carrot mixture. Turn into an oiled baking dish. Sprinkle with almonds. Bake 15 minutes.

Yield: Four servings.

CARROT LOAF

3 cups grated raw carrots
2 cups cooked brown rice
(see page 217)
1 cup raw peanuts or cashews
1 cup raw peanut butter
2 cups soy milk
1 tablespoon sage
2 eggs, lightly beaten

1. Preheat the oven to 325 degrees.

2. Mix together the carrots, rice and peanuts.

3. Blend together the peanut butter and soy milk either in an electric blender or with a rotary whisk. Add sage and eggs.

4. Pour milk mixture over carrot mixture and mix well.

5. Turn into an oiled casserole and bake 45 minutes or until set.

Yield: Six servings.

AVOCADO BURGERS

1 medium-size avocado, peeled
  and pitted
1 cup cooked soybeans
  (see page 157)
½ small onion, chopped
1 teaspoon prepared mustard
1 tablespoon tomato puree
Sea salt to taste
Whole wheat bread crumbs
Oil

1. Mix all the ingredients except bread
crumbs and oil together in a blender and
blend until smooth. Turn into a bowl and
add bread crumbs until mixture can be
shaped into patties.

2. Form into hamburger-shaped patties
and fry in oil in a heavy skillet until
outside of each patty is brown and crisp.

Yield: Two servings.

LIMA BEAN LOAF

2 cups cooked lima beans
1 cup whole wheat bread crumbs
½ cup finely chopped green pepper
½ cup finely chopped onion
½ cup chopped nuts
2 eggs, well beaten
½ cup heavy cream
Vegetable salt to taste
Melted butter

1. Preheat the oven to 350 degrees.

2. Mix together the lima beans, bread
crumbs, green pepper, onion, nuts, eggs,
cream, salt and two tablespoons melted
butter. Turn into a well-buttered
9-by-5-by-3-inch loaf pan. Bake 45
minutes, basting three times with melted
butter during cooking.

Yield: Six servings.

BARLEY LENTIL KASHA

½ cup whole barley
1 cup lentils, soaked in water to
  cover 30 minutes, and drained
¼ cup soy grits
Boiling vegetable broth
1 tablespoon oil
1 onion, finely chopped
3 tablespoons chopped parsley
3 tablespoons brewer's yeast
1 teaspoon rosemary
Sea salt to taste

1. Combine the barley, lentils and grits in
a saucepan. Add broth until it is one-half
inch above the vegetables. Cover and
simmer 30 minutes or until barley and
lentils are tender.

2. Meanwhile, heat the oil and sauté the
onion in it until tender.

3. Add onion, parsley, yeast, rosemary and
salt to barley mixture and simmer 10
minutes. If mixture becomes too dry during
cooking, add a little more vegetable broth.

Yield: Six servings.

LENTIL-MILLET PATTIES WITH TOMATO SAUCE

1 cup dried lentils, picked over
   and washed
Water
¾ cup whole hulled millet
1 onion, chopped
Sea salt and freshly ground black
   pepper to taste (optional)
2 eggs, lightly beaten
Wheat germ
Oil for frying
Tomato sauce (see page 161)

1. Put lentils in saucepan with water to cover, bring to a boil and cook until tender, about 30 minutes.

2. Put millet and one and one-half cups water in a second saucepan, bring to a boil, cover and simmer 30 minutes or until tender and water is absorbed.

3. Drain lentils and mix with millet. Add onion, salt and pepper. Form mixture into patties. Dip into beaten eggs and then into wheat germ.

4. Heat oil to depth of one-quarter inch in heavy skillet and fry patties in it until golden. Drain on paper towels. Serve with tomato sauce.

Yield: Six servings.

LENTIL STEW

1 cup dried lentils, picked over
   and washed
Water
2 potatoes, peeled and diced
¼ cup safflower oil
1 onion, finely chopped
3 tablespoons rice polishings
Vegetable broth powder
   to taste
Sea salt to taste

1. Place lentils in a bowl, add water to cover and let soak one to two hours.

2. Pour lentils and water into a saucepan. Add potatoes and enough extra water to cover. Bring to a boil, cover and cook gently until vegetables are tender.

3. Heat one tablespoon of the oil in a small skillet and sauté the onion in it. Add to lentil mixture.

4. In a small saucepan, mix remaining oil with rice polishings and vegetable broth powder. Heat, stirring, until mixture thickens slightly. Add a little of the liquid from the lentil mixture.

5. Stir rice polishings mixture into lentil mixture, season with sea salt and simmer five minutes.

Yield: Four servings.

LENTIL AND BARLEY STEW

¼ cup butter
⅓ cup chopped onion
½ cup chopped celery
2½ cups skinned chopped fresh or canned tomatoes
2 cups water
½ cup dried lentils, picked over and washed
⅓ cup whole barley
½ teaspoon sea salt
⅛ teaspoon black pepper
⅛ teaspoon rosemary
⅓ cup shredded carrots

1. In a large heavy saucepan, melt the butter and sauté the onion in it until tender. Add celery and cook five minutes longer.

2. Add remaining ingredients except the carrots, bring to a boil, cover and simmer gently 25 minutes, stirring occasionally.

3. Add carrots and cook five minutes longer or until barley and lentils are tender.

Yield: Four servings.

LENTIL LOAF

2 cups cooked lentils, slightly mashed
1 cup cooked oatmeal or cooked brown rice (see page 217)
¼ cup soy grits
½ cup vegetable or meat broth
¼ teaspoon tarragon
1 medium-size onion, grated
½ teaspoon sea salt
2 tablespoons chopped parsley
3 tablespoons chopped nuts
1 egg, lightly beaten

1. Preheat the oven to 375 degrees.

2. In a bowl, combine the lentils and oatmeal. Soak the soy grits in the broth five minutes. Add to lentil mixture.

3. Add remaining ingredients and mix well. Turn into an 8½-by-4½-by-2½-inch loaf pan that has been oiled and then dusted with wheat germ. Bake 45 to 60 minutes.

Yield: Six to eight servings.

LENTIL BURGERS

2 cups cooked lentils
1 cup whole wheat bread crumbs
½ cup wheat germ
½ teaspoon sea salt
½ onion, grated
½ teaspoon celery seeds
Whole wheat flour
3 tablespoons oil

1. Mash the lentils slightly. Add bread crumbs, wheat germ, salt, onion and celery seeds. Mix well.

2. Form the mixture into eight patties. Coat with flour.

3. Heat the oil in a skillet and fry the patties on both sides in it until browned.

Yield: Eight servings.

CAJUN'S DELIGHT

⅓ cup dried lentils, picked over and washed

⅓ cup dried lima beans (speckled, if available), picked over and washed

Water

7 tablespoons oil

Sea salt

1 cup raw brown rice

3 cups boiling water

2 tablespoons Woodie's Bar-B-Q sauce (see note)

1 large green pepper, seeded and diced

3 or 4 medium-size hot peppers, seeded and chopped

2 ribs celery, diced

1 large onion, chopped

2 or 3 cloves garlic, finely chopped

1 cup homemade tomato sauce (see page 161) or canned tomato sauce

1½ tablespoons sesame seeds

1 cup chopped pecans

1½ cups shredded Cheddar cheese

1. Put the lentils and lima beans in a bowl with water to cover and let soak overnight. Drain. Place in a kettle with fresh water to cover, one tablespoon oil and salt to taste.

2. Cook until very tender and water has been absorbed or evaporated.

3. Meanwhile, rinse the rice and drain. Heat two tablespoons oil in a saucepan and sauté the rice in it five minutes. Add the boiling water and salt to taste, cover and cook until rice is tender, about 40 minutes.

4. Preheat the oven to 375 degrees.

5. Mash the lentils and lima beans. Stir in the Bar-B-Q sauce. Heat remaining oil and sauté the green pepper, hot peppers, celery, onion and garlic in it until tender. Add to lentils with tomato sauce.

6. Add rice, sesame seeds, pecans and one-half cup of the cheese. Mix well. Pour into a large oiled casserole. Bake 20 minutes. Sprinkle with remaining cheese and bake 15 minutes longer.

Yield: Eight servings.

Note: Woodie's Bar-B-Q sauce comes from Woodie's Pantry, 1041 East 7th Street, Long Beach, Calif., but a good robust substitute might suffice.

VEGETARIAN SAUSAGES

2 cups cooked soybeans
  (see page 157)
1 cup cooked dried lima beans
1 cup cooked dried navy beans
2 teaspoons vegetable salt
⅛ teaspoon paprika
1 tablespoon melted butter
¼ teaspoon powdered sage
¼ teaspoon thyme
¼ teaspoon marjoram
⅛ teaspoon summer savory
1 egg, lightly beaten
⅔ cup milk
1 cup corn meal
Soy oil

1. Preheat the oven to 500 degrees.

2. Press the soybeans, lima beans and navy beans through a colander. Add the salt, paprika, butter, sage, thyme, marjoram and savory.

3. Shape the bean mixture into sausage shapes. Combine the egg and milk. Dip sausages into the egg mixture and then into the corn meal. Place in a large shallow roasting pan well-oiled with soy oil. Bake until sausages are browned on all sides, turning during the cooking.

Yield: Four servings.

SOYBEAN SOUFFLÉ

3 cups warm soybean pulp or
  cooked soybeans forced through
  a food mill or colander
  (pulp should be fairly dry)
4 eggs, separated
1 tablespoon grated onion
2 tablespoons chopped parsley
Sea salt to taste
½ teaspoon thyme
¼ teaspoon marjoram

1. Preheat the oven to 325 degrees.

2. Beat the soybean pulp together with the egg yolks and heat gently, while stirring constantly, until mixture thickens slightly. Do not allow to boil.

3. Stir in the onion, parsley, salt, thyme and marjoram. Beat the egg whites until stiff but not dry and fold into soybean mixture. Pour mixture into a well-buttered 1½-quart soufflé or baking dish and bake 45 minutes or until set.

Yield: Six servings.

SOYBEAN AND NUT LOAF

4 cups cooked drained soybeans
(see page 157)
½ cup ground pecans
½ cup ground almonds
⅓ cup sesame seeds
⅓ cup flax seeds, soaked in warm
water 30 minutes and drained
2 tablespoons oil
1 cup chopped celery
1 cup chopped onions
1 teaspoon paprika
1 teaspoon oregano
1 teaspoon ground cumin

1. Preheat the oven to 350 degrees.

2. Grind the beans through a meat grinder and mix with the pecans, almonds, sesame seeds and flax seeds.

3. Heat the oil and sauté the celery and onions in it until tender. Add to bean mixture with remaining ingredients. Pack into a 9-by-5-by-3-inch loaf pan and bake one hour. (Alternately, the loaf mixture may be formed into patties and fried in a little oil in a skillet.)

Yield: Eight servings.

SOYBEAN AND VEGETABLE CASSEROLE

3 tablespoons oil
1 cup chopped celery
1 cup chopped onions
2½ cups skinned chopped fresh
tomatoes or canned tomatoes
2 cloves garlic, finely chopped
½ teaspoon sea salt
½ cup wheat germ
½ cup chicken broth
(see page 52)
3 tablespoons brewer's yeast
3 tablespoons soy flour
3 cups cooked soybeans
(see page 157)

1. Preheat the oven to 350 degrees.

2. Heat the oil in a skillet and sauté the celery and onions in it until tender. Mix onion mixture with remaining ingredients and turn into an oiled casserole. Bake 30 minutes.

Yield: Six servings.

PRESSURE-COOKED SOYBEANS

1 cup dried soybeans
1 large onion, grated
3¼ cups water
1 teaspoon sea salt
3 tablespoons unsulphured molasses
1 tablespoon sesame oil
¼ teaspoon cinnamon
¼ teaspoon ground cloves
¼ cup chopped dates
¼ cup chopped apple
2 tablespoons unsweetened coconut
1 tablespoon lime juice or lemon juice

1. Pick over and wash the soybeans. Mix beans with onion and water and soak overnight in the refrigerator. Place beans, onion, soaking liquid, salt, molasses, oil, cinnamon and cloves in a pressure cooker. Cooker should not be more than half full.

2. Close cover tightly, place pressure regulator on vent pipe, set for 15 pounds if there is a choice, and cook, according to manufacturer's directions, for 30 minutes.

3. Allow the pressure to reduce of its own accord. Remove pressure regulator and cover. Add the remaining ingredients and mix, while stirring over low heat.

Yield: Six servings.

Note: The soaked beans may be cooked in a regular covered saucepan for several hours. Add extra water as needed.

BAKED SOYBEANS I

2 cups cooked dried soybeans, with cooking liquid reserved (see page 157)
1 large onion, chopped
¼ cup oil or bacon drippings
2 tablespoons unsulphured molasses
4 teaspoons sea salt, or to taste
½ teaspoon dry mustard
Hot water

1. Preheat the oven to 300 degrees.

2. Combine the beans with the onion and oil or drippings. Place in a bean crock or casserole with narrow top opening.

3. In a measuring cup, combine the molasses, salt, mustard and enough hot water to fill the cup. Pour over the beans. Add enough reserved soybean cooking liquid to cover beans.

4. Cover dish and bake six to eight hours. Add more water as necessary to maintain level until the last hour, then uncover and do not add any more water.

Yield: Four to six servings.

BAKED SOYBEANS II

1 pound yellow soybeans, picked over and washed
Cold water
¼ cup oil
1 small onion, chopped
1 green pepper, seeded and diced
¾ cup tomato paste
½ teaspoon kelp
2 tablespoons honey
1½ teaspoons sea salt
2 tablespoons molasses

1. Place the beans in a large freezer container, or several smaller ones, and cover the beans with cold water. There should be plenty of room for the beans to expand.

2. Let soak five hours and then place in the freezer for at least 24 hours. (This reduces length of cooking time required.)

3. Place frozen beans and liquid in a large kettle. Bring to a boil and simmer gently until tender, adding more water if necessary.

4. Beans will take two and one-half hours to three and one-half hours to cook.

5. Meanwhile, heat the oil and sauté the onion and green pepper in it until tender. Transfer to a three-quart casserole. Add the tomato paste, kelp, honey, salt and molasses.

6. Preheat the oven to 325 degrees.

7. Add the beans and cooking liquid to the casserole. Mix well and add more water if beans are not covered. Bake, uncovered, about one and one-half hours or until browned.

Yield: Eight servings.

SOY BURGERS

1 can (15½ ounces) soybeans, drained and rinsed, or 2 cups cooked soybeans (see page 157)
1 small onion, finely grated or chopped
2 eggs, lightly beaten
1 cup wheat germ
1 tablespoon vegetable broth seasoning
1 tablespoon tamari (soy sauce)
1 tomato, skinned and put through an electric blender until smooth

1. Preheat the oven to 350 degrees.

2. Mash the soybeans with a potato masher.

3. In a large bowl, combine all the ingredients.

4. Using a small ice cream scoop, measure out portions of mixture onto a lightly oiled baking sheet. Flatten each scoop slightly.

5. Bake 25 minutes, turn and bake 15 minutes longer.

Yield: Four servings.

SOY-RICE BURGERS

1½ cups (15½-ounce can) soybeans, drained, or dried soybeans, soaked, cooked and drained (see page 157)
1 cup cooked brown rice (see page 217)
2 tablespoons chopped onion
2 eggs, lightly beaten
½ teaspoon sea salt
½ teaspoon celery salt
1 cup whole wheat bread crumbs
¼ teaspoon paprika
2 tablespoons chopped parsley
½ cup wheat germ
8 slices whole wheat bread

1. Grind the soybeans, using the coarse blade of the meat grinder. Mix soybeans with other ingredients except the wheat germ and bread slices.

2. Form into four burger patties. Roll in the wheat germ.

3. Broil over charcoal fire, or under the broiler, until lightly browned. Alternately, the burgers may be baked on a baking sheet in a 350-degree oven for 35 minutes.

4. Serve between whole wheat bread slices.

Yield: Four servings.

SOYBEAN PATTIES

1½ cups cooked soybeans
(see page 157)
1 egg, lightly beaten
2 scallions, chopped
¼ cup non-fat dry milk solids
½ cup wheat germ
¼ cup cottage cheese
1 tablespoon tamari (soy sauce)
¼ teaspoon sea salt
⅛ teaspoon freshly ground
black pepper
⅛ teaspoon kelp
⅛ teaspoon dry mustard
⅛ teaspoon ginger
1 tablespoon sesame oil
Sesame seeds

1. Puree the soybeans in an electric blender, using a minimum of the cooking liquid. Turn into a bowl and add all other ingredients except the oil and sesame seeds.

2. Mixture should be of a consistency easily shaped. If mixture is too wet, add more wheat germ; if too dry, a little bean cooking liquid.

3. Shape into six flat patties and roll in sesame seeds. Let dry 15 minutes. Heat the oil in a skillet and fry the patties five to eight minutes on each side.

Yield: Six servings.

BROILED SOY CAKES

2 cups cooked soybeans
(see page 157)
1 cup diced celery with leaves
½ cup cooked wild rice
½ cup chopped onion
2 eggs
¼ cup butter
½ cup wheat germ
½ teaspoon sea salt
¼ cup finely chopped green
pepper
Melted butter (optional)
Parsley sprigs and tomato slices

Mix the soybeans, celery, rice, onion, eggs, butter, wheat germ, salt and green pepper together very well and form into cakes. Broil until golden, turn and broil second side. If browning seems slow, brush with a little melted butter. Garnish with parsley sprigs and tomato slices.

Yield: Six servings.

MILLET-STUFFED PEPPERS

1 cup whole hulled millet
3 cups water
Sea salt to taste
4 medium-size green peppers,
    halved lengthwise and seeded
⅓ cup sesame oil
1½ cups chopped onions
1 clove garlic, chopped
½ cup sliced mushrooms
3 tablespoons chopped parsley
1 teaspoon oregano
½ teaspoon basil
1 teaspoon tamari (soy sauce)
2 eggs, lightly beaten
½ cup cottage cheese
8 slices tomato
Grated Cheddar cheese

1. Put millet, water and salt in a saucepan. Bring to a boil and simmer, covered, until tender, about 30 minutes. Drain.

2. Steam the pepper halves over boiling water five minutes.

3. Preheat the oven to 350 degrees.

4. In a large heavy skillet, heat the oil and sauté the onions and garlic in it until tender. Add mushrooms and cook two minutes longer.

5. Stir in parsley, oregano, basil and soy sauce.

6. Add cooked millet, the eggs and cottage cheese and cook, stirring gently, a minute or two. Fill pepper halves with millet mixture.

7. Set in a baking dish with one-half inch of hot water in the bottom. Top each pepper half with a tomato slice and some cheese.

8. Bake 25 to 30 minutes.

Yield: Four servings.

MILLET STEW

1 tablespoon sesame oil
½ cup chopped onion
1 cup peeled butternut squash
    cubes (about ½-inch cubes)
1 cup whole hulled millet
4½ cups water
1 tablespoon tamari (soy sauce)

1. Heat the oil in a saucepan and sauté the onion in it. Add the squash and cook five minutes longer.

2. Add millet, water and tamari, bring to a boil, cover and boil 45 minutes. Stir to mix and let stand 10 minutes before serving.

Yield: Four servings.

MILLET 'N VEGETABLES

1 cup chopped carrots
½ cup chopped onion
1 cup diced peeled potato
½ cup chopped parsnip or white turnip
1 cup shredded cabbage
¼ cup chopped parsley
½ cup whole hulled millet
1 teaspoon sea salt
2½ cups water or vegetable broth, approximately
1 tablespoon oil

1. Place all the vegetables in a heavy porcelainized iron casserole. Add parsley, millet, salt and two and one-half cups water. Bring to a boil, cover and cook gently 45 minutes.

2. If mixture seems too thick, add a little water, or broth, and cook 15 minutes longer. Drizzle oil over surface before serving.

Yield: Four servings.

MILLET SOUFFLÉ

3 eggs, separated
1¾ cups cooked millet (see page 212)
½ teaspoon sea salt
⅓ cup plus ¼ cup grated Cheddar cheese
⅔ cup milk

1. Preheat the oven to 350 degrees.

2. Beat the egg yolks lightly. Mix with the millet, salt, one-third cup cheese and the milk.

3. Beat the egg whites until stiff but not dry and fold into millet mixture. Pour into a 1½-quart soufflé dish. Sprinkle top with remaining cheese. Set soufflé dish in a pan of hot water and bake about 20 minutes or until set.

Yield: Four servings.

MILLET CASSEROLE I

1 cup whole hulled millet
4 cups water
Sea salt to taste
2 onions, finely chopped
1 clove garlic, finely chopped
2 cups tomato puree
2 cups wheat germ
2 tablespoons oil
2 tablespoons chopped fresh basil
2 tablespoons chopped parsley
½ teaspoon celery seeds

1. Place millet, water and salt in a saucepan, bring to a boil, cover and simmer until tender, about 30 minutes.

2. Preheat the oven to 350 degrees.

3. Add remaining ingredients to the cooked millet and turn into oiled 9-by-5-by-3-inch loaf pan or casserole. Bake one hour or until set.

Yield: Six servings.

Note: One-half cup grated Cheddar cheese can be added if desired.

MILLET CASSEROLE II

2 tablespoons safflower oil
1 cup whole hulled millet
½ cup diced carrot
¼ cup diced celery
1 tablespoon chopped green pepper
1 tablespoon vegetable salt or to taste
½ teaspoon oregano
½ teaspoon basil
¼ teaspoon chervil
¼ teaspoon summer savory
Water or vegetable broth

1. Heat the oil in a heavy skillet and brown the millet in it, stirring constantly. Add carrot, celery and green pepper and cook three minutes.

2. Place mixture in saucepan, and add remaining ingredients including enough water, or broth, to extend one inch above millet-vegetable mixture. Bring to a boil, cover and cook 15 minutes.

3. Place pan over hot water and continue cooking until millet is tender, about 20 minutes.

Yield: Six servings.

FARINATA (CORN MEAL, KALE AND BEANS)

1 pound red kidney beans,
  picked over and washed
Water
1 large unpeeled onion
2 unpeeled cloves garlic
3 ribs celery
4 sprigs parsley, tied together
Sea salt to taste
1 tablespoon tamari (soy sauce)
2 pounds kale, stems and tough
  veins removed
2 quarts boiling water
1½ cups stoneground
  corn meal
1 cup olive oil

1. Put the beans in a bowl, cover with water and let soak overnight. Next morning, drain, cover with fresh water and add onion, garlic, celery, parsley, salt and tamari. Bring to a boil and simmer, covered, until tender, about 30 minutes.

2. Break the kale into pieces and cook in the boiling water until tender.

3. Remove the onion, garlic, parsley and celery from beans and discard.

4. Drain the kale, adding the liquid to the bean mixture. Stir the corn meal and salt to taste into the boiling bean mixture, beating vigorously to prevent lumping. Cover and simmer slowly 30 minutes or until corn meal is done.

5. Add kale and oil. Check seasoning. Serve hot. Or, slice when cold and fry in oil.
Yield: Twelve servings.

BROWN RICE AND CHEESE CASSEROLE

2 eggs, lightly beaten
½ cup heavy cream
⅓ cup water
1½ cups cooked brown rice
  (see page 217)
1¼ cups grated Cheddar cheese
Sea salt to taste
¼ cup chopped green pepper
2 tablespoons grated onion

1. Preheat the oven to 350 degrees.

2. Beat the eggs together with the cream and water. Stir into the rice. Add cheese, salt, green pepper and onion. Mix well.

3. Turn into an oiled casserole and bake 45 minutes or until set.
Yield: Two servings.

VEGETARIAN RICE CASSEROLE

¼ cup oil
1 onion, finely chopped
1 large carrot, diced
1 cup shredded Chinese cabbage
1 cup snow peas
1 cup shredded spinach leaves
1 cup shredded romaine or escarole
1½ cups bean sprouts (see page 195)
2 tablespoons sesame seeds
½ cup finely chopped walnuts
Sea salt to taste
Tamari (soy sauce) to taste
4 cups cooked brown rice (see page 217)
2 eggs, lightly beaten

1. Heat the oil in a large heavy skillet and sauté the onion and carrot in it until onion is tender. Add Chinese cabbage, snow peas, spinach and lettuce. Cover pan and cook, without added liquid, until wilted.

2. Add bean sprouts, sesame seeds, walnuts, salt and tamari. Cover and steam three minutes. Mix in the rice and reheat.

3. Make a well in the center of the vegetable mixture and add the eggs. Cook, stirring, until eggs are cooked. Check seasoning. Transfer to a casserole and keep warm for serving.

Yield: Six to eight servings.

BROWN RICE ORIENTAL STYLE

3 tablespoons sesame oil
2 bunches scallions, chopped
1 clove garlic, finely chopped
4 ribs celery, diced
1 can (5 ounces) water chestnuts, sliced
2 cups bean sprouts (see page 195)
3 tablespoons chopped parsley
1 teaspoon oregano
½ teaspoon basil
¾ cup sunflower seed kernels
2 tablespoons grated fresh ginger
¾ cup honey
½ cup soy sauce
1 tablespoon lemon juice
Sea salt to taste
4 cups cooked brown rice (see page 217)
1 cup drained mandarin orange segments (optional)

1. In a wok, or a heavy iron skillet, heat the oil. Add scallions and cook quickly one minute. Add garlic and celery and cook one minute.

2. Add water chestnuts, bean sprouts and parsley. Cook, stirring, one minute. Stir in the oregano, basil and sunflower seed kernels.

3. Combine the ginger, honey, soy sauce and lemon juice and stir into the vegetable mixture. Add salt. Stir in the cooked rice and reheat. Garnish with orange slices.

Yield: Four servings.

RICE-STUFFED GREEN PEPPERS

6 large sweet green peppers
¼ cup oil
1 small onion, finely chopped
1 cup diced celery
½ cup sliced mushrooms
⅓ cup chopped nuts
½ cup shredded Cheddar cheese
3 cups cooked brown rice
(see page 217)
Sea salt to taste
3 tablespoons freshly grated
Parmesan cheese

1. Cut a thin slice off top of peppers; remove seeds and core. Trim slices and chop good parts to use later.

2. Preheat the oven to 375 degrees.

3. Heat the oil in a large heavy skillet and sauté the onion in it until tender. Add reserved chopped pepper, the celery and mushrooms and cook five minutes longer.

4. Stir in the nuts, Cheddar cheese, brown rice and salt. Mix well. Use mixture to stuff peppers. Set in an oiled baking dish with one-half inch of hot water in the bottom. Sprinkle tops of stuffed peppers with Parmesan cheese.

5. Bake 35 to 45 minutes or until tender.

Yield: Six servings.

RICE OMELET

1 tablespoon unbleached white
flour
½ cup milk
3 eggs, separated
½ teaspoon sea salt
1½ cups cooked brown rice
(see page 217)

1. Mix the flour in a small saucepan with a small quantity of the milk until smooth. Gradually stir in remaining milk. Bring to a boil, stirring.

2. Beat the egg yolks lightly. Add with salt and rice to milk mixture.

3. Beat the egg whites until stiff but not dry and fold into rice mixture. Pour mixture into a very hot, well-buttered omelet pan: Cook until well browned on bottom.

4. Place under preheated broiler to brown and cook top surface. Fold over onto plate.

Yield: One serving.

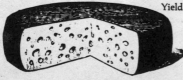

NOODLE CASSEROLE

1 cup ricotta or large curd cottage
  cheese
1 cup yogurt (see page 311)
¼ cup melted butter
Sea salt and freshly ground black
  pepper to taste (optional)
1 egg, lightly beaten
⅛ teaspoon nutmeg
⅓ cup freshly grated Parmesan
  cheese
8 ounces whole wheat noodles,
  cooked al dente (see page 309)

1. Preheat the oven to 300 degrees.
2. Mix together all ingredients except the noodles. Drain noodles and rinse with cold water. Add cheese mixture and toss.
3. Turn into a buttered casserole or baking dish and bake 45 to 60 minutes.

Yield: Six servings.

BUCKWHEAT AND PEANUT CASSEROLE

4 cups peeled sliced potatoes
½ cup whole buckwheat
2 medium-size onions, finely
  chopped
½ green pepper, seeded and
  chopped
1 teaspoon sea salt
½ cup shelled raw peanuts
3 cups water

1. Preheat the oven to 350 degrees.
2. Make a layer of half the potatoes in a buttered 1½-quart casserole. Add buckwheat, onions, green pepper and salt. Top with remaining potatoes.
3. In an electric blender, finely chop the peanuts, add water and blend until mixture is smooth. Pour over casserole. Cover and bake one hour or until buckwheat is cooked.

Yield: Six servings.

BUCKWHEAT GROATS LOAF

2 cups cooked buckwheat groats
  (see page 213)
2 cups cooked brown rice
  (see page 217)
3 cups steamed diced vegetables,
  including celery, carrot, turnip,
  parsnip, green pepper and potato
2 cups shredded Cheddar cheese
Sea salt to taste

1. Preheat the oven to 325 degrees.
2. Combine the groats, rice, vegetables and one cup of the cheese in a bowl. Mix well. Add salt.
3. Turn into an oiled casserole or ovenproof bowl. Sprinkle remaining cheese over the top and bake 40 minutes or until cheese is melted.

Yield: Six servings.

BUCKWHEAT-STUFFED CABBAGE ROLLS

1 medium-size onion, finely
  chopped
¼ cup oil
2 cups kasha (buckwheat groats)
Sea salt and freshly ground
  black pepper to taste
1 quart water
1 head cabbage (3 pounds)
Warm water or tomato sauce
  (see page 161)

1. Sauté the onion in the oil until tender. Add groats and cook, stirring, until coated with oil.

2. Add salt, pepper and one quart water and bring to a boil. Cover and simmer 20 minutes or until water has been absorbed.

3. Meanwhile, core the cabbage and steam over boiling water until leaves are soft.

4. Preheat the oven to 350 degrees.

5. Separate the cabbage leaves and place two to three heaping tablespoonfuls groats mixture on each big leaf. Roll up, tucking in the sides as you go. Use two smaller leaves together for making other rolls.

6. Place rolls in an oiled baking dish or casserole. Pour warm water or tomato sauce over rolls until liquid reaches three-quarters the way up the layers of rolls. Cover and bake two hours or until cabbage is tender.

Yield: Ten servings.

WILD RICE AND BUCKWHEAT LOAF

½ cup whole buckwheat
½ cup raw brown rice
½ cup raw wild rice
1 quart water or vegetable
  broth, approximately
2 tablespoons oil
2 medium-size onions, chopped
  finely
1 cup chopped celery
1½ teaspoons sea salt
¼ cup chopped parsley
2 teaspoons ground cumin

1. Place buckwheat, rice and wild rice in a kettle. Add one quart water. Bring to a boil, cover and simmer until tender, about 40 minutes. Add more water as necessary during cooking.

2. Preheat the oven to 350 degrees.

3. Heat the oil in a skillet and sauté the onion and celery in it until tender. Add to cooked grains with remaining ingredients. Turn into an oiled casserole and bake one hour.

Yield: Six servings.

WHEAT LOAF

1 cup finely ground walnuts or
   pecans
1 cup wheat germ
1 cup grated mild Cheddar cheese
¾ cup tomato juice (see page 27)
3 eggs, well beaten
1 large onion, finely chopped
1 teaspoon thyme
¼ teaspoon marjoram
Sea salt to taste

1. Preheat the oven to 350 degrees.
2. Mix together the nuts, wheat germ and cheese. Add remaining ingredients and mix well. Turn into an oiled 8½-by-4½-by-2½-inch loaf pan. Bake 45 minutes. Serve like meat loaf.

Yield: Four to six servings.

WHEAT GERM LOAF

1½ cups wheat germ
   Nut milk (see page 25)
1 cup finely chopped walnuts
1 onion, finely chopped
1 green pepper, finely chopped
¼ cup lemon juice
1 tablespoon oil
1 egg, lightly beaten
   Tomato sauce (see page 161)

1. Preheat the oven to 325 degrees.
2. Put the wheat germ in a bowl and add nut milk slowly until wheat germ will not absorb any more. It is hard to estimate the amount because wheat germ varies.
3. Drain off any excess nut milk and add walnuts, onion, green pepper, lemon juice, oil and egg. Turn into an oiled 8½-by-4½-by-2½-inch loaf pan and bake about 30 minutes. Serve with tomato sauce.

Yield: Four servings.

WHEAT AND NUT LOAF

¼ cup safflower oil
1 onion, finely chopped
4 eggs, lightly beaten
3 cups cooked brown rice
(see page 217)
1 quart milk
3 cups stoneground whole wheat
raisin bread crumbs
1 teaspoon sea salt
3 tablespoons dried sage
2 cups finely chopped walnuts
Tomato sauce (see page 161)

1. Preheat the oven to 350 degrees.

2. Heat the oil and sauté the onion in it until tender. Mix the eggs and rice together. Pour two cups of the milk over the raisin bread crumbs and let stand five minutes.

3. In a large bowl, combine the onion mixture, rice mixture, crumb mixture, salt, sage, walnuts and remaining milk. Pack into an oiled 9-by-5-by-3-inch loaf pan or 2-quart casserole.

4. Place pan or casserole in pan of hot water and bake one hour. Serve hot with tomato sauce.

Yield: Eight servings.

NUT CASSEROLE

⅓ cup raisins
⅓ cup finely chopped dried
apricots
Cold water
2 cups cooked brown rice
(see page 217)
1½ cups unblanched almonds,
slivered, or ground in mouli
or Moulinex grinder
½ cup butter, melted
Sea salt to taste
1 tablespoon raw sugar or honey

1. Soak the raisins and apricots in water to cover for 30 minutes. Drain.

2. Preheat the oven to 350 degrees.

3. Combine the rice, fruits and nuts in an oiled casserole. Stir in the butter, salt and sugar or honey. Bake 30 minutes or until firm.

Yield: Six servings.

CHEESE AND NUT LOAF

3 tablespoons oil
1 onion, chopped
1½ cups chopped celery
1 cup chopped cashews
1 cup chopped walnuts
2 cups cooked brown rice
(see page 217)
2 cups (1 pound) cottage cheese
2 tablespoons chopped chives
¼ cup toasted sesame seeds
¼ cup chopped parsley
½ teaspoon thyme
Sea salt to taste
3 eggs, lightly beaten
¼ cup wheat germ

1. Preheat the oven to 375 degrees.

2. Heat the oil in a skillet and sauté the onion in it until tender. Add the celery and cook five minutes longer.

3. Combine the cashews, walnuts, rice, cottage cheese, chives, sesame seeds, parsley, thyme, salt and eggs in a large bowl. Stir in the cooked onion mixture.

4. Oil a 9-by-5-by-3-inch loaf pan and dust generously with wheat germ. Turn the cheese-rice-nut mixture into the pan and sprinkle remaining wheat germ over the surface. Bake one hour. Unmold to serve.

Yield: Eight to ten servings.

NUT LOAF

2 cups finely ground mixture of
nuts such as sunflower
seed kernels, almonds, walnuts
and cashews
1 medium-size onion, finely
chopped
3 cloves garlic, finely chopped
3 ribs celery, finely chopped
2 eggs, lightly beaten
¾ cup wheat germ
3 tablespoons brewer's yeast
1 cup cooked brown rice
(see page 217) or
raw rolled oats
1 tablespoon tamari (soy sauce)
½ teaspoon chopped fresh
rosemary or ⅛ teaspoon dried
rosemary
½ teaspoon chopped fresh sage or
¼ teaspoon dried sage
1 teaspoon caraway seeds
Sea salt to taste

1. Preheat the oven to 350 degrees.

2. Mix all ingredients together in a large bowl until well blended. Turn into an oiled 9-by-5-by-3-inch loaf pan and bake 40 minutes. Serve like a meat loaf. The nut loaf, when cold, can be spread on crackers with cream cheese.

Yield: Six servings.

SUNFLOWER SEED LOAF

1½ cups sunflower seed kernels,
  ground in an electric blender
  or Moulinex grinder
¾ cup sesame seeds, ground in
  an electric blender or Moulinex
  grinder
½ cup chopped walnuts or pecans
1 cup cooked dried lentils
½ cup grated raw beets or carrots
3 tablespoons chopped onion
2 eggs, lightly beaten
1 tablespoon apple cider vinegar
2 teaspoons lemon juice
½ cup diced celery
½ cup chopped parsley
Sea salt to taste
Chopped fresh sage or crumbled
  dry sage to taste

1. Preheat the oven to 325 degrees.
2. In a large bowl, combine all the
ingredients. Mix well. Turn into an oiled
casserole or baking dish and bake 40
minutes.

Yield: Six servings.

EGGS GRINNELL

1 quart lamb's quarters, spinach or
  other spring green, well washed
  and drained
1 cup chicken broth (see page 52)
1 cup grated Cheddar cheese
4 eggs
Sea salt and freshly ground black
  pepper to taste
2 tablespoons milk

1. Preheat the oven to 350 degrees.
2. Place the greens and broth in a large
kettle, cover and cook until tender. Drain
well and chop. Cooking liquid can be used
in soup, stew or gravy.
3. Press the cheese on bottom and sides
of a buttered eight-inch pie plate. Break
eggs over cheese, positioning one in each
quadrant. Season with salt and pepper.
Dribble milk over eggs. Arrange chopped
greens in collars around eggs. Bake until
eggs are set, about 10 minutes.

Yield: Four servings.

EGG FOO YONG

2 tablespoons oil
1 cup diced celery
½ cup chopped onion
½ cup sliced mushrooms
½ cup sliced water chestnuts
2 cups bean sprouts
  (see page 195)
5 eggs, lightly beaten
Sea salt to taste
Soy sauce to taste
4 cups cooked brown rice (see
  page 217)

1. Heat the oil in a skillet and sauté the celery and onion in it until crisp-tender. Add mushrooms, water chestnuts and bean sprouts and cook two minutes longer.

2. Stir in the eggs, salt and soy sauce. Drop by serving spoonfuls onto hot, well-oiled skillet and brown lightly on both sides. Serve with brown rice.

Yield: Four servings.

RED AND SWEET CURRY

¼ cup oil
2 large sweet onions, finely
  chopped
2 cups tomato puree
2 tablespoons brown sugar
1 teaspoon curry powder
2 tablespoons water
3 tart apples, cored and finely
  diced
1 cup fresh peas
½ cup shredded or diced
  fresh coconut
4 cups cooked brown rice
  (see page 217)

1. Heat the oil in a heavy skillet and sauté the onions in it until tender. Add puree and sugar and bring to a boil. Mix curry powder with water and stir into mixture. Cook two minutes.

2. Add apples, peas and coconut and heat through, about five minutes. Serve over brown rice.

Yield: Four servings.

7
VEGETABLES

National nutrition surveys conducted in recent years have shown that the average American diet is lacking in fresh fruits and vegetables.
This chapter aims to show that fresh vegetables that are not overcooked—served alone or in combinations—can add variety, flavor, texture, color and essential nutrients to the diet.
Bought-in-season fresh vegetables are usually cheaper than their frozen, boil-in-the-bag and canned counterparts and infinitely preferable at all seasons. Undercooking, rather than overcooking, and utilization of all cooking liquids in soups, stews, beverages or gravies are probably the two most important rules to bear in mind for successful vegetable cookery.
The recipes in this chapter rely on such natural supplements as seeds, nuts and herbs to enhance flavor and frequently food value too. And dried peas and beans, for which various recipes are included, are splendid sources of essential nutrients, especially protein. Combining a whole grain, such as brown rice, with beans or dulse provides nutritional value beyond the value of either eaten alone.
Many of the recipes in this chapter, and in those on salads and vegetarian main dishes, have been contributed by people who garden or farm organically.
Some urban dwellers can buy produce that is labeled "organically grown" if they are willing to pay a premium price. All of the recipes listed here will give best results with the freshest produce available.

JERUSALEM ARTICHOKES

1½ pounds Jerusalem
  artichokes, peeled
Boiling salted water
3 tablespoons butter
Sea salt to taste
⅛ teaspoon nutmeg

1. Put the artichokes and boiling salted water to cover in a saucepan, cover and boil until tender, about 20 minutes.

2. Drain artichokes and mash together with butter, salt and nutmeg.

Yield: Four servings.

Note: Cooked Jerusalem artichokes can also be served in a cheese sauce. Raw chopped peeled Jerusalem artichokes can be used in salads or as dippers when cut into sticks, and are delicious pickled.

ASPARAGUS CASSEROLE

1 tablespoon butter
1 tablespoon unbleached
  white flour
1 cup milk
4 hard-cooked eggs, sliced
1½ cups cooked asparagus cut
  slantwise into one-inch pieces
Sea salt and freshly ground
  black pepper to taste
  (optional)
½ cup buttered bread crumbs

1. Preheat the oven to 350 degrees.

2. Melt the butter, blend in the flour and gradually stir in the milk. Bring to a boil, stirring until mixture thickens.

3. Fold in the eggs, asparagus, salt and pepper. Pour into a buttered baking dish, sprinkle with the crumbs and bake 15 minutes.

Yield: Four side servings or two main dish servings.

GREEN BEANS
WITH SUNFLOWER SEED KERNELS

¼ cup butter
½ teaspoon marjoram
½ teaspoon basil
½ teaspoon chervil
 1 teaspoon chopped parsley
 1 teaspoon chopped chives
⅛ teaspoon savory
⅛ teaspoon thyme
 1 pound green beans
 1 small onion, chopped
 1 clove garlic, finely chopped
Boiling salted water
¼ cup sunflower seed kernels
Sea salt and freshly ground
   black pepper to taste

1. Mix butter with marjoram, basil, chervil, parsley, chives, savory and thyme.

2. Wash beans and remove ends. In a large skillet, place onion and garlic in boiling salted water (the water should only just cover the bottom of the pan). Add beans, cover and cook until crisp-tender.

3. Pour off excess liquid. Add herb butter and sunflower seed kernels and swirl around to melt butter. Add salt and pepper and toss over medium heat one minute.

Yield: Four to six servings.

SPANISH GREEN BEANS

 2 tablespoons butter
 1 tablespoon whole wheat flour
1½ cups tomato juice
   (see page 27)
 1 quart whole cooked green
   beans, drained
 1 cup grated Swiss or Cheddar
   cheese
 1 onion, finely chopped
 1 green pepper, seeded and
   finely chopped
Sea salt to taste
 1 cup buttered whole wheat
   bread crumbs

1. Preheat the oven to 275 degrees.

2. Melt the butter and stir in the flour. Gradually blend in the tomato juice. Bring to a boil, stirring, and cook until thickened.

3. Combine the beans, cheese, onion, green pepper and salt and mix well. Pour into an oiled baking dish. Pour tomato mixture over all.

4. Sprinkle with crumbs and bake 45 minutes.

Yield: Eight servings.

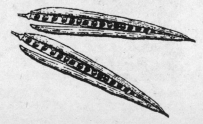

PICKLED BEETS

2 bunches young beets, tops
  removed, scrubbed
Water
2 slices onion
2 tablespoons mustard seeds
1 bay leaf
2 whole cloves
1 teaspoon sea salt
1 teaspoon raw sugar
¾ cup cider vinegar

1. Peel the beets and place peelings in a saucepan with water to cover. Bring to a boil and simmer 10 minutes. Strain and set liquid aside.

2. Preheat the oven to 250 degrees.

3. Place a slice of onion in each of two quart jars. Fill jars with raw whole small beets or sliced larger ones. Add one tablespoon mustard seeds to each jar.

4. To reserved liquid add bay leaf, cloves, salt, sugar and vinegar. Bring to a boil and immediately pour over the beets.

5. Set covers in place loosely and set jars on oven shelf. Cook one hour. Secure covers tightly. Cool and store several days or weeks before using.

Yield: Two quarts.

SWEET AND SOUR CABBAGE

4 cups shredded red or green
  cabbage
3 onions, grated
Juice of 2 lemons
4 tart apples, cored and diced
¼ cup apple cider
3 tablespoons honey
3 tablespoons oil
1 tablespoon caraway seeds
½ cup raisins
⅛ teaspoon ground allspice

Place all the ingredients in a kettle or saucepan, bring to a boil and simmer gently for 10 minutes, stirring occasionally.

Yield: Six servings.

CELERY AND CABBAGE

3 tablespoons butter
3 tablespoons water
1½ cups diagonally sliced celery
1 small head cabbage, shredded
1 tablespoon cider vinegar
Sea salt and freshly ground
  black pepper to taste (optional)
1 tablespoon brown sugar
1 cup yogurt (see page 311)
1 tablespoon caraway seeds

1. Place butter, water, celery and cabbage in a saucepan. Heat to boiling, cover and cook 10 minutes, stirring at least three times.

2. Add vinegar, salt, pepper and sugar. Cover and cook until cabbage is barely tender, about five minutes. Stir in the yogurt and caraway seeds. Reheat but do not boil.

Yield: Six servings.

RICE-STUFFED CABBAGE ROLLS

¼ cup oil
1 medium-size onion, finely
  chopped
2 tablespoons chopped green
  pepper
Sea salt to taste
4 cups cooked brown rice
  (see page 217)
1 medium-size head cabbage,
  core removed and cabbage
  steamed whole until leaves are
  limp, about 10 minutes
1½ cups homemade tomato sauce
  (see page 161)

1. Preheat the oven to 350 degrees.

2. Heat the oil in a skillet and sauté the onion in it until tender. Add green pepper, salt and rice.

3. Separate cabbage leaves carefully and spoon about one-quarter cup to one-third cup filling onto each leaf. Put two smaller leaves together to make all rolls uniform. Roll cabbage leaves around rice filling, tucking in sides. Place in an oiled baking dish. Pour tomato sauce over all and bake 45 minutes.

Yield: Six to eight servings.

TOASTED CARROTS

8 large carrots, scrubbed and
  quartered lengthwise
1 tablespoon boiling water,
  approximately
⅛ teaspoon sea salt
1 teaspoon brown sugar
1 tablespoon butter
1 cup wheat germ

1. Place the carrots in a saucepan and add
the water. Cover tightly and simmer gently
until tender, about 15 minutes. Add more
water if necessary to prevent scorching.

2. Preheat the oven to 350 degrees.

3. Add salt and sugar and shake to coat
carrots.

4. Roll the carrot sticks in wheat germ.
Place on a buttered baking sheet and bake
15 minutes or until toasted.

Yield: Eight servings.

CARROT CASSEROLE

6 to 8 large carrots, scrubbed
  and cut into ¼-inch slices
¼ cup boiling salted water
¼ cup brown sugar
2 tablespoons lemon juice, or to
  taste
½ teaspoon grated lemon rind
½ cup honey
½ teaspoon cinnamon
⅛ teaspoon ground cloves
¼ cup raisins
2 tablespoons butter

1. Place carrots and water in a saucepan.
Cover tightly and simmer gently until
almost tender, about 10 minutes.

2. Preheat the oven to 300 degrees.

3. Drain the carrots, reserving cooking
liquid, and arrange in a buttered baking
dish.

4. Combine reserved liquid with remaining
ingredients except butter. Pour over
carrots. Dot with the butter and bake
30 minutes, basting occasionally. Serve hot.

Yield: Six servings.

BASIL CARROTS

2 tablespoons butter
6 medium-size carrots, thinly
  sliced diagonally
¼ teaspoon sea salt
1 tablespoon chopped fresh basil
  or ½ teaspoon dried basil

Melt the butter in a heavy skillet. Add
remaining ingredients, cover and simmer
gently 10 to 12 minutes or until carrots are
crisp-tender. No water is needed.

Yield: Six servings.

FRUITED CARROTS

3 tablespoons butter
1 cup fresh orange juice
  (2 oranges)
¼ cup brown sugar
8 carrots, scrubbed and scraped,
  left whole
2 oranges, peeled and sliced
⅛ teaspoon cinnamon
⅛ teaspoon nutmeg

1. Melt the butter in a skillet. Stir in the orange juice and sugar. Cook two minutes, stirring constantly, over low heat.

2. Add the carrots. Arrange the orange slices over the carrots. Sprinkle with the cinnamon and nutmeg. Cook, stirring, over fairly high heat until juice has almost evaporated. Carrots will be crisp-tender.

Yield: Six servings.

MINTED CAULIFLOWER

1 medium-size head cauliflower,
  broken into flowerets and
  steamed until crisp-tender
½ cup chopped fresh mint leaves
1 clove garlic, finely chopped
½ cup olive oil
⅓ cup wine vinegar
Sea salt to taste
Freshly ground black pepper
  to taste

1. Place hot cooked cauliflower pieces on a platter or in a serving bowl. Sprinkle with the mint and garlic and toss with the oil.

2. Refrigerate one hour. Toss with the vinegar, salt and pepper. Drain and use as an appetizer or as a vegetable or salad with lamb.

Yield: Six servings.

Note: The cauliflower can be combined with other cooked vegetables, or hard-cooked egg slices can be added to make it a luncheon main course.

CAULIFLOWER, ONIONS AND SESAME SEEDS

2 large Spanish onions, thinly
  sliced
¼ cup oil
1½ tablespoons raw sugar
1 medium-size head cauliflower,
  broken into flowerets
Sea salt to taste
½ cup tomato juice
  (see page 27)
2 tablespoons toasted sesame
  seeds

1. Sauté the onions in the oil in a skillet until tender and lightly browned. Add the sugar and cook two minutes longer.

2. Add cauliflower, salt and tomato juice. Cover and cook over medium heat until cauliflower is crisp-tender.

3. Sprinkle with seeds just before serving.

Yield: Six servings.

CAULIFLOWER CURRY

2 tablespoons oil
¼ teaspoon mustard seeds
1 clove garlic, finely chopped
2 onions, finely chopped
1 tomato, skinned and diced
1 cup yogurt (see page 311)
¾ cup water
¾ teaspoon grated fresh ginger
½ teaspoon ground cumin
¼ teaspoon turmeric
½ teaspoon ground coriander
1 head cauliflower, broken into
  flowerets and steamed for eight
  minutes or until crisp-tender

1. Heat the oil in a skillet or casserole. Add the mustard seeds and when they pop add the garlic and onions and cook until wilted.

2. Add remaining ingredients except the cauliflower and heat to just below the boiling point. Add cauliflower and cook over very low heat 20 minutes.

Yield: Six servings.

CHICK-PEAS

2 cups dried chick-peas
Cold water
4 vegetable broth cubes
  or powder
¼ cup cider vinegar
¼ cup soy oil
2 cloves garlic, very finely minced
Sea salt to taste
Freshly ground black pepper
  to taste

1. Pick over and wash the chick-peas and place in a bowl. Pour in enough water to cover the peas. Let stand overnight.

2. Next day, drain the peas and place in a kettle with five cups of water. Bring to a boil, cover and simmer two hours or until tender.

3. Add remaining ingredients and simmer until tender, about 30 minutes.

Yield: Six servings.

CHICK-PEA SAUCE

1 cup dried chick-peas
Cold water
¼ cup lemon juice
Sea salt to taste

1. Pick over and wash the chick-peas and place in a bowl. Pour in water to cover. Let soak overnight.

2. Add lemon juice and blend in an electric blender until smooth, adding more water if necessary. Season with salt. Serve cold over salads or warm over vegetables.

Yield: About two and one-half cups sauce.

CHICK-PEA CASSEROLE

2 tablespoons oil

2 medium-size onions, finely chopped

4 cups cooked dried (see page 137) or drained canned chick-peas

2 large tomatoes, skinned and chopped

1 6-ounce can tomato paste

1 cup water

1 teaspoon ground coriander

1 teaspoon ground cumin seed

¼ teaspoon turmeric

2 tablespoons chopped parsley

1. Heat the oil in a saucepan and sauté the onions in it until wilted. Add chick-peas, tomatoes, tomato paste, water, coriander, cumin and turmeric and simmer 30 minutes.

2. Sprinkle with parsley.

Yield: Six servings.

BOLLOS DE MAZORCA (STUFFED CORNHUSKS)

6 ears of corn with husks

1 egg, lightly beaten

3 tablespoons raw sugar or honey

1 teaspoon sea salt

3 ounces soft cream cheese

¼ cup melted butter

1 teaspoon baking powder

¼ cup yellow corn meal

2 cups water

1. Remove the husks from the corn and set aside. Scrape the kernels from the cobs and reserve cobs.

2. Place kernels in electric blender and blend very briefly at low speed. Do not liquefy. Scrape from the blender into a bowl and add egg, sugar, salt, cream cheese, butter, baking powder and corn meal. Mixture should be on the heavy side.

3. Divide the mixture into 12 and place each portion on a double husk, roll to enclose and then wrap in aluminum foil.

4. Place a layer of corncobs in the bottom of a kettle and add water. Place packages on top of cobs, cover and steam 45 minutes or until done.

Yield: Six servings.

RATATOUILLE

1 medium-size eggplant, peeled
  and sliced
Sea salt
⅓ cup olive oil
3 cloves garlic, finely chopped
1 medium-size onion, finely
  chopped
3 zucchini, washed and sliced
2 tablespoons flour
2 green peppers, seeded and diced
4 tomatoes, skinned and chopped
⅓ cup sliced pitted black olives

1. Sprinkle the eggplant slices with salt and set aside.

2. Heat the oil in a skillet and sauté the garlic and onion in it until tender but not browned. Toss the zucchini with one tablespoon of the flour and add to the skillet.

3. Rinse the eggplant slices, pat dry and dust with remaining flour. Add to the skillet. Cook over medium heat five minutes. Cover and cook 45 minutes. Add the green pepper and tomatoes and cook, uncovered, until all vegetables are tender and excess liquid has evaporated. Serve warm or cold, garnished with olives.

Yield: Six servings.

EGGPLANT PARMIGIANA

1 large eggplant
6 large tomatoes, skinned
1 pound whole-milk mozzarella,
  thinly sliced

1. Preheat the oven to 400 degrees.

2. Peel the eggplant and slice crosswise into paper-thin slices. Blend the tomatoes in an electric blender until smooth.

3. Butter a large casserole or baking dish and make alternate layers of eggplant, mozzarella and tomato puree, making the top layer cheese. Bake 45 minutes.

Yield: Six servings.

Note: One-half pound of whole-milk ricotta can be added in layers and zucchini cut into lengthwise strips can be substituted for the eggplant.

EGGPLANT AND SQUASH

1 medium-size zucchini or summer squash, washed and thickly sliced
1 medium-size eggplant, peeled and cubed
Boiling salted water
4 tomatoes, skinned and diced
3 tablespoons oil
1 small onion, finely chopped
1 clove garlic, finely chopped
1 bay leaf
1 tablespoon chopped parsley
Sea salt and pepper to taste
¼ cup freshly grated Parmesan cheese

1. Place the squash and eggplant in a saucepan. Cover with boiling salted water and simmer three minutes. Drain vegetables. (The liquid can be used in soups, stews or gravies.)

2. Combine squash and eggplant with tomatoes.

3. Heat the oil in a skillet and sauté the onion in it until tender. Add the garlic, bay leaf, parsley, salt, pepper and squash mixture. Simmer gently, uncovered, until vegetables are crisp-tender.

4. Pour mixture into a shallow heatproof serving dish, sprinkle with the cheese and brown under a preheated broiler.

Yield: Four servings.

EGGPLANT CROQUETTES

2 large eggplants, peeled and cubed
Boiling salted water
½ cup unbleached white flour
2 eggs, lightly beaten
⅛ teaspoon nutmeg
2 slices whole wheat bread, soaked in water and squeezed dry
2 tablespoons grated Swiss or Parmesan cheese
Sea salt to taste
2 tablespoons chopped parsley
Unbleached white flour
1 cup soy oil, approximately

1. Put the cubed eggplant in a saucepan and cover with boiling salted water. Cover and simmer 15 minutes or until eggplant is tender. Use liquid in soups or stews.

2. Drain the eggplant and chop very finely. Mix with the eggs, nutmeg, bread, cheese, salt and parsley until well blended.

3. Shape the mixture into cutlets, cylinders or patties. Dredge in flour. Heat the oil in a large heavy skillet and fry the croquettes until they are browned on all sides.

Yield: Six to eight servings.

EGGPLANT CASSEROLE I

3 tablespoons butter
1 onion, finely chopped
3 ribs celery, chopped
½ cup diced green pepper
¼ cup canned tomatoes or 1 small tomato, skinned, seeded and diced
½ cup water
½ teaspoon basil
1 medium-size or ½ large eggplant, peeled and cubed
2 tablespoons chopped parsley
Sea salt and pepper to taste
½ teaspoon oregano
2 slices whole wheat bread
Water
2 eggs, lightly beaten

1. Preheat the oven to 325 degrees.

2. Melt the butter in a heavy skillet and sauté the onion and celery in it until tender. Add the green pepper, tomatoes, water, basil, cubed eggplant, parsley, salt, pepper and oregano. Bring to a boil and simmer until tender.

3. Meanwhile, soak the bread in water. Squeeze out excess water and mix bread crumbs with the eggs and add to the eggplant mixture. Place in a buttered casserole or baking dish and bake, covered, 30 minutes. Uncover and bake 15 minutes longer.

Yield: Four to six servings.

EGGPLANT CASSEROLE II

1 tablespoon oil
¼ cup mustard seeds
1 teaspoon dried lentils
1 large onion, chopped
1 medium-size eggplant, peeled and finely chopped
1 teaspoon grated fresh ginger
1 tablespoon chopped parsley
Sea salt to taste
1 large tomato, skinned and chopped
1 cup yogurt (see page 311)

1. Heat the oil in a skillet and add the seeds. Heat gently until the seeds make popping sounds. Add the lentils.

2. Add the onion and sauté until wilted. Add the eggplant, ginger, parsley and salt. Cook two minutes. Add tomato, cover and cook 30 minutes. Let cool to room temperature and stir in the yogurt.

3. The dish may be served at room temperature or slightly warmed.

Yield: Six servings.

EGGPLANT HUSH PUPPIES

2 large eggplants, peeled and
cubed
Sea salt
½ cup yellow corn meal
1 cup whole wheat flour
1½ teaspoons baking powder
2 tablespoons grated or finely
chopped onion
Oil for deep-frying

1. Put the eggplant cubes into a colander and steam, covered, over boiling water until tender, about 25 minutes.

2. Sprinkle with salt and set aside.

3. Meanwhile, combine the corn meal, flour, baking powder and one and one-half teaspoons salt in a bowl. Push the eggplant through the colander into the bowl in small amounts, mixing in enough eggplant to make a medium-stiff dough.

4. Stir in the onion. Set the mixture aside for 15 to 30 minutes.

5. Drop the mixture by teaspoonfuls into deep oil heated to 365 degrees and fry until golden. Drain on paper towels.

Yield: Six servings.

LETCHO (HUNGARIAN VEGETABLE STEW)

¼ cup oil
3 large onions, chopped
4 green peppers, seeded and cut
into strips
3 tomatoes, washed and diced
1 eggplant, peeled and diced
Sea salt or vegetable salt to taste

1. Heat the oil in a heavy skillet or casserole and sauté the onions in it until tender and golden.

2. Add the green peppers, tomatoes and eggplant. Bring to a boil, season with salt, cover and simmer until all vegetables are tender, about 20 minutes.

Yield: Six servings.

BAKED EGGPLANT

2 large onions, sliced
1 medium-size eggplant, sliced
   into ¼-inch slices
6 tomatoes, sliced
1 cup olive oil, approximately
Sea salt to taste
1 teaspoon sweet paprika
⅛ teaspoon cayenne pepper
¼ teaspoon marjoram
¼ cup grated Parmesan cheese
¼ cup heavy cream

1. Preheat the oven to 350 degrees.

2. In a well-oiled casserole or baking dish, place alternate layers of onions, eggplant and tomatoes until all are used.

3. Combine the oil, salt, paprika, cayenne and marjoram and pour over the vegetables. The oil should come about three-quarters way up the vegetables.

4. Cover and bake 40 minutes. Increase oven heat to 400 degrees. Combine the cheese and cream and pour over the top of the vegetables. Bake, uncovered, until top is browned, about 10 minutes.

Yield: Six to eight servings.

EGGPLANT PROVENCALE

2 tablespoons olive oil
   or safflower oil
1 medium-size eggplant, washed
   (unpeeled) and diced
2 cloves garlic, finely chopped
1 green pepper, seeded and
   chopped
3 tomatoes, washed and diced
1 teaspoon sea salt
1 teaspoon basil
1 tablespoon chopped parsley
2 tablespoons lecithin granules
   (optional)

1. Heat the oil in a heavy skillet or casserole and sauté the eggplant and garlic in it until lightly browned and almost tender.

2. Add the green pepper, tomatoes, salt, basil and parsley, bring to a boil and simmer, uncovered, five minutes. Sprinkle with lecithin if desired.

Yield: Four servings.

SPRING GREENS PUREE

1 pound young lamb's quarters,
  violet leaves, mustard greens,
  dandelion greens or other wild
  or cultivated spring greens,
  combined or used separately
1 tablespoon butter
1 tablespoon oil
1 clove garlic, crushed
Water if necessary
Sea salt to taste
Freshly ground pepper to taste
  (optional)
1 tablespoon heavy cream
1 hard-cooked egg, chopped

1. Wash and drain the greens but do not dry thoroughly. Place in a large saucepan with the butter, oil and garlic. Cook two minutes, stirring constantly.

2. Remove the garlic and cook greens five to seven minutes longer or until tender. Do not overcook. Add a tablespoon or two of water if necessary to prevent scorching.

3. Transfer the greens to an electric blender. Add salt, pepper and cream and blend until smooth. Reheat.

4. Serve garnished with the egg.

Yield: Six servings.

BEET GREENS

2 quarts beet greens, well washed
  and shaken dry
Sea salt to taste
2 tablespoons oil
1 small onion, finely chopped
1 tablespoon flour

1. Place the greens, with only water clinging to the leaves, in a large kettle, add salt, cover tightly and cook until wilted.

2. Meanwhile, heat the oil and sauté the onion in it until golden. Sprinkle with the flour and stir to mix.

3. Add onion-flour mixture to cooked greens and heat, stirring, until mixture thickens slightly.

Yield: About four servings.

Note: The contributor grows all her vegetables organically.

DANDELION GREENS I

6 to 8 quarts tender young
  dandelion leaves, well washed
  (a dishpan full)
Cold water
4 slices thick lean bacon
1 egg, lightly beaten
¼ cup brown sugar
¼ cup cider vinegar
2 hard-cooked eggs, chopped

1. Put the dandelion greens in a large
kettle and cover with water. Bring to a boil,
turn off the heat and let stand 10 minutes.
Drain well.

2. In a skillet, fry the bacon until crisp.
Remove bacon, crumble and reserve bacon
bits.

3. Combine the egg, sugar, vinegar and
one-quarter cup water and pour into the
bacon drippings in the skillet. Heat slowly,
while stirring, until slightly thickened.

4. Remove from the heat, add greens and
stir to coat evenly.

5. Serve garnished with reserved bacon
bits and chopped eggs.

Yield: Six servings.

DANDELION GREENS II

8 quarts long tender dandelion
  leaf rosettes, cut off at base of
  leaves, separated and well
  washed (about ½ bucketful)
1 quart boiling salted water
6 thick slices bacon, diced
½ cup sour cream or yogurt
  (see page 311)
1 cup water
1 egg
2 to 3 tablespoons vinegar
Sea salt and freshly ground black
  pepper (optional)
1 small onion, finely chopped
Slices of buttered homemade
  whole grain bread, several days
  old

1. Place the dandelion greens in a large
kettle with the boiling water and simmer,
covered, until tender, about eight minutes.

2. Drain and squeeze out the excess water.

3. In a skillet, brown the bacon pieces.

4. Pour off and discard all but two to three
tablespoons of the bacon drippings. Leave
the bacon in the skillet.

5. In a bowl, combine the sour cream or
yogurt, the water, egg, vinegar, salt and
pepper. Pour into the skillet and heat
gradually with the bacon drippings and
bacon until hot, but do not allow to boil.

6. Add the greens and the onion and mix
thoroughly. Serve over the bread slices.

Yield: Six servings.

COMFREY GREENS

2 quarts tender young comfrey
  leaves, washed well and coarsely
  shredded
⅓ cup boiling salted water
Sea salt to taste
2 tablespoons butter

1. Place the greens and water in a saucepan, bring to a boil, cover and cook until tender, about 10 minutes.

2. Drain very well. Add salt and butter and toss well.

Yield: Four servings.

RADISH AND SPINACH GREENS

Tops from about 18 radishes
  (2 bunches), trimmed, washed
  and shredded
1 cup shredded spinach leaves
1 tablespoon oil
½ cup sour cream or yogurt
  (see page 311)
Sea salt to taste

1. Combine the radish and spinach greens.

2. Heat the oil in a heavy skillet, add greens and cook quickly, tossing with a pancake turner, until wilted. Reduce heat and simmer, covered, five minutes. Arrange on a hot platter.

3. Add sour cream or yogurt to skillet. Do not heat, but stir around in hot pan until warm. Add salt and pour over greens.

Yield: Three to four servings.

SPINACH-NUT RING

2 tablespoons oil
1 small onion, finely chopped
½ cup diced celery
½ green pepper, seeded and diced
2 cups cooked well-drained
  spinach, chopped
1 cup finely chopped nuts
1 teaspoon lemon juice
2 eggs, lightly beaten
¼ teaspoon nutmeg
1 cup soft bread crumbs
Sea salt to taste
3 tablespoons wheat germ

1. Preheat the oven to 375 degrees.

2. Heat the oil and sauté the onion in it until tender. Add celery and green pepper and cook two minutes longer. Mix in the spinach.

3. Stir in the remaining ingredients except the wheat germ.

4. Oil a one-quart ring mold and sprinkle with the wheat germ to give an even coating.

5. Pour in the spinach mixture. Set mold in a pan of hot water and bake 40 minutes or until set.

Yield: Six servings.

BROWN RICE AND SPINACH CASSEROLE

2 quarts washed spinach leaves
2 tablespoons butter
2 tablespoons unbleached white flour
2 cups milk
½ cup vinegar
½ cup freshly grated Parmesan or Swiss cheese
Sea salt to taste
¼ teaspoon nutmeg
6 cups cooked brown rice (see page 217)
½ cup buttered whole wheat bread crumbs

1. Preheat the oven to 325 degrees.

2. Place the spinach in a large kettle with just the water clinging to the leaves, cover and cook until wilted. Drain well, squeeze out excess water and chop.

3. Melt the butter, stir in the flour and gradually blend in the milk. Stir in the vinegar. Mixture will curdle but as it heats, and is stirred, it will smooth out. Heat, stirring, until mixture thickens. Stir in the cheese, salt and nutmeg.

4. Mix the spinach and rice into the sauce and pour into a buttered casserole. Sprinkle top with bread crumbs and heat in the oven for 20 minutes.

Yield: Eight to ten servings.

Note: The dish may be prepared early in the day, stored in the refrigerator and heated for 45 to 60 minutes before serving.

GREEN VEGETABLE SAUCE

2½ cups water
⅓ cup chopped scallions
1 cup shredded romaine or escarole
1 cup shredded spinach
¼ cup shredded beet tops
½ pitted avocado, peeled
2 tablespoons chopped parsley
2 teaspoons chopped fresh mint leaves
2 teaspoons chopped fresh basil (optional)
Kelp to taste
Lime juice to taste

1. Place the water and scallions in an electric blender and blend until smooth. While blending at low speed, gradually add the lettuce, spinach, beet tops, avocado, parsley, mint and basil.

2. Season mixture with kelp and lime juice.

Yield: About five cups.

Note: The mixture can be eaten as a cold soup or heated and served as a soup or as a sauce over whole wheat noodles or brown rice.

GREEN SAUCE AND NOODLES

1 large bunch Italian parsley
1 large bunch fresh basil
3 cloves garlic
½ cup olive oil
½ cup melted butter
Sea salt and pepper to taste
1 pound homemade noodles or spaghetti, cooked al dente and drained (see page 308)
Freshly grated Parmesan cheese

1. Place parsley and basil leaves in an electric blender. Add garlic, oil, butter, salt and pepper and blend until smooth. Pour into a saucepan.

2. Warm, but do not allow to boil.

3. Pour over noodles or spaghetti. Sprinkle with cheese.

Yield: Six servings.

LEEKS

2 large leeks, washed well and sliced
½ cup boiling water
1 tablespoon raisins
Sea salt to taste
1 tablespoon flour
2 teaspoons soft butter

1. Place the leeks, water and raisins in a saucepan. Cover and simmer until tender, about 15 minutes.

2. Season with salt. Mix flour and butter together and gradually whisk into the leek mixture. Heat, stirring, until mixture thickens.

Yield: Four servings.

LEEK AND VEGETABLE STEW

6 large leeks, washed well and sliced into ½-inch slices, including some of the green part
2 large potatoes, peeled and thinly sliced
4 carrots, scrubbed and thinly sliced
¼ head cabbage, shredded
1½ cups water
¼ teaspoon kelp
Vegetable salt or sea salt to taste
3 slices bacon, or 2-inch piece slab bacon, scored

1. In a large heavy casserole, place the leeks, then potatoes, next the carrots and last a layer of the cabbage. Pour the water over all.

2. Season with the kelp and salt. Add the bacon. Cover tightly and cook very slowly until all vegetables are tender, about 40 minutes.

Yield: Eight servings.

LENTILS

2 cups (1 pound) dried lentils
1½ quarts water
3 or 4 beef neck bones or ham bone
1 small onion, sliced
1 carrot, quartered
2 ribs celery with leaves, quartered
1 clove garlic, crushed
Sea salt to taste

1. Pick over the lentils; wash and drain. Place in a kettle with the water, bones, onion, carrot, celery, garlic and salt.

2. Bring to a boil, cover and simmer until lentils are tender, about one and one-half hours. Discard bones.

Yield: Two quarts lentils.

SWEET AND SOUR LENTILS

2 cups beef broth (see page 53)
1 bay leaf, crushed
Sea salt to taste
1 cup picked-over and washed dried lentils, yellow or green split peas or black-eyed peas
1 clove garlic, finely chopped
⅛ teaspoon ground cloves
⅛ teaspoon nutmeg
3 tablespoons oil
3 tablespoons apple cider
3 tablespoons cider vinegar
3 tablespoons brown sugar, molasses or honey

1. Bring the broth to a boil in a kettle and add the bay leaf, salt and lentils or peas. Cover and simmer gently 30 minutes.

2. Add remaining ingredients. Stir to mix well. Cook five minutes or until lentils or peas are tender.

Yield: Four servings.

LENTILS, SPANISH STYLE

1 cup cooked lentils
1 cup homemade tomato sauce (see page 161)
½ green pepper, diced

Combine all ingredients and heat to a boil.

Yield: Four servings.

CURRIED LENTILS

¼ cup oil
1 onion, quartered and thinly sliced
1 clove garlic, chopped
2 tablespoons finely chopped fresh ginger
2 bay leaves, chopped
8 whole cloves
2 tomatoes, quartered
2 to 4 tablespoons Madras-style curry powder
1 teaspoon turmeric
6¼ cups water, approximately
1½ pounds dried lentils, preferably those with a reddish cast, cleaned and drained
2½ teaspoons sea salt

1. Heat the oil in a heavy three- to four-quart saucepan until hot. Add the onion and heat until lightly browned.

2. Add the garlic, ginger, bay leaves and cloves and cook one minute. Add tomatoes and continue cooking.

3. Mix the curry powder and turmeric with one-quarter cup of the water. Add curry powder mixture to the pan and cook, stirring, three minutes, adding a tablespoon of water if necessary to prevent sticking.

4. Add the lentils and salt and cook two minutes. Add remaining water. Bring to a boil, cover and simmer one hour or until lentils are tender and the liquid is absorbed. More water may be added during the cooking if necessary.

Yield: Eight servings.

OKRA STEW

2 tablespoons oil
1 large onion, sliced
1 clove garlic, chopped
1 can (6 ounces) tomato paste
4 medium-size tomatoes, skinned and diced
¼ cup lemon juice
1 teaspoon raw sugar or brown sugar
Sea salt and freshly ground black pepper to taste (optional)
1 pound small okra
Bulghur pilaf (see page 213)

1. Heat the oil in a saucepan and sauté the onion and garlic in it until tender but not browned.

2. Add tomato paste, tomatoes, lemon juice, sugar, salt and pepper. Bring to a boil, cover and simmer 20 minutes.

3. Wash the okra and remove the stem from each by cutting the thin cone-shaped skin off the top. Do not pierce the okra or the juices will run out.

4. Add okra to tomato mixture and simmer, covered, 30 minutes. Serve with pilaf.

Yield: Six servings.

STEWED OKRA

1 pound okra
Lightly salted water
2 tablespoons butter
1 large sweet onion, sliced
⅓ cup chopped nuts
2 large tomatoes, sliced
1 fresh hot chili pepper, finely
    chopped
1 sweet green or red pepper,
    seeded and cut into strips
Water
⅓ cup homemade tomato sauce
    (see page 161)
2 large potatoes, peeled and diced
Sea salt to taste

1. Place the okra in a bowl and cover with lightly salted water. Let stand one hour.

2. Heat the butter in a skillet and sauté the onion in it until tender. Add nuts and cook two minutes longer. Drain okra, reserving soaking liquid. Add okra to skillet.

3. Add tomatoes, chili pepper and sweet pepper.

4. Measure the reserved liquid into a saucepan and make up to three cups with water. Bring to a boil and pour over vegetables in skillet.

5. Stir in the tomato sauce, potatoes and salt. Cover tightly and simmer over low heat until vegetables are tender, about 30 minutes.

Yield: Six servings.

PARSNIP PIE

Crust:
¾ cup rolled oats
¼ cup chestnut flour
¼ cup whole wheat flour
    Sea salt to taste
    Water
Filling:
5 large parsnips, peeled, sliced
    and steamed until tender
1 tablespoon sesame butter
    or tahini (sesame paste)
    Sea salt to taste

1. Preheat the oven to 350 degrees.

2. For the crust, mix together the oats, chestnut flour, whole wheat flour and salt. Stir in enough water to make a moist but not sticky dough.

3. Pat the mixture into an oiled nine-inch pie plate to form a pie shell. Bake 10 minutes.

4. Meanwhile, for the filling, mash the parsnips and stir in sesame butter and salt.

5. Fill crust and bake 30 minutes. Serve with ham or poultry.

Yield: Six servings.

PEAS AND ONIONS

4 cups shelled fresh peas
3 small white onions, thinly sliced
1 sprig parsley
2 stalks fresh basil
¼ cup butter
¼ teaspoon sea salt
6 small cauliflowerets
½ cup water
3 Boston lettuce leaves

1. Place peas, onions, parsley, basil, butter, salt, cauliflowerets and water in a saucepan. Cover with lettuce leaves and tight-fitting pan cover.

2. Bring to a boil and cook over medium heat until peas are tender, about 12 minutes.

Yield: Six servings.

ITALIAN PEPPER CASSEROLE

¼ cup safflower oil
1 large onion, sliced
6 Italian sweet green peppers, seeded and quartered
3 medium-size tomatoes, skinned and sliced
1 teaspoon sea salt

1. Heat the oil in a heavy skillet and sauté the onion in it until tender.

2. Add remaining ingredients, cover and simmer over low heat until ingredients are very soft and a sauce has formed.

Yield: Four servings.

POKEBERRY OR POKE SALET

Pokeberry shoots, 6 to 8 inches long, snapped off rootstalks before leaves form
Boiling salted water
Butter

Place the shoots in a large skillet, cover with water and boil seven minutes. Drain. Serve topped with dots of butter.

POKEWEED AU GRATIN

36 young pokeweed stalks
Boiling water
1 tablespoon butter
2 teaspoons chopped onion
1 tablespoon flour
1½ cups milk, scalded
Sea salt to taste
⅛ teaspoon mace
1 cup grated Cheddar cheese
¼ cup toasted whole wheat bread
crumbs

1. Cut off lower, tough parts of stalks, stripping off all but uppermost leaves. Wash well and place in a saucepan with boiling water to half-cover stalks. Cover and cook until tender, about 15 minutes. Drain well. Arrange stalks in a buttered shallow baking dish.

2. Melt the one tablespoon butter in a small saucepan and sauté the onion in it until tender. Stir in the flour and cook one minute.

3. Gradually blend in the milk; bring to a boil, stirring. Add salt and mace and cook over hot water 15 minutes, stirring often.

4. Preheat the oven to 400 degrees.

5. Remove sauce from the heat and stir in cheese. Pour over the pokeweed. Cover loosely with aluminum foil and heat 15 minutes. Sprinkle with toast crumbs before serving.

Yield: Four servings.

POTATOES WITH YOGURT

2 tablespoons oil
1 pound small red-skinned new
potatoes, boiled until tender
and peeled
¼ teaspoon ground cloves
½ teaspoon cinnamon
½ teaspoon ground cardamom
2 bay leaves, crumbled
¼ cup water
½ teaspoon grated fresh ginger
¾ cup yogurt (see page 311)
Sea salt to taste

1. Heat the oil in a skillet and add the potatoes. Cook quickly until lightly browned. Remove potatoes and drain on paper towels; keep warm.

2. Add the cloves, cinnamon, cardamom, bay leaves and water to skillet and bring to a boil. Stir in the ginger and yogurt.

3. Reheat but do not boil. Add potatoes and salt.

Yield: Six servings.

NEW POTATOES

2 pounds tiny new potatoes,
scrubbed or scraped to
remove skins
Boiling water
2 teaspoons sea salt
2 teaspoons raw sugar
1 clove garlic, halved and crushed
¼ cup butter, melted
2 tablespoons lemon juice
½ teaspoon paprika

1. Place the potatoes in the boiling water in a saucepan so that they are covered. Add the salt, sugar and garlic. Cover and simmer 10 to 15 minutes or until potatoes are barely tender.

2. Drain potatoes and toss with the butter, lemon juice and paprika. Serve hot or cold.

Yield: Six servings.

Note: The contributor says he serves these potatoes cold as a snack instead of peanuts.

TZIMMES DELUXE

2 large yams, peeled and cut
into cubes
2 carrots, sliced
½ cup pitted prunes
1 cup water
1 apple, cored and cubed
Honey to taste

1. Put the yams, carrots, prunes and water in a saucepan. Bring to a boil, cover and simmer 25 minutes or until tender.

2. Add apple and honey and cook 25 minutes longer.

3. Preheat the oven to 300 degrees.

4. Turn the mixture into a heatproof serving dish and bake, uncovered, 15 to 20 minutes.

Yield: Four servings.

MOLASSES YAMS

6 medium-size yams, cooked,
peeled and mashed
¼ cup butter
⅓ cup unsulphured molasses
1 teaspoon sea salt
2 teaspoons grated orange rind

1. Preheat the oven to 400 degrees.

2. Combine all the ingredients and mix well. Turn into an oiled 1½-quart casserole. Bake 20 minutes.

Yield: Six servings.

SWEET POTATO AND APPLE

6 medium-size sweet potatoes
Boiling salted water
½ cup molasses
½ cup butter
4 medium-size red apples, cored and cut into ½-inch slices
¼ cup orange juice
1 tablespoon grated orange rind
½ teaspoon salt

1. Scrub the sweet potatoes, cover with the boiling salted water, cover and simmer 30 minutes or until the potatoes are tender.

2. Meanwhile, heat one-quarter cup of the molasses with one-quarter cup of the butter in a skillet. Add the apple slices and turn to coat with the mixture. Simmer very gently until barely tender, about 10 minutes, turning twice during the cooking.

3. Drain the potatoes, peel and mash or puree in a food mill. Add the remaining butter, remaining molasses, the orange juice, orange rind and salt. Beat until light and fluffy.

4. Mound the mixture on top of the apple rings and serve immediately.

Yield: About ten servings.

CURRIED SOYBEANS

1½ cups dried soybeans
Cold water
2½ tablespoons butter
¾ cup yogurt (see page 311) or sour cream
2 tablespoons curry powder, or to taste
Sea salt if needed

1. Pick over and wash the beans and place in a large bowl. Cover with cold water and let stand overnight.

2. Place beans and soaking liquid in a kettle and cook, covered, until tender, about three and one-half hours, maintaining only enough water so that beans do not scorch.

3. Drain excess liquid (it can be used in soups or stews) from beans. Add butter to beans. Combine the yogurt or sour cream with the curry powder and salt (if needed) and stir into the beans. Reheat but do not boil.

Yield: Six to eight servings.

SOYBEAN PISTOU

4 cloves garlic
1 tablespoon dried basil
4 tablespoons tomato paste
½ cup olive oil
½ cup grated Parmesan cheese
2 cups cooked soybeans with
  a little cooking liquid

1. In an electric blender or a mortar and pestle, mash together the garlic, basil and tomato paste. While blending on low speed or beating with an electric mixer, add the oil drop by drop until mixture begins to thicken. Then add oil more quickly.

2. Beat in the cheese and the few tablespoons of soybean cooking liquid. Pour mixture over the beans and serve warm or cold.

Yield: Four servings.

Note: Cut string beans, sliced zucchini or carrots (cooked until barely tender) may be mixed with the soybeans.

SOYBEANS WITH TOMATO SAUCE

1 cup dried soybeans
2 tablespoons oil
Cold water
1 cup tomato sauce
  (see page 161)
½ teaspoon sea salt
1¼ teaspoons vegetable broth
  powder
1 tablespoon soy sauce

1. Place the soybeans and oil in a large bowl. Cover well with cold water and let soak overnight.

2. Next day, drain the beans and discard liquid. Place beans and remaining ingredients in a pressure cooker. Close cover tightly. Place pressure regulator on vent pipe (set for 15 lbs. if there is a choice of pressures) and cook according to manufacturer's instructions for 45 minutes.

3. If pressure regulator ceases to rock during cooking, the vent pipe may have become clogged; cool cooker rapidly. At the end of the cooking time, allow pan to cool of its own accord. Do not remove pressure regulator until pressure is completely reduced.

Yield: Six servings.

COOKING DRIED SOYBEANS

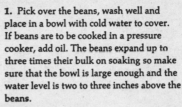

2 cups (1 pound) dried soybeans, green or yellow
Cold water
¼ cup oil if beans are to be cooked in pressure cooker
Sea salt to taste (optional)

1. Pick over the beans, wash well and place in a bowl with cold water to cover. If beans are to be cooked in a pressure cooker, add oil. The beans expand up to three times their bulk on soaking so make sure that the bowl is large enough and the water level is two to three inches above the beans.

METHOD I

2. To cook the beans in a kettle, place in a heavy kettle with soaking liquid and extra water if necessary to almost cover. Add salt if desired, bring to a boil and simmer over low heat three to four hours, or until tender.

METHOD II

3. Alternately, to cook the beans in the oven, preheat the oven to 325 degrees. Place the beans, soaking liquid and enough extra water to barely cover beans in a heavy casserole. Add salt if desired, cover tightly and bake two hours or until beans are barely tender. Remove cover and bake at least 30 minutes longer or until tender.

METHOD III

4. To cook the beans in a pressure cooker, place beans, oil, cooking liquid and salt if desired in the cooker, adding enough water to cover beans. Do not fill pressure cooker more than half full. Close cover tightly. Place pressure regulator on vent pipe (set for 15 lbs. if there is a choice of pressures) and cook according to manufacturer's instructions for 30 minutes. If pressure regulator ceases to rock, the vent pipe may have become clogged; cool cooker rapidly. At the end of the 30 minutes cooking at

15 lbs. pressure, allow pan to cool of its own accord. Do not remove pressure regulator until pressure is completely reduced.

Yield: Eight to ten cups cooked beans.

Note: To make a pulp or puree of soybeans, force the cooked beans through a coarse sieve, food grinder or electric blender. Other seasonings such as brewer's yeast, diced onion, chopped celery and bay leaves may be added during the last hour of cooking in methods I and II.

SOYBEAN CHEESE OR CURD

1½ cups dried yellow soybeans
    Cold water
    Sea salt to taste
  ⅓ cup lemon juice

1. Place the beans in a large bowl and cover with cold water. Let soak at least 20 hours, changing the soaking water four times, at approximately four-hour intervals. Drain.

2. Place beans in a large heavy kettle with one and one-half quarts of fresh water and the salt. Bring to a boil and cook 30 minutes, stirring almost constantly to prevent the mixture from sticking.

3. Remove from the heat and add lemon juice. Mix gently. Let stand a few minutes, then pour through a sieve lined with a double thickness of wet muslin. Drain well. The curd left in the muslin is the cheese. It can be used in salads and in cooked dishes.

Yield: About four cups cheese.

Note: Soybean curd can be made by setting soy milk in a warm place to sour. Strain as above.

SQUASH BLOSSOMS

24 squash blossoms picked in the
    early morning, washed, drained
    and placed in a towel
3 eggs
½ teaspoon sea salt
½ cup unbleached white flour
½ teaspoon baking powder
1 tablespoon chopped parsley
½ clove garlic, finely chopped
1 tablespoon freshly grated
    Parmesan cheese
Oil

1. Allow the blossoms to remain in the towel while preparing the batter so that the excess water drains from them.

2. Beat together the eggs, salt, flour and baking powder. Batter should be a fairly thick coating consistency. Add parsley, garlic and cheese.

3. Heat oil to depth of one-half-inch in a heavy saucepan. Dip blossoms in the batter and fry, one at a time, in the oil until golden. Drain on paper towels.

Yield: Four to six servings.

Note: The contributor takes two or three small comfrey leaves, rolls them together tightly, dips them into the same batter and fries them until golden.

SQUASH PUFF

3 cups mashed cooked acorn
    squash
½ cup molasses
3 tablespoons whole wheat flour
1¼ teaspoons salt
¼ teaspoon nutmeg
¼ teaspoon ginger
3 eggs, separated
¼ cup finely chopped pecans or
    walnuts

1. Preheat the oven to 350 degrees.

2. In a large bowl, blend together the squash, molasses, flour, salt, nutmeg, ginger and egg yolks. Beat the egg whites until stiff but not dry. Fold into the squash mixture.

3. Turn into an oiled 1½-quart baking dish. Sprinkle nuts around outside edge and bake one hour or until golden and crusty.

Yield: Six servings.

YELLOW SQUASH

3 large yellow summer squash, sliced
1 onion, finely grated
1 clove garlic, finely chopped
2 tablespoons oil
½ teaspoon salt
1 tablespoon honey
⅓ cup diced celery
2 tablespoons chopped parsley
½ teaspoon oregano
1 tablespoon whole wheat flour
¼ cup sunflower seed kernels

1. Place the squash, onion, garlic, oil, salt, honey, celery, parsley and oregano in a skillet. Bring to a boil, reduce heat, cover and cook slowly until squash is barely tender, about 15 minutes.

2. Sprinkle the flour over all and cook, stirring, until liquid in skillet thickens. Stir in the sunflower seed kernels.

Yield: Four servings.

FRIED GREEN TOMATOES

8 large firm green tomatoes
Unbleached white flour
¼ cup butter
⅓ cup brown sugar
Sea salt and freshly ground black pepper to taste
1 cup heavy cream

1. Cut off and discard a thin slice from top and bottom of each tomato. Cut each tomato into three thick slices. Dip each slice in flour.

2. Heat the butter in a heavy skillet. Add tomato slices and sprinkle half the sugar over slices. Fry until browned on the bottom. Turn slices, sprinkle with remaining sugar and brown second side.

3. Turn slices and reduce heat. Season with salt and pepper. Add cream and heat until hot but do not allow to boil. Tomato slices should remain firm.

Yield: Six to eight servings.

BASIC TOMATO SAUCE

12 large ripe tomatoes, skinned and chopped
2 green peppers, seeded
2 onions, chopped
2 carrots, chopped
6 ribs celery, diced
2 tablespoons snipped fresh chives
2 tablespoons chopped parsley
2 tablespoons chopped fresh basil
2 cloves garlic, finely chopped

1. Combine all the ingredients in a stainless steel, or porcelainized steel, pan or casserole. Bring to a boil and simmer, uncovered, 45 minutes. Puree (in a blender) if desired.

2. Refrigerate overnight before using or freezing for future use.

Yield: About two quarts.

Note: The contributors grow all the ingredients for this sauce in their organically-run garden.

BAKED TOMATOES

3 cups corn kernels cut from the cobs
3 tomatoes, skinned and diced
4 shallots, finely chopped
2 eggs, separated
Sea salt and freshly ground black pepper to taste (optional)
3 tablespoons buttered whole wheat bread crumbs

1. Preheat the oven to 375 degrees.

2. Combine the corn kernels, tomatoes, shallots, egg yolks, salt and pepper.

3. Beat egg whites until stiff but not dry and fold into vegetable mixture. Pour into a buttered baking dish, casserole or soufflé dish.

4. Sprinkle with the crumbs and bake until set, about 40 minutes.

Yield: Six servings.

BAKED HONEYED TURNIP

1 medium-size yellow turnip, peeled and cubed
½ cup chicken broth or beef broth (see pages 52, 53)
2 tablespoons dark honey, or to taste

1. Preheat the oven to 325 degrees.

2. Place the turnip in a buttered casserole. Mix broth with honey and pour over.

3. Cover and bake one hour or until tender.

Yield: Four servings.

VEGETABLES AND RICE

2 carrots, finely diced
1 onion, sliced
2 ribs celery, diced
1 zucchini or yellow squash, washed and diced
½ green pepper, seeded and diced
1 tomato, seeded and chopped
¼ cup boiling salted water
¼ cup halved raw unblanched almonds
4 cups cooked brown rice (see page 217), chilled several hours so that the grains separate
Sea salt to taste (optional)

1. Place carrots, onion, celery, squash and green pepper in a saucepan with the tomato and water. Cover tightly, bring to a boil and simmer gently over low heat until carrots are tender, about 15 minutes. Stir in the almonds.

2. Add rice and stir to mix. Reheat over very low heat while stirring. Season with salt if desired.

Yield: Eight servings.

VEGETABLE MÉLANGE

¼ cup soy oil
2 medium-size onions, chopped
4 cloves garlic, finely chopped
½ bunch broccoli flowerets, chopped
1 large carrot, chopped
½ pound mushrooms, sliced if large
8 cups cooked brown rice (see page 217)
½ cup mung bean and alfalfa sprouts (see page 195)
Tamari (soy sauce) to taste

1. Heat the oil in a large skillet or kettle and sauté the onions, garlic, broccoli and carrot in it until crisp-tender. Add mushrooms and cook three minutes longer.

2. Add rice, toss and reheat. Sprinkle with the sprouts and tamari and heat five minutes longer.

Yield: Eight to twelve servings.

Note: The contributor uses organically-grown vegetables to make this dish.

CIAMBOTTA
(ITALIAN VEGETABLE STEW)

2 medium-size potatoes, unpeeled, scrubbed and sliced lengthwise
1 onion, sliced
3 small zucchini, washed and sliced lengthwise
1 green pepper, seeded and sliced lengthwise
⅓ cup olive oil
1 unpeeled clove garlic
2 bay leaves
1 teaspoon oregano
Sea salt and freshly ground black pepper to taste (optional)

Put all the ingredients into an enameled or porcelainized heavy saucepan or casserole. Cover, bring to a boil and cook slowly, stirring frequently, 20 minutes. Let stand, covered, 10 minutes before serving.

Yield: Two servings.

Note: The contributor uses organically-grown vegetables to prepare this dish.

BAKED ZUCCHINI

1½ cups dry bread crumbs
Sea salt to taste
3 medium-size zucchini, washed and cut slightly on the diagonal into ½-inch slices
2 eggs, lightly beaten
¼ cup butter
3 tablespoons grated Parmesan or Cheddar cheese

1. Preheat the oven to 350 degrees.
2. Combine the bread crumbs and salt. Dip the zucchini slices into the beaten eggs and then into the seasoned crumbs. Arrange the slices on a buttered jellyroll pan.
3. Place a small dot of butter on each slice and sprinkle with cheese. Bake 40 minutes or until tender.

Yield: Six servings.

Note: The contributor uses organically-grown zucchini.

8
SALADS

Salads depend more on the freshness and quality of the raw ingredients
than on any fanciful recipes. Growing your own vegetables, fruits
and herbs is the ultimate, if not always practical, insurance
of an adequate source of supply.

Many of the recipes in this chapter are from organic gardeners across the
country who believe their produce is superior in every way. City dwellers
can trek to the few organic farms selling retail or to the nearest roadside
farm stand for fresh-picked produce, or can pay premium prices at
health food stores and organic co-ops, but seldom have any real
guarantee on growth conditions of the produce.

The recipes here offer unusual ingredient combinations and ways of
preparation for salads, regardless of the source of the fresh fruits and
vegetables. When the cook's imagination takes over to utilize available
supplies, the choice of a suitable and flavorful dressing can make the
difference between the delectable and the mundane. In this chapter
particular emphasis is placed on providing recipes for a variety of
salad dressings made from natural ingredients that will
enhance even the simplest duo of salad greens.

SPECIAL DINNER SALAD

2 cups shredded romaine
2 cups shredded spinach leaves
1 tablespoon safflower oil
3 slices cooked crumbled crisp warm bacon
1 hard-cooked egg, grated
1 dozen cooked shelled deveined shrimp
4 thin carrot sticks
4 ripe olives
1 tomato, cut into wedges
1 tablespoon chopped fresh basil
1 tablespoon snipped fresh dill weed
Lemon juice to taste
Sea salt and freshly ground black pepper to taste

1. Combine the romaine and spinach in a salad bowl. Add the oil and toss until all the leaves glisten.

2. Add bacon, egg, shrimp, carrot sticks, olives, tomato, basil and dill. Toss. Add lemon juice, salt and pepper.

Yield: Two servings.

SPRINGTIME SALAD

2 cups leaf lettuce, torn apart
2 cups dandelion greens, torn apart
1 cup shredded comfrey leaves
1 cup shredded plantain leaves
1 bunch radishes, thinly sliced
Honey dressing:
1 teaspoon sea salt
¼ teaspoon dry mustard
¼ teaspoon freshly ground black pepper
2 tablespoons honey
⅓ cup apple cider vinegar
1 cup oil

1. Combine all the salad greens and the radishes in a salad bowl and toss to mix.

2. Place all the dressing ingredients except the oil in an electric blender and blend on low speed. Turn the speed to high and very gradually blend in the oil. Pour dressing over the greens and toss. Serve at once.

Yield: Twelve servings.

THE HEARTY SALAD BOWL

1½ quarts washed, drained and crisped Buttercrunch, Bibb or Boston lettuce
1 cup chopped celery
1 cup sliced radishes
1 large Bermuda onion, chopped
2 tomatoes, cut into wedges
1 green pepper, cut into thin strips
½ cucumber, skin scored and thinly sliced
1 cup diced Cheddar cheese
1 cup julienne strips cooked turkey breast, ham or beef
2 hard-cooked eggs, sliced
Homemade dressing

1. In a large salad bowl, combine the lettuce, celery, radishes, onion, tomatoes, green pepper and cucumber. Toss to mix.

2. Arrange the cheese, turkey or meat and eggs attractively over the surface. Toss with the dressing, at the table, just before serving.

Yield: Four servings.

Note: The contributor specializes in growing the new type Bibb lettuce, called Buttercrunch, on his organic farm.

GRATED SALAD

3 cups grated cabbage
2 cups grated carrots
½ cup finely chopped peeled broccoli stalks
⅓ cup sesame seeds, ground in Moulinex grinder or left whole
1 tomato, diced
½ avocado, peeled, pitted and cubed, then dipped in lemon juice to prevent darkening
½ cup chopped cucumber
¼ cup chopped green pepper
¼ cup chopped celery
Homemade dressing

1. In a large salad bowl, combine the cabbage, carrots, broccoli stalks and sesame seeds.

2. Use the tomato, avocado, cucumber, green pepper and celery to garnish the salad in an attractive pattern.

3. At the table, toss with dressing.

Yield: Eight servings.

SALAD NICOISE LONDON STYLE

2 green peppers, seeded and
   diced
4 radishes, sliced
4 tomatoes, cut into wedges
1½ cups diced celery with leaves
½ cup diced fennel or 1
   tablespoon snipped fresh dill
   weed
6 cooked unmarinated artichoke
   bottoms
1 can (6½ or 7 ounces) tuna fish,
   drained and roughly flaked
8 flat anchovy fillets, chopped
3 hard-cooked eggs, cut into
   wedges
4 cold cooked new potatoes,
   sliced
1 cup diced cooked green beans
Salad greens
Dressing (see below)

Combine all the ingredients except salad
greens and dressing. Add dressing. Toss to
mix. Chill briefly. Turn into a bowl lined
with salad greens.

Yield: Six servings.

Dressing:
1 cup oil
¼ cup cider vinegar
½ teaspoon dry mustard
Sea salt and freshly ground
   black pepper to taste
1 tablespoon chopped fresh
   tarragon
1 tablespoon chopped parsley
1 tablespoon chopped chives
1 tablespoon chopped fresh
   chervil

Shake or beat all the ingredients together
in a jar or bowl and chill well before using.

Yield: About one and one-third cups.

FULL MEAL SALAD

1 clove garlic, crushed
½ cup diced celery
½ cup sliced onions
¼ cup chopped green scallion
2 apples, scrubbed and finely chopped including core
1½ cups chopped raw broccoli flowerets
4 radishes, sliced
2 hard-cooked eggs, chopped or sliced
½ cup diced green pepper
6 cold cooked new potatoes, skins left on
½ cup tangerine sections
1 cup mixed nuts
2 cups diced hard cheeses (2 or 3 kinds)
1 head romaine lettuce, core chopped and leaves shredded
½ cup diced raw yellow turnip
The hard core of one large cabbage, chopped
1 cup raisins
1½ cups whole wheat or rye bread toast cubes
2 tablespoons butter
1½ to 2 cups homemade mayonnaise (see page 186)

1. Rub a salad bowl with the clove of garlic.

2. Combine all the ingredients except the toast cubes, butter and mayonnaise in the bowl and mix well.

3. Sauté the toast cubes in the butter.

4. Add enough of the mayonnaise to moisten the salad. Toss well. Sprinkle with the sautéed toast cubes.

Yield: Six servings.

AUGUST SALAD

1½ cups fresh peas

12 tiny carrot thinnings or 4 regular-size ones, scrubbed or scraped and sliced

Water

6 ribs celery with leaves, diced

1 bunch tiny radishes, sliced

1 green pepper, seeded and chopped

4 to 6 scallions, sliced, including some of the green

4 ears of corn, steamed four minutes, kernels scraped off

4 cooked new potatoes, diced

2 cooked beets, diced

1 cup cooked green beans

Homemade French dressing (see page 188)

Sea salt to taste

Buttercrunch or Boston lettuce leaves

2 hard-cooked eggs, sliced

3 tomatoes, cut into wedges

1. Place the peas and sliced carrots in a saucepan. Add enough water to barely cover the bottom of the saucepan, cover and simmer eight minutes.

2. Drain the vegetables, use water for soup, and put vegetables in a bowl. Cool and chill. Add celery, radishes, green pepper, scallions, corn, potatoes, beets and green beans.

3. Toss with dressing, adding salt while tossing. Turn mixture into a salad bowl lined with lettuce leaves. Garnish with egg slices and tomato wedges. "Place in the middle of a picnic table, with a big spoon, and get out of the way!"

Yield: Eight servings.

Note: The contributor describes picking the carrot thinnings, scallions, corn, etc., from her garden in the original recipe. These add enormously to the flavor of the finished dish. The contributor is co-author of "Moment in the Sun," and author of the environmental novel "The Year of the Last Eagle."

GREEN BEAN SALAD I

1½ pounds green beans, ends removed
½ medium-size onion, finely chopped
2 tablespoons wine vinegar
1 teaspoon honey
3 tablespoons oil
¼ teaspoon nutmeg
Sea salt and freshly ground black pepper to taste
3 tablespoons sunflower seed kernels

1. Steam the beans over boiling water until they are crisp-tender. Do not overcook. Drain.

2. Meanwhile, combine onion, vinegar, honey, oil and nutmeg and pour over hot beans. Cool and chill.

3. Season with salt and pepper and sprinkle with sunflower seed kernels.

Yield: Six servings.

GREEN BEAN SALAD II

1 pound fresh young green beans
Boiling salted water
5 tablespoons oil
2 large Spanish onions, finely chopped
4 hard-cooked eggs
2 ribs celery, chopped
½ green pepper, chopped
¼ cup chopped walnuts
2 tablespoons wine vinegar
Sea salt to taste
Freshly ground black pepper to taste (optional)

1. Cut the beans slantwise into one-inch pieces and cook in the boiling water until barely tender. Do not overcook.

2. Heat three tablespoons oil in a skillet and sauté the onions in it until tender and lightly golden in color.

3. In a large wooden salad bowl, chop the beans and add onions. Grate the eggs over the beans and onions. Add celery, green pepper and nuts.

4. Add remaining oil, the vinegar, salt and pepper and toss.

Yield: Six servings.

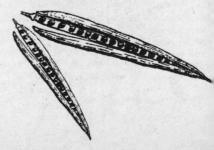

DANDELION SALAD

½ clove garlic
1 quart young tender dandelion
   leaves, picked before flower
   blossoms, torn up
2 tablespoons chopped parsley
1 tablespoon chopped scallions
2 tablespoons finely chopped
   onion
1 cup watercress sprigs
1 tablespoon lemon juice
2 tablespoons sesame paste
   (tahini)
⅛ teaspoon tarragon
⅛ teaspoon summer savory
Sea salt to taste

1. Rub a salad bowl with the garlic
clove. Add the dandelion greens, parsley,
scallions, onion and watercress.

2. Beat together the lemon juice and
sesame paste. Add tarragon, savory and
salt and pour over greens mixture. Toss
with wooden spoon and fork.

Yield: Four servings.

Note: The contributor dries the dandelion
roots and makes a coffee substitute.

ROMAINE AND RADISH SALAD

1 quart torn romaine leaves
8 radishes, quartered
1 scallion, chopped
¼ cup walnut pieces
½ unpeeled cored apple, diced
4 dates, chopped
1 tablespoon raisins
2 tablespoons snipped fresh dill
   weed
2 tablespoons chopped parsley
Dressing:
⅓ cup yogurt (see page 311)
1 tablespoon lemon juice
1 tablespoon honey
1 tablespoon sesame seeds,
   toasted
Blue cheese to taste (optional)

1. Combine all the salad ingredients in
a wooden bowl.

2. Mix together the yogurt and other
dressing ingredients. Pour over the salad
and toss.

Yield: Four to six servings.

CUKE SALAD

2 large cucumbers, peeled and
chopped
1 small onion, finely chopped
¾ cup yogurt (see page 311)
1 teaspoon prepared mustard
1 tablespoon vinegar
½ teaspoon sea salt
⅛ teaspoon freshly ground black
pepper
½ teaspoon celery seeds
6 Boston lettuce cups

Put the cucumbers in a salad bowl and add
all remaining ingredients except the lettuce.
Mix well. Chill two hours and serve in
Boston lettuce cups.

Yield: Six servings.

MEDITERRANEAN CUCUMBER SALAD

2 small firm cucumbers
1 cup yogurt (see page 311)
3 tablespoons monukka raisins
¼ cup chopped walnuts
1 small onion, finely chopped
Sea salt and freshly ground black
pepper to taste
1 tablespoon finely chopped fresh
mint leaves

1. Peel cucumbers, slice lengthwise and
remove and discard seeds.

2. Dice cucumbers and place in a bowl.
Add remaining ingredients and mix well.
Chill and serve very cold.

Yield: Four servings.

MUSHROOM SALAD

⅓ cup clam juice
⅓ cup oil
2 tablespoons vinegar
½ teaspoon sea salt
¼ teaspoon tarragon
¼ pound mushrooms, sliced
1 red onion, thinly sliced
1 to 1½ quarts salad greens
(escarole, chicory, romaine,
Boston and leaf lettuce), crisped
1 tomato, cut into wedges

1. In a glass or ceramic bowl, combine the
clam juice, oil, vinegar, salt and tarragon.
Beat with a rotary beater until well
blended.

2. Add mushrooms and onion. Chill well.

3. Place crisped salad greens in a salad
bowl. Add mushroom-onion mixture and
toss. Garnish with tomato wedges and
serve immediately.

Yield: Six servings.

ZUCCHINI SALAD

3 small young zucchini
(about 1 pound)
3 scallions, finely chopped
2 tablespoons snipped fresh dill
weed
1 tablespoon chopped parsley
¼ teaspoon oregano
1 cup yogurt (see page 311)
1 tablespoon lemon juice
1 teaspoon honey

1. Wash the zucchini and dice very finely.
Place in a salad bowl with the scallions,
dill, parsley and oregano.

2. Combine the yogurt, lemon juice and
honey and pour over the zucchini. Toss to
mix well. Refrigerate 30 minutes or longer
before serving.

Yield: Four to six servings.

MARINATED ZUCCHINI

2 medium-size zucchini
½ cup oil
½ cup vinegar
1 clove garlic, finely chopped
1 tablespoon grated onion
1 tablespoon chopped fresh mint
leaves

1. Wash the zucchini and slice thinly. Heat
the oil in a skillet and sauté the zucchini in
it until tender and lightly browned, turning
often.

2. Place the zucchini in a bowl and allow
to cool. Stir in the remaining ingredients
and chill well before serving.

Yield: Four servings.

CORN SALAD

1 cup cooked corn kernels, cut
from the cob
1½ cups cottage cheese, well
drained
1 tablespoon chopped green
pepper
1 tablespoon chopped parsley
Sea salt to taste

Toss all ingredients together and store in a
covered container in the refrigerator until
serving time.

Yield: Four servings.

RAW BEET SALAD

1 bunch small young beets (tops removed for a tossed salad bowl), peeled
2 cups shredded red cabbage
1 cup shredded carrots
½ cup lemon juice
¼ cup honey
¼ cup oil
Sea salt or vegetable salt to taste

1. Grate the beets finely into a salad bowl. Add the cabbage and carrots.

2. Beat together the lemon juice, honey, oil and salt and pour over beet mixture. Toss and chill well.

Yield: Eight to ten servings.

HARD BREAD SALAD

1 loaf stale Italian bread (whole wheat is best)
Water
2 tomatoes, sliced
1 large sweet Spanish onion, thinly sliced
1 cucumber, peeled and diced
⅓ cup oil
⅓ cup vinegar
Sea salt and freshly ground black pepper to taste

1. Cut the bread into bite-size chunks. Sprinkle lightly with water and place in a salad bowl.

2. Add remaining ingredients and toss thoroughly.

Yield: Four servings.

MARINATED BROCCOLI SALAD

1 bunch broccoli, broken into small flowerets (discard stems or use in grated salad— (see page 166)
Boiling salted water
½ cup oil
½ cup lemon juice
Sea salt and freshly ground black pepper to taste
1 clove garlic, finely chopped

1. Put the broccoli in a large skillet and add boiling water to cover the bottom of pan to depth of one-half inch. Cover and simmer until broccoli is crisp-tender, about eight minutes. Drain.

2. Meanwhile, beat together remaining ingredients.

3. Pour dressing over hot broccoli. Chill well before serving.

Yield: Six to eight servings.

CABBAGE SLAW WITH CASHEW DRESSING

1 small head green cabbage,
  finely shredded
1 cup shredded fresh pineapple
1 cup cashews, ground in a
  Moulinex grinder
¼ cup water
¼ cup honey
2 tablespoons cider vinegar
Sea salt to taste

1. Place cabbage and pineapple in a salad bowl.

2. Mix the ground cashews with the water to make a stiff paste. Add honey, vinegar and salt. Pour over cabbage and pineapple and toss.

Yield: Six to eight servings.

TEXAS COLE SLAW

2 cups finely shredded cabbage
½ green pepper, diced
½ carrot, shredded
½ peeled cucumber, seeded and
  chopped
1 sweet onion, finely sliced
3 tablespoons brown sugar
2 tablespoons red wine vinegar
1 tablespoon cold water
1 tablespoon white vinegar
2 tablespoons oil
1 tablespoon sea salt
1 clove garlic, finely chopped

1. Combine the cabbage, pepper, carrot, cucumber and onion in a ceramic or glass bowl. Mix together the remaining ingredients and pour over the vegetables.

2. Allow to marinate in the refrigerator a few hours or overnight.

Yield: Six servings.

SLAW WITH VINEGAR DRESSING

2 cups shredded cabbage
1 apple, cored and grated
½ cup grated carrot
½ cup pecans, chopped
½ cup sunflower seed kernels
1 cup heavy cream
2 tablespoons honey
2 tablespoons apple cider vinegar
Sea salt to taste

1. Combine the cabbage, apple, carrot, pecans and sunflower seed kernels in a salad bowl.

2. Combine remaining ingredients and mix well. Pour over cabbage and chill well.

Yield: Four servings.

FRUITED CABBAGE SALAD

1 small head red cabbage, finely shredded

½ large Hawaiian or sugar pineapple, peeled, cored and finely shredded

2 apples, cored and grated

1 celery root (celeriac), peeled and grated or finely shredded

1 cup coarsely chopped pecans

Combine all the ingredients in a bowl. Toss to mix. Chill well. There will be enough juice from the pineapple and apples to serve the salad without further dressing.

Yield: Eight servings.

SHREDDED CABBAGE SALAD

3 cups shredded green cabbage

½ cup chopped parsley

¼ cup chopped scallions, green tops included

¼ cup honey

1 teaspoon vegetable salt

¼ cup cider vinegar

2 tablespoons safflower oil or sesame oil

Sliced radishes or black olives

1. Combine the cabbage, parsley and scallions and chill well.

2. Combine the honey, salt, vinegar and oil. Shake well; chill. Pour dressing over vegetables and toss lightly.

Yield: Six servings.

SAUERKRAUT SALAD

2 cups fresh sauerkraut, drained

2 medium-size apples, cored and finely diced

1 onion, halved and then cut into thin slices

3 tablespoons oil

1 tablespoon grated horseradish, or to taste

½ cup chopped nuts

Combine all ingredients and chill well before serving.

Yield: Six servings.

CARROT SALAD I

1 large carrot, finely grated
1 tablespoon finely chopped onion
¼ cup currants
Sea salt to taste
2 tablespoons lemon juice

Combine all ingredients and chill well.
Yield: Two servings.

CARROT SALAD II

1 pound carrots, cut into ¼-inch-thick slices
Boiling salted water
¾ cup homemade tomato juice (see page 27)
½ cup honey or raw sugar
½ cup oil
¼ cup vinegar
2 tablespoons water
¾ teaspoon sea salt
Few leaves fresh thyme or ¼ teaspoon dried thyme
1 small green pepper, seeded and slivered
1 small sweet red onion, cut into thin rings

1. Place carrots in a saucepan and add boiling water to come one-quarter the way up the carrots. Cover and simmer until carrots are crisp-tender, about 10 minutes. Drain, and use liquid in soup.
2. Combine remaining ingredients and mix well. Pour over the hot carrots and store, covered, in the refrigerator overnight. Stir well and drain before serving.
Yield: Six servings.

LITTLECHEW

1 cup finely grated carrots
½ cup finely grated raw young beets
1 cup shredded romaine
1 cup alfalfa sprouts (see page 195)
½ avocado, peeled, pitted and mashed
Lemon juice
Sea salt to taste

1. In a salad bowl, combine the carrots, beets, romaine and alfalfa sprouts.
2. Mash the avocado with a fork or in an electric blender, adding enough juice to make a thick puree. Season with salt.
3. Pour avocado over salad and toss.
Yield: Three or four servings.

WATERCRESS WITH CREAM CHEESE

1 package (8 ounces) cream
 cheese
¼ cup blanched slivered almonds
2 tablespoons butter
3 cups watercress sprigs
Homemade French dressing
 (see page 188)

1. Divide the cream cheese into 16 to 20
pieces. Roll each piece into a ball and allow
it to come to room temperature for serving.

2. Sauté the almonds in the butter in a
small skillet until golden. Drain on paper
towel.

3. Arrange the watercress on four salad
plates. Place four or five of the cheese balls
neatly on each portion of watercress.
Sprinkle with the almonds and spoon the
dressing over all as desired just before
serving.

Yield: Four servings.

EGGPLANT SALAD

1 medium-size eggplant
1 small onion, chopped
2 ribs celery with leaves, chopped
2 hard-cooked eggs, chopped
¼ cup oil
¼ cup lemon juice
Kelp to taste
Vegetable salt to taste
Romaine
Tomato wedges and cucumber
 slices
2 tablespoons chopped parsley

1. Preheat the oven to 400 degrees.

2. Place eggplant directly on oven shelf
and bake 30 minutes or until tender and
soft to the touch.

3. Peel and chop eggplant and put into a
bowl. Add onion, celery and eggs. Mix well.

4. Add the oil, lemon juice, kelp and
vegetable salt. Mix well and chill.

5. Scoop eggplant mixture onto bed of
romaine and garnish with tomato and
cucumber. Sprinkle with the parsley.

Yield: Four servings.

PICKLED BEET SALAD

4 bunches beets, leaves removed
   for use in green salads
Boiling water
1 quart apple cider vinegar
1 cup honey
½ cup maple syrup or honey
8 red onions, thinly sliced
1 teaspoon sea salt
3 teaspoons kelp
3 teaspoons chopped fresh
   tarragon
1 quart safflower oil
½ cup brewer's yeast

1. Wash the beets and place in a kettle with boiling water to cover. Cook until tender, about 35 minutes. Skin beets and slice or dice.

2. Meanwhile, heat remaining ingredients except oil and yeast to boiling. Cool. Gradually beat in the oil and yeast and pour over the beets.

Yield: About twelve servings.

CHICK-PEA PLATTER

2 cans (1 pound each) chick-peas,
   drained, or 1 cup dried
   chick-peas, soaked, cooked and
   drained
⅓ cup chopped scallions
2 tablespoons chopped parsley
¼ cup oil
2 tablespoons lemon juice
½ teaspoon sea salt
⅛ teaspoon dry mustard
Freshly ground black pepper to
   taste
Salad greens

1. Combine the chick-peas, scallions and parsley. Blend together the oil, lemon juice, salt, mustard and pepper and pour over the vegetables. Toss lightly. Chill well, at least one hour, tossing twice during chilling.

2. Serve on bed of crisp salad greens.

Yield: About ten servings.

SWEET POTATO SALAD

2 cups grated raw sweet potato
(for those who cannot tolerate
raw sweet potato, steam or boil
potatoes in their skins until
barely tender, peel, cool and
grate)
2 cups finely chopped green
peppers
1 cup finely ground peanuts,
pecans, cashews or almonds
2 tablespoons homemade
mayonnaise, approximately
(see page 186)
Salad greens
½ cup diced cucumber

1. Combine the sweet potato, green
peppers and nuts in a bowl. Stir in the
mayonnaise to barely moisten, or to taste.

2. Spoon onto a bed of salad greens.
Garnish with the cucumber.

Yield: Eight servings.

TOSSED SALAD

1 quart buckwheat or curly leaf
lettuce, torn apart
2 cups sprouted alfalfa seeds
(see page 195)
2 tablespoons sprouted mung
beans (see page 195)
2 tablespoons sprouted chick-peas
(see page 195)
2 tablespoons sprouted lentils
(see page 195)
¼ to ⅓ cup finely chopped
dandelion or sorrel leaves
3 tablespoons chopped fresh mint
leaves
3 tablespoons sesame seeds
Oil and lemon juice to taste
Sea salt to taste

1. Combine the lettuce, alfalfa seeds,
mung beans, chick-peas, lentils, dandelion
or sorrel leaves and mint in a salad bowl.
Toss.

2. Sprinkle with the sesame seeds and toss
with oil, lemon juice and salt.

Yield: Six servings.

TABOOLEY

1 cup medium-fine bulghur
   (cracked wheat)
½ cup olive oil
Juice of 4 lemons (about ¾ cup)
1 bunch scallions, finely chopped
   including green part
2 large bunches parsley, chopped
4 large tomatoes, very finely
   chopped
1 small bunch celery, very finely
   chopped
2 small cucumbers, very finely
   chopped
Vegetable salt to taste
Romaine lettuce leaves

1. In a large ceramic or glass crock, make a layer of the bulghur. Add the olive oil and lemon juice.

2. Layer the vegetables in the order listed, scallions first and cucumbers last. Sprinkle vegetable salt over the top.

3. Cover the crock loosely and store in the refrigerator until ready to serve, at least 24 hours, and up to two weeks.

4. To serve, toss the salad so that all ingredients are well mixed. Check seasoning. Salad may be served on a bed of lettuce, or Lebanese style, wrapped by the fingers in single leaves of lettuce and eaten out-of-hand.

Yield: Six to eight servings.

MARINATED SOYBEAN SALAD

3 cups hot cooked drained
   soybeans (see page 157)
¾ cup oil
⅓ cup vinegar
Sea salt and freshly ground
   black pepper to taste
1 clove garlic, finely chopped
½ cup chopped scallions
½ cup chopped green pepper
⅓ cup chopped celery
2 tablespoons chopped parsley
2 tablespoons snipped fresh dill
   weed

1. Place the hot beans in a bowl. Combine the oil, vinegar, salt, pepper and garlic and pour over hot beans. Cover and marinate in the refrigerator several hours.

2. Stir in remaining ingredients. Chill again.

Yield: Four servings.

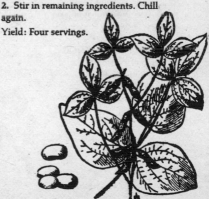

BLUEBERRY RICE SALAD

2 cups cooked cold brown rice
  (see page 217)
2 cups fresh blueberries
½ cup unsweetened shredded
  coconut
½ cup chopped pecans or almonds
  Honey
½ cup soy milk powder
⅛ teaspoon sea salt
⅔ cup oil (cold)
2 tablespoons lemon juice
  Wheat germ

1. In a serving bowl, combine the rice, berries, coconut, nuts and honey (one-quarter cup, or to taste).

2. In an electric blender, place the soy milk powder, salt and one tablespoon honey. While blending at high speed add oil slowly until mixture becomes thick.

3. Stir in the lemon juice. Fold soy cream into rice mixture and sprinkle with wheat germ.

Yield: Four servings.

SANDRAHENE SALAD

1 carrot, coarsely grated
1 apple, washed and grated
  whole
2 ribs celery, grated
6 radishes, grated
1 cup shredded red cabbage
¼ cup chopped parsley
1 cup finely chopped raisins,
  dried apricots and dates mixed
¼ cup unblanched toasted
  almonds, roughly chopped
1 cup oil
½ cup lemon juice
½ cup coconut water (drained
  from a fresh coconut)
1½ teaspoons sea salt
2 tablespoons honey
  Wheat germ

1. In a salad bowl, combine carrot, apple, celery, radishes, cabbage, parsley, dried fruits and almonds. Toss to mix.

2. In a jar, place remaining ingredients except the wheat germ; shake to mix well. Pour over salad bowl ingredients and toss. Sprinkle with wheat germ.

Yield: Four servings.

TROPICAL SUN SALAD

1 large cantaloupe, cubed or
  made into melon balls
8 bananas, sliced
½ pound cherries, halved and
  pitted
1 pint strawberries, halved
4 fresh peaches, pitted and sliced
1 fresh pineapple, peeled, cored
  and cubed
2 cups seedless grapes
1 cup mandarin orange segments
  (optional)
1 can (8 ounces) papaya juice or
  nectar
1 quart bottled or canned guava
  juice
1 quart homemade strawberry ice
  cream (see page 327)

1. Combine all the ingredients except the
ice cream in a large salad bowl. Chill for at
least three hours.

2. Add scoops of the ice cream just before
serving.

Yield: Twelve to sixteen servings.

Note: Other fresh fruits can be added or
substituted, and salad can be served with
cottage cheese sprinkled with wheat germ
instead of ice cream if you prefer.

OLYMPIAN SALAD

8 unsulphured dried peach
  halves
Spring water
Lettuce leaves (Boston, romaine
  or leaf)
1½ cups alfalfa sprouts
  (see page 195)
1 cup blanched almonds, flaked
  or finely grated in a Moulinex
  grinder
Honey to taste (optional)

1. Place the peaches in a jar. Cover with
water, cover the jar and refrigerate one to
two days. Drain the peaches.

2. Arrange the drained peaches on a bed
of lettuce leaves. Top with the sprouts.
Sprinkle with the nuts or make a nut cream
dressing by beating the nuts with honey
and a little water until mixture is thick and
smooth. Spoon the nut cream over the
sprouts.

Yield: Six to eight servings.

MELON SALAD

1 large cantaloupe, cubed or
  made into melon balls
1 cup grated or cubed Swiss
  cheese
¼ cup raisins
3 tablespoons sunflower seed
  kernels
2 cups watercress sprigs
Lemon juice or homemade
  dressing

1. Combine the melon, cheese, raisins and
sunflower seed kernels.

2. Arrange the watercress on two salad
plates. Pile the melon mixture on top of the
watercress. Sprinkle with juice or dressing.

Yield: Two servings.

FRESH ORANGE SALAD

2 navel oranges
1 grapefruit (optional)
Freshly ground black pepper
Sea salt to taste
⅓ to ½ cup olive oil
2 tablespoons chopped walnuts
Salad greens
Warm whole wheat bread

1. Peel and section the oranges and
grapefruit. Cut each section into two or
three pieces and place in a salad bowl. Add
all the juice.

2. Add about two turns of the pepper mill
and salt to taste. Pour the oil over all, toss
and chill.

3. Sprinkle with the nuts and serve on
salad greens, with warm whole wheat
bread.

Yield: Three servings.

APPLE-BANANA SALAD

6 pounds sweet apples, some red
  and some yellow
3 to 4 bananas
1 cup toasted peanuts
Homemade mayonnaise
  or salad dressing
  (see page 186)
12 Boston lettuce cups

1. Core the apples but do not peel. Cut
into bite-size pieces and place in a salad
bowl. Slice bananas and add to apples.

2. Sprinkle with nuts and toss with
mayonnaise or dressing. Serve in lettuce
cups.

Yield: Twelve servings.

Note: The contributor's orchard is
organically maintained.

APPLE SLAW

1 small head green cabbage,
  finely shredded
1 carrot, grated
2 tablespoons chopped celery
1 tablespoon chopped green
  pepper
1 large apple, cored and finely
  chopped
1 tablespoon grated onion
Dressing:
1 tablespoon honey
½ teaspoon sea salt
Few grains cayenne pepper
1 tablespoon vinegar
1 tablespoon homemade
  mayonnaise (see page 186)

1. Combine the cabbage, carrot, celery,
green pepper, apple and onion in a salad
bowl.

2. Beat together the dressing ingredients.
Pour over the salad mixture and toss well.
Let stand at least 20 minutes in refrigerator
before serving.

Yield: Eight servings.

APPLE-LEMON SALAD

4 lemons, washed
6 to 8 red-skinned apples,
  cored but unpeeled
Brown sugar
½ cup dry white wine,
  approximately

1. Using a very sharp knife, slice the
lemons very thin. Remove seeds and make
a layer of lemon slices in a serving bowl.

2. Cut the apples twice the thickness of the
lemon slices. Sprinkle a little brown sugar
over the lemon layer, top with apple slices,
sprinkle with sugar and continue with
layers until all fruit is used. Do not use too
much sugar.

3. Pour about one-half cup white wine over
all and chill four hours. If the wine is
absorbed by the apples, add a little more
during the chilling.

Yield: Twelve servings.

Note: This is good served as a relish with
pork or ham.

HOMEMADE MAYONNAISE

1 egg
1 teaspoon prepared mustard
½ teaspoon sea salt
1 teaspoon raw sugar
3 tablespoons apple cider vinegar or lemon juice
1 cup safflower oil

1. Put the egg, mustard, salt, sugar, vinegar and one-half cup of the oil in an electric blender. Blend until smooth.

2. Continue blending while adding remaining oil very slowly in a steady stream into the center of the egg mixture. Remove mayonnaise with a small rubber spatula into a jar. Store, covered, in the refrigerator.

Yield: About two cups.

Note: If the mayonnaise curdles, blend one egg in a clean electric blender and gradually pour the curdled mayonnaise back in while blending at high speed.

CASHEW MAYONNAISE

½ cup raw cashews
1 teaspoon kelp or dulse
½ teaspoon paprika
1 clove garlic, crushed
1 cup water
1 cup oil
⅓ cup lemon juice
¼ teaspoon chervil
¼ teaspoon summer savory

1. Put the cashews, kelp or dulse, paprika, garlic and water in an electric blender. Blend until smooth.

2. While still blending, gradually add the oil until mixture is thick. Add the lemon juice, chervil and savory.

Yield: About two and one-half cups.

Note: This dressing is good with vegetable and fruit salads.

EGGLESS MAYONNAISE

1 cup evaporated milk
1 teaspoon sea salt
¼ cup lemon juice
1 cup oil
1 teaspoon raw sugar

Put all the ingredients in an electric blender and blend until smooth.

Yield: About three cups.

THICK MAYONNAISE

1 slice onion
2 egg yolks
½ teaspoon dry mustard
¼ teaspoon paprika
⅛ teaspoon thyme
⅛ teaspoon chervil
⅛ teaspoon summer savory
⅛ teaspoon marjoram
¼ teaspoon vegetable salt
1 teaspoon sea salt
3 teaspoons honey
1½ cups oil
3 tablespoons cider vinegar

1. Place all the ingredients except the oil and vinegar in an electric blender and blend until smooth.

2. While still blending add the oil, one tablespoon at a time, until mixture thickens. When one-half cup of the oil has been used, add the vinegar. Add remaining oil very slowly.

Yield: About two and one-half cups.

AVOCADO DRESSING

1 ripe avocado, peeled, pitted and mashed or pureed
1 cup yogurt (see page 311)
1 tablespoon tamari (soy sauce)
⅛ teaspoon oregano

Combine all ingredients and mix well.

Yield: About two and one-half cups.

Note: This dressing is good served over tossed green salads garnished with sprouts.

AVOCADO-TOFU DRESSING

3 cloves garlic
⅓ cup corn germ oil
½ bunch parsley, chopped
2 slices fresh gingerroot
1 ripe avocado, peeled and pitted
1 cup fresh tofu, soybean curd or cheese (see page 158)
Tofu liquid or water
1 teaspoon tamari (soy sauce)
½ cup raw nut butter or sprouted sunflower seed kernels
1 peeled lemon, pulp and juice
1 teaspoon kelp

Put the garlic, oil, parsley and ginger in an electric blender. Blend until smooth. Add remaining ingredients and blend until thick and smooth, using enough tofu liquid or water to blend easily. The dressing should be consistency of thin mayonnaise.

Yield: About three and one-third cups.

CAESAR SALAD DRESSING

¼ cup lemon juice
¼ cup water
¼ cup cider vinegar
¼ to ½ teaspoon vegetable salt
¼ teaspoon freshly ground black pepper
1 clove garlic, finely chopped
1 tablespoon anchovy paste
1 teaspoon honey
3 tablespoons grated Romano cheese
¾ cup oil

1. Put in an electric blender the lemon juice, water, vinegar, salt, pepper, garlic, anchovy paste, honey and cheese.
2. Blend until smooth.
3. While blending on medium speed, add the oil gradually until the mixture thickens. Chill well.

Yield: About one and one-half cups.

CHEESE AND TOMATO DRESSING

1 cup goat's milk cottage cheese
¼ cup homemade mayonnaise (see page 186)
1 tomato, skinned and mashed
1 teaspoon lemon juice
2 or 3 tablespoons tamari (soy sauce)
½ teaspoon oregano
½ teaspoon thyme
1 teaspoon vegetable salt
1 clove garlic, very finely chopped

1. By hand, or in an electric blender, blend the cottage cheese and mayonnaise together until smooth.
2. Mix the tomato, lemon juice, tamari, oregano, thyme, salt and garlic together until well blended. Combine the two mixtures.

Yield: About two cups.

FRENCH DRESSING

¼ teaspoon dry mustard
⅛ teaspoon freshly ground black pepper
¾ teaspoon sea salt
¼ teaspoon paprika
2 teaspoons raw sugar
¾ cup olive oil or peanut oil
¼ cup vinegar
2 tablespoons tomato juice (see page 27)

Shake all ingredients together in a bottle.

Yield: About one and one-quarter cups.

Note: This dressing is particularly good on raw spinach salad.

FRUIT AND OIL DRESSING

   1 tablespoon oil
   3 tablespoons orange juice or
     pineapple juice
1½ tablespoons papaya juice

Shake ingredients together in a jar and use on salads.

Yield: About one-quarter cup.

FRUIT SALAD DRESSING

  3 eggs, separated
¾ cup lemon juice
¾ cup honey

1. Beat the egg whites until stiff but not dry. Set aside.

2. Beat the egg yolks with the lemon juice and honey in the top of a double boiler. Cook, stirring, until mixture thickens. Cool. Fold in the whites.

Yield: About two cups.

HOMEMADE TAHINI

1½ tablespoons lime juice
  1 teaspoon oil
  1 teaspoon kelp
  6 tablespoons water
  ½ cup sesame seeds, finely
     ground in a Moulinex grinder

Put the lime juice, oil, kelp and water in an electric blender and blend at medium speed while adding the ground sesame seeds. Continue blending until mixture is like thick heavy cream.

Yield: About three-quarters cup.

Note: Use on sprout salad or any other salad.

RUSSIAN DRESSING

1 cup cottage cheese
1 tablespoon vinegar or lemon
  juice
¼ cup tomato juice, approximately
  (see page 27)
1 hard-cooked egg, chopped

1. Put the cottage cheese and vinegar or lemon juice in an electric blender. Add one-quarter cup tomato juice and blend until very smooth, adding more tomato juice if necessary.

2. Stir the egg into the dressing just before using.

Yield: About one cup.

HONEY CREAM DRESSING FOR FRUITS

2 eggs
½ cup honey
½ cup lemon juice
¼ cup orange juice
⅛ teaspoon sea salt
½ cup heavy cream, whipped
2 teaspoons grated orange rind
Unsweetened flaked or shredded coconut

1. Beat the eggs in a small saucepan and stir in the honey, lemon juice, orange juice and salt.

2. Cook, stirring, over low heat until mixture coats the back of the spoon. Cool thoroughly.

3. Fold in the cream and orange rind. Serve over fresh fruit salad and sprinkle with coconut.

Yield: About two and one-half cups.

PEANUT DRESSING

2 tablespoons raw peanut butter
¼ cup water
2 tablespoons lemon juice

Mix the ingredients together with a fork and serve over sliced banana and apple salad.

Yield: About three-quarters cup.

BASIC TOFU DRESSING

Spring water
1 cup tofu, soybean curd or cheese (see page 158)
1 clove garlic
2 tablespoons tamari (soy sauce)
Juice and pulp of half a lemon
¼ teaspoon kelp
1 teaspoon lecithin
¼ teaspoon oregano
¼ teaspoon marjoram

Adding only the minimum water that is necessary, place all ingredients in an electric blender and blend until thick and creamy.

Yield: About one and one-half cups.

Note: Variations are possible by adding one of the following:

2 large mushrooms
1 small tomato
2 tablespoons chopped scallion.

SALAD DRESSING I

¼ cup corn germ oil
7 pickled plums (available where macrobiotic ingredients are sold)
1 scallion, chopped
Tamari (soy sauce) to taste

Place oil, plums and scallion in an electric blender and blend until smooth. Season with tamari.

Yield: About three-quarters cup.

SALAD DRESSING II

3 tablespoons tahini (sesame paste)
3 tablespoons tamari (soy sauce)
Water

Mix tahini and tamari together with enough water to make the correct consistency for a salad dressing.

Yield: About one-third cup.

SALAD DRESSING III

2 teaspoons vegetable salt or coarse kosher salt
1½ teaspoons coarsely ground black pepper
2 cloves garlic, cut into pieces
½ teaspoon dry mustard
1 teaspoon prepared mustard
1 teaspoon dried tarragon
1 teaspoon lemon juice
3 to 5 tablespoons vinegar (such as imported Dessaux Fils)
2 tablespoons French olive oil (such as Monks)
10 tablespoons soy oil
1 egg yolk

Combine all ingredients in an electric blender and blend until thick and smooth.

Yield: About two cups.

Note: The contributor suggests making green salads more interesting by adding thinly sliced Jerusalem artichokes, raw cauliflowerets, thinly sliced raw mushrooms, carrots, nuts or crumbled cheeses . . . not all at once, though, she warns.

GREEN DRESSING

¼ cup safflower oil
2 tablespoons cider vinegar
¼ cup chopped watercress
1 egg
⅛ teaspoon sea salt
1 sprig fresh dill
1 sprig fresh thyme or ⅛ teaspoon dried thyme
½ teaspoon brown sugar

Place all ingredients in an electric blender and blend until smooth. Store in tightly covered jar in the refrigerator.

Yield: About three-quarters cup.

HERB DRESSING

¼ cup apple cider vinegar
2 tablespoons water
2 teaspoons vegetable broth flavoring (such as Vi-Gor-Cup)
1 teaspoon Meadowbrook brand salad herbs or your own choice of several herbs
1 teaspoon sea salt
⅔ cup sesame oil

Put in a jar all ingredients except the oil. Shake well. Add oil and shake again. Chill several hours before using.

Yield: About one cup.

SESAME DRESSING

½ cup ground sesame seeds
1 cup water, approximately
1 teaspoon kelp
Juice of ½ lemon
½ clove garlic

Place seeds and one cup water in an electric blender and blend until smooth. Add remaining ingredients and blend until smooth, adding more water if necessary to give dressing the correct consistency.

Yield: About one cup.

Note: Add one-half cup chopped onions, one-half cup chopped celery and one-half cup mixed alfalfa, mung bean and lentil sprouts. Blend until smooth for a mock tuna-sandwich spread.

THOUSAND ISLAND DRESSING

1 cup homemade mayonnaise
    (see page 186)
1 tablespoon chopped chives
½ green pepper, seeded and
    chopped
2 hard-cooked eggs, chopped
2 tablespoons chili sauce
1 tablespoon lemon juice
1½ teaspoons raw sugar
½ teaspoon celery salt
¼ teaspoon sea salt
½ teaspoon paprika
½ sweet red pepper, seeded
    and finely diced

Combine all the ingredients until well mixed.

Yield: About two and one-half cups.

PERFECT DRESSING

1 ripe avocado, peeled, pitted and
    mashed
1 large grapefruit, peeled and
    sectioned
1 large tomato, skinned and diced

Place the ingredients in an electric blender and blend until smooth.

Yield: About three cups.

Note: The contributor recommends this dressing for raw vegetable salads, and it can be used as a dip.

YARROW VINEGAR

½ cup cider vinegar
5 or more young yarrow leaves
    (3 to 4 inches long)

Put the vinegar and leaves in an electric blender and blend at low speed until leaves are finely chopped. Let leaves settle, then taste vinegar. If stronger flavor is desired, add more leaves, one at a time, until desired flavor is attained.

Yield: One-half cup.

Note: This vinegar can be used in making any dressing or mayonnaise where an unusual flavor is desired.

9
SPROUTS

Most people associate bean sprouts with Chinese restaurants, dark, damp cellars and cans of bleached, less-than-crisp sprouts on supermarket shelves. Growing your own sprouts from a wide variety of seeds and grains can be an adventure in horticulture and gastronomy, even for the city apartment dweller.

Researchers working at such reputable institutions as Yale, the University of Pennsylvania, the University of Minnesota and McGill University have demonstrated that the nutritional value of seeds increases dramatically during the first two to three days of sprouting. The vitamin C content of soybeans increases more than 500% by the third day. There are significant increases in many of the B vitamins and in vitamin E in many sprouted seeds, while the protein level remains generally high. Starch content is reduced as it is converted to sugar. However, no two varieties of seeds follow the same nutritional content pattern during sprouting. Some sources for the nutritional value of sprouted seeds are given in the Ingredient Chart at the end of this book.

Sprouts can be palatable snacks, or added to soups, salads, vegetable dishes, sandwich fillings, omelets, breads and beverages, or used as garnishes, so they are well worth the small investment it takes to produce them.

In choosing seeds to sprout, buy only those which have not been chemically treated and are sold specifically for sprouting or eating. They are available in health food stores, some garden supply houses and by mail order from growers and suppliers.

Among the most popular seeds and grains for sprouting are alfalfa, mung beans, lentils, chick-peas, watercress, sunflower, wheat and flax. They are relatively inexpensive when one considers that one-half cup swells to one and one-half cups after soaking and explodes into one quart of edible sprouts, costing about one cent a serving. Avoid tomato seeds and potato sprouts because they are poisonous.

Sophisticated equipment sold in health food stores and by mail order is not necessary for successful sprouting. Below are three simple methods utilizing equipment found in most homes. One variety can be sprouted in one receptacle, or two, such as alfalfa and lentils, can be sprouted together.

General Methods for Sprouting Seeds and Grains

For all methods, first pick over the seeds carefully, retaining only clean whole seeds for sprouting. Wash one-quarter cup of the seeds well, place in a bowl or jar and cover with lukewarm water. Let stand overnight. Drain, retaining the soaking liquid for a beverage or use in a soup or stew. Rinse the seeds thoroughly, pouring off all excess water.

Method I

Place two to three tablespoons of the soaked seeds in a quart jar, cover top of jar with cheesecloth or nylon mesh and secure tightly. Place the jar on its side, so that seeds form a thin layer, in a dark place where it is warm and humid. At least three times every day rinse the sprouts by pouring lukewarm water into the jar, swirling around and pouring out excess. Seeds should be kept moist but not wet. Depending on the variety of seeds, sprouts will develop in three to five days. They should be removed before rootlets appear, but when the first young leaves appear the jar may be placed in direct sunlight for development of green chlorophyll. Rinse and drain the sprouts when they have reached the optimum length (see below) and store in covered containers in the refrigerator. They will keep for three to five days. Use the whole sprouted seed.

Method II

The soaked seeds, two to three tablespoons at a time, can be spread on several layers of dampened paper towels, flannel or muslin fitted into a colander or over a perforated plastic tray. Enclose the colander or tray in an opaque plastic bag for darkness and humidity but do not forget to rinse the seeds thoroughly three times a day as in Method I. One end of the bag must be left loose for ventilation, and the opaque bag can be replaced by a clear bag when the first leaves appear. Follow the general directions in Method I for harvesting and storing.

Method III

The seeds can be placed in a new, porous, clay flowerpot,
well soaked in water, with a cloth screen over
the bottom hole and entirely covered with muslin.
In general, sprouts are best harvested when they reach
the length of the seed or grain.
Harvesting schedule for some popular seed and grain sprouts:

Seeds	Best when
alfalfa sprouts	about one inch long
chick-peas	one-half inch to three-quarters inch long
flax	about three-quarters inch long
lentil seeds	no longer than one inch
mung bean sprouts	one and one-half inches to two and one-half inches long
sesame and sunflower	as soon as sprouts are visible
soybeans	one-half inch long

Whenever possible, sprouted seeds should be used without cooking for full retention of all nutrients. If some of the larger sprouts seem to be tough, they may be blanched in steam or boiling water for a moment or two before being added to a dish. To use in breads and other baked goods, it is a good idea to grind the sprouts through a food grinder. In this form they can be added to a cooked cereal without their presence being obvious, though many people prefer the texture and appearance that sprouts give to pancakes, salads and sandwiches.

According to the publication *Natural Life Styles*, it is possible to travel with bean sprouts wrapped between thick damp towels, or in a jar, as long as the sprouts are kept moist. *Natural Life Styles* subscribers suggest taking seeds along on camping trips this way.

Following are a number of recipes calling for various kinds of sprouts.

BEAN SPROUT LUNCH

1½ quarts shredded salad greens
    including escarole, spinach,
    romaine and Boston lettuce
½ bunch watercress
½ cup diced celery
½ cucumber, skin scored, thinly
    sliced
2 hard-cooked eggs, sliced
½ cup julienne strips Swiss or
    Cheddar cheese
½ cup julienne strips baked ham
    slices
½ cup julienne strips cooked
    chicken breast
1 cup alfalfa, flax or sunflower
    sprouts (see page 195)
½ cup homemade mayonnaise
    (see page 186)
¼ cup homemade French dressing
    (see page 188)

1. Place the salad greens in the bottom of a large shallow bowl. Sprinkle watercress and celery over the greens.

2. Divide the surface area into sixths and arrange cucumber slices in one section, then the eggs, cheese, ham, chicken and sprouts in the other sections.

3. Combine the mayonnaise and dressing. Toss salad with the mixture at the table just prior to serving.

Yield: Six servings.

HIZIKI AND RICE

¾ cup dried hiziki (seaweed),
    available in some health food
    stores and in Oriental food
    stores
1 tablespoon sesame oil
½ pound mushrooms
3 scallions, cut into ½-inch
    strips
1½ cups plus 3 tablespoons water
½ pound green beans
½ cup peeled diced turnip
1 tablespoon tamari (soy sauce)
¾ cup mung bean sprouts
    (see page 195)
1 tablespoon brown rice flour
6 cups cooked brown rice
    (see page 217)

1. Wash the hiziki well in running water. Heat the oil in a saucepan and sauté the seaweed, mushrooms and scallions in it over low heat until tender.

2. Add one and one-half cups water, the green beans and turnip. Cover and simmer until tender, about 25 minutes.

3. Add tamari and bean sprouts; bring to a boil. Mix rice flour with remaining water and stir into mixture. Serve with brown rice.

Yield: Six servings.

CHICKEN CHOW MEIN

2 tablespoons safflower oil
3 medium-size onions, chopped
1 cup sliced mushrooms
3 cups chopped celery or Chinese cabbage
2 cups chicken broth (see page 52)
2 teaspoons soy sauce or to taste
2 teaspoons arrowroot
Water
2 cups slivered cooked chicken
1 cup mung bean sprouts (see page 195)
4 cups cooked brown rice (see page 217)

1. Heat the oil in a wok or skillet and stir-fry or sauté the onions in it until golden. Add mushrooms and celery and cook briefly.

2. Stir in the broth and soy sauce. Bring to a boil.

3. Mix arrowroot with a little water until smooth and whisk into onion mixture. Add chicken and sprouts. Reheat, but do not boil. Serve over rice.

Yield: Four servings.

BEAN SPROUT OMELET

4 eggs, lightly beaten
2 tablespoons water
Sea salt and freshly ground black pepper to taste
1½ tablespoons butter
1 cup alfalfa, lentil, soy or mung bean sprouts (see page 195)
1 tablespoon chopped parsley

1. Combine eggs, water, salt and pepper.

2. Heat the butter in a heavy omelet pan. Pour in the egg mixture and immediately stir with a fork until mixture begins to set on the bottom.

3. Continue cooking, without stirring, until bottom is golden. Sprinkle with sprouts and parsley. Fold over and tip onto warm platter.

Yield: One serving.

CUCUMBER AND OLIVE SALAD

1 large cucumber, peeled and diced
12 stuffed olives
⅓ cup diced Swiss cheese
1 bunch watercress
1 cup alfalfa, flax or lentil sprouts
French dressing (see page 188)

1. Combine the cucumber, olives and cheese.

2. Toss watercress and sprouts together and arrange on four salad plates. Top with cheese mixture and serve dressing separately or spooned over.

Yield: Four servings.

MUSHROOM AND SPROUT SALAD

2 cups alfalfa, lentil or radish
  seed sprouts (see page 195)
2 cups sliced mushrooms
3 cups small or torn-up spinach
  leaves
¼ cup chopped scallions
  French dressing (see page 188)
1 to 2 tablespoons prepared
  mustard

1. In a salad bowl, combine the sprouts,
mushrooms, spinach and scallion.

2. Mix dressing with mustard and toss
with spinach mixture just before serving.

Yield: Four servings.

GREEN REVOLUTION BREAKFAST

1 apple, cored and diced, or 1
  slice fresh pineapple, cubed
¼ cup soaked raisins
¾ cup 5-inch lengths wheat grass
  clipped into one-inch lengths
  Water or apple juice
1½ tablespoons wheat germ
1 tablespoon lecithin granules
2 tablespoons unhulled sesame
  seeds, ground in a Moulinex
  grinder

1. Put the apple or pineapple, the raisins,
wheat grass and enough water or juice to
blend in an electric blender. Blend until
smooth.

2. Combine remaining ingredients in a
cereal bowl and pour the wheat grass
mixture over all.

Yield: One serving.

LUCERNE SALAD

1 cucumber, skin scored, thinly
  sliced
4 tomatoes, thinly sliced
Homemade French dressing
  (see page 188)
Salad greens
1 cup alfalfa sprouts
  (see page 195)

1. Place the cucumber slices and tomato
slices alternately in a shallow dish. Pour
dressing over and allow to marinate in the
refrigerator an hour or so.

2. Garnish the outside edges of the dish
with salad greens and sprinkle sprouts over
the top of the cucumbers and tomato slices.

Yield: Six servings.

SPROUTED CHICK-PEA SALAD

2 cups sprouted chick-peas
  (see page 195)
1 clove garlic, finely chopped
¼ cup chopped scallions
1 tomato, diced
¼ cup chopped parsley
2 tablespoons wine vinegar
½ cup olive oil
Sea salt and freshly ground black
  pepper to taste

Combine all ingredients and toss to mix.

Yield: Four to six servings.

SWEET AND SOUR BEAN SPROUTS

1 pound (about 1 quart) mung
  bean sprouts (see page 195)
2 cups water
3 tablespoons sugar
¾ teaspoon sea salt
⅓ cup wine vinegar
¼ cup olive oil
¼ teaspoon freshly ground
  black pepper (optional)

1. Place sprouts in a saucepan with the water, one tablespoon of the sugar and one-half teaspoon of the salt. Stir and cook one minute.

2. Drain well and cool.

3. Combine remaining ingredients and pour over sprouts. Allow to marinate in the refrigerator overnight. The sprouts will keep in the refrigerator for a week or so.

Yield: Twelve servings.

BEAN SPROUT SALAD

2 ribs celery, finely chopped
½ cup chopped walnuts
1½ cups mung bean or soybean
  sprouts (see page 195)
½ teaspoon caraway seeds
2 Boston lettuce cups
Honey and lemon juice to taste

1. Combine the celery, nuts, sprouts and seeds. Spoon into lettuce cups.

2. Dress to taste with honey and lemon juice mixed together.

Yield: Two servings.

SAUTÉED BEAN SPROUTS

3 tablespoons oil
1 scallion, finely chopped
1 quart mung bean, soybean,
   chick-pea or sprouted
   wheat berries (see page 195)
1 slice fresh ginger, finely
   chopped
1 tablespoon soy sauce
⅓ cup sliced water chestnuts

1. Heat the oil in a wok or heavy skillet.
Add scallion and cook 30 seconds. Add
sprouted wheat berries and cook one
minute.

2. Add ginger, soy sauce and water
chestnuts. Cover and cook four minutes.
Serve hot.

Yield: Four to six servings.

SPROUT SLAW

2 cups grated carrots
2 cups sprouted alfalfa, lentil,
   millet and fenugreek seeds
   mixed in any proportion
   (see page 195)
1 cup diced celery
½ cup chopped nuts
2 tablespoons chopped parsley
2 tablespoons grated onion
¼ cup raisins
1 cup homemade mayonnaise,
   approximately (see page 186)
1 hard-cooked egg, cut into
   wedges

1. In a salad bowl, combine the carrots,
sprouts, celery, nuts, parsley, onion and
raisins.

2. Add enough mayonnaise to moisten
and toss to mix.

3. Garnish with egg wedges.

Yield: Six servings.

RED CABBAGE AND SPROUTS

3 tablespoons safflower oil
4 cups shredded red cabbage
2 cups mung bean sprouts
   (see page 195)
1 tablespoon caraway seeds
Sea salt and freshly ground
   black pepper to taste
1 tablespoon soy sauce
1 tablespoon vinegar

1. In a wok or heavy skillet, heat the oil.
Sauté the cabbage in it three minutes. Add
sprouts and sauté two minutes longer.

2. Add remaining ingredients and reheat.
Toss lightly and serve hot.

Yield: Six servings.

SPROUT AND HAZELNUT SALAD

2 cups sprouted alfalfa seeds with
green leaves (see page 195)
Herb dressing (see page 192)
Salad greens
⅓ cup finely chopped hazelnuts

Toss sprouts with dressing. Arrange on
bed of salad greens and sprinkle with nuts.
Serve at once.

Yield: Four servings.

SPROUTED TABOOLEY SALAD

2 cups sprouted wheat berries
(¼ inch) (see page 195)
1 cucumber, peeled and diced
1 green pepper, seeded and diced
1 tomato, diced
1 scallion, chopped
¼ cup celery, diced with leaves
2 tablespoons chopped parsley
Vegetable salt to taste
½ cup oil
½ cup lemon juice

1. Combine all the ingredients in a large
ceramic or glass bowl or crock. Toss to mix.

2. Cover and refrigerate at least overnight
before serving. Mixture will keep several
days in the refrigerator.

Yield: Six to eight servings.

SPROUTED WHEAT STICKS

3 to 4 cups sprouted
wheat berries (see page 195)
¼ cup caraway seeds, ground
in Moulinex grinder
1 egg, lightly beaten
Corn meal

1. Preheat the oven to 400 degrees.

2. Grind the sprouted wheat berries
through the finest blade of a meat grinder.
Mix with the seeds and egg.

3. Shape into cigar shapes, roll in corn
meal and set on an oiled baking sheet. Let
dry five minutes.

4. Bake 10 minutes, reduce oven heat to
325 degrees and continue baking until
done, about five minutes longer.

Yield: About one dozen sticks.

SPROUTED WHEAT BALLS

2 cups sprouted wheat berries
   (see page 195)
1 cup unblanched almonds
1 large onion
2 cups whole wheat bread crumbs
1 teaspoon sea salt
3 tablespoons oil
1 cup milk, approximately
Oil for frying

1. Put the sprouted wheat berries, almonds and onion through the fine blade of a meat grinder. Turn into a bowl.

2. Add the crumbs, salt, three tablespoons oil and enough milk to make a mixture that holds together.

3. Form into one-inch balls. Heat enough oil to cover the bottom of a heavy skillet to ⅛-inch depth. Fry the balls in the oil until golden. Drain on paper towels.

Yield: Four servings.

BROILED SPROUTED WHEAT PATTIES

2 cups sprouted wheat berries
   (see page 195)
1 cup nuts
1 onion, quartered
1 cup milk
1 tablespoon soy flour
1 teaspoon sea salt
3 tablespoons brewer's yeast
1 sprig parsley
1 egg
2 cups whole wheat bread crumbs,
   approximately

1. Put all the ingredients except the bread crumbs in an electric blender and blend until smooth. Turn into a bowl.

2. Stir in enough crumbs to make a mixture that is stiff enough to be molded into patties.

3. Form into six patties and place on an oiled baking sheet. Broil under a preheated broiler until browned; turn and brown second side.

Yield: Six servings.

10
GRAINS & CEREALS

Much has been written and said in recent years on the disadvantages of
packaged, processed foods containing a minimum of essential nutrients
and quantities of non-nutritive additives. One of the most widely
publicized studies was on ready-to-eat cereals by Robert Choate,
former government advisor on the hunger problem, in 1970.

The recipes in this chapter may persuade the reader to try alternates.
Cook brown rice and fix a couple of the combination dishes calling for it.
Compare the nutritive values with other kinds of rice from the sources
suggested in the Ingredient Chart.

Savor the texture and flavor of a homemade cereal, fruit and honey mixture
and calculate the cost per serving compared with
store-bought packages.

Explore the culinary possibilities of little-known cereals such as millet,
which has a delicate flavor, while containing a complete protein and
little starch; bulghur, the cracked wheat staple of Mediterranean lands,
and kasha or buckwheat groats.

Cooking cereals and whole grains takes a little extra time so make sure
to get a bonus by fixing extra and using it later in combination dishes
included in this chapter and among the vegetarian main dishes.

NUT-APPLE BREAKFAST

2 tablespoons sunflower seed
   kernels
2 tablespoons sesame seeds
2 tablespoons unblanched
   almonds
2 tablespoons hazelnuts
2 tablespoons pumpkin seeds
2 tablespoons wheat germ
2 tablespoons date sugar
½ cup dried apples
½ cup raisins
Milk

1. In a Moulinex grinder, grind the
sunflower seed kernels, sesame seeds,
almonds, hazelnuts and pumpkin seeds.
Stir in the wheat germ and date sugar.

2. In an electric blender, grind the apples
until fine. Add with raisins to nut mixture.
Mix well. Serve in cereal bowls with milk.
Mixture can be stored in plastic bag or
covered container in the refrigerator.

Yield: Four servings.

BREAKFAST NUTRIMENT

2 cups pecans, chopped in an
   electric blender
1 tablespoon wheat germ
1 unpeeled apple, cored and
   finely diced
1 banana, sliced
1 unpeeled pear, cored and diced
1 cup raisins
1 teaspoon brown sugar
Reconstituted non-fat dry
   milk solids

Combine all the ingredients except
the milk. Moisten with milk and serve.

Yield: Four to six servings.

SIMPLE BREAKFAST

¼ cup wheat germ
¼ cup sunflower seed kernels,
   coarsely ground
¼ cup sesame seeds
⅛ cup rice polishings
⅛ cup chopped walnuts
Milk

Combine all ingredients except milk and
mix well. Serve in cereal bowl with milk.

Yield: One serving.

HONEY-OATS CEREAL

½ pound rolled oats
2 cups wheat germ
1 cup almonds
1 cup cashews
1 cup sunflower seed kernels
⅛ teaspoon sea salt
1 cup honey
⅔ cup water
1 teaspoon vanilla
⅔ cup oil

1. Preheat the oven to 350 degrees.

2. Combine the oats, wheat germ, almonds, cashews, sunflower seed kernels and salt.

3. In a separate bowl, combine the remaining ingredients. Pour over dry ingredients and mix well. Spread out on a baking sheet and bake 15 minutes.

4. Turn mixture over and bake 15 minutes longer. Serve with milk. Store, when cool, in covered container in the refrigerator.

Yield: Eight servings.

NEW ENGLAND MIX

1 cup rolled oats, crushed
2 cups water
¼ cup honey
1 cup hazelnuts, ground finely in Moulinex grinder
½ cup walnuts, ground in Moulinex grinder
¾ cup raisins
1 carrot, grated
1 cup sprouted sunflower seed kernels (see page 195)
1 cup lemon juice
¾ cup heavy cream
2 cups grated whole, washed apples, core included
Yogurt (see page 311)

1. Place the oats in a bowl, add water, cover and let soak overnight. Next day, add remaining ingredients except yogurt and work with the hands to mix well.

2. Serve topped with yogurt.

Yield: Twelve servings.

HEAVENLY MUNCH

2 pounds rolled oats
½ teaspoon sea salt
1¼ cups soy oil
⅓ cup honey
¾ cup non-fat dry milk solids
1 cup soy flour
1¾ cups wheat germ
1 pound finely chopped dates
1½ cups unsweetened coconut
1¾ cups sesame seeds
1½ cups chopped dried bananas (optional)
1 cup sunflower seed kernels
1½ cups raisins
1½ cups nuts
1 cup pumpkin seeds
1 cup squash seeds

1. Preheat the oven to 300 degrees.

2. Place rolled oats in a large bowl and add salt, oil and honey, mix well.

3. In another large bowl, combine all remaining ingredients and mix well. Stir in the oats mixture and mix well again.

4. Spread out enough of the mixture to cover a large baking sheet and bake 15 minutes. Transfer to a bowl to cool. Repeat with remaining oats mixture. Serve as dry snack or in cereal bowl with milk. Store in tightly covered container in the refrigerator.

Yield: About thirty-six servings.

READY-TO-EAT CEREAL

1 bag (3 pounds) Crunchy Granola or Vitagrains with Nuts
¾ cup unsweetened coconut meal
1 cup sunflower seed kernels
¾ cup chopped nuts
10 ounces wheat germ
½ cup soy grits
½ cup sesame seeds
¼ cup raw sugar (optional)
½ cup raisins
½ cup chopped figs
½ cup chopped dried apricots

1. Combine all the ingredients and mix well. Store in jars in the refrigerator.

2. Serve with milk and fresh fruit, if desired.

Yield: About twenty-four servings.

PECAN CRUNCH

½ cup soy oil
½ cup honey
½ cup spring water
5 cups rolled oats
½ cup wheat germ
½ cup sesame seeds
½ cup sunflower seed kernels
½ cup pumpkin seeds
½ cup monukka raisins
1½ cups chopped pecans
Milk

1. Preheat the oven to 350 degrees.

2. Mix together the oil, honey and water and pour over the oats. Spread mixture in a big shallow pan, at least 12-by-18 inches. Bake 30 minutes or until golden, stirring frequently after first 15 minutes to prevent overbrowning.

3. Combine remaining ingredients except milk and mix with toasted oats mixture. Serve in cereal bowls with milk. Store in refrigerator.

Yield: Sixteen servings.

PUFFED BROWN RICE

4 cups cooked brown rice, cooked so that grains are separate and dry (see page 217)
1 quart soy oil or sesame oil

1. Spread the rice out and let dry for three days, turning occasionally. It should be hard.

2. Heat the oil in a deep cooker to 360 degrees.

3. Place one-quarter cup rice at a time in a stainless steel basket or sieve and lower into the hot oil. Fry about 20 seconds or until lightly golden. Drain on paper towel. Serve as cereal or snack.

Yield: About two quarts.

APPLICIOUS

2 cups old-fashioned rolled oats
¾ cup raisins
3 apples, peeled, cored and cubed
3 cups applesauce
2 cups milk
Honey or maple syrup to taste

Mix all ingredients together.

Yield: About four servings.

ISLAND BREAKFAST CEREAL

1 cup hazelnuts
1 cup blanched almonds
3 cups quick-cooking rolled oats
¾ cup wheat germ
1 cup currants
⅔ cup snipped dried apricots
¾ cup brown sugar
Cream and fresh fruit

1. Preheat the oven to 350 degrees.

2. Spread the hazelnuts and almonds in a single layer on large baking sheet and bake five to eight minutes, shaking pan occasionally.

3. Place hazelnuts between towels and rub to remove skins. Blow away. Chop nuts and combine with oats, wheat germ, currants, apricots and brown sugar. Serve with cream and fruit. Store in a covered container in the refrigerator.

Yield: Eight servings.

Note: The contributor has to import the nuts, wheat germ and apricots.

UNCOOKED HIGH-ENERGY CEREAL

2 pounds quick-cooking rolled oats, crushed
½ pound sunflower seed kernels
½ pound wheat germ
¼ pound unblanched almonds, ground
¼ pound hazelnuts, ground
¼ pound Brazil nuts, ground
½ pound monukka raisins
5 bananas, sliced
½ cup chopped dates
½ cup snipped dried apricots
Honey or cider

Combine all the ingredients except the honey or cider and mix well. Serve in cereal bowls with honey or cider.

Yield: Twenty-four servings.

CORN MEAL MUSH

1 cup boiling water
1 cup stoneground yellow corn
meal
1 cup cold water
1 teaspoon sea salt
Honey and milk

1. Place boiling water in a saucepan. Mix together the corn meal and cold water and gradually stir into boiling water.

2. Add salt and cook, stirring, about 20 minutes. Serve with honey and milk. Or, corn meal mush can be served in place of potatoes at dinner.

Yield: Four servings.

Note: The contributors of this recipe grow their own corn organically.

PISTACHIO-RAISIN BRUNCH LOAF

2 cups boiling water
1 teaspoon sea salt
1 tablespoon safflower oil
6 ounces (about 1 cup)
stoneground yellow corn meal
¼ cup butter
¼ cup raisins
¼ cup non-dyed shelled
pistachios
2 eggs, lightly beaten
Dry bread crumbs or wheat germ
Butter
Maple syrup or honey

1. Bring water to a rolling boil in a saucepan, add salt and oil and gradually pour in the corn meal while stirring constantly. Heat, stirring, until mixture is thickened and smooth.

2. Add raisins and pistachios. Cook for 15 minutes, stirring occasionally, adding a little extra water if mixture seems dry.

3. Pour into a greased baking dish to give a one-half-inch-thick layer. Cool. Cut into squares. Dip into the eggs and then into bread crumbs or wheat germ.

4. Heat enough butter to cover the bottom of a heavy skillet and brown the squares in the butter; turn and brown other side, adding more butter as necessary. Serve with maple syrup or honey.

Yield: Four servings.

CORN MEAL MUSH AND SOY GRITS

1 cup yellow corn meal
1 teaspoon sea salt
½ cup non-fat dry milk solids
½ cup soy grits
Boiling water
1 cup cold milk
2 cups scalded milk
Potato starch
Butter

1. Mix the corn meal, salt and milk solids together.

2. Place grits in a small bowl and cover with boiling water. Let stand five minutes; drain. Add to corn meal mixture.

3. Stir in the cold milk. Stir corn meal mixture gradually into the simmering scalded milk in a saucepan. Heat, stirring, five minutes or until thick and smooth. Pour into an oiled 9-by-13-inch pan. Cool. Cut into squares or rounds.

4. Dip squares or rounds into potato starch. Heat enough butter to cover the bottom of a heavy skillet and fry the corn meal pieces in the butter until browned on both sides.

Yield: Four to six servings.

MILLET WITH CHEESE

1 recipe millet cereal, prepared as in Millet Cereal with broth (see page 212)
2 tablespoons water
2 tablespoons butter
1 cup grated Cheddar cheese

Place millet, water, butter and half the cheese in a saucepan. Heat, stirring, until cheese melts. Serve in dish, sprinkled with rest of cheese.

Yield: Four servings.

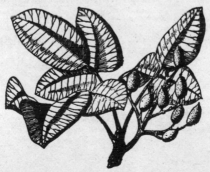

MILLET CEREAL

½ cup whole hulled millet
1½ cups water, milk or
    meat broth
Sea salt to taste

1. Combine the millet, water, milk or broth and the salt in a saucepan. Bring to a boil, cover and let simmer 30 minutes or until millet is cooked.

2. Plain, made with water or milk, the cereal can be eaten for breakfast with honey and cream. Made with broth, the cereal can be the basis for many savory dishes, such as the one below, to take the place of starchy vegetables.

Yield: About four servings.

MILLET PILAF

1 cup whole hulled millet
2 tablespoons oil
2 onions, chopped
1 carrot, quartered
1 teaspoon sea salt
¼ teaspoon freshly ground black
    pepper
1 quart chicken broth, beef broth
    or lamb broth, approximately
1 cup sliced mushrooms
1 cup sour cream

1. Preheat the oven to 350 degrees.

2. Place the millet in a dry, heavy casserole and brown slowly over low heat. Remove millet. Add oil to casserole and sauté onions in it until lightly browned.

3. Return millet to casserole and add carrot, salt and pepper. Pour one quart broth over all and bake, tightly covered, one and one-half hours or until millet is tender. It may be necessary to add more broth during cooking. When millet is fully cooked it is like rice with each grain separate.

4. Stir in the sour cream and serve with fowl, game or lamb. Millet pilaf can be served as a main dish.

Yield: Six servings.

KASHA

1 cup kasha (buckwheat
   groats)
1 egg, lightly beaten
½ teaspoon salt
⅓ cup finely chopped onion
2½ cups boiling water
3 tablespoons butter (optional)
3 tablespoons chopped parsley

1. Mix the kasha with the egg and heat the mixture in a dry skillet over medium to low heat, stirring occasionally until all the grains become separate. Do not let mixture scorch.

2. Add remaining ingredients. Bring to a boil, cover tightly and simmer 25 minutes or until grain is tender and has absorbed all the liquid. Fluff with a fork before serving.

Yield: Six to eight servings.

Note: For use as a breakfast cereal, omit onion and parsley and serve with honey and cream or fruit.

BULGHUR PILAF

1 cup bulghur (cracked wheat),
   rinsed in cool water
   and drained
2 cups water, approximately
3 tablespoons butter
1 onion, finely chopped
2 cups chicken broth or beef
   broth (see pages 52, 53)
¼ teaspoon sage
Sea salt to taste
¼ teaspoon summer savory
2 tablespoons chopped parsley

1. Preheat the oven to 200 degrees.

2. Place the bulghur and two cups water in a saucepan. Bring to a boil, cover tightly and simmer 40 minutes or until tender, adding more water during cooking if necessary. Spread out the bulghur on baking sheets and dry in the oven.

3. Bulghur can be left whole for a chewy product or cracked by passing through a coffee mill. Store in closed container in refrigerator.

4. Heat the butter in a heavy casserole and add one cup of the dried bulghur and the onion. Sauté five minutes.

5. Add the broth, sea salt, savory and parsley. Cover tightly and simmer over low heat until water is absorbed, about 25 minutes.

Yield: Four servings.

MILLET BREAKFAST CEREAL

1 cup whole hulled millet
1 quart water or milk
1 teaspoon sea salt
1 cup chopped unpeeled cored
  apples
1 cup raisins
Honey and cream

1. Put the millet, water or milk and the salt in a saucepan. Bring to a boil, cover and let simmer 45 minutes or until millet is soft.

2. Add apples and raisins and cook 15 minutes longer. Serve with honey and cream.

Yield: Four to six servings.

FOUR-GRAIN HOMEMADE CEREAL

1 pound whole rye, ground in
  seed grinder to medium fine
1 pound whole oats, ground in
  seed grinder to medium fine
1 pound wheat germ
½ pound whole bran, ground
  in seed grinder if coarse
1 pound yellow corn meal
  (optional)
To cook:
2½ cups water
  Sea salt to taste
  1 cup mixed cereal
  2 tablespoons rice polishings
  Raisins and milk or nut milk

1. Combine the rye, oats, wheat germ, bran and corn meal and mix well. Store in covered jars in refrigerator and use as needed. The mixture yields three and one-half pounds.

2. To cook cereal, heat the water to boiling. Add salt and one cup of the mixed cereal while beating vigorously. Bring to a boil and then set in a warm place (in a thermos bottle or on yogurt maker) until next morning. Reheat. Add rice polishings and serve with raisins and milk.

Yield: Two servings.

BREAKFAST RICE

1 cup raw brown rice
4 cups milk
1 cup raisins
Maple syrup

1. Grind the rice in an electric blender until kernels are half the original size. Combine rice with milk and raisins in a saucepan.

2. Bring to a boil, cover and simmer until rice is cooked, about 10 to 15 minutes. Serve with maple syrup.

Yield: Four servings.

CRACKED WHEAT CEREAL

1 cup whole wheat grains
4 cups water or milk
½ teaspoon sea salt
Cream and honey

1. Spread the wheat grains on a pan and place under broiler set at 400 degrees. Toast until grain smells toasted; do not allow to burn.

2. Grind the toasted grains in a coffee mill or Moulinex grinder and discard any floury residue.

3. Place one cup cracked toasted wheat in a saucepan with water or milk and the salt. Heat, stirring, until mixture boils. Reduce heat and cook slowly, stirring occasionally, until tender, about 40 minutes. Alternately, the mixture can be cooked in the top of a double boiler over boiling water for one hour.

4. Serve with cream and honey.

Yield: Four servings.

BARLEY PILAF

¼ cup oil, approximately
1 pound mushrooms, sliced
2 onions, sliced
1¾ cups whole hulled barley
1 quart boiling vegetable broth, chicken broth or beef broth (see pages 52, 53), approximately
3 tablespoons brewer's yeast
Sea salt to taste
2 tablespoons snipped fresh dill weed

1. Preheat the oven to 350 degrees.

2. Heat one-quarter cup oil in a heavy skillet and sauté the mushrooms in it five minutes. Remove mushrooms and set aside. Add onions to skillet and sauté until golden. Remove and set aside.

3. Add the barley to the skillet and cook, stirring, until all the grains are coated with oil, adding more oil if necessary.

4. Return mushrooms and onions to the skillet. Add one quart broth, the yeast, salt and dill. Mix and turn into an oiled casserole. Cover and bake 30 minutes, adding more broth if pilaf becomes too dry.

Yield: Six servings.

GARDEN STATE COUSCOUS

2 cups couscous
½ cup water
¼ cup butter
1 cup cubed carrots
1 cup diced celery
1 green pepper, seeded and
    cubed
1 cup 1-inch pieces green beans
1½ cups shredded red cabbage
1 cup tiny broccoli flowerets
1 cup fresh peas
Sea salt to taste
3 cups boiling vegetable broth
1 cup button mushrooms
2 cups cooked dried chick-peas
    or drained canned chick-peas

1. Spread the couscous on a baking sheet, sprinkle with the water and lightly mix with the fingers to moisten all grains.

2. Place grains in a muslin-lined colander over a pan of boiling water, or in a special couscous pot. Cover and steam 20 minutes. Stir grains; steam 20 minutes longer. Stir in butter.

3. Meanwhile, place carrots, celery, green pepper, beans, cabbage, broccoli and peas in a heavy saucepan. Add salt and pour broth over all. Cover and cook vegetables until barely crisp-tender, about 10 minutes. Add mushrooms and chick-peas and cook five minutes longer.

4. To serve, arrange the couscous in a large deep dish (a paella pan is ideal) and pile couscous into a conical shape. Arrange the drained vegetables around neatly and pour some vegetable broth over the couscous.

Yield: Six servings.

JERRY'S RICE

1½ cups raw brown rice, rinsed
    and drained
½ cup whole wheat berries,
    rinsed and drained
½ cup pine nuts
6 cups water
1 teaspoon sea salt

Place all ingredients in a heavy kettle. Bring to a boil, cover and let simmer gently one hour. Do not remove cover during cooking.

Yield: Four to six servings.

BROWN RICE
(METHOD I – BOILING)

1 cup raw brown rice, rinsed
and drained
2 to 3 cups water
Sea salt to taste

Place the rice, water and salt in a saucepan, bring to a boil, cover tightly and cook over low heat 45 minutes or until rice is tender and has absorbed the liquid. Do not stir during cooking. The larger amount of water will give a softer rice grain.

Yield: About four cups cooked rice.

BROWN RICE
(METHOD II – PRESSURE COOKING)

1 cup raw brown rice, rinsed
and drained
2 cups water
½ teaspoon sea salt

1. Place the rice, water and salt in a pressure cooker. Cover tightly. Place pressure regulator in place. Heat the pan until the regulator joggles evenly, or reaches 15 pounds pressure.

2. Reduce the heat to maintain the regulator just joggling gently and cook 40 minutes. Allow pan to cool by itself, about 20 minutes.

3. Remove the regulator when pressure has been reduced, open pan and serve rice.

Yield: About four cups cooked rice.

Note: Cooking for a shorter time, say 20 minutes, will give a firmer grain.

BROWN RICE
(METHOD III – BAKING)

1 cup raw brown rice, rinsed
and drained
2 to 3 cups water
Sea salt to taste
2 tablespoons butter

1. Preheat the oven to 350 degrees.

2. Place all ingredients in a casserole and bring to a boil on top of stove. Cover and bake 40 minutes.

Yield: About four cups cooked rice.

GREEN RICE

1 egg
1 cup milk
½ cup finely chopped parsley
1 small onion, finely chopped
2 cups cooked brown rice
  (see page 217)
½ cup grated Cheddar cheese
Vegetable salt to taste
2 teaspoons olive oil

1. Preheat the oven to 325 degrees.

2. Beat the egg lightly and gradually beat in the milk. Stir in remaining ingredients except the oil and mix well.

3. Place oil in a casserole. Turn the rice mixture into the casserole and bake 30 minutes or until set.

Yield: Four servings.

GLORY RICE

2 cups cooked brown rice
  (see page 217)
2 cups grated Cheddar cheese
½ teaspoon sea salt
2 cups milk
3 eggs, lightly beaten
3 tablespoons chopped parsley
¼ cup melted butter
1 onion, finely chopped
Blanched slivered almonds
Sunflower seed kernels

1. Preheat the oven to 350 degrees.

2. Combine all the ingredients except the almonds and sunflower seed kernels. Turn into an oiled casserole. Top with almonds. Bake 35 minutes or until set.

3. Garnish with sunflower seed kernels.

Yield: Four servings.

FRUIT AND RICE

3¾ cups chicken broth
  (see page 52)
2 cups raw brown rice, rinsed
  and drained
1 medium-size onion, chopped
3 carrots, sliced
1 cup whole dried apricots
1 teaspoon sea salt
¼ teaspoon saffron
½ cup whole unblanched
  almonds

1. In a large saucepan, heat the broth to boiling and add the rice, onion, carrots, apricots, salt and saffron.

2. Bring to a boil, cover and simmer gently 45 minutes or until rice is tender. Serve garnished with almonds.

Yield: Four to six servings.

Note: This can be served with curries, fowl and fish or as a luncheon main dish.

BROWN RICE WITH CHICKEN

4 tablespoons oil
1 cup raw brown rice, rinsed and drained
3 cups boiling chicken broth (see page 52)
2 ribs celery, chopped
2 onions, chopped
1 cup diced cooked chicken
1 tablespoon dry white wine (optional)
1 tablespoon finely ground unblanched almonds

1. Heat three tablespoons of the oil in a saucepan and add rice. Cook rice in oil until all grains are coated.

2. Add broth, cover and simmer gently until rice is almost tender, about 40 minutes.

3. Meanwhile, heat remaining oil and sauté the celery and onions in it until tender. Add to rice along with wine and almonds and cook five minutes longer.

Yield: Four servings.

BROWN RICE AND PUMPKIN SEED STUFFING

2 onions
3 ribs celery with leaves
Giblets from chicken or turkey
3 cups water
1 bay leaf
Sea salt to taste
2 tablespoons oil
1 cup raw brown rice
¼ cup pumpkin seeds
¼ cup chopped parsley
½ teaspoon sage
¼ teaspoon marjoram

1. Slice one onion and dice one rib celery. Place in a saucepan. Add giblets, water, bay leaf and salt. Bring to a boil, cover and simmer 45 minutes.

2. Remove giblets. Discard skin and bones and dice meat. Reserve.

3. Boil broth rapidly until two cups remain. Reserve.

4. Chop remaining onion. Heat the oil in a saucepan, add the chopped onion and sauté.

5. Add rice to saucepan and cook three minutes longer. Add reserved broth, bring to a boil, cover and simmer until rice has absorbed all the liquid, about 45 minutes.

6. Finely chop remaining celery and add with pumpkin seeds, parsley, sage, marjoram and the reserved meat. Season with salt. Use to stuff a five-pound chicken or turkey.

Yield: About one and one-half quarts.

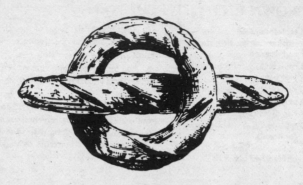

11

BREADS

This chapter is a collection of recipes for breads with different textures,
flavors and nutritive contributions to add variety and pleasure
to family meals, snacks and lunch boxes.

Try offering a child a slice of hot buttered bread straight from the
oven as an after-school snack. He could get to like the bread
better than store-bought cookies.

There are quick breads, leavened with baking powder and baking soda,
yeast breads and, for the really adventurous, a few unleavened loaves.
Most of the recipes call for whole grains, that is, the entire kernel ground
into flour so that nothing is lost. Stoneground grains are favored where
possible because the slow-moving stones generate less heat and cause less
damage than high-speed mills. Slow-moving stones
leave more flavor in the flour, too.

In their ability to absorb moisture, whole wheat flours vary tremendously,
depending on the strain of wheat, the area where it is grown and the
climatic conditions of storage and usage. Therefore, especially in yeast
mixtures, it is difficult to give exact amounts of liquid or flour needed.
Experience in dealing with doughs will tell you
how the dough should feel.

Wheat flour is the only grain with any appreciable amount of gluten. Gluten is the protein that forms the structure of the bread; it is developed by kneading. The quantity of gluten in unbleached white flour is greater than in whole wheat flour, and many recipes call for a combination of the two for that reason.

Other grains, such as corn, buckwheat, rye and oatmeal, are mixed with the wheat flours in the recipes. Hard wheats contain most gluten, with Deaf Smith County, Tex., wheat having up to 20 per cent gluten. A good bread flour should have at least 12 per cent. If stoneground whole wheat flour is sifted for a recipe, retain the bran siftings left in the sieve that contain all manner of good things to add to coarser breads, breakfast cereals and cooked hot puddings.

Enriched white flour is not used in the recipes. This is flour that has had roughly 16 elements removed in processing and four synthetic elements put back in. This flour is usually sold in a bleached form.

Fresh stoneground whole grains have not been fumigated and have a relatively short shelf-life. They should be bought in small quantities and stored in tightly closed containers in the refrigerator.

Most of the mixed-grain breads in this chapter are fortified with a variety of natural, nutritious additions such as soy flour, soy grits, raw wheat germ and brewer's yeast.

Yeast is the favored raising agent and is available as baker's compressed yeast, bulk dry active yeast and packaged dry active yeast. The latter contains BHA as a preservative. (One tablespoon dry active yeast = one 1½-ounce cake compressed yeast.)

Some natural foods purists eschew baking powder and baking soda completely as unnecessary synthetic chemicals, but for most people their use makes a wide selection of nourishing quick breads more palatable. Some groups consider Rumford brand (a phosphate-based powder) less obnoxious than regular double-acting or tartrate-type baking powders.

Whole grain breads tend to be heavier in texture, and you have to work harder, by kneading, to develop the gluten to get a good-textured loaf. Whole grain breads should not be allowed to over-rise, especially after shaping, and just prior to baking, or they will collapse later due to lack of structure.

There's as much art as science in bread making because you're dealing with living things, such as yeast, that need warmth and moisture and tender loving care.

BROWN RICE AND WHOLE WHEAT MUFFINS

1¼ cups whole wheat flour
2 teaspoons baking powder
½ teaspoon sea salt
2 tablespoons brown sugar or molasses
1 cup cold (not chilled) cooked brown rice (see page 217)
¼ cup butter, melted
2 eggs, lightly beaten
⅔ cup milk

1. Preheat the oven to 425 degrees.

2. In a bowl, combine the flour, baking powder, salt and brown sugar, if used, and mix well.

3. Add the rice, butter, eggs, milk and molasses, if used. Spoon mixture into oiled and floured muffin tins. Bake 15 to 20 minutes or until done.

Yield: One dozen medium-size muffins.

Note: The rice gives a crunchy texture to the muffins.

BRAN MUFFINS

2 cups stoneground whole wheat flour
1½ cups whole bran or ¾ cup whole bran and ¾ cup wheat germ
¾ teaspoon sea salt
1¼ teaspoons baking soda
2 tablespoons raw sugar
2 cups yogurt (see page 311)
1 egg, lightly beaten
½ cup honey, preferably a light honey such as clover
2 tablespoons soft butter
1 cup raisins

1. Preheat the oven to 425 degrees.

2. In a large bowl, combine the whole wheat flour, bran, salt, baking soda and sugar.

3. Beat together the yogurt, egg, honey and butter in a second bowl. Add dry ingredients and fold in with a few quick strokes. Fold in the raisins.

4. Fill oiled muffin tins two-thirds full. Bake 15 to 20 minutes or until done.

Yield: About two dozen two-inch muffins.

THREE-GRAIN MUFFINS

⅓ cup stoneground corn meal
⅓ cup raw sugar
⅓ cup soy flour
1 cup whole wheat flour
¾ teaspoon sea salt
1 teaspoon baking soda
1 large egg, lightly beaten
1 cup yogurt (see page 311)
⅓ cup butter, melted

1. Preheat the oven to 350 degrees.

2. In a bowl, combine the corn meal, sugar, soy flour, whole wheat flour, salt and baking soda.

3. Mix the egg and yogurt together lightly and stir into the dry ingredients. Stir in the butter.

4. Fill muffin tins two-thirds full and bake 25 minutes or until done.

Yield: One dozen muffins.

Note: These are noted as poor keepers because they are so good.

CORN MUFFINS

1½ cups corn meal
½ cup whole wheat flour
2 teaspoons aluminum-free baking powder (Rumford)
½ teaspoon sea salt
½ cup honey
½ cup molasses
1 egg, lightly beaten
1¼ cups cow's or goat's milk
¼ cup melted butter

1. Preheat the oven to 400 degrees.

2. Combine the corn meal, whole wheat flour, baking powder and salt in a bowl.

3. Add the honey, molasses, egg, milk and butter. Stir just enough to moisten ingredients (batter should be lumpy). Fill well oiled two-inch muffin tins two-thirds full. Bake 20 to 25 minutes.

Yield: Twelve muffins.

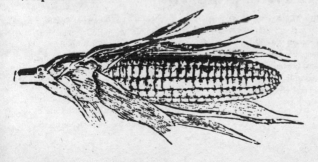

WHEAT GERM MUFFINS

1 egg, well beaten
⅓ cup raw sugar
1¼ cups milk
⅓ cup melted butter
1 cup unbleached white flour
½ teaspoon sea salt
4 teaspoons baking powder
1 cup wheat germ

1. Preheat the oven to 425 degrees.

2. Beat together the egg, sugar, milk and butter.

3. Sift together the flour, salt and baking powder and mix into the egg mixture. Stir in the wheat germ lightly.

4. Fill muffin cups two-thirds full and bake 20 minutes or until done.

Yield: About sixteen muffins.

BUCKWHEAT-CORN MUFFINS

1 cup buckwheat flour
½ cup corn meal
2½ teaspoons baking powder
½ teaspoon sea salt
1 to 2 tablespoons brown sugar
2 eggs
1¼ cups milk
¼ cup butter, melted

1. Preheat the oven to 400 degrees.

2. Mix together the buckwheat flour, corn meal, baking powder, salt and sugar.

3. Combine the eggs, milk and butter and stir into the dry ingredients until just moistened (batter will be thin).

4. Fill muffin tins two-thirds full and bake 15 to 20 minutes or until done.

Yield: One dozen muffins.

WHOLE WHEAT MUFFINS

3 cups whole wheat flour
⅓ cup brown sugar or raw sugar
1 teaspoon sea salt
4½ teaspoons baking powder
2 eggs, beaten
1⅓ cups milk
⅓ cup melted butter

1. Preheat the oven to 375 degrees.

2. Sift whole wheat flour, sugar, salt and baking powder into a bowl.

3. Combine the eggs, milk and melted butter and stir into the dry ingredients until they are just moistened.

4. Fill oiled muffin tins two-thirds full and bake 20 minutes, or until done.

Yield: Eighteen medium-size muffins.

SUNFLOWER MUFFINS

3 eggs, separated
2 tablespoons soy oil
2 tablespoons honey
½ cup shredded unsweetened
   coconut
¼ cup wheat germ
1 cup sunflower seed meal
½ cup rice polishings
½ teaspoon sea salt
1 cup raisins
½ cup apple juice

1. Preheat the oven to 350 degrees.

2. Beat the egg yolks lightly and mix with remaining ingredients except for egg whites. Beat the egg whites until stiff but not dry. Fold into the batter.

3. Fill oiled muffin tins two-thirds full and bake 25 to 30 minutes.

Yield: About one dozen medium-size muffins.

Note: No baking powder or other leavening is necessary in this recipe. The muffins are chewy and quite heavy textured.

PEANUT BUTTER-APRICOT MUFFINS

½ cup stoneground whole
   wheat flour
¼ cup unbleached white flour
1 tablespoon wheat germ
¼ teaspoon sea salt
½ teaspoon baking soda
3 tablespoons natural peanut
   butter with defatted
   wheat germ
1 tablespoon butter
½ cup unsulphured dried apricots
Boiling water
2 tablespoons blackstrap
   molasses
1 egg
½ cup buttermilk
1 tablespoon raw sugar
⅛ teaspoon cinnamon

1. Preheat the oven to 400 degrees.

2. In a bowl, mix together the whole wheat flour, unbleached flour, wheat germ, salt and baking soda.

3. With two knives, cut in the peanut butter and the butter until well distributed.

4. Pour boiling water over apricots. Let stand three minutes. Drain apricots and dice finely using scissors. Add to peanut butter mixture.

5. Combine the molasses, egg and buttermilk and add all at once to peanut butter mixture. Stir only until dry ingredients are moistened.

6. Spoon mixture into eight oiled 2½-inch muffin tins. Combine sugar and cinnamon and sprinkle over muffins. Bake 15 minutes or until done.

Yield: Eight muffins.

BLUEBERRY MUFFINS

4 cups whole wheat flour
1 teaspoon sea salt
⅓ cup raw sugar
1 tablespoon baking powder
1 tablespoon brewer's yeast
1 cup milk, approximately
¼ cup soy oil
2 eggs, lightly beaten
1 cup blueberries

1. Preheat the oven to 400 degrees.

2. In a mixing bowl, combine the flour, salt, sugar, baking powder and yeast. Stir in enough milk to make a stiff dough.

3. Stir in the oil, eggs and blueberries. Spoon into oiled muffin tins so that they are two-thirds full. Bake 30 minutes or until done.

Yield: About three dozen two-inch muffins.

BANANA OATMEAL MUFFINS

1 cup quick-cooking oats
1 cup unbleached white flour
1 teaspoon sea salt
2 tablespoons brown sugar
2 eggs, separated, at room temperature
½ cup milk, scalded
⅓ cup oil
1 teaspoon vanilla
1 small banana, mashed

1. Preheat the oven to 375 degrees.

2. Combine the oats, flour, salt and sugar in a bowl.

3. Lightly beat the egg yolks and stir in the hot milk. Beat until very light and thick. Beat in the oil, vanilla and mashed banana. Sprinkle the dry ingredients over the yolk mixture and fold in gently.

4. Beat the egg whites until stiff but not dry and fold into batter. Spoon into oiled muffin tins until they are two-thirds full.

5. Bake 30 minutes or until golden and done. Cool on a rack.

Yield: About twenty muffins.

SPICY APPLE-CARROT MUFFINS

½ cup non-instant dry milk solids

3 teaspoons baking powder

½ teaspoon sea salt

½ teaspoon allspice

½ teaspoon nutmeg

1 teaspoon cinnamon

2½ cups stoneground whole wheat flour

1 cup honey

1 cup safflower or other oil

4 eggs

1 teaspoon vanilla

1 cup grated unpeeled apple

1 cup grated carrot

1. Preheat the oven to 400 degrees.

2. In a large bowl, combine the milk solids, baking powder, salt, allspice, nutmeg, cinnamon and flour.

3. Combine the honey, oil and eggs and stir into dry ingredients. Fold in the apple and carrot. Spoon into oiled muffin tins.

4. Bake 15 to 20 minutes or until done.

Yield: About two dozen medium-size muffins.

YOGURT MUFFINS

2 eggs, lightly beaten

1 cup yogurt (see page 311)

2 tablespoons oil

¼ cup molasses

1½ cups whole wheat flour

2 tablespoons soy flour

1 teaspoon sea salt

¼ cup raisins

¼ cup chopped nuts

1. Preheat the oven to 375 degrees.

2. Combine the eggs and yogurt. Beat in the oil and molasses. Sift together the whole wheat flour, soy flour and salt.

3. Add the egg mixture to the dry ingredients and stir until just moistened. Stir in the raisins and nuts.

4. Fill oiled muffin tins two-thirds full. Bake 20 minutes or until done.

Yield: One dozen muffins.

Note: These muffins have no raising agent and will be compact in texture.

BARLEY FLOUR DROP BISCUITS

1 cup barley flour
¼ teaspoon sea salt
2 teaspoons baking powder
2 tablespoons butter
⅓ to ½ cup buttermilk
1 egg

1. Preheat the oven to 425 degrees.

2. Sift the barley flour, salt and baking powder into a bowl.

3. With a pastry blender or two knives, cut the butter into the dry ingredients.

4. With fork, beat one-third cup buttermilk and the egg together and stir into the flour mixture just to moisten. If necessary, add a little more milk. Dough should be soft but firm enough to hold its shape when dropped from a spoon onto an oiled baking sheet.

5. Bake 12 to 15 minutes or until done.

Yield: Ten to twelve small biscuits.

"DEAF SMITH" WHEAT BISCUITS

2 cups sifted whole wheat flour (Deaf Smith County Flour)
4 teaspoons baking powder
½ teaspoon sea salt
¼ cup oil
¾ to 1 cup milk

1. Preheat the oven to 450 degrees.

2. Mix together the flour, baking powder and salt and sift into a bowl. Add the oil and mix very well. (This will take several minutes, and complete mixing of the oil into the dry ingredients is crucial.)

3. Stir in enough milk to make a soft dough that is not sticky. Mix just enough to moisten dry ingredients.

4. With the hands, or a rolling pin, pat out the mixture to three-quarter-inch thickness on a floured board. Cut with a two-inch biscuit cutter. Place on an oiled baking sheet and bake 20 minutes or until done.

Yield: About eighteen biscuits.

Note: Deaf Smith County, Tex., has some of the most fertile soil and best farming country in the nation. Much of the produce is organically grown.

WHOLE WHEAT POPOVERS

3 eggs
1½ cups milk
1 cup sifted stoneground whole wheat flour
¾ teaspoon sea salt
3 tablespoons melted butter

1. Preheat the oven to 475 degrees.

2. Place eggs, milk, sifted flour and salt in an electric blender and blend for one-half minute or, if using an electric mixer, beat at high speed one minute.

3. Stir in the melted butter.

4. Place one teaspoon of oil in the bottom of eight iron popover forms or six large muffin tins. Heat two minutes in the oven.

5. Fill forms, or tins, three-quarters full and bake 15 minutes. Lower oven heat to 350 degrees and bake 25 minutes longer. For drier popovers, prick each one, turn oven off and let them stand in the hot oven five minutes longer. Serve hot.

Yield: Six to eight popovers.

Note: Rye popovers can be made by substituting one-half cup rye flour and one-half cup unbleached white flour for the whole wheat flour.

WHEAT GERM WAFERS

½ cup unbleached white flour
2 teaspoons baking powder
½ teaspoon sea salt
1 teaspoon raw sugar
¾ cup wheat germ
2 tablespoons firm butter
¼ cup ice water

1. Preheat the oven to 350 degrees.

2. Sift the flour, baking powder and salt into a bowl. Add sugar and one-half cup of the wheat germ. With two knives, cut in the butter until it is well distributed.

3. Stir in water quickly but gently. Gather dough into a ball and place on a floured board. Roll to one-half-inch thickness, sprinkle with remaining wheat germ and continue to roll until dough is wafer thin.

4. Cut with a two-inch cutter. Place on ungreased baking sheet. Bake 15 minutes or until done.

Yield: About eighteen wafers.

QUICK HEALTH BREAD

1¾ cups milk
2 cups whole bran
1¼ cups whole wheat flour
¼ cup soy flour
¼ cup flax seed meal
½ teaspoon kelp or vegetable salt
2 teaspoons baking powder
1 tablespoon wheat germ
3 eggs, well beaten
⅓ cup unsulphured molasses
1 cup monukka raisins
1 cup chopped pecans

1. Preheat the oven to 350 degrees.

2. Pour the milk over the bran and let stand 10 minutes.

3. Sift together the whole wheat flour, soy flour, flax seed meal, kelp and baking powder. Add wheat germ.

4. Add eggs to bran-milk mixture and stir into the dry ingredients. Stir in the molasses and mix well. Stir in the raisins and nuts.

5. Pour into two well-oiled 8½-by-4½-inch loaf pans.

6. Bake about 45 minutes or until done.
Yield: Two small loaves.

CORN BREAD

1¾ cups stoneground yellow corn meal
¼ cup stoneground whole wheat flour
¼ cup non-instant dry milk solids
3 teaspoons baking powder
1 teaspoon sea salt
1 egg, lightly beaten
1 tablespoon honey or dark brown sugar
2 tablespoons oil
1½ cups milk

1. Preheat the oven to 425 degrees.

2. In a bowl, combine the corn meal, flour, milk powder, baking powder and salt.

3. Add remaining ingredients and stir just enough to moisten. Turn into an oiled eight-inch square baking pan. Bake 20 to 25 minutes or until done. Serve hot.
Yield: Six servings.

MEXICAN CORN BREAD

1 cup stoneground whole wheat
  flour
1 cup stoneground yellow corn
  meal
4 teaspoons baking powder
½ teaspoon sea salt
½ teaspoon chili powder
¼ cup non-instant dry milk solids
¼ cup honey
2 eggs, lightly beaten
½ cup oil
½ cup milk
¼ cup finely chopped onion
2 tablespoons chopped pimento
¼ cup diced green pepper
2 tablespoons chopped jalapeña
  chili peppers

1. Preheat the oven to 425 degrees.

2. In a bowl, combine the flour, corn meal, baking powder, salt, chili powder and powdered milk.

3. Add remaining ingredients and mix just enough to moisten.

4. Turn into an oiled eight-inch square baking pan and bake about 20 minutes or until done.

Yield: Six servings.

SPOON BREAD

3 cups milk
1 cup stoneground yellow corn
  meal
1 teaspoon sea salt
1 teaspoon baking powder
1 tablespoon raw sugar
2 tablespoons oil
3 eggs, separated

1. Preheat the oven to 350 degrees.

2. Heat two cups of the milk in a saucepan. When milk begins to simmer, add the corn meal and continue to cook, stirring until mixture is thick.

3. Remove from the heat and add salt, baking powder, sugar, oil and remaining cup of milk. Beat the egg yolks lightly and add to corn meal mixture.

4. Beat the egg whites until stiff but not dry and fold into corn meal mixture. Turn into a buttered two-quart souffle dish and bake one hour or until well puffed and brown on top.

5. Serve by the spoonful directly from the dish and top with butter.

Yield: Six to eight servings.

LOGAN BREAD

(This is a bread developed for numerous Canadian ascents on Mount Logan. A 2-by-2-inch square will sustain a man for a day, according to Malcolm "Tink" Taylor, Holderness, N.H.)

    1 quart water
    4 pounds whole wheat flour
1½ pounds raw sugar or brown sugar
  12 ounces non-fat dry milk solids
    2 tablespoons baking powder
    2 tablespoons sea salt
    2 cups honey
    1 cup blackstrap molasses
1¼ cups oil
    1 cup sesame seeds
1½ cups wheat germ

1. Preheat the oven to 300 degrees.
2. Mix all the ingredients together very well and turn into a greased roasting pan. Bake one hour. Cut into squares and then allow to air-dry until squares are semi-dry.

Yield: Enough to sustain two men 16 days.

HONEY DATE LOAF

    2 tablespoons butter
  ½ cup honey
    1 egg
    1 teaspoon grated lemon rind
    2 teaspoons lemon juice
1½ cups unbleached white flour
  ¼ teaspoon sea salt
  ⅛ teaspoon baking soda
    1 teaspoon baking powder
  ½ cup buttermilk
    1 cup chopped dates
  ½ cup chopped walnuts

1. Preheat the oven to 350 degrees.
2. Cream the butter and gradually beat in the honey. Beat in the egg, lemon rind and lemon juice.
3. Combine the flour, salt, baking soda and baking powder and add alternately with the buttermilk to the batter. Fold in the dates and walnuts.
4. Turn the mixture into an oiled 9-by-5-by-3-inch loaf pan.
5. Bake 50 to 60 minutes or until done.

Yield: One loaf.

FRUITY AND NUTTY TEA LOAF

½ cup fresh blueberries
1½ cups unbleached white flour
  or whole wheat flour
⅔ cup raw sugar
2¼ teaspoons baking powder
½ teaspoon sea salt
½ cup oatmeal
  2 eggs, lightly beaten
⅓ cup soft butter
  1 cup mashed ripe bananas
½ cup chopped pecans
¼ cup raisins

1. Preheat the oven to 350 degrees.

2. Sprinkle the blueberries with two tablespoons flour.

3. Sift together remaining flour, sugar, baking powder and salt. Stir in the oatmeal.

4. Blend together the eggs, butter and bananas. Add to dry ingredients, stirring until combined. Add pecans, raisins and blueberries gradually and stir only enough to distribute them evenly through the batter.

5. Pour the batter into an oiled and floured 8½-by-4½-inch loaf pan. Bake one hour. Allow loaf to cool in the pan 15 minutes. Remove from pan gently and cool completely. Wrap cooled loaf in aluminum foil and store overnight before slicing.

Yield: One loaf.

NUT BUTTER LOAF

  2 cups unbleached white flour
  4 teaspoons baking powder
  1 teaspoon sea salt
  1 tablespoon wheat germ
¼ cup raw sugar or
  ⅛ cup honey
⅔ cup natural non-homogenized
  nut butter (cashew, peanut or
  almond)
1¼ cups milk or yogurt
  (see page 311)
  honey butter (see page 307)

1. Preheat the oven to 350 degrees.

2. Sift together the flour, baking powder and salt. Add wheat germ and sugar, if used.

3. Combine the honey, if used, with the nut butter and the milk or yogurt until thoroughly blended. Add to dry ingredients and mix well. Turn soft mixture into an oiled 8½-by-4½-inch loaf pan. Bake 50 minutes or until done. Remove from the pan and cool.

4. Wrap in moisture-proof wrapper and store one day before slicing. Serve with honey butter.

Yield: One loaf.

FAT-FREE DATE BRAN BREAD

¾ pound dates, diced
2 cups boiling water
2 large eggs, at room temperature
¾ cup raw sugar
1½ cups whole wheat flour
2 teaspoons baking powder
1 teaspoon baking soda
2 cups unbleached white flour
1 teaspoon vanilla
2 cups whole bran
1 cup chopped nuts
¼ teaspoon sea salt

1. Place the dates in a bowl. Pour the boiling water over dates and let cool.

2. Preheat the oven to 350 degrees.

3. Beat the eggs until very light and thick. Gradually beat in the sugar until mixture makes a rope when dropped from the beaters.

4. Sift together the whole wheat flour, baking powder and baking soda.

5. Fold one cup of the whole wheat flour mixture into the egg mixture. Fold in half the dates, half the soaking water, white flour and vanilla.

6. Stir in remaining whole wheat flour mixture, remaining dates and water, the bran, nuts and salt. Turn mixture into a 10-inch tube pan with bottom buttered and floured. Bake 50 minutes or until done. Cool in pan 20 minutes before turning out.

Yield: Twelve to sixteen servings.

Note: This is a very solid-textured bread.

ORANGE-NUT BREAD

3 cups whole wheat flour
1 cup wheat germ
⅔ cup non-fat dry milk solids
2½ cups milk or yogurt (see page 311)
1 cup blackstrap molasses
⅓ cup vegetable oil
2 cups chopped walnuts
4 teaspoons cinnamon
1 teaspoon kelp
4 teaspoons baking powder
Orange skin of two oranges, removed with a potato peeler and finely chopped

1. Preheat the oven to 350 degrees.

2. Combine all the ingredients in a large bowl and mix well.

3. Spoon dough into three buttered and brown paper-lined 3-by-7-inch loaf pans. Press down well into the corners. Bake 45 minutes or until done.

Yield: Three small loaves.

WHOLE WHEAT BANANA BREAD

½ cup butter
¾ cup brown sugar or raw sugar
1 egg
1 cup unsifted stoneground whole wheat flour
½ cup unsifted unbleached white flour
1 teaspoon baking soda
¾ teaspoon sea salt
1¼ cups mashed ripe bananas (two large or three small)
¼ cup buttermilk or yogurt (see page 311)

1. Preheat the oven to 350 degrees.

2. Cream the butter and sugar together until very light and creamy. Beat in the egg.

3. Sift together the whole wheat flour, white flour, baking soda and salt. Combine the bananas and buttermilk, stirring just enough to mix.

4. Add dry ingredients alternately with banana mixture to butter mixture, stirring just enough to combine well.

5. Turn into an oiled 9-by-5-inch loaf pan.

6. Bake 50 to 60 minutes or until done. Cool in the pan 10 minutes. Remove from the pan and finish cooling on a rack.

Yield: One loaf.

PUMPKIN BREAD

1 cup honey
1 cup brown sugar
1 cup oil
3 cups pumpkin puree
1 cup chopped dates
1 cup chopped walnuts
1 teaspoon sea salt
1 teaspoon cinnamon
1 teaspoon ground cloves
4 teaspoons baking soda
2 cups unbleached white flour
2½ cups whole wheat flour
½ cup wheat germ

1. Preheat the oven to 350 degrees.

2. Combine the honey, brown sugar, oil, pumpkin, dates, walnuts, salt, cinnamon, cloves and baking soda in a large bowl. Mix well.

3. Stir in the remaining ingredients.

4. Spoon the mixture into three well-oiled 8½-by-4½-inch loaf pans and bake one hour or until done. Cool in the pan 20 minutes before turning onto a rack to finish cooling.

Yield: Three loaves.

STEAMED DATE-NUT LOAF

½ cup whole wheat flour
½ cup stoneground yellow corn meal
¼ cup wheat germ
1 tablespoon brewer's yeast
2 tablespoons Familia or Crunchy Granola or Honey-Almond Crunch
2 tablespoons sesame seeds
½ teaspoon sea salt
½ teaspoon baking soda
½ teaspoon baking powder
½ teaspoon vanilla
½ cup buttermilk
1 egg, lightly beaten
¼ cup blackstrap molasses
¼ cup honey
¼ cup chopped almonds
½ cup chopped pitted dates
¼ cup raisins

1. Combine all the ingredients in a large bowl and mix well.

2. Pour mixture into a one-pound coffee tin or one-quart pudding mold that has been lightly greased with safflower oil. Cover tin with aluminum foil and secure tightly. Place plastic cover over foil to keep it in place.

3. Place the tin on a rack in a large kettle of boiling water so that the water extends halfway up the tin. Cover the kettle.

4. Keep the kettle of water simmering for three and one-half hours, maintaining the level of boiling water by replenishing as needed. The bread is done when it is firm to the touch on the top surface.

5. Remove from the tin and serve warm or cool on a rack. The bread will keep in the refrigerator two weeks and can be mailed. Yield: One loaf.

PARKER HOUSE ROLLS

2 cups soy milk, lukewarm
1 tablespoon dry active yeast
Oil
⅓ cup honey
2 teaspoons sea salt
4 cups whole wheat pastry flour
2 cups unbleached white flour,
   approximately

1. Combine the soy milk and yeast and set aside for five minutes. Stir to dissolve yeast. Add one-third cup oil, the honey and salt.

2. Stir in the whole wheat flour and enough of the unbleached flour to make a soft dough. Mix well.

3. Turn onto a floured board and knead until the dough is smooth and elastic, about 10 minutes.

4. Place dough in a clean buttered bowl, cover and let rise until doubled in bulk, about one and one-half hours.

5. Punch down. Roll dough out to one-third-inch thickness and cut into 2½-inch rounds. Brush rounds with oil and fold in half so that upper half extends beyond lower half. Press edges together lightly.

6. Place rolls in rows on an oiled baking sheet or jellyroll pan. Cover and let rise in a warm place until doubled in bulk, about 35 minutes.

7. Preheat the oven to 350 degrees.

8. Bake 35 minutes or until done.

Yield: About four dozen rolls.

BUTTERMILK ROLLS

2 cakes compressed yeast or 2
tablespoons dry active yeast
¼ cup honey
1½ cups buttermilk, heated to
lukewarm
½ cup melted butter
5 cups unbleached white flour,
approximately
1 teaspoon baking soda
1 teaspoon sea salt

1. Crumble the compressed yeast and
place it, or the dry yeast, in a bowl. Add
the honey and, while stirring, pour in the
buttermilk. Continue to stir until yeast is
dissolved.

2. Stir in the melted butter.

3. Mix in two cups of the flour, the baking
soda and salt. Beat well, cover and set in a
warm place until mixture rises about two
inches up the bowl, about 25 minutes.

4. Stir down and add enough of the
remaining flour to make a soft dough. Beat
well. Cover and let rise in a warm place
until nearly doubled in bulk, about 30
minutes. Punch down.

5. Divide the dough into 24 pieces and
form each piece into a ball. Place one inch
apart in oiled layer pans or on baking
sheets.

6. Cover and let rise until doubled in bulk,
about 10 minutes.

7. Preheat the oven to 400 degrees.

8. Bake the rolls about 20 minutes or until
golden brown.

Yield: Two dozen rolls.

PERFECT PECAN ROLLS

2 cups soy milk, heated to
  lukewarm
1 tablespoon dry active yeast
½ cup honey
⅓ cup plus 3 tablespoons oil
2 teaspoons grated orange rind
2 teaspoons sea salt
1 cup monukka raisins
3 cups whole wheat flour
¼ cup soy flour
3 cups unbleached white flour,
  approximately
½ cup date sugar
1 teaspoon ground coriander
1½ cups chopped pecans
½ cup melted butter
½ cup raw sugar or brown sugar

1. Place the soy milk in a bowl and add the yeast, honey and one-third cup oil. Stir until the yeast dissolves.

2. Add the orange rind, salt, raisins, whole wheat flour, soy flour and enough unbleached flour to make a dough that is sticky but can be kneaded.

3. Turn out onto a floured board and knead until smooth and elastic. Place dough in an oiled bowl, turn to oil top, cover and let rise in a warm place until doubled in size.

4. Punch down. Divide into two pieces. Roll each piece into a rectangle about 12-by-6 inches. Brush with remaining oil. Sprinkle with date sugar and coriander. Sprinkle each rectangle with one-half cup of the pecans.

5. Roll each rectangle like a jellyroll and cut into about 15 slices. Butter generously three nine-inch layer pans or 30 large muffin tins. Sprinkle with raw sugar or brown sugar and the remaining pecans.

6. Place rolls, cut side down, one-half inch apart in pans, or in muffin tins. Cover and let rise until doubled in bulk.

7. Preheat the oven to 375 degrees.

8. Bake 25 to 35 minutes or until rolls are done. Immediately turn upside down onto serving dish. Serve warm.

Yield: About thirty rolls.

HONEY WHOLE WHEAT ROLLS

2 tablespoons dry active yeast
½ cup lukewarm water
1 tablespoon raw sugar
⅓ cup sweet butter
⅓ cup honey
2 tablespoons sea salt
1 cup boiling water
1⅔ cups cold water
3 cups whole wheat flour
2 cups oatmeal
4 cups unbleached white flour, approximately
1 teaspoon ground cardamom

1. In a cup, combine the yeast, lukewarm water and sugar. Set in a warm place until mixture starts to bubble.

2. In a large bowl, place the butter, honey and salt. Pour the boiling water over and stir to melt the butter. Pour in the cold water and stir in the yeast mixture which has started to bubble.

3. Stir in the whole wheat flour, oatmeal and enough of the white flour to make a fairly stiff dough. Work in the cardamom.

4. Turn dough onto a lightly floured board and knead until dough is smooth and satiny and all traces of stickiness are gone.

5. Place the dough in a clean buttered bowl; turn to butter top of dough. Cover and set in a warm place until doubled in bulk, about one and one-half hours.

6. Punch down and turn onto the floured board. Pull off pieces of dough the size of a large plum. Roll each piece into a rope one-quarter inch in diameter. Knot the rope and place on an oiled baking sheet two inches apart. Repeat until all the dough is used.

7. Cover and set in a warm place to rise until doubled in bulk, about 30 minutes.

8. Preheat the oven to 375 degrees.

9. Bake rolls 30 minutes or until golden and done. Cool on racks.

Yield: Three dozen rolls.

HAMBURGER ROLLS

2 tablespoons dry active yeast
½ cup lukewarm water
1 tablespoon honey
1 cup milk, scalded and cooled to
    lukewarm
⅓ cup oil
⅓ cup raw sugar
2 teaspoons sea salt
2 eggs, well beaten
4 to 4½ cups unsifted whole
    wheat flour

1. Mix together the yeast, water and honey in a large bowl and set in a warm place while assembling rest of ingredients.

2. Combine the milk, oil, sugar and salt. Stir into the yeast mixture. Beat in the eggs and enough flour to make a soft, somewhat sticky dough. Mix well in the bowl. Cover and refrigerate overnight.

3. Two hours before serving time, remove dough from the refrigerator and let stand at room temperature 30 minutes. Turn onto a lightly floured board and knead well.

4. Pinch off pieces of dough about the size of a large egg and flatten into a hamburger bun shape. Place on lightly oiled baking sheets, cover and let rise until doubled in bulk, about 30 minutes.

5. Preheat the oven to 375 degrees.

6. Bake the rolls 15 to 20 minutes or until lightly browned. Cool on a rack.

Yield: About two dozen hamburger buns.

Note: This mixture can be shaped into hot dog rolls or Parker House and clover leaf rolls.

CURRANT BUNS

½ cup apple juice, heated to just
  below simmering point
1 cake compressed yeast or
  1 tablespoon dry active yeast
¼ cup honey
¼ cup oil
1 cup oatmeal
2 eggs
4 cups whole wheat flour
2 cups unbleached white flour,
  approximately
½ teaspoon sea salt
1 cup currants
Milk

1. Cool the apple juice to lukewarm and
stir in the yeast.

2. In a large bowl, mix together the honey
and oil. Stir in the yeast mixture and add
the oatmeal. Mix thoroughly.

3. Beat in the eggs and let mixture rest
10 minutes.

4. Slowly add the whole wheat flour,
stirring vigorously. Then, work in enough
of the unbleached flour to make a dough
that leaves the sides of the bowl clean.

5. Knead in the sea salt and the currants
and continue to knead either in the bowl
or on a floured board until dough becomes
smooth and elastic, about 10 minutes.

6. Place dough in a clean oiled bowl, turn
to oil top, cover with a damp towel and let
rise in a warm place until dough doubles in
bulk, about one hour.

7. Punch dough down and let rise to double
its size again, about 30 minutes.

8. Divide the dough into 12 balls and
place them on two oiled large heavy
baking sheets. With a sharp knife, slash a
superficial X on the top of each ball. Cover
and let rise in a warm place until doubled
in bulk.

9. Preheat the oven to 350 degrees. Place
a pan of water on the bottom of the oven.

10. Bake 40 minutes or until buns sound
hollow when tapped on the bottom.
Remove to a rack; brush with milk. Cool
under a damp cloth.

Yield: One dozen buns.

WHOLE WHEAT COFFEECAKE DOUGH

Basic Dough:
    2 tablespoons dry active yeast
    ½ cup lukewarm water
    ½ cup plus 1 teaspoon raw
       sugar or brown sugar
    2 eggs, lightly beaten
    1 teaspoon sea salt
    ½ cup melted butter
    1 teaspoon grated lemon rind
    ½ cup evaporated milk
    ½ cup hot water
    3½ to 4 cups sifted whole wheat
       flour

1. In a small bowl, mix together the yeast, warm water and one teaspoon of the sugar.

2. In a large bowl, combine the eggs, remaining sugar, the salt, butter, lemon rind, milk and hot water and mix well. Stir in the yeast mixture.

3. Add enough of the flour to make a soft dough. Beat well. Cover and let rise 15 minutes. Turn onto a floured board and knead until dough is smooth and satiny, about 10 minutes.

4. Place in a buttered bowl, turn to butter top, cover and let rise until more than doubled in bulk, about one hour.

5. Punch down; now the dough is ready to shape and flavor according to your whim.

Yield: Enough dough for two coffeecakes.

For Coffeecake Twist:
    1 recipe basic dough as above
    ⅔ cup plus 1 tablespoon soft
       butter
    ½ cup brown sugar
    1½ teaspoons cinnamon
    2 tablespoons raw sugar
    ¼ cup honey
       Slivered almonds

1. Cover the punched-down dough with a towel and let rest five minutes.

2. Divide dough in half and roll out each half into a rectangle 9-by-12 inches. Brush each half with the one-third cup butter. Combine the brown sugar and cinnamon and sprinkle half over the first rectangle.

3. Roll like a jellyroll and place in form of a crescent ring with ends pinched together, or twisted into a knot, on a buttered baking sheet. Repeat with second half of dough.

4. Cover and let rise until doubled in bulk, about one hour.

5. Preheat the oven to 350 degrees.

6. Bake 20 to 30 minutes. Watch carefully because the coffeecakes burn easily.

7. Meanwhile, place the remaining butter, the raw sugar and honey in a small saucepan and bring to a boil, stirring.

8. Brush hot glaze over hot coffeecakes and sprinkle with almonds. Cool on a rack.

Yield: Two coffeecakes.

BAGELS

8 cups whole wheat flour
1 tablespoon sea salt
2 cakes compressed yeast
2 cups lukewarm potato water
  (see note)
⅓ cup honey
¼ cup oil
4 eggs, lightly beaten
2 tablespoons raw sugar
2 quarts boiling water

1. Sift flour and salt into a bowl. Soften yeast in one-third of the potato water and stir into flour.

2. Add honey and oil to remaining potato water and stir into flour mixture. Add eggs and beat to form a dough.

3. Turn onto a lightly floured board and knead for 10 minutes. The dough should be quite firm. Add more flour if necessary.

4. Return dough to clean buttered bowl, cover and let rise at room temperature until doubled in bulk, about one and one-half to two hours.

5. Preheat the oven to 450 degrees.

6. Knead dough again until smooth and elastic.

7. Pinch off pieces of dough and roll into ropes six inches long and three-quarters inch wide.

8. Bring the ends of the dough together and pinch to form doughnut shape.

9. Drop raw sugar into kettle of boiling water. Drop bagels into the water one at a time and when they come to the surface turn them over. Boil one minute longer.

10. Place bagels on oiled cookie sheet and bake 10 to 15 minutes or until golden brown and crisp.

Yield: About thirty bagels.

Note: Potato water is made by boiling peeled diced potatoes in excess water until they are tender. Drain and use liquid.

CARAWAY PUFFS

1 tablespoon dry active yeast
1⅓ cups whole wheat flour
2 teaspoons caraway seeds
1 cup cream-style cottage cheese (the contributor uses her own hoop cheese mixed with cream)
¼ cup water
2 tablespoons honey
1 tablespoon butter
1 teaspoon sea salt
1 egg
2 teaspoons chopped onion
1 cup unbleached white flour

1. In the large bowl of an electric mixer, combine the yeast, whole wheat flour and caraway seeds. In an electric blender, combine the cottage cheese, water, honey, butter, salt, egg and onion. Blend until smooth.

2. Add blended ingredients to dry ingredients and beat at low speed one-half minute. Beat three minutes longer at high speed. Stir in unbleached white flour.

3. Place the dough in a clean buttered bowl, cover and let rise until doubled in bulk, about one and one-half hours.

4. Divide the dough among 12 well-buttered large muffin tins. The tins should be about half full. Cover and let rise until doubled in bulk.

5. Preheat the oven to 400 degrees.

6. Bake 12 to 15 minutes. Serve hot.

Yield: One dozen large muffins.

Note: The muffins can be frozen and reheated.

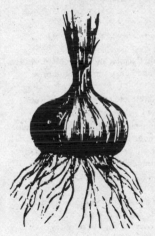

PIZZA DOUGH

1½ teaspoons dry active yeast
½ cup lukewarm water
1½ cups unbleached white flour,
   or a combination of rye,
   barley and buckwheat flours
1 tablespoon oil

1. Dissolve the yeast in the warm water.

2. Stir in the flour and the oil. Knead the dough on a lightly floured board until smooth and satiny, about three minutes.

3. Place dough in a clean buttered bowl, turn to butter top, cover and let rise in a warm place until doubled in bulk, about 40 minutes.

4. Preheat oven to 400 degrees.

5. Spread the dough over well-oiled 12-inch to 14-inch pizza pan. Bake eight to 10 minutes and then crust is ready for the topping of your choice and three to five minutes further baking.

Yield: Six servings.

SUGARLESS DOUGHNUTS

½ cup milk
½ cup sour cream
2 tablespoons butter
2 teaspoons honey
1 cake compressed yeast
3 egg yolks
½ teaspoon sea salt
1 teaspoon cinnamon
Grated rind of one lemon
2 cups whole wheat flour
½ cup unbleached white flour
Oil for deep-frying

1. Scald the milk and sour cream. Add butter and honey and let stand until lukewarm.

2. Crumble and stir in the yeast until dissolved. Add egg yolks and salt.

3. Beat in cinnamon, lemon rind, whole wheat flour and unbleached white flour. Dough will be soft. It can be placed in refrigerator and punched down when necessary or left at room temperature until light.

4. Roll dough to one-half-inch thickness. Cut with doughnut cutter and set on board, covered, for five minutes.

5. Fry, a few at a time, until golden, in oil heated to 375 degrees. Drain on paper towels and serve warm.

Yield: About eighteen doughnuts.

YEAST-RAISED WHOLE WHEAT DOUGHNUTS

2 tablespoons dry active yeast
1½ cups lukewarm water
2 teaspoons raw sugar
¼ cup honey
¼ cup oil
3 eggs, well beaten
1 teaspoon sea salt
⅓ cup non-fat dry milk solids
4½ cups sifted whole wheat flour, approximately
Oil for deep-frying
Sugar

1. Sprinkle the yeast over one-half cup of the water and stir in the sugar. Set aside for 10 minutes, or until yeast is bubbling actively.

2. Stir in remaining water, the honey, oil, eggs, salt and milk solids. Mix well. Stir in enough of the sifted flour to make a soft dough. Let stand 10 minutes.

3. Turn out onto a floured board and knead until dough is smooth and elastic, about 10 minutes. Place in a clean oiled bowl, cover and let rise until doubled in bulk, about 40 minutes.

4. Roll out dough to one-half-inch thickness and cut with a doughnut cutter. Place rings well apart on a lightly floured baking sheet.

5. Cover and let rise in a warm place until almost doubled in bulk.

6. Meanwhile, heat the deep oil to 375 degrees. Fry the doughnuts, a few at a time, until golden, turning once. Drain on paper towels, and sugar-coat if desired.

Yield: About three dozen doughnuts.

BREADSTICKS

1 tablespoon dry active yeast
1½ cups lukewarm water
1 teaspoon sea salt
1 tablespoon raw sugar
4 cups whole wheat flour,
approximately
1 egg, beaten
Coarse salt

1. Dissolve the yeast in the warm water.

2. Combine the salt, sugar and three cups of the flour in a bowl. Stir in the yeast mixture and enough of the remaining flour to make a fairly stiff dough.

3. Preheat the oven to 425 degrees.

4. Turn dough onto a lightly floured board and knead until smooth and satiny. Divide dough into 48 pieces and roll each one into rope one-half inch in diameter and nine inches long. Place on oiled baking sheet.

5. Brush with the beaten egg and sprinkle generously with coarse salt. Bake 12 to 15 minutes or until browned.

Yield: Four dozen breadsticks.

SOUR DOUGH BREAD

Starter:
1 tablespoon dry active yeast
2 cups unbleached white flour
2 cups lukewarm water
Bread:
1½ cups starter
3 cups lukewarm water
2 tablespoons raw sugar
1 tablespoon sea salt
5 cups unbleached white flour,
or 3 cups unbleached white
flour and 2 cups whole wheat
flour, approximately
¼ cup melted butter, cooled
1½ cups whole wheat flour
Corn meal
Butter

1. Combine all the starter ingredients in a large ceramic or glass bowl; mix well. Let stand, uncovered, in a warm place for 24 to 48 hours, stirring occasionally.

2. Remove the amount of starter (one and one-half cups) needed for the bread and place in a large bowl. Replenish the remaining starter by adding one cup of warm water and one cup of unbleached white flour. Let mixture stand in a warm place a few hours and then refrigerate for future use.

3. To the one and one-half cups of starter in the bowl, add the remaining lukewarm water, sugar, salt and two and one-half cups of the unbleached white flour. Beat until smooth.

4. Let stand in a warm place 12 to 18 hours. Stir batter down. Mix in the melted butter and whole wheat flour and enough of the remaining unbleached white flour to make a moderately stiff dough.

5. Turn onto a lightly floured board and knead until smooth and satiny, about 10 minutes. Place in a clean buttered bowl, turn to grease the top, cover and let rise until doubled in bulk, about two hours.

6. Punch down the dough and shape into two round loaves. Place on an oiled baking sheet sprinkled with corn meal. Brush the tops with butter. Cover and let rise in a warm place until doubled in bulk, about one and one-half hours.

7. Preheat the oven to 400 degrees.

8. Bake 40 to 50 minutes or until bread sounds hollow when tapped on the bottom. Cover with aluminum foil if bread starts to overbrown. Cool on a rack.

Yield: Two loaves.

Note: Store the unused starter in a glass or ceramic container loosely covered with wax paper. The starter should be replenished or used at least once every 10 days. Before using, the starter should be left at room temperature until mixture starts to bubble again, about 12 hours. Remove the amount needed for a recipe and replenish the remainder by adding one cup flour and one cup warm water.

WHOLE WHEAT SOUR DOUGH ONION BREAD

6½ to 8½ cups whole wheat flour
¾ cup lukewarm water
5 medium-size onions, skinned and grated or liquefied in an electric blender
1 teaspoon cumin seeds
½ teaspoon chili powder (optional)
Corn meal
Water

1. Sixty to 72 hours before you wish to eat the bread, combine one-half cup of the flour and one-half cup of the lukewarm water in a large glass, or ceramic, bowl and let stand, uncovered, at room temperature for 50 to 60 hours. The dough should bubble and increase in volume. Stir if necessary and add more warm water if evaporation seems excessive. At the end of the time, the starter should be bubbly, good and smelly and increased in volume.

2. Eight to 12 hours before you wish to eat the bread, mix together the onion, starter, remaining water and the cumin seeds. (The contributor adds no salt to his bread.)

3. Knead enough of the remaining flour into the mixture to give a firm, spongy, non-sticky dough. This chore takes at least 30 minutes but is very important. The dough must be stiff. Form dough into a large ball, cover with plastic wrap or a damp towel and let mixture stand at warm room temperature two to three hours. If you use a towel, remoisten it every hour to prevent it from sticking to the dough.

4. Knead the dough again very well. Divide the dough into three and shape each into a round or oval shape and place on a baking sheet that has been buttered and sprinkled with corn meal. Cover bread as before and let rise for not less than five hours.

5. If the loaves flatten out instead of rising, the dough is too soft and sticky. Harder work incorporating more flour is needed next time. The longer the loaves stand the stronger the flavor.

6. Preheat the oven to 375 degrees.

7. Brush the loaves with water and bake 30 minutes. Brush with water again and bake another 20 minutes or until the bread tests done. It will sound hollow on the bottom when tapped. Brush with water again. If bread starts to brown too fast, lower the heat to 325 degrees.

8. Cool the loaves on a rack.

Yield: Three loaves or about four pounds of bread.

Note: This is a heavy-textured bread that is a meal in itself and should not be compared with any regular bread.

To avoid repeating the entire procedure again for more loaves, pinch off a piece of the raw dough as a starter for the next batch. This starter should be used within three days for full potency.

SOUR DOUGH BISCUITS

2 cups unbleached white flour or whole wheat flour, approximately
1 cup starter (replenish remainder as suggested in Step 2 and note for Sour Dough Bread)
⅔ cup milk, scalded and cooled to lukewarm
1 tablespoon raw sugar
2 teaspoons baking powder
½ teaspoon baking soda
1 teaspoon sea salt
½ cup butter

1. In a large bowl, combine one-half cup flour, the starter, milk and sugar. Mix well. Cover loosely with wax paper and let stand in a warm place at least 18 hours.

2. Preheat the oven to 425 degrees.

3. Mix together one and one-half cups flour, the baking powder, baking soda and salt. Cut in the butter until mixture resembles coarse oatmeal.

4. Stir in the starter mixture. Add more flour if necessary to make a dough of biscuit consistency. Turn onto a lightly floured board and knead 10 strokes.

5. Roll or pat into rectangle one-half-inch thick; cut with floured biscuit cutter. Place on ungreased baking sheet and bake 10 to 12 minutes.

Yield: About eighteen biscuits.

SOUR DOUGH PANCAKES

2 cups starter (retain ½ cup to
replenish as suggested in
Step 2 and note for
Sour Dough Bread)
1 cup milk or water
2 cups unbleached white flour
or whole wheat flour,
approximately
2 eggs, lightly beaten
¼ cup raw sugar
¼ cup oil
1 teaspoon baking powder
1 teaspoon sea salt
½ teaspoon baking soda
(optional if dough is extra sour)

1. Combine the two cups starter, the milk
and flour in a large bowl and mix well.
Cover loosely with wax paper and let stand
in a warm place overnight.

2. Next morning, add remaining
ingredients and stir until batter is smooth.
Spoon two to three tablespoons of the
batter at a time onto a hot oiled griddle
and cook over high heat until browned.
Turn to cook second side. If the batter is
too thin, add a little extra flour; if batter
seems too thick, add milk.

Yield: About four dozen small pancakes.

SOUR DOUGH MUFFINS

1 cup starter (replenish
remainder as suggested in
Step 2 and note for
Sour Dough Bread)
2 cups milk, scalded and
cooled to lukewarm
5 cups unbleached white flour
or whole wheat flour,
approximately
3 tablespoons raw sugar
1½ teaspoons sea salt
1 teaspoon baking soda
2 tablespoons oil
1 tablespoon dry active yeast
Corn meal

1. Combine the starter, milk and two cups
of the flour in a large bowl; mix well. Cover
loosely with wax paper and let stand in a
warm place overnight.

2. Stir down and add sugar, salt, baking
soda, oil and yeast. Add enough remaining
flour to make a moderately stiff dough.
Turn onto a lightly floured board and
knead until smooth and satiny, about 10
minutes.

3. Sprinkle work surface with corn meal
and roll out the dough to three-eighth-inch
thickness. Cut with a four-inch cutter,
cover and let rise at room temperature until
doubled in bulk.

4. Bake the muffins about 12 to 15 minutes
on each side on a lightly oiled griddle
preheated to 275 degrees. To serve, split
and toast.

Yield: About one dozen muffins.

WHOLE WHEAT ENGLISH MUFFINS

1 tablespoon dry active yeast
2 tablespoons lukewarm water
1 cup hot water
½ cup milk, scalded and cooled
2 teaspoons raw sugar
1 teaspoon sea salt
4 cups whole wheat flour,
   approximately
3 tablespoons soft butter
10 muffin rings or 7-ounce tuna
   cans with both ends removed,
   scrubbed and well buttered

1. Dissolve the yeast in the warm water and set aside for 10 minutes. Combine hot water, milk, sugar and salt in a bowl.

2. Stir in the yeast mixture. Add two cups of the flour and beat well.

3. Cover mixture with a damp towel and let rise in a warm place for about one and one-half hours or until mixture collapses back into the bowl.

4. Beat in the butter and beat or knead in the remaining flour. Set greased muffin rings or tuna cans on cold buttered griddle and half-fill each with muffin batter. Cover and let rise until doubled in bulk, about 30 minutes.

5. Heat the griddle to 400 degrees. When muffins are set and browned, remove rings and turn to brown other side. Cool slightly on a rack.

6. To split for toasting, use a fork or fingernails.

Yield: Ten muffins.

OATMEAL MUFFINS

½ cup rolled oats
3 tablespoons brown sugar
1 tablespoon butter
1 teaspoon vegetable salt
1 cup milk, scalded
1 cake compressed yeast
2 cups unbleached white flour

1. Combine the oats, sugar, butter and salt in a mixing bowl. Pour the milk over all. Cool to lukewarm.

2. Crumble the yeast and add to cooled mixture. Beat in the flour. Fill oiled muffin tins half-full of the batter. Let rise in a warm place until mixture fills pans.

3. Preheat the oven to 425 degrees.

4. Bake 20 to 25 minutes.

Yield: About one dozen two-inch muffins.

UNLEAVENED BREAD

3½ cups stoneground whole
    wheat flour
½ cup stoneground yellow
    corn meal
3 teaspoons cinnamon
1½ cups homemade applesauce
    (made with minimum of water
    and lightly sweetened with
    honey- see page 316)
1½ cups raisins
⅔ cup molasses
½ cup water

1. In a large bowl, combine the whole wheat flour, corn meal and cinnamon. In a small saucepan, place the applesauce, raisins, molasses and water and heat until almost simmering.

2. Stir into the dry ingredients to make a dough. Turn onto a lightly floured board and knead, or knead in the bowl, for at least 10 minutes.

3. Place dough in a clean buttered bowl, turn to butter top, cover and let stand eight hours or longer, at room temperature.

4. Knead again briefly and form into a round loaf. Place on an oiled baking sheet. Let stand while oven heats.

5. Preheat the oven to 350 degrees.

6. Bake the loaf for about one hour and 40 minutes or until done.

Yield: One loaf.

Note: This solid loaf should not be compared with raised breads as far as texture is concerned.

SALT-RISING BREAD

2 medium-size raw potatoes, peeled and sliced
¼ cup yellow corn meal
3 tablespoons plus ½ cup raw sugar
½ teaspoon baking soda
1 teaspoon baking powder
½ teaspoon plus 1 tablespoon sea salt
Boiling water
7½ to 8½ cups unbleached white flour
2 cups lukewarm water
½ cup melted butter

1. In a plastic container or ceramic bowl, place the potatoes, corn meal, three tablespoons sugar, the baking soda, baking powder and one-half teaspoon salt. Pour enough boiling water over to cover. Stir and set in a warm place overnight.

2. Next day the mixture should be bubbling with a froth on the top. If mixture is not, discard and start again. If it is working, pour off the liquid. It should measure about one and one-half cups. If a little corn meal goes into the liquid it will not hurt.

3. Discard the potato-corn meal residue.

4. Place the one and one-half cups liquid in a bowl and stir in one and one-half cups of flour to make a thick creamy batter. Cover and set in a warm place until mixture doubles in bulk, about two hours.

5. Add the warm water, butter, remaining salt and remaining sugar. Stir in enough of the remaining flour to make a soft dough.

6. Turn onto a lightly floured board and knead until smooth and elastic, about 15 minutes.

7. Divide the dough in half and form each half into either a round or oblong shape and place in a greased eight inch deep cake pan or a greased 9-by-5-by-3-inch loaf pan.

8. Cover and let rise until doubled in bulk, about two to three hours.

9. Preheat the oven to 350 degrees.

10. Bake the loaves 45 minutes or until they sound hollow when tapped on the bottom.

Yield: Two loaves.

STEAMED YEAST BREAD

1 tablespoon dry active yeast
¼ cup lukewarm water
½ cup whole wheat flour
½ cup stoneground corn meal
⅓ cup non-fat dry milk solids
½ teaspoon sea salt
1 cup raisins or chopped dates, dried apricots or figs
¾ cup yogurt (see page 311)
½ cup honey
½ cup wheat germ

1. Dissolve the yeast in the warm water. Combine the whole wheat flour, corn meal, milk solids, salt and raisins or dates, apricots or figs. Mix well.

2. Combine the yeast mixture with the yogurt and honey and stir into the dry ingredients. Add the wheat germ. Spoon into two well-buttered two-cup cans. Cover and let rise until doubled in bulk, about 45 minutes.

3. Cover cans with brown paper and set on a rack in a kettle of boiling water so that the water extends halfway up the cans.

4. Cover the kettle and steam the bread one and one-half to two hours or until bread is firm and done. Cool in the cans and then cut the bottom of the can off and push the bread out gradually so that it can be sliced evenly.

Yield: Two small loaves.

Note: Molasses can be used in place of the honey. The dried fruits can be replaced by one-half cup nuts and three-quarters cup mashed ripe bananas. Applesauce can be used in place of the yogurt and bran flakes in place of the wheat germ.

SOYA-CAROB BREAD

1½ tablespoons dry active yeast
3¼ cups lukewarm water
½ cup honey
½ cup oil
½ cup non-fat dry milk solids
½ cup sunflower seed meal
1 teaspoon sea salt
8 cups soya-carob flour,
approximately (see note)

1. Dissolve yeast in one-half cup of the water and set aside until mixture becomes frothy.

2. Add honey, oil and remaining water to the yeast mixture.

3. Mix together the milk solids, sunflower meal, salt and four cups of the soya-carob flour. Add to the liquid ingredients and mix well.

4. Add enough of remaining flour to make a dough for kneading. Knead in the bowl, or on a floured board, until smooth and elastic, about 10 minutes. Place in a clean oiled bowl, turn to oil top, cover and let rise until doubled in bulk, about one and one-half hours.

5. Punch down. Divide dough into three portions and shape each portion into a loaf to fit a well-buttered 8½-by-4½-by-2½-inch loaf pan. Cover and let rise again until doubled in bulk.

6. Preheat the oven to 375 degrees.

7. Bake 45 to 60 minutes or until loaves sound hollow when tapped on the bottom.

Yield: Three loaves.

Note: Soya-carob flour is a mixture of soya flour, toasted soya meal, carob pod (St. John's Bread) pieces and wheat gluten and makes an interesting, although not strictly natural, bread.

CORN AND WHEAT BREAD

½ cup plus one tablespoon
    stoneground yellow corn meal
3 tablespoons safflower oil
¼ cup molasses
2¼ teaspoons sea salt
¾ cup boiling water
1 tablespoon dry active yeast
    (or 1 cake compressed yeast)
¼ cup warm water
1 egg, lightly beaten
2½ cups whole wheat flour,
    approximately

1. Combine one-half cup corn meal, the oil, molasses, two teaspoons salt and the boiling water in a mixing bowl. Let stand until lukewarm. Mix well.

2. Sprinkle the yeast over the warm water and stir to dissolve.

3. Add the yeast mixture, egg and one and one-half cups of the whole wheat flour to corn meal mixture. Beat well. Work in enough of the remaining flour to make a smooth dough that can be kneaded.

4. Knead until smooth. Place dough in an oiled 9-by-5-by-3-inch loaf pan. Cover and let rise in a warm place until dough reaches top of pan, about three hours.

5. Preheat the oven to 375 degrees.

6. Combine the remaining corn meal and salt and sprinkle over loaf. Bake 35 minutes or until well browned and done. Turn onto a wire rack to cool.

Yield: One loaf.

YEAST-RAISED CORN BREAD

2 cakes compressed yeast or
    2 tablespoons dry active yeast
1 cup milk, heated to lukewarm
2 eggs, lightly beaten
1 tablespoon oil
2 tablespoons honey
1 cup stoneground yellow corn
    meal
1 cup whole wheat flour
¼ teaspoon sea salt
3 tablespoons brewer's yeast

1. Soften the compressed or dry active yeast in the milk. Blend in the remaining ingredients. Turn into a buttered eight-inch square pan. Cover and set in a warm place to rise until almost doubled, about 30 minutes.

2. Preheat the oven to 350 degrees.

3. Bake the bread 30 minutes or until done.

Yield: Six servings.

CORN AND MOLASSES BREAD

1 tablespoon dry active yeast
1 teaspoon raw sugar
¼ cup lukewarm water
3 tablespoons butter
1 tablespoon sea salt
3 tablespoons molasses
½ teaspoon ground cloves
1 cup boiling water
¼ cup cold water
1½ cups whole wheat flour
2 cups yellow corn flour
    (use only the product sold in
    health food stores)
1 tablespoon grated lemon rind
½ cup raisins, soaked for three
    minutes in boiling water,
    drained and patted dry

1. Dissolve the yeast and sugar in the warm water. Set aside.

2. In a mixing bowl, combine the butter, salt, molasses, cloves and boiling water. Stir until butter melts, then add cold water to cool the mixture. Continue to stir mixture until it is lukewarm.

3. When the molasses mixture is lukewarm, stir in the yeast mixture. Add the whole wheat and corn flours and beat with a wooden spoon five to 10 minutes or until the mixture is smooth and elastic.

4. Turn the dough into a clean buttered bowl. Cover with a towel and let rise in a warm place until doubled in bulk, about one hour.

5. Punch the dough down by stirring with a wooden spoon. Stir in the lemon rind and raisins. Place mixture in a well-buttered 9-by-5-by-3-inch loaf pan.

6. Cover with a towel and let rise in a warm place until the dough is just above the rim of the pan, about 50 minutes.

7. Preheat the oven to 350 degrees.

8. Bake the bread for one hour or until done and cover the top loosely with aluminum foil if top begins to brown too much. Turn onto a rack to cool. Do not slice until bread is cold.

Yield: One loaf.

BLUEBERRY BREAD

¼ cup stoneground yellow
corn meal
1 cup boiling water
1 tablespoon oil
¼ cup molasses
1 egg, well beaten
1 tablespoon dry active yeast
¼ cup lukewarm water
3 cups unbleached white flour,
approximately
2 cups blueberries

1. Stir the corn meal into the boiling water and stir until mixture thickens. Remove from the heat and stir in the oil, molasses and egg.

2. Dissolve the yeast in the warm water. When corn meal mixture is lukewarm, stir in the dissolved yeast.

3. Beat in enough flour to make a stiff dough. Turn the mixture onto a floured board. Knead until mixture is smooth and elastic, about 10 minutes.

4. Place dough in a cleaned buttered bowl; turn to butter the top.

5. Cover the bowl and let dough rise in a warm place until doubled in bulk, about one hour.

6. Punch dough down and roll into 10-inch square. Sprinkle the blueberries over the square and press in gently.

7. Roll up the dough like a jellyroll, tuck under the ends and place, seam side down, in a well-greased 9-by-5-by-3-inch loaf pan. Cover and let rise until doubled in bulk, about 45 minutes.

8. Preheat the oven to 375 degrees.

9. Bake the loaf 45 to 50 minutes or until loaf sounds hollow when tapped on the bottom. Cool on a rack. Do not slice until thoroughly cool.

Yield: One loaf.

BARBARA'S BASIC REFRIGERATOR BREAD

8 to 10 cups unbleached white
    flour, approximately
4 tablespoons dry active yeast
¼ cup raw sugar or brown sugar
2 tablespoons sea salt
1 cup non-fat dry milk solids
½ cup wheat germ
½ cup lard or butter
1 quart hot tap water
Melted butter

1. In a large bowl, combine six cups of the flour with the dry yeast, sugar, salt, milk solids and wheat germ. Stir well.

2. In a second bowl, combine the lard or butter and the hot water. Stir to melt and then add to flour mixture. Mix well.

3. Add more flour, a cup at a time, stirring well after each addition until dough is soft but leaves the sides of the bowl clean.

4. Turn onto a well-floured board and knead until very smooth and elastic, about 10 minutes. Cover with plastic wrap and a towel and let rest 20 minutes. Punch down the center of the dough and reshape into a ball.

5. Divide the dough into four portions. Roll each into a rectangle double the size of an 8½-by-4½-by-2½-inch loaf pan. Roll up tightly like a jellyroll, tuck under the ends and place in four well-buttered 8½-by-4½-by-2½-inch loaf pans. Brush surface of loaves with melted butter.

6. Cover loaves loosely with plastic wrap and refrigerate two to 24 hours at moderately cold setting.

7. Preheat the oven to 400 degrees.

8. Remove loaves from refrigerator and let stand 10 minutes.

9. Just before baking, carefully puncture any surface bubbles. Bake 35 to 40 minutes on rack set low in the oven. Remove from pans, brush crust with butter, and cool on racks.

Yield: Four loaves.

Note: This is a firm-textured bread which can be sliced very thinly, using an electric knife, for low-calorie sandwiches.

CRUSTY WHITE BREAD

5 cups unbleached white flour
1 teaspoon sea salt
1 tablespoon dry active yeast
1 cup lukewarm water
¼ cup clarified melted butter
  (milky solids discarded)
  or olive oil
⅔ cup plus one tablespoon milk
1 egg, lightly beaten

1. Combine the flour and salt.

2. Dissolve the yeast in the warm water, add butter or oil and two-thirds cup milk and mix very well.

3. Combine yeast mixture with flour mixture and mix well. This takes the place of kneading so mixing should be done vigorously and well. Place in oiled bowl.

4. Cover and let rise in a warm place until dough is doubled in bulk and is very light, about one and one-half hours.

5. Punch down, turn onto a board and pat or roll to one-half-inch thickness. Cut dough in half and roll each half like a jellyroll with tapered ends. Place, seam side down, on oiled baking sheet.

6. Cover and let rise in a warm place until half-risen.

7. When half-risen, slash tops of loaves diagonally with a sharp knife. Combine remaining milk with the egg and brush over loaves. Set in a warm place to rise until very light, another hour or so.

8. Preheat the oven to 400 degrees.

9. Place a pan of hot water on the bottom of the oven. Bake the loaves in the middle of the oven for about 15 minutes. Reduce oven heat to 350 degrees and bake 15 minutes longer or until well browned.

Yield: Two loaves.

BREAD-PERFECT EVERY TIME

2½ teaspoons sea salt
Oil
2 tablespoons honey
2 cups skim milk or
  reconstituted non-fat dry
  milk solids, scalded
1 tablespoon dry active yeast or
  1 cake compressed yeast
3 tablespoons lukewarm water
6 cups sifted whole wheat
  pastry flour or unbleached
  white flour, approximately
Melted butter (optional)

1. Place the salt, three tablespoons oil and the honey in a bowl. Pour the milk over all and cool to lukewarm.

2. Dissolve the yeast in the lukewarm water and add to the cooled milk mixture.

3. Stir in enough flour to make a stiff dough. Turn onto a floured board and knead for 10 minutes or until dough is smooth and elastic. It will lose its stickiness as it is kneaded.

4. Place dough in a clean oiled bowl; brush top lightly with oil. Cover and set in a warm place to rise until doubled in bulk, about two hours. (When dough is pressed lightly with a finger, an impression will remain.)

5. Punch dough down, fold and turn so that smooth side is on top. Let rise again until almost doubled in bulk, about 30 minutes.

6. Divide into two pieces and let rest, covered with a cloth or bowl upside down, on the board for 10 minutes.

7. Roll or pat each piece of dough until it is twice the size of an 8½-by-4½-inch loaf pan. Fold in the sides and then the edges. Roll tightly into a loaf shape and set, seam side down, in pans.

8. Cover pans and let dough rise until doubled in bulk, about one hour.

9. Preheat the oven to 400 degrees.

10. Bake bread 35 to 45 minutes or until it sounds hollow when tapped on the bottom. Cool on a rack. Brush with melted butter if a soft crust is desired.

Yield: Two loaves.

GOLDEN BRAIDS

3 tablespoons dry active yeast
¾ cup lukewarm water
½ cup plus 2 tablespoons raw
  sugar
½ cup butter
1 cup boiling water
3 tablespoons oil
1 tablespoon sea salt
¼ cup honey
7 eggs
9 cups unbleached white flour,
  approximately
1 cup wheat germ
1 tablespoon water
Sesame seeds or poppy seeds
  (optional)

1. Dissolve the yeast in the warm water in a quart container. Add two tablespoons of the sugar and let stand in warm place.

2. Meanwhile, place the butter in a large mixing bowl of an electric mixer and add the boiling water. When butter is melted, add the oil, salt, remaining sugar and the honey.

3. Add six eggs, one at a time, with the mixer set at low speed. Add yeast mixture and beat.

4. Add four cups of the flour and the wheat germ and mix well. Add enough of the remaining flour to make a cohesive dough that can be kneaded.

5. Turn out onto a floured board and knead, drawing in just enough flour to prevent sticking, until smooth and satiny, about 10 minutes.

6. Place dough in a clean buttered bowl, turn to butter top, cover and let rise in a warm place until doubled in bulk, about one hour.

7. Punch down and divide dough into four pieces. Divide each of the four pieces into three and form each of the thirds into a rope by rolling between the palms of the hands. Each rope should be about 12 inches long.

8. Form three ropes into a tight braid. Repeat with other ropes.

9. Place each braid in a greased and floured 9-by-5-by-3-inch loaf pan. Cover and let rise until dough reaches top of pan, about one hour.

10. Preheat the oven to 350 degrees.

11. Lightly beat the remaining egg with one tablespoon water.

12. Brush the tops of the braids with the egg mixture and sprinkle with the sesame seeds or poppy seeds if desired. Bake 30 minutes. Rearrange loaves during baking if they are not browning evenly. Turn oven off and wait five minutes before removing loaves from oven.

13. Loaves should shake free from pans. Place each loaf on a rack to cool. When cool, place in a plastic bag to freeze.

Yield: Four loaves.

DILLED BATTER BREAD

¾ cup evaporated milk
¾ cup boiling water
2 teaspoons caraway seeds
1 tablespoon grated onion
1 tablespoon snipped fresh dill weed
2 tablespoons raw sugar
2 teaspoons sea salt
¼ cup butter
2 tablespoons dry active yeast
½ cup lukewarm water
2 eggs, beaten
4 to 4½ cups sifted whole wheat flour
Melted butter

1. In a large bowl, combine the milk, boiling water, caraway seeds, onion, dill, sugar, salt and butter. Stir to melt the butter. Cool to lukewarm.

2. Dissolve the yeast in the warm water. Add to the milk mixture along with the eggs and beat well.

3. Beat in enough of the flour to give a soft, sticky dough.

4. Beat vigorously for three minutes. Cover and let dough rise in a warm place until doubled in bulk. Stir down and beat for one minute.

5. Turn into an oiled two-quart round casserole. Let rise 10 to 15 minutes.

6. Preheat the oven to 375 degrees.

7. Bake 40 minutes or until loaf sounds hollow when tapped on the bottom. Brush with melted butter for a soft crust.

Yield: One loaf.

HEALTH LOAF

2 tablespoons dry active yeast
1 tablespoon honey
3 cups lukewarm water
¼ cup safflower oil
1 egg, lightly beaten
¼ cup honey or molasses
1½ teaspoons sea salt
8 to 9 cups unsifted stoneground whole wheat flour (preferably Deaf Smith County Flour)
½ cup non-fat dry milk solids
½ cup low-fat soy flour
¼ cup brewer's yeast
3 tablespoons wheat germ
1 cup sunflower seed kernels

1. In large mixing bowl of an electric mixer, place the dry active yeast, one tablespoon honey and one-half cup of the lukewarm water. Let stand 10 minutes.

2. Stir yeast mixture and add to it the oil, egg, honey or molasses, salt and remaining warm water.

3. Mix in four cups of the whole wheat flour. Mix at moderate speed for seven to 10 minutes or until mixture becomes very elastic.

4. Add the milk solids, soy flour, brewer's yeast and wheat germ. Mix well. Work in enough of the remaining whole wheat flour to make a dough that can be kneaded. It will be slightly sticky at first.

5. Turn onto a floured board and knead five to eight minutes or until smooth and elastic.

5. Place dough in a well-oiled very large bowl; turn to oil top of dough. Cover with a damp towel and let rise in a warm place until doubled in bulk, about one hour.

6. Sprinkle the sunflower kernels over the dough, punch dough down and mix in the seeds as well as possible. Shape dough into three balls, cover and let rest 10 minutes.

7. Shape into three loaves and place in well-oiled 9-by-5-by-3-inch loaf pans. Cover and let rise until barely doubled in bulk, about 30 minutes.

8. Do not let bread rise too high or it will fall. Place loaf pans in cold oven. Turn oven temperature to 400 degrees and turn oven on. After 15 minutes reduce oven heat to 375 degrees and bake 25 to 35 minutes longer or until loaves sound hollow when tapped on bottom.

Yield: Three loaves.

HEALTH BREAD

- 2 cups milk, scalded
- 2 cups cold water
- 2 tablespoons raw sugar
- ½ teaspoon ground ginger
- 2 tablespoons dry active yeast
- ¼ cup molasses
- ¼ cup soy oil
- 4 teaspoons sea salt
- 2½ cups whole wheat flour
- ¼ cup wheat germ
- 1 tablespoon bone meal (optional)
- 1 tablespoon potato flour (optional)
- 1 tablespoon non-fat dry milk solids (optional)
- 1 tablespoon lecithin (optional)
- 4½ cups unbleached white flour, approximately

1. Combine the milk and cold water. Measure one half of the liquid mixture into a small bowl and add the sugar and ginger. Stir well. Add the yeast and let stand 10 minutes.

2. To the balance of the milk mixture, add the molasses, oil and salt. Beat a few seconds and then add to the yeast mixture.

3. In a large bowl, combine the whole wheat flour, wheat germ, bone meal, potato flour, dry milk and lecithin.

4. Combine the yeast mixture and the whole wheat flour mixture and beat thoroughly by hand for four minutes or with an electric mixer at medium speed. (This is in place of kneading.)

5. Work in enough of the unbleached flour so that the dough leaves the sides of the bowl clean. Cover and let rise in a warm place until doubled in bulk, about 45 minutes.

6. Punch down. Divide the dough into three pieces. Shape each piece into a loaf and fit into an oiled 9-by-5-by-3-inch loaf pan. Cover and let rise until doubled in bulk, about 30 minutes.

7. Preheat the oven to 400 degrees.

8. Bake loaves 15 minutes. Reduce oven heat to 375 degrees and bake 35 to 45 minutes longer or until done. When done, the loaves will sound hollow when tapped on the bottom.

Yield: Three loaves.

SIX LOAVES TO FEED A FAMILY OF FIVE FOR A WEEK

Basic dough:

   3 tablespoons dry active yeast
      or 3 cakes compressed yeast

   ⅓ cup raw sugar, honey or
      molasses

   6 cups lukewarm water

   8 cups unbleached white flour

   2½ tablespoons sea salt

   1½ cups non-fat dry milk solids

   ⅓ cup wheat germ

   1 cup soy flour

   6 tablespoons oil

Pumpernickel:

   4 teaspoons caraway seeds

   1½ cups whole bran (only variety
      sold in health food stores)

   3½ cups rye flour, approximately

   1 egg white, lightly beaten

   1 tablespoon water

Regular bread:

   3½ cups unbleached white flour,
      approximately

1. To prepare basic dough, place the yeast, sugar, honey or molasses and warm water in a large bowl and let stand five minutes.

2. Stir the yeast mixture. Add the white flour and salt and beat at least 300 strokes. Add the milk solids, wheat germ, soy flour and oil and mix well. Divide the dough between two four-quart bowls.

3. For the pumpernickel bread, add the caraway seeds and whole bran to one bowl. Let stand five minutes. Stir 70 strokes. Add enough rye flour to make a dough and turn onto a floured board. Knead seven to 10 minutes.

4. Place dough in a clean oiled bowl; turn to oil top of dough. Cover with wax paper and a damp towel. Let rise in a warm place until doubled in bulk, about one and one-half hours. Punch down and let rise 30 minutes more. Remove to board, pound out the bubbles and shape dough into three oval loaves. Place on an oiled baking sheet, oil tops, cover and let rise in a warm place until doubled in bulk. Slash each top with three slantwise cuts.

5. Preheat the oven to 350 degrees.

6. Paint the tops of the loaves with egg white mixed with water. Bake 50 to 60 minutes, or until done. Cool on a rack.

7. For the regular bread, add enough of the white flour to the second bowl to make a medium-soft dough. Turn onto a floured board and knead seven to 10 minutes.

8. Place dough in a clean oiled bowl; turn to oil the top. Cover with wax paper and damp towel. Let rise in a warm place until doubled in bulk, about 45 minutes. Punch down, turn so that smooth side is up and let rise again 25 minutes.

9. Turn onto the board and punch out the bubbles. Divide the dough into three pieces. Shape each piece into a loaf and place in a well-oiled 8½-by-4½-inch loaf pan. Oil tops of loaves, cover and let rise until doubled in bulk, about 30 minutes.

10. Preheat the oven to 350 degrees.

11. Bake loaves 25 minutes or until they sound hollow when tapped on the bottom. Cool on a rack.

Yield: Three pumpernickel and three regular loaves.

MIXED WHOLE GRAIN BREAD

1 tablespoon dry active yeast
¼ cup lukewarm water
1 teaspoon raw sugar
1¼ cups boiling water
⅓ cup honey
1 tablespoon sea salt
3 tablespoons butter
1½ cups whole wheat flour
1 cup rye flour
1 cup oatmeal
1 tablespoon grated orange rind

1. In a small cup, combine the yeast, warm water and sugar and set aside.

2. In a mixing bowl, combine the boiling water, honey, salt and butter. Stir until the butter is melted. Allow mixture to cool to lukewarm.

3. Stir in the yeast mixture and then the whole wheat and rye flours and oatmeal. Stir vigorously with a wooden spoon until well mixed.

4. Place the dough in a buttered bowl; turn to grease the top. Cover and let rise in a warm place until doubled in bulk, about one hour.

5. Stir the dough down and add the orange rind. Turn into a well-buttered 9-by-5-by-3-inch loaf pan. Cover and let rise in a warm place until doubled in bulk, about 55 minutes.

6. Preheat the oven to 350 degrees.

7. Bake the bread for one hour. When the loaf is tapped on the bottom, it should sound hollow. Cool on a rack. Do not cut until bread is thoroughly cooled.

Yield: One loaf.

QUICK BRAN BREAD

4½ to 5½ cups unbleached
    white flour
2 tablespoons raw sugar or
    brown sugar
2 teaspoons sea salt
2 tablespoons dry active yeast
2 cups whole bran
1 cup milk
½ cup water
2 tablespoons honey
⅓ cup butter
2 eggs, lightly beaten
¼ cup wheat germ

1. In a large bowl, combine one cup of the flour, the sugar, salt and yeast. Stir in the bran.

2. Combine the milk, water, honey and butter in a saucepan and heat until warm, 120 to 130 degrees. Pour into the dry ingredients and beat two minutes at medium speed of electric mixer, scraping the bowl occasionally.

3. Add the eggs, wheat germ and enough of the remaining flour to make a thick batter.

4. Beat at high speed two minutes. Stir in enough of the remaining flour to make a soft dough. Turn out onto a lightly floured board and knead until mixture is smooth and elastic, about 10 minutes.

5. Place the dough in a buttered bowl; turn to grease top. Cover and let rise in a warm place until doubled in bulk, about 45 minutes.

6. Punch down. Turn onto the board. Divide dough in halves. Shape each half into a loaf and place in an oiled 8½-by-4½-by-2½-inch loaf pan. Cover and let rise in a warm place until doubled in bulk, about 60 minutes.

7. Preheat the oven to 375 degrees.

8. Bake loaves in lower half of oven for 30 to 35 minutes or until loaves sound hollow when tapped on the bottom.

Yield: Two loaves.

MIXED-GRAIN BREAD

1½ cups milk, scalded
2 tablespoons butter
1 tablespoon dry active yeast
¼ cup lukewarm water
1 egg, lightly beaten
2 teaspoons sea salt
2 tablespoons honey
2 tablespoons molasses
1 cup unbleached white flour
1 cup rye flour
½ cup buckwheat flour
¾ cup wheat germ
¾ cup rolled oats
3 tablespoons brewer's yeast
2 cups whole wheat flour, approximately

1. Combine the milk and butter and set aside until lukewarm.

2. Sprinkle the dry active yeast over the warm water and stir to dissolve.

3. When the milk mixture is lukewarm, stir in the yeast mixture, egg, salt, honey and molasses. Mix well.

4. Stir in the unbleached white flour, rye flour and buckwheat flour and beat very hard several minutes. Beat in the wheat germ, oats and brewer's yeast and beat or knead well.

5. Add enough whole wheat flour to make a dough that can be kneaded on a board but is slightly sticky. Turn onto a floured board and knead until smooth and not sticky, about 15 minutes.

6. Place in a clean, buttered bowl, turn to butter top of dough, cover and let rise in a warm place until doubled in bulk, about one and one-half hours.

7. Punch down the dough, knead briefly, then divide dough into two halves. Shape each half into a loaf and place in a well-oiled 8½-by-4½-by-2½-inch loaf pan. Cover and let rise until doubled in bulk, about 45 minutes.

8. Preheat the oven to 375 degrees.

9. Bake loaves 40 to 45 minutes or until they sound hollow when tapped on the bottom. Cool on a rack.

Yield: Two loaves.

THREE-WHEAT BREAD

3 cups lukewarm water
½ cup honey
2 tablespoons molasses
3 tablespoons dry active yeast
1 tablespoon sea salt
¼ cup oil
5 cups stoneground whole wheat flour
3 cups unbleached white flour, approximately
1 cup cracked wheat

1. Mix together the warm water, honey, molasses and yeast. Let stand five minutes. Stir in the salt, oil, whole wheat flour, two cups unbleached white flour and the cracked wheat. Mix well.

2. Turn the dough out onto a floured board and gradually incorporate enough of remaining flour to make a dough that is not sticky. Knead until smooth and satiny, about 10 minutes.

3. Place in a clean oiled bowl; turn to oil top of dough. Cover and let rise in a warm place until doubled in bulk, about one and one-half hours. Punch down, fold and turn so that smooth side is up. Cover and let rise again about 45 minutes.

4. Divide the dough into two. One portion may be frozen at this stage if not needed. Shape each dough portion into a round loaf and place on a cookie sheet. Cover and let rise until doubled in bulk, about 45 minutes.

5. Preheat the oven to 350 degrees.

6. Bake 50 minutes or until loaf sounds hollow when tapped on the bottom.

Yield: Two loaves.

HALF & HALF BREAD

1 tablespoon dry active yeast
2 cups milk, heated to lukewarm
½ cup safflower oil
2 eggs, lightly beaten
¼ cup raw sugar
3½ cups unbleached white flour, approximately
3½ cups whole wheat flour

1. Dissolve the yeast in the milk. Add the oil, eggs and sugar and mix well.

2. Place three and one-half cups unbleached white flour and the whole wheat flour in a large bowl and stir in the milk mixture. Mix well and turn onto a floured board. Knead until smooth and satiny, about 10 minutes, adding only enough unbleached white flour during the kneading to prevent sticking.

3. Place dough in a clean oiled bowl. Turn to oil the top of the dough. Cover and let rise in a warm place until doubled in bulk, about one hour.

4. Punch down and knead briefly. Shape the dough into two loaves. Place in oiled 8½-by-4½-inch loaf pans. Cover and let rise again until doubled in bulk, about 45 minutes.

5. Preheat the oven to 375 degrees.

6. Bake loaves 15 minutes, lower oven heat to 325 degrees and bake 40 minutes longer or until loaves sound hollow when tapped on the bottom.

7. Brush tops of hot loaves with butter for a soft crust. Cool on a rack.

Yield: Two loaves.

DELICIOUS OATMEAL BREAD

1½ cups boiling water
1 cup rolled oats
¾ cup molasses
3 tablespoons soft butter
2 teaspoons sea salt
1 tablespoon dry active yeast
2 cups lukewarm water
8 cups unbleached white flour, approximately
Butter

1. Pour the boiling water over the oats and let stand 30 minutes.

2. Add the molasses, soft butter and salt. Dissolve the yeast in the warm water and add to the oat mixture.

3. Beat, and work in, enough of the flour to make a medium-soft dough. Turn onto a floured board and knead until smooth, about 10 minutes.

4. Place the dough in a clean buttered bowl, turn to butter the top, cover and let rise in a warm place until doubled in bulk, about one hour.

5. Turn onto the board and knead again.

6. Divide and shape the dough into two loaves and place in well-oiled 9-by-5-by-3-inch loaf pans. Cover and let rise until doubled in bulk, about 45 minutes.

7. Preheat the oven to 400 degrees.

8. Bake the loaves five minutes, lower the oven heat to 350 degrees and bake 40 minutes longer or until loaves sound hollow when tapped on the bottom. Brush tops of loaves with butter for a soft crust.

Yield: Two loaves.

OATMEAL-DILL BREAD

2 cups whole wheat flour
2 tablespoons dry active yeast
¼ cup chopped onion
½ cup hot water
2 cups cream-style cottage cheese
(the contributor uses
her own hoop cheese)
Butter
2 teaspoons sea salt
¼ cup raw sugar
2 eggs
1 cup quick-cooking or
regular rolled oats
2 tablespoons dill seeds
1½ cups unbleached white flour

1. In the large bowl of an electric mixer, place the whole wheat flour and yeast.

2. In an electric blender, combine the onion, water, cottage cheese, three tablespoons butter, the salt, sugar and eggs. Blend until smooth. Add to the dry ingredients and beat two minutes.

3. Stir in the oats, dill seeds and unbleached flour. Turn into a clean buttered bowl, cover and let rise in a warm place until doubled in bulk, about one hour.

4. Stir down and turn into a well-buttered 1½-quart casserole. Let rise, uncovered, until almost doubled in bulk, about 45 minutes.

5. Preheat the oven to 350 degrees.

6. Bake 35 minutes or until loaf sounds hollow when tapped on the bottom. Brush top with butter for a soft crust.

Yield: One loaf.

RAISIN PUMPERNICKEL

2¼ cups cold water
¾ cup stoneground corn meal
2 teaspoons sea salt
½ cup molasses
2 tablespoons oil
2 tablespoons dry active yeast
¼ cup lukewarm water
2 teaspoons honey
3 to 3½ cups whole wheat flour
3 to 3½ cups rye flour
1 cup raisins
Butter (optional)

1. Stir the cold water into the corn meal in a saucepan and heat, stirring, over medium heat until mixture comes to a boil and thickens.

2. Remove from the heat and stir in the salt, molasses and oil. Cool to lukewarm.

3. Sprinkle the yeast over the warm water and stir to dissolve. Add the honey and let stand in a warm place 10 minutes.

4. Add yeast mixture to corn meal mixture. Stir in two cups each whole wheat flour and rye flour to form a soft dough.

5. Turn mixture onto board dusted with some of remaining flour. Knead the dough, gradually incorporating enough of the remaining flours to make a non-sticky dough. Knead 10 minutes or until very smooth and satiny.

6. Knead in the raisins. Place the dough in a clean oiled bowl, oil top of dough lightly, cover and let rise in a warm place until doubled in bulk, about one hour.

7. Punch down the dough and divide in half. Shape each half into a well-rounded loaf and place on an oiled baking sheet dusted with corn meal.

8. Cover and let rise until doubled in bulk, about 45 minutes.

9. Preheat the oven to 375 degrees.

10. Bake 45 minutes or until done. Rub surface with butter for a soft crust; place in the draft from a window for crisp crust. Cool on a wire rack.

Yield: Two loaves.

OLD COUNTRY PUMPERNICKEL

¾ cup stoneground corn meal
1½ cups cold water
1½ cups boiling water
1½ teaspoons sea salt
  2 tablespoons unsulphured
    molasses
  2 tablespoons safflower oil
  2 tablespoons dry active yeast
    or two cakes compressed yeast
¼ cup lukewarm water
  2 cups mashed potatoes
  1 cup wheat germ
3¼ cups rye flour
4¼ cups whole wheat flour,
    approximately
  1 egg white, lightly beaten
  4 tablespoons sesame seeds

1. Mix the corn meal with the cold water in a saucepan. Stir in the boiling water and cook, stirring, until thick.

2. Add salt, molasses and oil and set aside until lukewarm.

3. Dissolve the yeast in the lukewarm water.

4. Add the dissolved yeast, mashed potatoes and wheat germ to the cooled corn meal mixture. Let stand five minutes.

5. Add the rye flour and enough of the whole wheat flour to make a fairly stiff dough. Knead in the bowl or on a lightly floured board until smooth and satiny.

6. Place in an oiled bowl, turn dough to oil top, cover and let rise until doubled in bulk, about one and one-half hours. Divide dough into two equal portions.

7. Roll each piece of dough into a rectangle twice as big as a 9-by-5-by-3-inch pan. Fold the ends of each into the center, press sides to seal, and fold over to fit in a well-oiled 9-by-5-by-3-inch pan. Cover loaves and let rise until doubled in bulk, about one hour.

8. Preheat the oven to 375 degrees.

9. Brush loaves with egg white and sprinkle each with two tablespoons sesame seeds. Bake one and one-half hours or until loaves sound hollow when tapped on the bottom.

Yield: Two loaves.

CRACKED RYE BREAD

2 cups boiling water
2 tablespoons butter
2 tablespoons raw sugar
1½ tablespoons sea salt
2 cups cold water
2 tablespoons dry active yeast
7 cups unbleached white flour, approximately
2½ cups extra-coarse rye meal (sold in health food stores)

1. In a large mixing bowl, combine the boiling water, butter, sugar and salt. Stir until butter melts. Add cold water and stir mixture until it is lukewarm.

2. Stir in the yeast and let stand five minutes to dissolve.

3. Stir in three cups of the unbleached white flour and the rye meal. Beat vigorously until mixture is smooth. Work in enough of the remaining flour to make a fairly stiff dough.

4. Turn out onto a floured board and knead until smooth and satiny, about 10 minutes.

5. Place the dough in an oiled bowl, oil the top of the dough, cover with a cloth and place in a warm place to rise until doubled in bulk, about one and one-half hours.

6. Punch the dough down and shape into two loaves. Place in well-buttered 9-by-5-by-3-inch loaf pans. Cover and let rise until dough reaches the top of pan, about 45 minutes.

7. Preheat the oven to 350 degrees.

8. Bake loaves one hour or until they sound hollow when tapped on the bottom.

9. Alternately, half the dough can be made into rolls by removing pieces of dough after the first rising, kneading into balls and placing them on a buttered cookie sheet to rise, covered, until doubled in bulk. They will take 30 minutes' baking time in the same 350-degree oven.

Yield: Two loaves or one loaf and sixteen rolls.

BERKELEY RYE BREAD

4⅓ cups stoneground whole
    wheat flour
  1 cup rye flour
  1 cup rye meal
    (coarsely ground rye flour)
  ⅓ cup soy flour
  ⅓ cup wheat germ
  1 tablespoon sea salt
  2 tablespoons caraway seeds
  1 tablespoon dry active yeast
2½ cups lukewarm water
  ⅓ cup molasses, preferably
    blackstrap
    Soy oil

1. In a large bowl, combine the whole wheat flour, rye flour, rye meal, soy flour, wheat germ, salt and caraway seeds. Mix very well.

2. Dissolve the yeast in one-half cup of the water. Mix remaining water with the molasses. Add yeast mixture to molasses mixture.

3. Add the yeast-molasses mixture to the dry ingredients and mix well. The mixture will appear sticky at first but as it is kneaded it will gradually leave the sides of the bowl clean.

4. Continue to knead the bread in the bowl, adding only a minimum of whole wheat flour extra, until the dough is smooth and satiny.

5. Remove the dough to a lightly floured board and knead three to four minutes longer. (Long kneading is essential to success in all whole grain breads.)

6. Place dough in a clean buttered bowl; turn to butter top of dough. Cover and let rise in a warm place until doubled in bulk, about one and one-half hours. Turn out onto board and divide into four pieces.

7. Knead each portion and form into an oval-shaped loaf. Cut slashes at an angle on the top and place on an oiled baking sheet. Brush the outside of the loaves with oil, cover and place in a warm place to rise until doubled in bulk, about one hour.

8. Preheat the oven to 350 degrees.

9. Bake loaves 45 minutes or until loaves sound hollow when tapped on the bottom.

Yield: Four loaves.

GRAHAM-RYE BREAD

1 tablespoon dry active yeast
¼ cup lukewarm water
1 teaspoon raw sugar
1⅔ cups milk, scalded
Butter
2 teaspoons sea salt
⅓ cup molasses
1 cup whole wheat flour
1 cup rye flour
2 cups unbleached white flour, approximately
½ cup soy flour
½ cup non-fat dry milk solids

1. Sprinkle the yeast over the warm water and stir to dissolve. Add the sugar and set in a warm place.

2. Combine the milk, two tablespoons butter, the salt and molasses. Stir to melt the butter and let stand until lukewarm.

3. When yeast mixture is bubbling well and milk mixture is lukewarm, combine the two mixtures.

4. Stir in the whole wheat flour, rye flour, two cups unbleached white flour, the soy flour and milk solids. Mix well to a medium-soft dough, adding more unbleached flour if necessary.

5. Turn onto a floured board and knead until smooth and elastic, about 10 minutes. Place in a clean buttered bowl, turn to butter top of dough, cover and let rise in a warm place until doubled in bulk, about one and one-half hours.

6. Punch down, divide into two and shape each half into a loaf. Place in well-oiled 8½-by-4¼-by-2½-inch loaf pans, cover and let rise until doubled in bulk, about one hour.

7. Preheat the oven to 375 degrees.

8. Bake 50 minutes or until loaves sound hollow when tapped on the bottom. Cool on a rack. Brush tops with butter for soft crust.

Yield: Two loaves.

RYE AND WHOLE WHEAT BREAD

1½ cups milk, scalded
⅓ cup oil
2 tablespoons molasses
2 tablespoons honey
2 teaspoons sea salt
2 tablespoons dry active yeast
½ cup lukewarm water
2 tablespoons caraway seeds
2½ cups rye flour, approximately
2 cups whole wheat flour
Butter, oil or cream

1. Place the milk in a large bowl and add the oil, molasses, honey and salt. Let stand until lukewarm.

2. Dissolve the yeast in the warm water and add with seeds to the cooled milk mixture. Set in a warm place until mixture bubbles actively. Stir in one and one-half cups each rye flour and whole wheat flour. Beat mixture very well by hand or with the dough hook of an electric mixer. Add remaining whole wheat flour and enough remaining rye flour to give a dough that can be kneaded.

3. Knead on a lightly floured board until very smooth and satiny. This takes about 15 minutes and must be done well to develop gluten.

4. Place dough in a clean oiled bowl, oil top surface, cover and set in a warm place until doubled in bulk, about one hour.

5. Punch down and knead for five minutes. Divide into two and shape each half into a loaf to fit a 9-by-5-by-3-inch loaf pan or deep metal pan of seven cups capacity. Cover and set in a warm place until dough just reaches tops of pans. Do not let dough over-rise or it will collapse.

6. Preheat the oven to 375 degrees.

7. Bake loaves 40 minutes or until they sound hollow when tapped on the bottom. Cool on a rack. Brush tops with butter, oil or cream for soft crust.

Yield: Two loaves.

CRACKED WHEAT BREAD

5 cups lukewarm water
3 tablespoons dry active yeast
2 cups cracked wheat, sold in
   health food stores as cereal
2 eggs, lightly beaten
½ cup raw sugar or brown sugar
1 tablespoon sea salt
2 cups non-fat dry milk solids
¼ cup melted butter
1 cup soy granules
½ cup wheat germ
8 to 9 cups unbleached white
   flour, approximately
⅓ cup sesame seeds

1. Combine the warm water and the yeast; stir to dissolve.

2. Add the cracked wheat and set the mixture aside for one hour to soften the wheat.

3. Reserve two tablespoons beaten eggs. Combine remaining eggs with the sugar, salt, milk solids, butter, soy granules and wheat germ and mix very well.

4. Add the unbleached flour cup by cup until you have a dough that is soft enough to knead (it will be a little sticky to begin with). Turn onto a lightly floured board and knead until dough loses its stickiness and becomes smooth and elastic, about 10 minutes.

5. Place dough in a well-buttered bowl; turn to butter top. Cover with clear plastic wrap and a damp towel and set in a warm place to rise until doubled in bulk, about one hour.

6. Punch down. Divide dough into four portions and shape each portion into a loaf. Place loaves in well-buttered 9-by-5-by-3-inch loaf pans. They should be less than two-thirds full.

7. Brush loaves with reserved egg, sprinkle with sesame seeds, cover and let rise in a warm place until dough reaches top of pans, 45 to 60 minutes.

8. Preheat the oven to 350 degrees.

9. Bake the loaves 40 to 45 minutes or until loaves sound hollow when tapped on the bottom. Cool on a rack. When cooled, they can be frozen.

Yield: Four loaves.

Note: Dough can be made into large sandwich rolls or dinner rolls.

ONE-BOWL WHEAT GERM BREAD

1 cup brown rice flour
1 cup whole wheat flour
1 cup unbleached white flour
2 teaspoons sea salt
½ cup wheat germ
2 tablespoons dry active yeast
2 tablespoons soy oil
1¼ cups very hot water
2 tablespoons honey

1. In a bowl, mix together the rice flour, whole wheat flour and unbleached flour very well.

2. In the large bowl of an electric mixer, mix one cup of the flour mixture with the salt, wheat germ and dry yeast. Stir in the oil.

3. While beating at medium speed, gradually add the hot water and honey. Beat two minutes at high speed, scraping the bowl occasionally.

4. Add ½ cup flour mixture, or enough flour mixture to make a thick batter. Beat two minutes at high speed.

5. Stir in enough of the remaining flour mixture to make a stiff dough. Turn onto a floured board and knead until dough is smooth and elastic, about 10 minutes.

6. Split the dough into two pieces and form each into a round ball. Place on an oiled baking sheet. Cover and let rise in a warm place until doubled in bulk, about one hour.

7. Preheat the oven to 350 degrees.

8. Bake loaves 20 to 25 minutes.

Yield: Two small loaves.

Note: This bread has a texture much like that of shortcake.

ANNMARIE'S BEST BREAD

¼ teaspoon dry active yeast
2 cups lukewarm water
3 to 4 cups whole wheat flour, approximately
½ cup rye flour
½ cup soy flour
½ cup corn meal
½ cup buckwheat flour
2 teaspoons sea salt
1 tablespoon corn oil or soy oil

1. In the evening, sprinkle the yeast into one-half cup of the water and let stand.

2. In the meantime, place one-half cup of the whole wheat flour, the rye flour, soy flour, corn meal and buckwheat flour into a large enamel or glass pot. Mix thoroughly.

3. Add the salt, oil and remaining water. The mixture should form a heavy batter. Stir yeast mixture and add to the batter. Beat the mixture very well.

4. Cover with a cloth and a tight-fitting cover to prevent a crust from forming. Set in a warm place and let stand overnight.

5. Next day, stir down with a wooden spoon and stir in enough of the remaining whole wheat flour to form a dough that can no longer be stirred.

6. Turn onto a floured board and knead until smooth and elastic, using only enough flour to prevent sticking to the fingers. This will take at least 20 to 30 minutes. Dough should be smooth and have a consistency similar to your earlobe.

7. Shape the dough into a loaf and place in a well-oiled 9-by-5-by-3-inch loaf pan; turn to oil top. Prick three times with a fork, cover and set in a warm place to rise for one and one-half hours.

8. Preheat the oven to 275 degrees.

9. Bake bread one and one-half hours or until it dislodges easily from the pan. Cool on a rack. For long storage, place in plastic bag in refrigerator. Then bread will have to be toasted or fried.

Yield: One loaf.

Note: This is a heavy-textured bread.

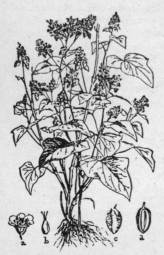

HIGH-PROTEIN WHOLE WHEAT BREAD

¾ cup milk, scalded
3 tablespoons raw sugar
4 teaspoons sea salt
⅓ cup butter
⅓ cup molasses
½ cup cold water
1 cup lukewarm water
2 tablespoons dry active yeast
4½ cups unsifted stoneground whole wheat flour
½ cup non-instant dry milk solids
2 cups unbleached white flour, approximately
½ cup soy flour

1. Place the milk in a bowl and add the sugar, salt, butter, molasses and cold water. Cool to lukewarm.

2. Place the warm water in a small bowl, sprinkle the yeast over the water and let stand five minutes or until yeast is dissolved.

3. Measure two and one-half cups of the whole wheat flour into the large bowl of an electric mixer. Combine cooled milk mixture and yeast mixture and stir into flour.

4. Beat three minutes at medium speed of electric mixer, scraping sides of bowl occasionally.

5. Sift the milk solids with one cup of the unbleached flour. Mix with remaining whole wheat flour and the soy flour. Add half this mixture to the large bowl and beat at high speed three minutes, scraping bowl occasionally. Stir in remaining flour mixture and enough additional unbleached flour to make a soft dough.

6. Turn onto a lightly floured board and knead until smooth and elastic, about 10 minutes.

7. Place in a clean well-buttered bowl, turn to butter top, cover and let rise in a warm place until doubled in bulk.

8. Punch down, divide in half, roll into balls, cover and let rest 10 minutes. Shape into two loaves and place in well-buttered 9-by-5-by-3-inch loaf pans. Cover and let rise in warm place until doubled in bulk, about one hour.

9. Preheat the oven to 400 degrees.

10. Bake 25 to 30 minutes or until loaves sound hollow when tapped on the bottom. Cool on racks.

Yield: Two loaves.

SPROUTED WHOLE WHEAT BREAD

3 cups lukewarm water
2 tablespoons dry active yeast
1 tablespoon sea salt
¼ cup honey
3 tablespoons oil
3½ cups unbleached white flour
2 cups wheat sprouts (see page 195), ground in a meat grinder
2 cups whole wheat flour, approximately

1. In a large mixing bowl, place one cup of the water. Sprinkle the yeast over the water and set aside for five minutes.

2. Stir to dissolve yeast. Add the remaining water, the salt, honey and oil and mix well.

3. Stir in the unbleached white flour and beat the dough until it is smooth and elastic. Cover and let rise in a warm place until doubled in bulk, about 45 minutes.

4. Stir in the ground sprouts and enough of the whole wheat flour to make a medium-soft dough. It will be slightly sticky.

5. Turn the dough onto a floured board and knead until very smooth and elastic, about 10 minutes. Place in a clean oiled bowl, turn to oil top of dough, cover and let rise in a warm place until doubled in bulk, about one hour.

6. Turn onto the board and knead briefly. Divide dough into two and shape into two loaves. Place in well-oiled 9-by-5-by-3-inch loaf pans, cover and let rise until doubled in bulk, about 45 minutes.

7. Preheat the oven to 375 degrees.

8. Bake loaves 25 minutes, lower oven heat to 300 degrees and bake 35 minutes longer or until the loaves sound hollow when tapped on the bottom. Cool on a rack.

Yield: Two loaves.

ORGANIC WHOLE WHEAT BREAD

2 packages compressed yeast (or two tablespoons dry active yeast may be substituted)
½ cup lukewarm water
3 cups milk, scalded and cooled to lukewarm
Melted butter
1 cup unsulphured molasses
1 tablespoon sea salt
6 cups sifted organic whole wheat flour
6 cups sifted unbleached organic white flour, approximately

1. Crumble or sprinkle the yeast into the warm water and stir to dissolve.

2. Add cooled milk, one-half cup melted butter, the molasses and salt to yeast mixture.

3. Work in the whole wheat flour, beating very well. Work in enough of the unbleached white flour to give a dough that can be kneaded, although it will be a bit sticky at the beginning.

4. Turn onto a floured board and knead vigorously until it hurts, at least 15 minutes.

5. Turn dough into a buttered bowl; turn to butter top.

6. Cover and let rise in a warm place until doubled in bulk, about one and one-half hours.

7. Divide the dough into four and shape each quarter into a loaf. Place in well-buttered 8½-by-4½-by-2½-inch loaf pans, cover and let rise until doubled in bulk, about 45 minutes.

8. Preheat the oven to 400 degrees.

9. Brush tops of loaves with melted butter. Bake the loaves 30 to 40 minutes or until loaves sound hollow when tapped on the bottom. Cool on a rack.

Yield: Four loaves.

LEONARD'S SPECIAL BREAD

2 tablespoons dry active yeast
3 cups lukewarm water
½ cup honey
½ cup molasses
¼ cup sunflower oil
1 teaspoon sea salt
½ cup sesame seeds
1 cup monukka raisins
5 to 6 cups stoneground whole wheat flour
1 cup rye flour
1 cup rolled oats

1. Sprinkle the yeast over the warm water in a large bowl. Set aside five minutes. Stir to dissolve. Add the honey, molasses, oil, salt, seeds and raisins.

2. Stir in four and one-half cups whole wheat flour and mix very well.

3. Stir in the rye flour and rolled oats. Add enough remaining whole wheat flour to make a dough that will knead but is slightly sticky to begin with.

4. Turn onto a floured board and knead until very elastic, about 15 minutes.

5. Place dough in a well-oiled bowl, turn dough to oil top, and cover. Let rise in a warm place until doubled in bulk, about one and one-half hours.

6. Punch down and knead again briefly. Divide into two, shape into loaves and place in two well-buttered 9-by-5-by-3-inch loaf pans. Cover and let rise until doubled in bulk, about one hour.

7. Preheat the oven to 350 degrees.

8. Bake the loaves 40 minutes or until loaves sound hollow when tapped on the bottom.

Yield: Two loaves.

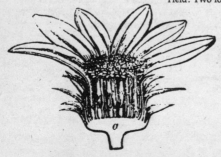

BETTIE'S WHOLE WHEAT BREAD

2 cakes compressed yeast
3 cups lukewarm water
2 cups wheat germ
1 tablespoon kelp
1 cup blackstrap molasses
¼ cup lecithin granules
½ cup brewer's yeast
⅓ cup oil
6 cups whole wheat flour,
    approximately

1. Crumble the yeast over one cup of the water and set aside five minutes.

2. Stir well and add wheat germ, kelp, molasses, lecithin, brewer's yeast, oil and remaining water. Mix very well.

3. Work in enough of the flour to give a fairly sticky dough. Turn onto a floured board and knead, using only enough flour to keep hands from sticking. Sticky bread dough gives a lighter loaf. Knead until smooth and elastic, about 10 minutes.

4. Place dough in an oiled bowl, turn to oil the top, cover and let rise until doubled in bulk, about two and one-half hours.

5. Punch down, cover and let rise one hour longer.

6. Turn the dough out onto the board again and knead five minutes. Divide dough into four pieces, shape into small loaves and fit into well-buttered 3-by-7-inch loaf pans.

7. Cover and let rise 30 minutes.

8. Place loaves in cold oven. Turn oven to 325 degrees and light. Bake one hour or until loaves are done.

Yield: Four small loaves.

HONEY WHOLE WHEAT BREAD

2 cups milk, scalded
1 tablespoon sea salt
½ cup honey
3 tablespoons oil
2 tablespoons dry active yeast
⅓ cup lukewarm water
4½ cups unsifted whole wheat
    flour, approximately
½ cup wheat germ
¼ cup soy flour (optional)
2 tablespoons brewer's yeast
    (optional)
Heavy cream, oil or fat

1. Place milk in a large bowl. Add salt, honey and oil. Mix well and set aside to cool to lukewarm.

2. Dissolve the dry active yeast in the warm water. If there is some doubt that yeast is still active, or to hasten its growth, add one teaspoon of honey and set in a warm place for 10 minutes. Mixture will bubble if yeast is active.

3. Add yeast mixture to cooled milk mixture.

4. Beat in three cups of the flour and continue beating until smooth.

5. Work in wheat germ, soy flour, brewer's yeast and enough of the remaining flour to make a dough that can be kneaded.

6. Knead the dough on a lightly floured board until smooth and elastic. This will take at least 10 minutes. (There is less gluten in whole wheat flour than in regular white flour and so it takes more kneading to develop whole wheat flour dough.)

7. Place the dough in a clean oiled bowl, oil the top, cover and set in a warm place to rise until doubled in bulk, about one hour.

8. Punch down, knead until smooth, put back in the bowl, cover and let rise again, about 45 minutes.

9. Punch down and divide into two. Shape dough into two loaves and place in oiled 8-by-4½-by-2½-inch bread tins or five-cup capacity deep round cake tins or charlotte molds.

10. Cover and let rise in a warm place until loaves just reach top of pans; do not let over-rise.

11. Preheat the oven to 375 degrees.

12. Bake loaves 45 minutes or until loaves sound hollow when tapped on the bottom. Cool on a rack. Brush with heavy cream, oil or fat for a soft crust.

Yield: Two loaves.

NO-KNEAD QUICK WHOLE WHEAT BREAD

2 tablespoons dry active yeast
3 cups lukewarm water
¼ cup molasses
¼ cup raw sugar or brown sugar
6 cups whole wheat flour
½ cup soy flour
¾ cup non-fat dry milk solids
3 tablespoons wheat germ
2 tablespoons brewer's yeast
4 teaspoons sea salt
¼ cup oil

1. Mix together the yeast and warm water. Add the molasses and sugar and let stand 10 minutes, until yeast dissolves and mixture starts to bubble.

2. Meanwhile, mix together the whole wheat flour, soy flour, milk solids, wheat germ, brewer's yeast and salt.

3. Stir the yeast mixture and add half the flour mixture and the oil. Beat vigorously and add only as much more flour mixture as can be beaten in easily.

4. Continue to beat the mixture until it is smooth and elastic, at least 10 minutes. With the spoon and the hands, work in the remaining flour mixture.

5. Turn into two well-oiled 8½-by-4¼-inch loaf pans. Cover and let rise until mixture has doubled in bulk, about 45 minutes.

6. Preheat the oven to 375 degrees.

7. Bake the loaves 50 minutes or until they sound hollow when tapped on the bottom.

Yield: Two loaves.

SPOON-STIRRED WHOLE WHEAT BREAD

1 tablespoon dry active yeast
2 cups lukewarm water
2 tablespoons honey
1½ teaspoons sea salt
2 tablespoons oil
4½ cups sifted whole wheat flour
Corn meal
Cold water
4 tablespoons sesame seeds
Melted butter

1. Dissolve the yeast in the lukewarm water. Add honey, salt and oil and mix well.

2. Stir in the flour and beat well with a wooden spoon. Cover bowl and set in a warm place for about an hour. Every 10 minutes work through the dough vigorously with the wooden spoon.

3. Turn dough onto a lightly floured board and divide in half. Shape each half into a ball, cover with the bowl or a towel and let rest 10 minutes.

4. Roll each ball into a 12-by-9-inch rectangle. Roll tightly, like a jellyroll, starting with the long side. Seal the edge. Place on a well-oiled baking sheet that has been sprinkled with corn meal.

5. Make diagonal slashes across tops of loaves. Brush loaves with water, cover and let rise until doubled in bulk, about 30 minutes.

6. Preheat the oven to 375 degrees.

7. Brush the loaves with water again and sprinkle each with two tablespoons seeds. Bake 35 to 40 minutes or until loaves sound hollow when tapped on the bottom. Brush with melted butter and cool on a rack.

Yield: Two loaves.

HEARTY BREAD

- 3 tablespoons dry active yeast
- 4 cups lukewarm water
- ⅔ cup molasses
- 2 tablespoons oil
- 1 cup rye flour
- 6 to 8 cups whole wheat flour
- 1 tablespoon sea salt
- 1 cup non-fat dry milk solids
- 3 tablespoons brewer's yeast
- ½ cup fine bulghur wheat
- ½ cup stoneground yellow corn meal
- ½ cup rolled oats
- ½ cup sesame seeds
- ½ cup sunflower seed kernels
- ½ cup whole wheat berries
- 1 cup raisins
- Butter

1. Dissolve the dry active yeast in the water. Stir in the molasses and oil. Stir in the rye flour and mix well. Stir in enough whole wheat flour to make a batter which can be beaten. Beat 300 strokes or for 10 minutes. This develops the gluten and is very important.

2. Gradually work in, one at a time, the salt, milk solids, brewer's yeast, bulghur, corn meal, oats, sesame seeds, sunflower seed kernels, whole wheat berries and raisins. Mix well.

3. Add enough of the remaining whole wheat flour to make a moderately stiff dough that just pulls from the sides of the bowl.

4. Place dough in a clean oiled bowl, cover and let rise until doubled in bulk, about two hours. Punch down, turn onto a floured board and knead lightly.

5. Divide dough in half, shape each half into a loaf and place in a well-oiled 9-by-5-by-3-inch loaf pan. Butter tops.

6. Let rise until doubled in bulk.

7. Preheat the oven to 375 degrees.

8. Bake 50 minutes or until loaf sounds hollow when tapped on the bottom. Cool on a rack.

Yield: Two loaves.

12
PANCAKES, WAFFLES & PASTA

A good breakfast to start the day doesn't have to be bacon and eggs or come out of a package. Tempt the family into sitting down together with fruit-filled cottage cheese pancakes, nut-filled waffles or baked French toast served with honey and real maple syrup.
Homemade noodles and ravioli have always been the mark of a dedicated cook. Made with eggs and unbleached white flour or whole wheat flour, the noodles taste better, and cost less, than any store-bought product.

OLD-FASHIONED BUCKWHEAT HOT CAKES

2 cups lukewarm water
1 tablespoon dry active yeast
2 tablespoons brown sugar
2 cups buckwheat flour
1 cup unbleached white flour
1 cup milk, scalded and cooled to lukewarm
1 teaspoon sea salt

1. Mix together the warm water, yeast and sugar and stir until dissolved.

2. Sift the buckwheat flour and unbleached flour together and add to the yeast mixture. Stir in the milk and salt. Beat until smooth.

3. Cover and set in a warm place to rise for one hour. Mixture will be light and fluffy. Stir well and bake on a hot, oiled griddle until browned; turn and brown second side.

Yield: About two dozen hot cakes.

Note: To make the mixture overnight, use one-quarter of a cake of compressed yeast in place of the dry active yeast and add an extra one-half teaspoon sea salt.

DELICIOUS NUTRITIOUS PANCAKES

1 cup sifted whole wheat flour
1 cup sifted unbleached white flour
1 cup sifted soy flour
½ cup brown rice flour
½ cup peanut flour
1 cup non-fat dry milk solids
4 teaspoons baking powder
1 teaspoon sea salt
4 eggs
⅔ cup safflower oil
2 cups water, approximately
Butter, maple syrup or honey

1. Sift together twice the whole wheat flour, unbleached white flour, soy flour, rice flour, peanut flour, milk solids, baking powder and salt.

2. Blend the eggs, oil and two cups water in an electric blender, or beat well. Stir liquid ingredients into dry ingredients until mixture is of heavy cream consistency, adding extra water as necessary.

3. Ladle onto a hot, oiled griddle and cook until browned. Turn and brown the second side. Serve with butter, maple syrup or honey.

Yield: About twenty pancakes.

OATMEAL GRIDDLECAKES

½ cup whole wheat pastry flour
4 teaspoons baking powder
1 teaspoon sea salt
1½ cups rolled oats
1 egg, lightly beaten
1 tablespoon oil
1 teaspoon unsulphured
   molasses
¾ cup water
¾ cup milk

1. Sift together the pastry flour, baking powder and salt. Stir in the oats.

2. Combine egg, oil, molasses, water and milk. Pour into the dry ingredients and beat until smooth. Ladle mixture onto a hot, oiled griddle and cook until browned; turn and brown the second side.

Yield: About one dozen griddlecakes.

EASY WHEAT PANCAKES

1 cup sour milk or buttermilk
1 egg
1 tablespoon raw sugar or brown
   sugar
1 cup whole wheat flour
1 teaspoon baking soda
½ teaspoon sea salt
1 tablespoon oil or melted butter
Maple syrup or honey

1. In a bowl, mix the milk, egg, sugar, flour, baking soda, salt and oil together. Bake by ladlefuls on a hot, oiled griddle. Turn when bubbles form on top of the pancakes. Brown the second side.

2. Serve with syrup or honey.

Yield: About one dozen pancakes.

RAISED WHEAT PANCAKES

2 tablespoons dry active yeast
1½ cups lukewarm skim milk
1 tablespoon blackstrap or
   unsulphured molasses
2 eggs, lightly beaten
2 tablespoons corn oil
1 cup whole wheat flour
½ cup wheat germ
⅓ cup non-fat dry milk solids
1 teaspoon sea salt

1. Dissolve the yeast in the warm skim milk. Add the molasses, eggs and corn oil.

2. Add remaining ingredients and mix until blended. Ladle onto a hot, oiled griddle and cook until bubbles form; turn and brown the second side.

Yield: About ten pancakes.

BUCKWHEAT PANCAKES

¾ cup buckwheat flour
½ cup wheat germ
¼ cup whole wheat flour
3 tablespoons raw sugar
1¾ teaspoons double-acting
   baking powder
2 eggs, lightly beaten
3 tablespoons peanut oil
Milk or water

1. In a bowl, mix together the buckwheat flour, wheat germ, whole wheat flour, sugar and baking powder.

2. Stir in the eggs, oil and enough water or milk to make a batter the consistency of thick heavy cream. Ladle the mixture onto a hot, oiled griddle. When holes appear on the surface of the pancakes, turn to brown second side.

Yield: About eight large pancakes.

BARLEY FLOUR PANCAKES

1 egg, lightly beaten
⅓ cup sour cream
⅓ cup buttermilk
1 cup barley flour
1½ teaspoons baking powder
1 teaspoon sea salt
1 teaspoon sugar
Butter and honey

1. Beat the egg with the sour cream and buttermilk.

2. Sift together the barley flour, baking powder, salt and sugar. Stir in the egg mixture and let stand two minutes.

3. Ladle onto a hot, oiled griddle and cook until browned and puffy. Turn to brown the second side. Serve with butter and honey.

Yield: About eight pancakes.

GREAT SPECKLED PANCAKES

1 cup unbleached white flour
½ cup whole wheat flour
½ cup corn meal
4 teaspoons baking powder
½ teaspoon nutmeg
1 tablespoon raw sugar or
  brown sugar (optional)
½ cup non-fat dry milk solids
2 eggs, lightly beaten
¼ cup oil or melted butter
1 to 2 cups water

1. Sift the unbleached white flour, whole wheat flour, corn meal, baking powder, nutmeg, sugar and milk solids together into a bowl. Tip the coarse parts that are retained in the sifter into the bowl. (The purpose of the sifting is to mix the ingredients thoroughly.)

2. Using a rotary beater, beat in the eggs, oil and enough water to make a creamy batter that pours. Thicker batter will give thick puffy pancakes; a thinner batter, thinner crisper pancakes.

3. Ladle the mixture onto a hot, oiled griddle and cook until browned; turn and brown the second side.

Yield: About one dozen pancakes.

Note: The contributor says that you can double, triple or quadruple the recipe's dry ingredients and keep in a covered jar. The dry mixture can also be used for coating chicken or fish before frying. The pancake batter can be used as the base for corn pancakes. Stir in one cup fresh corn kernels, cut from the cob, to the basic recipe before frying on a griddle.

WHEAT GERM PANCAKE

6 eggs
5 tablespoons cottage cheese
⅔ cup wheat germ
¼ teaspoon vanilla
1 tablespoon butter
Maple syrup or honey

1. Put the eggs, cheese, wheat germ and vanilla into an electric blender and blend 30 seconds.

2. Heat the butter in a 10-inch heavy skillet. Pour in the egg mixture and cook over medium heat until browned on the bottom; turn and brown on the other side. Serve with syrup or honey.

Yield: Four servings.

CASHEW WHOLE GRAIN WAFFLES

5 eggs, separated
¼ cup oil
2 cups freshly ground whole grain flour (the contributor uses a mixture of barley, rye and buckwheat flours)
1½ teaspoons baking powder (Rumford brand if available)
1½ cups water
¾ cup ground raw cashews
Maple syrup, ground-up blueberries or peeled and cored pears, chopped

1. Beat the egg yolks and oil together. Sift the flour and baking powder together and add to yolk mixture with the water.

2. Stir in the ground cashews. Beat the egg whites until stiff but not dry and fold in. Bake the mixture on lightly oiled, preheated waffle iron.

3. Serve topped with syrup, blueberries or pears.

Yield: Eight to ten servings.

COTTAGE CHEESE PANCAKES I

1 cup cottage cheese
2 eggs, lightly beaten
2 tablespoons whole wheat flour
  or unbleached white flour
¼ cup wheat germ
1 tablespoon melted butter
Homemade applesauce
  (see page 316)
Cinnamon

1. Mix cottage cheese, eggs, flour, wheat germ and butter together until well blended.

2. Fry on a hot, oiled griddle until browned on one side. Turn and brown the other side.

3. Serve with applesauce, sprinkled with cinnamon.

Yield: About six pancakes.

COTTAGE CHEESE PANCAKES II

3 eggs, well beaten
8 ounces cottage cheese
½ cup less 1 tablespoon soy flour
½ cup less 2 tablespoons wheat
  germ
½ cup sunflower seed kernels
Honey

1. Beat the eggs with the cottage cheese until smooth.

2. Add the flour, wheat germ and sunflower seed kernels and mix until blended. Ladle the mixture onto a hot, oiled griddle and cook until browned; turn and brown the second side. Serve with honey.

Yield: Ten to twelve pancakes.

GOAT CHEESE PANCAKES

3 eggs, separated
¼ cup unbleached white flour
¼ teaspoon sea salt
¾ cup goat cottage cheese
Butter and maple syrup

1. Beat the egg yolks until light and lemon colored. Stir in the flour, salt and cheese.

2. Beat the egg whites until stiff but not dry and fold in. Ladle the mixture onto a hot, oiled griddle and cook until browned on one side. Turn and brown the second side. Serve with butter and maple syrup.

Yield: About one dozen pancakes.

STRAWBERRY PANCAKES

1 cup yogurt (see page 311)
2 eggs, lightly beaten
3 tablespoons oil
¼ teaspoon sea salt
2 cups whole wheat flour
Milk
1 pint strawberries
Honey to taste

1. In a bowl, mix together the yogurt and eggs. Stir in the oil, salt and flour.

2. Stir in enough milk to make a thick pancake batter consistency. Heat an oiled griddle and spoon quarter cups of the batter onto griddle. Cook until browned on one side; turn and brown the other side.

3. Slice the strawberries into a small saucepan. Add honey and heat gently to warm but do not allow to come close to boiling.

4. For each serving, place a pancake on a warm plate, top with some strawberries, then another pancake; garnish with more strawberries.

Yield: Six servings.

PUMPKIN CORNCAKES

½ cup stoneground corn meal
1 cup boiling water
⅞ cup evaporated milk
¼ cup cooked pumpkin puree
1 cup whole wheat flour
2 teaspoons baking powder
¾ teaspoon kelp or sea salt
1 tablespoon honey
1 egg, beaten
Maple syrup or honey

1. Gradually add the corn meal to the boiling water while stirring vigorously. Add milk and stir until smooth.

2. Stir in the pumpkin. Sift together the flour, baking powder and kelp or salt and stir into corn meal mixture.

3. Stir in one tablespoon honey and the egg. Ladle the mixture onto a preheated and oiled griddle to form small cakes. Bake until bubbles form on the surface; turn and cook until second side is browned.
Serve with syrup or honey.

Yield: Six servings.

BLENDER POTATO PANCAKES

2 medium-size potatoes, scrubbed
  or peeled, and quartered
1 egg yolk
Sea salt to taste
2 egg whites, beaten until stiff
  but not dry
Oil

1. Put the potatoes, egg yolk and salt into
an electric blender. Blend until smooth.
Pour into a bowl.

2. Fold in the beaten egg whites. Heat oil
to a depth of one-eighth inch in a heavy
skillet and ladle the mixture into the hot oil
to make small cakes. Cook until browned,
turn and cook to brown the second side.
Drain on paper towels.

Yield: Four servings.

LATKES OR POTATO PANCAKES

3 large potatoes
1 large onion
3 eggs
Sea salt to taste
2 tablespoons wheat germ
1 teaspoon unbleached white flour
Oil
Sour cream

1. Grate potatoes on flat stainless steel
grater. Grate onion on fine grater and add
to potatoes. Mix with the eggs. Alternately,
the potatoes, onion and eggs may be
blended in an electric blender if divided
into three batches.

2. Add salt, wheat germ and flour to
grated or blended potato mixture. Set aside
while heating oil. Add enough oil to just
cover the bottom of a large, heavy skillet
and heat.

3. Ladle the potato mixture by the
tablespoonful into the hot fat. Lower heat
slightly and fry quickly until browned;
turn and brown other side. Drain on paper
towels. Serve with sour cream.

Yield: Four servings.

POTATO PANCAKES

6 large potatoes, finely grated
into bowl of water
3 eggs, lightly beaten
¼ cup soy grits
3 tablespoons chopped parsley
2 small onions, finely grated
1 teaspoon tamari (soy sauce)
½ teaspoon sea salt
Oil for frying
Applesauce, cottage cheese and
yogurt (see page 311)

1. Squeeze the potatoes between the hands until dry. This removes excess liquid and surface starch.

2. Combine potatoes with grits, parsley, onions, tamari and salt and mix well.

3. Pour oil into a heavy skillet to a depth of one-quarter inch. Heat the oil. Drop the potato mixture by ladlefuls into the hot oil and fry until browned; turn to brown the second side. Drain on paper towels.

4. Serve with applesauce, cottage cheese and yogurt.

Yield: Three or four servings.

BREAKFAST POTATO PANCAKES

3 medium-size raw potatoes
½ tablespoon soy grits
½ tablespoon wheat germ
½ tablespoon soy flour
½ tablespoon rye flour
1 egg, lightly beaten
1 tablespoon kelp
1 large onion, grated
1 tablespoon sweet cream or
sour cream
Corn oil, peanut oil
or sesame oil
Yogurt (see page 311), sour
cream, applesauce or cranberry
sauce

1. Grate the potatoes and drain well on paper towels. Mix with the grits, wheat germ, soy flour, rye flour, egg, kelp, onion and cream.

2. Heat a griddle. Grease well with the oil and drop pancake mixture by the teaspoonful onto hot, greased griddle. Cook until browned. Turn and brown other side.

3. Serve with yogurt, sour cream, applesauce or cranberry sauce.

Yield: Four servings.

WHOLE WHEAT PANCAKES

1 cup unground whole wheat
1⅓ cups water
1⅛ cups non-fat dry milk solids
2 eggs
1 teaspoon sea salt
1 tablespoon raw sugar or
  molasses
3 tablespoons corn oil
1 tablespoon baking powder
Honey or maple syrup

1. Wash the whole wheat thoroughly. Place wheat and water in an electric blender and blend until smooth.

2. In a bowl, combine the milk solids, eggs, salt, sugar, corn oil and baking powder. Mix well. Pour in the blended wheat mixture and stir to mix.

3. Bake on a preheated, lightly oiled griddle. Serve with honey or maple syrup.

Yield: Four servings.

BAKED GERMAN PANCAKE

2 eggs
½ cup milk
⅛ teaspoon sea salt
1 tablespoon oil
1 cup whole wheat flour
½ teaspoon soy flour
1 teaspoon brewer's yeast
1 cup pureed cored peeled raw
  apples
¼ cup finely chopped walnuts
⅛ teaspoon nutmeg
¼ cup brown sugar
1 tablespoon honey or maple
  syrup

1. Preheat the oven to 450 degrees.

2. Put the eggs, milk, salt and oil in an electric blender and blend until well mixed.

3. In a bowl, combine the whole wheat flour, soy flour and brewer's yeast. Pour in the egg mixture and beat until smooth. Pour into a cold, oiled 9-inch or 10-inch pie plate.

4. Bake 10 minutes. Reduce oven heat to 350 degrees and bake 10 minutes longer or until done. Combine the remaining ingredients and spread over the top of the pancake.

Yield: Four servings.

WAFFLES

1¾ cups unbleached white flour
1 tablespoon baking powder
½ teaspoon sea salt
½ cup wheat germ
3 eggs, separated
¼ cup sunflower oil
1½ cups milk
½ cup chopped sunflower seed kernels
½ cup chopped pumpkin seeds
Honey

1. Sift into a bowl the flour, baking powder and salt. Add the wheat germ.

2. Combine the egg yolks and oil and beat well. Gradually beat in milk. Pour milk mixture into the dry ingredients and mix lightly. Stir in the sunflower seed kernels and pumpkin seeds.

3. Beat the egg whites until stiff but not dry and fold into the batter. Drop the mixture onto a preheated and oiled waffle iron and bake until light brown. Serve with honey.

Yield: Four servings.

THE HECTOR FAMILY'S WAFFLES

2 cups whole wheat flour
2 cups sifted soy flour
¾ cup corn meal
2 teaspoons sea salt
1 cup wheat germ
6 eggs, well beaten
1 tablespoon plus 1 teaspoon dry active yeast
1 cup lukewarm water
1 cup milk
1 cup oil
2 cups water, approximately
Butter and maple syrup

1. In a large bowl, mix together the whole wheat flour, soy flour, corn meal, salt and wheat germ. Stir in the eggs.

2. Dissolve the yeast in the lukewarm water and add to flour mixture. Stir in the milk, oil and enough water to make a waffle batter consistency. Let stand in a warm place until mixture shows signs of bubbling, about 15 minutes.

3. Cook the mixture in a lightly oiled, preheated waffle iron. Serve with butter and syrup.

Yield: Twenty large waffles.

RAISED WHOLE WHEAT WAFFLES

½ cup lukewarm water
3 tablespoons dry active yeast
2 cups lukewarm milk
¼ cup melted butter or oil
⅛ teaspoon salt
1 teaspoon sugar
2 cups whole wheat pastry flour
2 eggs, lightly beaten

1. In a large mixing bowl, place the water and yeast and stir to dissolve the yeast. Let stand five minutes in a warm place.

2. Add the milk, butter or oil, the salt and sugar.

3. Beat in the flour and the eggs but do not overbeat (batter will be thin). Set the mixture in a warm place until mixture just begins to rise, about 15 minutes.

4. Cook the mixture in a preheated, oiled waffle iron.

Yield: About four large waffles.

FRENCH TOAST

1 dozen eggs
1 pound cottage cheese
Sea salt and freshly ground black pepper to taste
6 slices homemade whole wheat cinnamon bread
Butter (optional)
Maple syrup or honey

1. Preheat the oven to 350 degrees.

2. Put the eggs, cottage cheese, salt and pepper in an electric blender and blend until smooth.

3. Arrange the bread slices, buttered if you wish, in a buttered 9-by-13-inch baking dish or large shallow heatproof dish.

4. Pour the egg-and-cheese mixture over bread and bake 30 minutes or until set and puffed. Serve with syrup or honey.

Yield: Six servings.

PANCAKE AND WAFFLE TOPPINGS

1. Honey-Almond Spread

½ cup honey
¼ cup butter
½ cup heavy cream
½ cup ground unblanched almonds

Combine honey, butter and cream in a small saucepan and bring to a boil. Boil five minutes or until mixture is consistency of thick syrup. Cool slightly. Stir in almonds.

Yield: About one and one-half cups.

2. Honey-Coconut Spread

¾ cup honey
2 tablespoons melted butter
¾ cup unsweetened grated coconut, toasted (see note)

Combine all ingredients.

Yield: About one and one-quarter cups.

Note: To toast coconut, spread on a baking sheet and bake in preheated 350-degree oven five to seven minutes, stirring or shaking often.

3. Fruited Honey Sauce

3 pears or apples, peeled, cored and finely diced
1 cup honey
1 teaspoon lemon juice
1 teaspoon butter
⅛ teaspoon cinnamon

Combine all ingredients in a small saucepan and cook slowly, stirring often, until fruit is tender.

Yield: About two cups.

4. Molasses and Orange Waffle Sauce

½ cup unsulphured molasses
¼ cup brown sugar
⅓ cup orange juice
¼ cup butter
1 tablespoon grated orange rind

Combine all the ingredients in a small saucepan and heat, stirring, until mixture is smooth and well blended. Serve warm over waffles.

Yield: About one cup.

5. Honey Butter

½ pound soft butter
3 tablespoons honey

Mix honey and butter together until well blended. Pack into a crock or serving jar and chill. Use on pancakes, waffles, hot breads and French toast.

Yield: About one cup.

HOMEMADE PASTA

2 cups whole wheat flour, sifted if
  bran is not considered desirable
1 teaspoon sea salt
2 eggs
1 egg white
1 tablespoon olive oil
⅓ cup wheat germ
Water
Sifted whole wheat flour

1. Make a pile of two cups flour and the salt on a board. Make a well in the center and add the eggs, egg white, olive oil and wheat germ.

2. With the fingers, gradually draw the flour into the wet ingredients, adding drops of water as it seems necessary to form the mixture into a ball of dough.

3. Knead the dough, using a minimum of sifted flour on the board, until dough is smooth and elastic, at least 10 minutes. Cover and let rest 10 minutes.

4. Divide the dough in half and roll each half until it is very thin. Dust lightly with flour and let dry 10 minutes.

5. Gently roll each rectangle of dough into a jellyroll shape and cut into one-quarter-inch to one-half-inch widths. Unfold bundles and set aside to dry.

Yield: About one pound noodles.

Note: It is advisable to use unbleached white flour if making spaghetti, and the use of a pasta machine makes shaping the dough easier still. The whole wheat pasta can be shaped into ravioli and tortellini. Once they are dry, the whole wheat noodles can be frozen or can be stored for a short while in a closed container.

WHOLE WHEAT NOODLES

2 cups whole wheat flour
1 teaspoon sea salt
1 egg
2 egg yolks
3 to 4 tablespoons water,
approximately
1 tablespoon oil

1. Place the flour and salt in a pile on a board. Make a well in the center. Add egg, egg yolks, about three tablespoons water and the oil to the well.

2. With the fingers, gradually mix the liquid ingredients into the flour.

3. Add enough water to make a stiff dough that can be kneaded. Knead the dough on a lightly floured board very well. The dough should be satiny smooth.

4. Divide into two and roll each half into a rectangle about 12-by-24 inches. This is hard work, especially at the beginning, but it is important that the dough is rolled paper thin. Let dry 30 minutes.

5. Roll the rectangles from the long side like a jellyroll and cut into one-eighth-inch noodles. Spread the noodles out and let dry very well before cooking or storing.

Yield: About three-quarters pound noodles.

13
YOGURT

Yogurt is a cultured milk product, made with lactobacillus bulgaricus, that has been known to man since Biblical times. It is a staple in the diets of many Middle Eastern countries, especially Lebanon and Syria, as well as in Bulgaria, Yugoslavia and India.
Compared with the milk from which it is made, which may come from a cow, goat, buffalo, reindeer, mare or ewe, yogurt has a slightly lower sugar content and protein that is more finely divided and readily digestible. In the human intestinal tract, the bacteria in yogurt produce lactic acid which controls, or in some instances may destroy, putrefying bacteria present which left unchecked can cause discomfort and often illness.
Despite some historians' and health enthusiasts' claims, yogurt is neither a panacea for all ills nor the long-sought-after elixir of life.

PREPARATION OF HOMEMADE YOGURT

Method I:

Using dry Bulgarian yogurt culture, available in health food stores

  1 quart raw, pasteurized, homogenized, skim, goat or soy milk, or reconstituted non-fat dry milk solids

  ¼ cup non-fat dry milk solids (optional)

  ⅓ ounce dry Bulgarian culture, approximately

1. Combine the liquid milk product and the extra non-fat dry milk solids if a thicker, more custard-like product is desired.

2. Heat the milk mixture in a heavy saucepan over direct heat, or in the top of a double boiler over simmering water, until mixture reaches 180 degrees. A thermometer is a useful tool in the making of uniformly good-quality yogurt.

3. Cool the milk mixture, suitably protected from surface contamination, to about 110 degrees, or lukewarm.

4. Stir in the culture and mix well. Pour the mixture into a warm sterilized quart jar, preferably with a wide mouth. Cover the jar with clear plastic wrap and set in a warm place such as those listed below.

a) Set jar in an insulated picnic cooler, warmed by two quart jars of hot water. Set the cooler in a place where it will not be disturbed for several hours and replenish the hot water jars if the temperature in the cooler goes below about 106 degrees.

b) Set the quart jar in a pan of medium-hot water over a pilot light on the stove and cover with a blanket. Do not disturb for several hours.

c) Line a kettle with thick foam rubber sheets and place in it the jar of milk mixture and one of hot water. Do not disturb.

d) Pour the milk mixture into a very clean, warmed thermos and set aside undisturbed.

e) Fill a box with green hay. Bury the jar of milk mixture in it, cover and set in the sun.

f) The warmth necessary for growth of the culture can often be maintained by merely wrapping the jar of warm milk in insulating material such as a blanket or newspaper.

g) Campers have been known to place jars of the milk mixture in the dying ashes of a campfire or to bury the jars under pine boughs with success.

h) A container warmed by a 15-watt light bulb or a night light makes an excellent place to leave the jar of milk mixture for the culture to grow undisturbed.

i) A commercial yogurt maker with four containers set on a warming device is available and sells for about $10.

5. Whatever the method of keeping the mixture warm, it is important that it is not disturbed, otherwise the whey tends to settle out from the curd. An average batch should be thickened in five hours and it should then be refrigerated several hours during which time it will thicken further.

6. The finished product should be thick, creamy and custardy in texture with a mild flavor and pleasant degree of acidity. Acidity can be increased by increasing the length of incubation time. The addition of extra milk solids gives a thicker product.

The yogurt will keep in the refrigerator for six to seven days. However, batches to be used as starters for culturing new jars of yogurt should not be more than three to five days old for best results. Successive batches of yogurt made with yogurt starter can be made for a month before flavor and texture deteriorate. It is then advisable to use another purchased dry culture or small quantity of store-purchased yogurt.

Scrupulous cleanliness is essential to successful yogurt making.

Method II:

Using homemade, or store-bought, yogurt as a starter
  1 quart raw, pasteurized, homogenized, skim, goat or soy milk or reconstituted non-fat dry milk solids
  ¼ cup non-fat dry milk solids (optional)
  1 teaspoon to 4 tablespoons yogurt

1. Combine the liquid milk with the non-fat dry milk solids and heat the mixture in a heavy saucepan, or in the top of a double boiler, until mixture registers 180 degrees on a thermometer.
2. Let milk mixture cool to 113 degrees.

3. Mix a little of the warm milk with the yogurt and then stir into the bulk of the milk mixture. Mix well. Keep in a warm place, undisturbed for several hours, using one of the methods suggested in Method I. The amount of yogurt used determines the length of time it takes to produce a thickened mixture. The longer the time, the more acid in flavor the yogurt will be. Time can vary from four to 15 hours. Refrigerate before using.

If a slightly sweet product is desired, a small quantity of honéy or maple syrup can be added to the milk mixture before the culture is added.

Uses for Yogurt

The cultured milk product can be sipped as a beverage, spooned as a dessert or enjoyed at any hour of the day as a snack or part of a meal. Yogurt can be spooned over fruit, cereal, vegetables, salads, curries, meat and poultry dishes and over hard-cooked eggs. Many of the recipes for breads, cakes, casseroles and soups in this book call for yogurt as an ingredient.

If the whey, or clear liquid, separates, it can be stirred back in or drunk as a beverage.

Yogurt can be frozen plain, or mixed with preserves, and served when it is the consistency of Italian ices. Yogurt pops for the children can be made with the aid of special molds and flat wooden sticks.

PANIR OR FRESH CURDS

1 pint whole milk, raw,
    pasteurized or homogenized
½ cup yogurt or 1 tablespoon
    lemon juice

1. Bring the milk to a boil. Add yogurt or lemon juice and bring to a boil again. The milk will curdle.

2. Strain it through a double thickness of muslin and tie to the water faucet or some other place where it can drain for one to two hours depending on how dry, or moist, you want the curds.

3. For a more solid product, lay the muslin-wrapped curds on a board, weight heavily and leave overnight. The solid curds can be cut into small squares and fried to a light golden brown color for adding to curry dishes such as a curry of peas and tomatoes.

4. Crumbly or solid, the cheese can be used in sandwiches and salads.

Yield: About one-half cup.

14
DESSERTS

Fresh and dried fruits are probably the most desirable desserts and
between-meal snacks, providing an abundance of natural
nutrients and few empty calories.
However, because of the habits of generations of America's cooks, people
have come to expect and enjoy pies, cakes, puddings and cookies.
It's hard to eliminate them from a family's diet suddenly. The children may
be satisfied with a banana or date chips once in a while but will insist on
their favorite cookie or cake when a special occasion comes around.
So in this book there's a fairly large offering of dessert recipes, all of which
attempt to cut down on the amount of sugar used and concentrate on
whole grains, unbleached white flour and nutritious additions to contribute
essential nutrients and a minimum of empty calories.
Use of some sweetening product is necessary to make desserts palatable.
The sweetening product best able to create an emulsion, the basis for texture
in many familiar cakes and cookies, is sugar. Thus both raw sugar and
brown sugar are included in the ingredients in the following recipes,
though in limited amounts.
A homemade raisin, oatmeal and whole wheat flour cookie with a small
percentage of sugar contributes essential nutrients to a child's lunch box,
or is a good after-school snack, when an apple or an orange will not satisfy
his acquired sweet tooth. Established food patterns are hard to change for
parents, too, so when switching from a highly refined and processed diet
including many convenience foods, these desserts are
good-tasting, beneficial alternates.

MYSTERY FRUIT THING

2 ripe bananas, thinly sliced
3 Red Delicious apples, cored and
   cut in very thin slices about
   the size of a nickel
3 tablespoons soy flour
3 tablespoons wheat germ
6 tablespoons honey
2 tablespoons butter
2 tablespoons lemon juice

1. Preheat the oven to 300 degrees.

2. Place one quarter of the banana slices
and apple pieces in the bottom of a baking
dish or casserole. Sprinkle with one
tablespoon soy flour and one tablespoon
wheat germ. Drizzle with two tablespoons
honey.

3. Top with another quarter of the fruits,
another tablespoon soy flour and wheat
germ and two tablespoons honey and so on,
ending with fruit layer.

4. Dot with the butter and sprinkle with
the lemon juice. Bake 30 minutes. Eat warm
or cooled.

Yield: Four servings.

SPICED FRUIT MISHMASH

2 cups fresh pineapple chunks
1½ pounds peaches, skinned,
   halved and pitted
1½ pounds apricots, skinned,
   halved and pitted
⅓ cup butter, melted
⅔ cup brown sugar
¼ teaspoon ground cloves
¼ teaspoon cinnamon
1 tablespoon curry powder, or to
   taste
Homemade vanilla ice cream

1. Preheat the oven to 350 degrees.

2. Arrange the fruits in layers in a shallow
casserole. Combine the butter, brown
sugar, cloves, cinnamon and curry powder
and sprinkle over fruits.

3. Bake 45 minutes. Serve warm with a
scoop of homemade ice cream.

Yield: Eight servings.

HOMEMADE APPLESAUCE I

2 pounds tart cooking apples, washed in distilled or spring water
½ cup boiling distilled or spring water
Wild honey to taste
Maple syrup to taste
¼ cup wheat germ
½ cup monukka raisins
2 tablespoons ground sunflower seed kernels
⅛ teaspoon nutmeg
⅛ teaspoon cinnamon
1 teaspoon lemon juice or grated lemon rind from organically grown fruit

1. Do not peel or core apples. Quarter them and place quarters in the boiling water. Cook, covered, until barely tender, about 15 minutes.

2. Press apples through a colander or food mill and add honey and maple syrup.

3. Add remaining ingredients.

Yield: Six servings.

HOMEMADE APPLESAUCE II

8 cups peeled and cored apple slices (even apparently wormy apples from a neglected orchard can be used if you're willing to pare away the bad parts)
2 cups water
2 teaspoons lemon juice
1 teaspoon cinnamon
½ teaspoon ground ginger
½ teaspoon ground cloves
½ teaspoon nutmeg
¼ teaspoon allspice
¼ teaspoon mace
Honey

1. In a six-quart kettle, place the apple slices, water and lemon juice. Bring to a boil and simmer until half the apples are mushy.

2. Add remaining ingredients including enough honey to sweeten to taste. Press the apple mixture with a potato masher, leaving some chunks for texture. Alternately, the mixture can be pureed in a food mill or electric blender.

Yield: Six servings.

Note: This same recipe can be used to cook homegrown peaches and pears.

EASY APPLE TREAT

4 cups homemade applesauce
  (see page 316), preferably made
  from McIntosh apples and
  not sweetened
½ cup raisins
⅓ cup chopped black walnuts
  (or regular walnuts can be
  substituted)
⅛ teaspoon cinnamon
Whipped cream

Combine the applesauce, raisins, walnuts
and cinnamon in a serving bowl and let
stand in a cool place at least four hours
before serving. Serve topped with whipped
cream.

Yield: Six servings.

APRICOT MOUSSE

½ pound dried organic apricots
1 orange, sliced thinly, including
  the skin
¼ cup blanched almonds
Water, if necessary
Whipped cream

1. Place the apricots, orange and almonds
in a small saucepan. Bring to a boil and
simmer until soft. Add water only if
necessary to prevent scorching.

2. Puree in an electric blender or a
food mill, again adding water if necessary
for blending or if mixture is too thick to go
through mill. Chill. Serve topped with
whipped cream.

Yield: Four servings.

THE LEOPARD MOUSSE AUX ABRICOTS

1 pound dried unsulphured
  apricots
Spring water
2 cups heavy cream or goat's
  cream, whipped
Honey to taste

1. Place the apricots in a bowl. Cover with
spring water and let soak overnight. Next
day, blend the apricots together with
soaking liquid, in small batches, in an
electric blender until smooth.

2. Fold in the whipped cream and honey.
Fill small pots de crème, individual soufflé
dishes or glass sherbets. Chill.

Yield: Six servings.

NATURAL COMPOTE

½ pound unsulphured pitted
    prunes
½ pound monukka raisins
½ pound dried pears
½ pound unsulphured dried apples
½ pound unsulphured dried
    apricots
½ pound unsulphured dried
    peaches
Boiling spring water

Mix all the fruits together and pack loosely into a crock or glass jar. Pour boiling spring water over fruit to cover. Let stand uncovered 36 to 48 hours. Fruit becomes puffy and soft and juice syrupy. Cover and refrigerate several hours before serving.

Yield: Eight servings.

RASPBERRY-STRAWBERRY DESSERT

1 pint fresh raspberries or
    10-ounce package frozen
    raspberries
Honey
1 quart strawberries, hulled,
    washed and sliced if very large
⅓ cup chopped walnuts
1 cup heavy cream, whipped
1 teaspoon cinnamon

1. Puree the raspberries in an electric blender. Pass through a fine sieve to remove the seeds. Sweeten to taste with honey.

2. Combine the puree, strawberries and walnuts in a bowl and chill thoroughly.

3. Sweeten the whipped cream with honey and add the cinnamon. Chill well. Serve fruit topped with cinnamon-flavored cream.

Yield: Six servings.

PINEAPPLE-NUTS DESSERT

1 large ripe pineapple, peeled,
    cored and thinly sliced
2 cups almonds very finely
    grated through a mouli or
    Moulinex grinder
1½ cups honey

1. Place a layer of pineapple in a glass bowl and sprinkle with some of the nuts and some of the honey. Repeat with layers of pineapple, nuts and honey until all are used.

2. Set in a cool place for at least two hours before serving.

Yield: Six servings.

POLYNESIAN DELIGHT

1 fresh ripe pineapple, peeled,
  cored and very finely chopped
1 cup unsweetened shredded
  coconut
3 tablespoons honey

Combine all the ingredients and serve at
room temperature or chilled.

Yield: Six servings.

RHUBARB DELIGHT

1 quart rhubarb cut into
  ½-inch pieces
¾ cup monukka raisins
¾ cup chopped dates
2 oranges, ground with rind
  and juice retained
2 quarts boiling spring water
1 teaspoon sea salt
¼ teaspoon cayenne pepper

1. Combine the rhubarb, raisins, dates,
ground oranges and orange juice in a
saucepan. Pour the boiling water over all.
Add the salt and cayenne.

2. Bring to a boil and simmer four to five
minutes. Pour into a porcelain or glass bowl
and let stand in a cool place overnight.

Yield: Six to eight servings.

FRESH RHUBARB SAUCE

1 cup finely diced young rhubarb
½ cup water
½ cup honey

Place all the ingredients in an electric
blender and blend until smooth. Serve in
stemmed glasses at room temperature or
chilled.

Yield: Two servings.

SIMPLEST DESSERT OF ALL

1 ripe banana

Peel banana and freeze. Serve frozen and
whole with napkin wrapped around bottom,
or sliced into serving dish.

Yield: One serving.

Note: Frozen banana has the consistency of
ice cream and tastes delicious.

CITRUS MOLD

1½ tablespoons unflavored gelatin
1 cup water
½ cup honey
¾ cup fresh or unsweetened canned grapefruit juice
2 tablespoons lemon juice
¼ cup orange juice
⅛ teaspoon sea salt
1½ medium-size grapefruit, sectioned
2 medium-size oranges, sectioned
½ cup chopped almonds or walnuts
2 apples, washed, cored and chopped (leave peel on)
1 banana, sliced
Sour cream or yogurt (see page 311)

1. Soak the gelatin in one-half cup of the water. Heat remaining water and honey to boiling and add to soaked gelatin. Stir to dissolve gelatin.

2. Add the grapefruit juice, lemon juice, orange juice and salt. Mix well and chill until mixture just shows signs of setting.

3. Fold in the fruit sections, nuts, apple and banana. Pour into a lightly oiled 1½- to 2-quart mold or serving dish. Chill well.

4. Serve from the dish, or unmold, and serve with sour cream or yogurt.

Yield: Six servings.

COLD FRUIT PUDDING

20-24 ounces (1½ boxes) mixed dried unsulphured fruit
1 cup raisins
3 tart apples, peeled, cored and quartered
1½ quarts water
½ cup raw sugar or brown sugar
1 cinnamon stick
¼ cup potato starch
3 tablespoons cold water
Whipped cream

1. Wash the dried fruit in warm water, drain, and place in a bowl with the raisins and apples. Pour the water over all. Add sugar and stir well. Let stand overnight.

2. Transfer fruit and liquid to a pan, add cinnamon stick and bring to a boil. Simmer slowly until fruit is tender but not mushy.

3. Strain off the cooking liquid into a second pan. Mix the potato starch with the cold water and stir into fruit liquid. Bring to a boil, stirring until mixture thickens and is clear, about three minutes.

4. Place the fruit in a serving bowl, pour the hot pudding over all, cool and chill. Serve with whipped cream.

Yield: Six servings.

LEOPARD COEUR À LA CRÈME

1 pound goat cottage cheese
(regular cottage cheese can be
substituted), at room
temperature
1 pound goat cream cheese
(regular cream cheese can be
substituted), at room
temperature
¼ teaspoon sea salt
2 cups heavy goat's cream or
heavy cream
1 pint strawberries

1. Line six coeur à la crème wicker baskets with a double thickness of muslin moistened in water.

2. Beat together the cottage cheese, cream cheese and salt until smooth.

3. Gradually beat in the cream. Pour the mixture into the prepared baskets. Draw the muslin over the top of the cheese mixture and place a small weight on each basket. Place baskets on a rack, over a platter, and let stand at cellar or refrigerator temperature overnight.

4. Unmold the baskets onto serving plates and garnish with strawberries.

Yield: Six servings.

NO-BAKE LEMON CHIFFON

8 eggs, separated
1 cup raw sugar
⅔ cup lemon juice, about 4
lemons
⅛ teaspoon sea salt
2 tablespoons unflavored gelatin
¼ cup cold water
1 teaspoon grated lemon rind
⅓ cup graham cracker crumbs

1. Place the egg yolks in the top of a double boiler with the sugar, lemon juice and salt.

2. Heat over simmering water, stirring, until mixture thickens.

3. Soak the gelatin in the cold water. Add to hot egg mixture and stir to dissolve gelatin. Cool until mixture starts to thicken.

4. Beat the egg whites until stiff but not dry and fold into cooled mixture. Fold in rind. Pour mixture into a well-buttered deep pie plate sprinkled with graham cracker crumbs on bottom and sides. Chill several hours before serving.

Yield: Six servings.

SOY BUTTERSCOTCH PUDDING

¼ cup raw sugar or brown sugar
¼ cup arrowroot
¼ teaspoon sea salt
1½ cups soy milk
¾ cup honey or unsulphured molasses
2 egg yolks, lightly beaten
2 tablespoons butter

1. In a saucepan, mix together the sugar, arrowroot and salt. Gradually blend in the milk. Stir in the honey or molasses and mix well.

2. Bring to a boil, stirring until mixture thickens. Spoon some of hot mixture onto the egg yolks. Mix well and return to the bulk of the mixture in the saucepan. Cook, stirring, until mixture thickens. Do not allow to boil.

3. Stir in the butter and pour into four individual dessert dishes. Cool and chill.

Yield: Four servings.

CONSCIOUSNESS III PUDDING

1 cup butter, melted
1 cup carob powder
1 teaspoon vanilla
2 eggs
2 tablespoons honey
1 pound whole milk ricotta cheese
1 cup chopped dates, pecans, walnuts or coconut, or ¼ cup sesame seeds or sunflower seed kernels (optional)

1. Combine the butter, carob powder and vanilla.

2. Place eggs in an electric blender and blend until frothy.

3. Add butter mixture and honey and blend until well mixed.

4. Add ricotta and blend until smooth. To take the dessert one step further, into Consciousness IV, add one of the optional ingredients. Pour into a serving bowl. Chill.

Yield: Eight servings.

DATE-WHEAT PUDDING

½ cup raw sugar
½ cup whole wheat flour
¾ teaspoon sea salt
½ cup cold water
2 cups boiling water
¾ cup diced pitted dates
Whipped cream

1. In the top of a double boiler, combine the sugar, flour and salt. Mix well. Stir in the cold water.

2. Gradually stir in the boiling water and cook over direct heat, stirring constantly, until mixture thickens, about 10 minutes.

3. Add dates. Place over simmering water, cover and cook, stirring occasionally, one and one-quarter hours. Cool and chill. Serve with whipped cream.

Yield: Four servings.

PERSIMMON PUDDING

2 cups wild persimmon pulp
2 cups raw sugar
1½ cups buttermilk
1 teaspoon baking soda
3 eggs, beaten
⅓ cup light cream
1½ cups unbleached white flour
1 teaspoon baking powder
⅛ teaspoon sea salt
½ teaspoon cinnamon
1 teaspoon vanilla
½ cup butter
Whipped cream

1. Preheat the oven to 325 degrees.

2. Mix the pulp with the sugar.

3. Combine the buttermilk and baking soda and stir until mixture stops foaming. Add to the pulp mixture along with the eggs and cream.

4. Sift the flour with the baking powder, salt and cinnamon and stir into pulp mixture.

5. Stir in vanilla. Melt the butter and pour into a 9-by-13-inch baking dish and swish butter around to grease sides. Pour excess into the pudding mixture.

6. Pour pudding into the dish and bake 45 minutes. Cool in the dish. Serve with whipped cream.

Yield: Twelve servings.

STRAWBERRY YOGURT DESSERT

2 tablespoons unflavored gelatin
½ cup concentrated strawberry
   syrup (Hain's brand)
1½ cups water
¼ cup honey
1 quart yogurt (see page 311)
2 cups strawberries, sliced
Wheat germ (optional)

1. Soften the gelatin in the strawberry syrup and one-half cup of the water. Boil remaining water and add to gelatin mixture.

2. Stir to dissolve gelatin. Add the honey and yogurt and beat with a rotary beater until smooth. Cool until mixture starts to thicken slightly.

3. Fold in the fruit and pour into a large, well-buttered deep pie plate liberally sprinkled with wheat germ or into a serving dish. Chill.

Yield: Six servings.

YOGURT SUNDAE

1 apple, cored and quartered
1 banana, cut lengthwise in half
¼ cup wheat germ
1 cup yogurt (see page 311)
¼ cup chopped nuts and seeds
   mixed

1. Place the cored unpeeled washed apple in a blender and blend until smooth. Divide the mixture between two sundae dishes. Top each with half a banana.

2. Sprinkle each dish with half of the wheat germ. Top each sundae with half a cup of yogurt and sprinkle with seeds and nuts.

Yield: Two servings.

PRUNANA WHIP

1 cup stewed pitted prunes
3 ripe bananas
½ teaspoon almond extract
¼ cup unsweetened shredded
   coconut (optional)

Place all the ingredients except the coconut in an electric blender and blend until smooth. Stir in the coconut if desired.

Yield: Four servings.

ORANGE-MILLET DESSERT

¼ cup whole hulled millet
2 cups milk
1 orange
¼ cup honey
2 eggs, separated
¼ cup slivered almonds

1. In the top of a double boiler, mix the millet with one-half cup of the milk. Scald remaining milk and stir into the millet.

2. Add grated rind of the orange and the honey. Cook over boiling water, stirring occasionally, until millet is tender and has absorbed about three quarters of the liquid, about 45 minutes.

3. Beat the egg yolks lightly, stir into the millet mixture and cook, stirring, until mixture thickens slightly. Cool to room temperature. Chill.

4. Beat the egg whites until stiff but not dry and fold into the dessert. Fold in the almonds. Section the orange and use as a garnish.

Yield: Four servings.

BLENDER VANILLA PUDDING

3 hard-cooked eggs, shelled
½ cup oil
¼ cup honey
½ cup water
1 teaspoon vanilla
¼ teaspoon almond extract
1 ripe banana, cut up

Place all ingredients in an electric blender and blend until smooth and thick. Chill well.

Yield: Four servings.

FRESH-SQUEEZED FRUIT SHERBET

3 cups pure fruit juice, either
fresh squeezed or made from
pure fruit concentrate

2 apples, peeled, cored and
quartered

2 ripe bananas

½ papaya or avocado, peeled and
pitted

½ cup berries, seedless grapes or
raisins

¼ cup oil

½ cup honey

Mix all the ingredients together and blend
in three separate batches in an electric
blender until smooth. Pour into ice cube
trays and freeze until solid.

Yield: Four to six servings.

QUICK FROZEN FRUIT DESSERT

1 cup heavy cream

1 tablespoon honey

1 pound frozen strawberries,
raspberries, peaches or cherries

1. Place the cream in an electric blender.
Add the honey.

2. Slowly add pieces of the frozen fruit
while blending on medium speed until
mixture is like slush, partly frozen but still
able to flow. Add as much of the fruit as
possible.

Yield: Four servings.

RAW NUT ICE CREAM

2 cups soy milk

1 cup almonds

1 cup pecans

½ cup sunflower seed kernels

½ cup sesame seeds

¼ cup flax seeds

½ cup honey

¼ cup oil

1 teaspoon vanilla

Mix all the ingredients together and blend
in an electric blender in batches until
smooth. Pour into ice cube trays and freeze
until solid.

Yield: Six to eight servings.

HOMEMADE STRAWBERRY ICE CREAM

2 cups strawberries, washed,
   sliced if large
1 cup honey
1 cup ice-cold water
1 cup soy milk powder
2 egg yolks
½ cup chilled salad oil

1. Combine the strawberries and honey,
cover and chill in the refrigerator at least
one hour.

2. Place the water and soy milk powder in
an electric blender. Blend until smooth and
thick. Add the egg yolks and blend well
again.

3. Add the oil slowly while blending on
low speed. Blend at high speed until
smooth and thick.

4. Add the strawberry mixture and blend
again. Pour into chilled ice cube trays and
freeze until mixture is solid round the
edges and slightly mushy in the middle.
Turn into the blender and blend until
smooth. Return to the trays; freeze again.

5. Repeat the freezing and blending twice
more, and serve frozen. Store any leftover
ice cream in covered glass jars in the
freezer.

Yield: Four servings.

MAPLE ELEGANCE

5 extra-large eggs, lightly beaten
1¼ cups hot pure maple syrup
⅛ teaspoon sea salt
2 cups heavy cream, whipped

1. Place the eggs in the top of a double
boiler.

2. Gradually pour the hot syrup into the
eggs while beating vigorously. Add the salt
and cook the mixture, over hot water, until
mixture thickens, stirring constantly. Cool.

3. Fold in the cream and spoon into parfait
goblets, individual soufflé dishes or a mold.
Freeze. Serve frozen, unmolded if frozen in
a mold.

Yield: Six servings.

GOAT'S MILK ICE CREAM

½ cup raw sugar, or maple syrup to taste

3 tablespoons unbleached white flour

3 eggs

6 cups sweet goat's milk (cow's milk can be used)

1 teaspoon vanilla

2 cups peeled pitted pureed apricots or peaches

1. Place the sugar or syrup, the flour, eggs and two cups of the milk in an electric blender and blend until smooth. Pour into a saucepan.

2. Heat, stirring, until mixture thickens. Cool.

3. Beat in remaining milk, the vanilla and fruit puree. Place in an electric ice cream maker and follow manufacturer's directions. Beat and freeze until firm. Scrape into a container and store in the freezer. Set in refrigerator 30 minutes or so before serving for best consistency.

Yield: Six servings.

BANANA ICE CREAM

1 cup milk

2 eggs, lightly beaten

⅔ cup honey

2 teaspoons vanilla

1 cup heavy cream, whipped

1 ripe banana, mashed

1. Beat the milk into the eggs. Add the honey and mix well.

2. Stir in the vanilla. Fold in the cream and then the banana. Turn into an ice cube tray and freeze until solid about one inch from the edges.

3. Turn into a mixer bowl and beat until smooth. Return to the tray and freeze again.

Yield: Six servings.

Note: Frozen strawberries can be used in place of the banana if desired.

HONEY ICE CREAM

2 cups milk
2 eggs, lightly beaten
1 tablespoon unflavored gelatin
2 tablespoons arrowroot
½ cup honey
2 cups heavy cream
2 tablespoons vanilla
½ cup non-fat dry milk solids

1. In a saucepan, place the milk, eggs, gelatin, arrowroot and honey. Bring to a boil, stirring until mixture thickens.

2. Cool mixture. Stir in the cream, vanilla and milk solids. Mix well. Pour into two freezer trays and freeze about one and one-half hours until mixture is frozen at least one inch from the edges.

3. Transfer mixture to a mixer bowl and beat until smooth. (An electric blender can be used instead of an electric mixer.)

4. Return to freezer trays and freeze again.

Yield: About one and one-quarter quarts.

Note: One and one-half cups fresh or frozen strawberries can be added to the cooled arrowroot mixture before adding the cream.

HONEY PECAN ICE CREAM

4 eggs, separated
¾ cup honey
3 teaspoons vanilla
2 cups heavy cream, whipped
⅛ teaspoon sea salt
1 cup chopped pecans

1. In the small bowl of an electric mixer, place the egg yolks, honey and vanilla. Beat until well blended and very smooth.

2. Fold the egg-and-honey mixture into the cream.

3. Beat the egg whites with the salt until stiff but not dry and fold into cream mixture. Fold in the nuts.

4. Pour into three ice cube trays and set in freezer. When solid, remove and pack into a quart container.

Yield: One quart.

APPLE CRUNCH

1½ cups sifted whole wheat flour
 1 cup rolled oats
 1 cup brown sugar
 ½ teaspoon sea salt
 ½ teaspoon baking soda
 ½ cup butter
Filling I:
 6 to 8 apples, peeled, cored and sliced
 ¼ cup raw sugar
 1 teaspoon cinnamon
 1 teaspoon lemon juice
Filling II:
 3 cups rhubarb cut in ½-inch slices
 ¼ cup raw sugar
 2 tablespoons tapioca
 1 egg
Filling III:
 1 pint blueberries
 ⅛ teaspoon mace or nutmeg
 1 tablespoon tapioca
 Ice cream (optional)

1. Preheat the oven to 350 degrees.

2. Place the flour, oats, sugar, salt and baking soda in a large bowl. With two knives or a pastry blender, work the butter into the dry ingredients until pieces are uniform and quite small.

3. If apple filling is being used, mix apples, sugar, cinnamon and lemon juice and place in bottom of a buttered nine-inch square pan.

4. Cover with oats mixture.

5. If rhubarb or blueberry filling is to be used, pat half the oats mixture into a buttered nine-inch square baking pan.

6. Combine the fruit with other ingredients indicated and place on top of the oats mixture. Place remaining oats mixture on top of fruit and bake 50 minutes or until done. Serve warm or cold, with ice cream if desired.

Yield: Six servings.

APPLE FRITTERS

1¾ cups whole wheat flour
 3 teaspoons single-acting baking powder (Royal brand)
 ½ teaspoon sea salt
 1 egg, lightly beaten
 1 cup milk
 1 tablespoon honey
 1 tablespoon safflower oil
 8 to 10 small apples, peeled, cored and chopped
 Oil for deep-frying
 Raw sugar

1. Mix together the flour, baking powder and salt.

2. Beat together the egg, milk, honey and oil. Pour into the dry ingredients and stir to mix. Stir in the apples.

3. Drop tablespoons of the apple batter into the deep oil heated to 365 to 375 degrees. Turn fritters as they rise to the surface, and fry until golden brown.

4. Drain on paper towels and dredge in sugar. Serve hot.

Yield: Six to eight servings.

APPLE SCROUNGE

5 to 6 cups unpeeled washed cored sliced apple drops (see note)

1½ cups chopped nuts (hazelnuts or hand-cracked butternuts are preferred)

¾ cup honey, or to taste

1 cup apple juice or water

1½ cups whole wheat flour

½ cup butter

¼ teaspoon sea salt

1½ teaspoons cinnamon

3 tablespoons brown sugar

Yogurt (see page 311) or sour cream, lightly sweetened with honey

1. Preheat the oven to 400 degrees.

2. Place the apple slices in a well-buttered baking dish or casserole. Sprinkle with the nuts. Drizzle the honey over and pour the juice or water over all.

3. Place the flour in a bowl and cut in the butter until mixture is like coarse corn meal.

4. Add the salt, cinnamon and sugar and sprinkle over apples. Cover the dish and bake 30 minutes, or until apples are tender. Uncover and bake 10 minutes longer to brown, or brown under the broiler. Serve warm with yogurt or sour cream.

Yield: Six servings.

Note: The contributor says, "Don't skip this recipe because you don't have a source of organic apples." She advises gaining permission from the owner of a neglected orchard to pick the apples dropped on the ground. "Scrounge around and carry home the unsprayed, wormy things. Nothing in this world tastes better than a juicy crisp apple right off the ground of a deserted orchard. It is well worth a bit of paring. And the worms are good for chicken feed."

BAKED APPLE DESSERT

6 to 8 baking apples, peeled, cored and thickly sliced

1 teaspoon cinnamon

2 tablespoons dark brown sugar

¾ cup unsweetened pineapple juice

½ cup finely chopped fresh pineapple or canned crushed pineapple (optional)

⅓ cup chopped walnuts

1. Preheat the oven to 350 degrees.

2. Place the apple slices in a well-buttered deep pie plate. Sprinkle the cinnamon and sugar over all. Pour the juice over apples and spoon the pineapple over all.

3. Sprinkle the walnuts over the top and bake 40 minutes. Cool and chill.

Yield: Six servings.

SWEET APPLE SNITZ AND DUMPLINGS

4 cups dried apples (about one
  pound)
4 cups water
Honey to taste
1 cup sifted whole wheat flour
1¼ teaspoons baking powder
¼ teaspoon sea salt
1 tablespoon brown sugar
Milk

1. Soak the dried apples in the water 30 minutes. Bring to a boil and simmer 30 minutes or until tender. Sweeten with honey.

2. Combine the flour, baking powder, salt and sugar in a bowl. Stir in enough milk to make a stiff dumpling batter.

3. Drop the batter by the tablespoon onto the top of the simmering apple mixture. Cover tightly and cook 15 minutes.

Yield: Eight servings.

Note: The contributor says this dish is fine after a hard day's work.

APPLE-OAT CRISP

6 medium-size Red Delicious,
  Cortland or Rome apples,
  washed, cored and thinly sliced
¾ cup plus 2 tablespoons dark
  brown sugar
½ teaspoon cinnamon
½ cup stoneground corn meal
¾ cup rolled oats
½ cup peanut oil

1. Preheat the oven to 300 degrees.

2. Oil a large heavy iron skillet. Place the unpeeled apple slices in the skillet and sprinkle with two tablespoons of the sugar and the cinnamon.

3. In a bowl, combine the corn meal, oats and remaining sugar. Pour in the oil and work with the fingers through the dry mixture. Mixture will be crumbly. Sprinkle over apples. Bake 40 minutes or until topping is brown. Do not overcook. Serve warm.

Yield: Six to eight servings.

BANANA SWEET POTATO PUDDING

2 ripe bananas, mashed
1 cup light cream
⅛ teaspoon sea salt
¼ cup chopped raisins
1 cup mashed cooked sweet
    potatoes
2 tablespoons brown sugar
2 egg yolks, lightly beaten

1. Preheat the oven to 300 degrees.

2. Combine all the ingredients in a large bowl and mix well. Turn into a well-buttered baking dish or casserole and bake about 45 minutes or until set and browned on top.

Yield: Four servings.

BLUEBERRY COBBLER

1 pint blueberries
⅓ cup water
1½ cups raw sugar
1 teaspoon grated lemon rind
1 cup whole wheat flour
½ teaspoon sea salt
1 teaspoon baking powder
⅓ cup butter

1. Preheat the oven to 350 degrees.

2. Combine the berries, water, three-quarters cup of the sugar and the rind in a heatproof casserole. Bring to a boil and simmer two minutes.

3. Meanwhile, combine remaining sugar with flour, salt and baking powder. Cut in the butter until mixture is crumbly.

4. Sprinkle crumbs over fruit. Bake about 25 minutes or until browned. Serve warm.

Yield: Four servings.

Note: Other berries can be used in place of the blueberries.

COTTAGE CHEESE BERRY SOUFFLÉ

4 eggs, well beaten
2 tablespoons wheat germ, or
  whole wheat bread crumbs
½ cup milk
¼ teaspoon sea salt
½ pound cottage cheese
2 cups sliced strawberries,
  blueberries, sliced peaches or
  applesauce
Honey to taste
Whipped cream

1. Beat together the eggs, wheat germ, milk and salt. Turn into a well-buttered two-cup ceramic, or glass, bowl. Cover bowl with aluminum foil. Set on a rack in a pan of boiling water, with the water extending at least two-thirds the way up the bowl. Cover pan and simmer very gently 15 minutes or until mixture is set. Cool, and chill if desired. Dessert may be eaten warm or cold.

2. Turn the mixture out onto a serving plate. Cover the outside of the mold with cottage cheese. Sweeten the fruit with honey and pour over cottage cheese.

3. Serve with whipped cream.

Yield: Four servings.

WHOLE WHEAT BERRY PUDDING

2 cups cooked whole wheat
  berries
3 cups milk
3 eggs, lightly beaten
¼ cup honey
1 cup raisins
1 tablespoon grated orange rind
⅛ teaspoon sea salt
⅛ teaspoon mace
2 cups fresh berries, sliced
  peaches or applesauce

1. Preheat the oven to 325 degrees.

2. Mix together all the ingredients except the fruit and turn into a well-buttered baking dish or casserole. Bake one hour or until set.

3. Serve warm or cold, topped with the fruit.

Yield: Six servings.

WHOLE WHEAT MOLASSES BREAD PUDDING

2¼ cups tiny cubes of whole
    wheat bread
½ cup raisins
2 eggs, lightly beaten
2½ cups milk
⅛ teaspoon sea salt
¼ cup unsulphured molasses
1 tablespoon butter
3 tablespoons honey or raw
    sugar
¼ teaspoon cinnamon

1. Preheat the oven to 350 degrees.

2. Place the bread cubes in a 1½-quart casserole. Sprinkle with the raisins.

3. Combine the eggs, milk, salt and molasses and pour over the bread. Dot with the butter. Drizzle the honey or sprinkle the raw sugar over all. Sprinkle with the cinnamon. Bake 30 to 35 minutes or until set.

Yield: Six servings.

BREAD PUDDING WITH ORANGE

½ cup raw sugar
2 tablespoons water
2 cups soy milk, scalded
6 tablespoons honey
1 tablespoon grated orange rind
1 teaspoon vanilla
6 slices whole wheat bread made
    into fine crumbs
2 tablespoons butter
4 eggs, beaten

1. Preheat the oven to 350 degrees.

2. Place the sugar and water in a small heavy skillet and heat gently, stirring until sugar has dissolved. Heat until mixture turns a pale golden color and pour immediately into a warmed, well-buttered 1½-quart baking dish.

3. Combine the milk, honey, rind, vanilla, bread crumbs and butter. Beat in the eggs. Pour into the baking dish and place in a pan of hot water. Bake 45 minutes or until set.

Yield: Six to eight servings.

CRANAPPLE COBBLER

3 large apples, cored and
    cut into small pieces
2 cups cranberries
2 teaspoons almond extract
¾ cup honey
½ cup finely chopped orange rind
1 cup wheat germ
1 teaspoon cinnamon
½ teaspoon kelp
¼ cup sweet butter
Yogurt (see page 311)

1. Preheat the oven to 425 degrees.

2. Mix together the apples, cranberries,
extract, honey and rind. Place in the bottom
of a well-buttered 1½- to 2-quart baking
dish or casserole.

3. Combine the wheat germ, cinnamon
and kelp and sprinkle over fruit mixture.
Dot with the butter and bake 40 minutes
or until bubbly and brown. Serve warm
with yogurt.

Yield: Six servings.

CRANBERRY CRUNCH

1 pound fresh cranberries
Honey to taste
1 cup rolled oats
½ cup whole wheat flour
1 cup brown sugar
½ cup butter
Homemade vanilla ice cream
    or whipped cream

1. Preheat the oven to 350 degrees.

2. Place the berries in saucepan and cook
until they pop and then a minute or two
longer. Do not let them get mushy.
Sweeten very lightly with honey. Cool
slightly.

3. Place the oats, flour and sugar in a bowl.
Cut in the butter with two knives, or a
pastry blender, until mixture is crumbly.

4. Place half the oat mixture in the bottom
of a buttered eight-inch square baking pan.
Cover with the cranberry mixture. Top
with remaining oat mixture. Bake 45
minutes or until done. Serve warm with
ice cream or whipped cream.

Yield: Six to eight servings.

STEAMED PERSIMMON PUDDING

1 cup wild persimmon pulp
1 cup raw sugar
2 tablespoons butter, melted
1 egg
½ teaspoon sea salt
1 cup unbleached white flour
½ cup milk
¼ teaspoon cinnamon
2 teaspoons baking soda

Combine all the ingredients in the order given. Pour into greased coffee can, bowl or mold. Cover with aluminum foil and set on a rack in a large kettle with water coming three-quarters the way up the can or bowl. Steam at least two hours. Serve warm.

Yield: Four servings.

Note: Nuts or dates may be added if desired.

PLANTATION PUDDING

1½ cups whole wheat flour
½ cup soy flour
¾ cup raw sugar
1 teaspoon cinnamon
¼ teaspoon sea salt
1 teaspoon ground ginger
¼ teaspoon ground cloves
⅓ cup butter
¾ cup hot water
¾ cup unsulphured molasses
1 teaspoon baking soda
Whipped cream

1. Preheat the oven to 350 degrees.

2. Sift the whole wheat flour with the soy flour, sugar, cinnamon, salt, ginger and cloves. Cut in the butter with two knives or a pastry blender until mixture resembles coarse meal.

3. Spread one third of crumb mixture in a buttered eight-inch square pan. Pat out evenly. Combine the hot water, molasses and baking soda, stir well and pour half the mixture over the crumbs.

4. Top with remaining crumbs. Drizzle remaining molasses mixture over crumbs to give a marbled appearance. Bake 25 to 30 minutes. Don't overbake. Serve warm with whipped cream.

Yield: Six servings.

INDIAN PUDDING

1 quart milk, scalded
5 tablespoons stoneground corn meal
2 eggs, well beaten
1 teaspoon sea salt
½ teaspoon ground ginger
½ teaspoon nutmeg
2 tablespoons butter
1 cup unsulphured molasses
½ cup raisins
Ice cream or whipped cream

1. Preheat oven to 325 degrees.
2. Pour the milk over the corn meal in a saucepan and bring to a boil, stirring. Cook over low heat, stirring constantly, until thick, smooth and creamy, about 15 minutes.
3. Pour corn meal mixture over the eggs. Add the salt, ginger, nutmeg, butter, molasses and raisins and pour into a greased baking dish. Bake one and one-half hours. Serve warm with ice cream or whipped cream.
Yield: Six servings.

OLD-FASHIONED TAPIOCA CREAM

1 cup large pearl tapioca
Water
4 cups milk
4 eggs, lightly beaten
¾ cup raw sugar
¼ teaspoon sea salt
1 teaspoon vanilla

1. Place tapioca in the top of a double boiler. Add water to cover and let stand for two hours.
2. Drain off excess water. Add the milk and cook, covered, over boiling water until tapioca is transparent, about one hour.
3. Beat together the eggs, sugar and salt. Gradually beat in the tapioca. Return to the double boiler and cook, stirring constantly, until mixture thickens. Do not allow to boil or it will curdle. Stir in vanilla and serve warm.
Yield: Six servings.

BAKED BROWN RICE WITH DATES

1 quart milk
½ cup raw brown rice
½ cup raw sugar or brown sugar
⅛ teaspoon sea salt
½ cup chopped dates
  Whipped cream

1. Preheat the oven to 300 degrees.

2. Place the milk, rice, sugar, salt and dates in a 1½-quart buttered casserole or baking dish. Stir to mix. Bake until a light brown skin forms over the surface. Stir the skin into the pudding and bake until another skin forms and stir that in. Continue stirring in the skins for two to two and one-half hours.

3. Bake, without stirring, until rice is tender and top is well browned. Serve with whipped cream.

Yield: Four servings.

CURRANT AND RICE PUDDING

3 cups milk
3 eggs, lightly beaten
½ teaspoon vanilla
½ cup raw sugar or brown sugar
⅛ teaspoon sea salt
2 cups cooked brown rice (see page 217)
½ cup chopped nuts
2 tablespoons currants
¼ teaspoon nutmeg
½ teaspoon cinnamon, or to taste

1. Preheat the oven to 325 degrees.

2. Beat the milk, eggs, vanilla, sugar and salt together. Add the rice, nuts, currants, nutmeg and cinnamon. Turn into a buttered casserole and bake 30 minutes or until pudding is the desired consistency. The longer the pudding bakes, the drier it will become.

Yield: Four servings.

SWEET PELLAO

4 cups cooked brown rice (see page 217)
½ cup raisins
¼ cup almonds, left whole or roughly chopped
½ teaspoon sea salt
½ teaspoon cinnamon
⅛ teaspoon mace
1/16 teaspoon saffron
Seeds from one whole cardamom pod, lightly crushed
6 tablespoons butter
3 tablespoons brown sugar

1. Mix together the rice, raisins, almonds, salt, cinnamon, mace, saffron and cardamom.

2. Melt the butter in a heavy skillet and add the brown sugar. Heat, stirring, until sugar dissolves. Add the rice mixture, spreading it over the pan, and heat over medium heat until mixture is warmed through and brown on the bottom.

Yield: Six servings.

HEAVENLY RICE

2 cups cold cooked brown rice (see page 217)
½ cup chopped dates
2 tablespoons honey
½ cup coarsely chopped nuts
1 cup very finely chopped fresh pineapple or canned crushed pineapple
Whipped cream
Fresh berries

1. Combine the rice, dates, honey, nuts and pineapple. Chill thoroughly.

2. Serve topped with whipped cream and berries.

Yield: Four servings.

BAKED RICE PUDDING

2 cups cooked brown rice (see page 217)
½ cup raisins
½ teaspoon grated lemon rind
1 teaspoon lemon juice
½ cup honey
½ teaspoon vanilla
3 eggs
2½ cups milk
¼ teaspoon sea salt

1. Preheat the oven to 325 degrees.

2. Place the rice, raisins, rind and juice in a buttered 1½-quart baking dish.

3. Beat together the remaining ingredients and pour over the rice and raisins. Stir to mix. Bake 30 minutes or until pudding is set.

Yield: Four servings.

PINEAPPLE-NOODLE PUDDING

½ cup soft butter
1 cup yogurt (see page 311)
3 eggs
1¼ teaspoons cinnamon
½ cup honey
1 teaspoon vanilla
½ pound ½-inch-wide
  (preferably crinkly) noodles,
  cooked, drained and cooled
  slightly
⅓ fresh pineapple, peeled, cored
  and cut into small pieces

1. Preheat the oven to 350 degrees.

2. Place the butter, yogurt, eggs, one teaspoon of the cinnamon, the honey and vanilla in an electric blender. Blend until smooth.

3. Place noodles and pineapple with juice in a bowl and pour the egg mixture over all. Mix well. Pour mixture into a buttered shallow baking dish, sprinkle with remaining cinnamon and bake one hour.

Yield: Six servings.

Note: Other juicy fruits, such as peaches and apricots, can be added to pineapple.

VELVET PUDDING

4 eggs, separated
1⅔ cups raw sugar
½ cup flour
¼ teaspoon sea salt
1 quart goat's milk, scalded
1 teaspoon vanilla

1. Preheat the oven to 350 degrees.

2. Combine the egg yolks, three-quarters cup of the sugar, the flour and one-eighth teaspoon of the salt in the top of a double boiler.

3. Gradually beat in the goat's milk and cook mixture over simmering water until mixture thickens, about five minutes. Add vanilla. Pour into a buttered baking dish and cool slightly.

4. Beat the egg whites until soft peaks form. Add remaining salt and remaining sugar gradually, while still beating, until mixture is very stiff and shiny.

5. Spread the meringue over the cooled pudding in the dish, place in a pan of hot water and bake 25 to 30 minutes.

Yield: Four servings.

COTTAGE CHEESE PUDDING

2 cups fresh goat's milk cottage cheese (regular cottage cheese can be substituted)
2 cups well-drained fresh, frozen thawed or canned pumpkin or squash pulp
4 eggs
½ cup raw sugar
⅛ teaspoon sea salt
¼ teaspoon nutmeg (optional)

1. Place all the ingredients except the nutmeg in an electric blender and blend until smooth.
2. Pour into six buttered or oiled custard cups. Sprinkle with nutmeg if desired. Place cups in a pan of hot water and bake until pudding is firm or until a silver knife inserted comes out clean, about 35 to 40 minutes. Cool and chill.

Yield: Six servings.

OIL PASTRY

2 cups soya-carob flour
½ teaspoon baking powder
1 teaspoon sea salt
⅔ cup oil
⅓ cup chilled spring water

1. Sift together the flour, baking powder and salt. Blend the oil and water together and immediately pour into the dry ingredients, stirring with a fork to distribute. Pour half of the mixture into a pie pan and press into place for bottom crust.
2. For top crust, flour wax paper, pour out remaining mixture onto paper, place another sheet of wax paper on top and roll out.

Yield: Enough for a two-crust pie.

WHEAT GERM PIE CRUST

1 cup wheat germ
1 cup whole wheat pastry flour
1 teaspoon sea salt
1 tablespoon blackstrap molasses
½ cup cold pressed sesame oil or corn oil
3 tablespoons cold water

1. Preheat the oven to 325 degrees.
2. Place all the ingredients in a bowl and cut mixture with a knife to blend. Turn into a 10-inch pie plate and press evenly over bottom and sides.
3. Bake 30 minutes or until done.

Yield: One baked pie shell.

WHOLE WHEAT PASTRY

1 cup whole wheat pastry flour
  (see step 2)
½ teaspoon salt
1 tablespoon wheat germ
¼ cup oil
2 tablespoons cold milk

1. Preheat the oven to 425 degrees.

2. Sift the flour before it is measured and discard or reserve any solids (bran husks) left in sieve to enrich another dish.

3. Place the cup of sifted flour in a bowl with the salt and wheat germ. Add the oil and milk and mix with a fork into a dough.

4. Between two pieces of wax paper, roll dough to fit an eight-inch pie pan. Peel off the top piece of wax paper and turn pastry side down into the pie pan.

5. Remove the second piece of wax paper and fit the pastry into the pan. Trim and decorate the edges.

6. Bake the pie shell about 15 minutes or until set and lightly browned.

Yield: One pie shell.

WHOLE WHEAT-RICE PASTRY

1 cup whole wheat pastry flour
  (see step 2)
1 cup brown rice flour
1 teaspoon salt
2 tablespoons wheat germ
⅓ cup oil
¼ cup plus 1 tablespoon cold milk

1. Preheat the oven to 400 degrees.

2. Sift the flour before it is measured and discard or reserve any solids (bran husks) left in sieve to enrich another dish.

3. Place the whole wheat flour, rice flour, salt and wheat germ in a bowl. Stir in the oil and milk to make a dough.

4. Roll out the dough between pieces of wax paper to a 10-inch round. Remove the top piece of paper. Turn the pastry side down into a nine-inch pie plate. Remove the second piece of wax paper and fit the pastry gently into the pan. Trim the edges and decorate. Bake 20 minutes or until set and lightly browned.

Yield: One pie shell.

WHOLE WHEAT-RICE PASTRY APPLE PIE

Crust:
    1 cup whole wheat pastry flour
       (see step 2)
    1 cup rice flour
    1 teaspoon sea salt
    ½ cup plus 2 tablespoons lard
       (see note)
    Ice water

Apple filling:
    4 cups sliced tart apples
    ⅔ cup raw sugar
    ½ teaspoon cinnamon
    1½ tablespoons whole wheat flour
    Grated lemon peel to taste

1. Preheat the oven to 425 degrees.

2. Sift the flour before it is measured and discard or reserve any solids (bran husks) left in sieve to enrich another dish.

3. Place the whole wheat flour, rice flour and salt in a bowl. With a pastry blender, or the fingertips, work the lard into the flours until mixture resembles coarse oatmeal.

4. Mixing with a fork, add enough ice water to make a dough. Roll out half the dough on a rice-floured board or between sheets of wax paper into a circle to fit a nine-inch pie pan. Fit the dough into the pan.

5. Combine all the ingredients for the filling and turn into the pastry-lined pie pan.

6. Roll out remaining pastry to cover the top of the pie. Place on pie, seal edges and decorate. Make steam holes. Bake 40 to 50 minutes or until filling is tender and pastry is done and slightly browned. Place aluminum foil over the pie if it tends to overbrown.

Yield: Six to eight servings.

Note: If this crust is to be used for a savory pie, chicken fat may be used instead of lard.

APPLE-CARROT PIE

Crust:

3 cups whole wheat flour
1 cup mixed flours (rice, soy, buckwheat, etc.)
½ teaspoon sea salt
⅔ cup cold pressed corn oil
Strong chilled peppermint tea

Filling:

4 medium-size Red Delicious or Cortland apples, washed, cored and finely chopped
1 cup carrot juice
3 tablespoons apple butter
¼ teaspoon cinnamon
¼ cup wheat germ
½ cup chopped almonds
⅓ cup raisins
Tahini (sesame paste)

1. For the crust, mix the flours and salt in a bowl. With the hands, mix in the oil until mixture almost forms a ball.

2. Add only enough tea to make a smooth dough. Knead the dough until it is the consistency of the earlobe. Do not overknead. Cover and let rest 30 minutes.

3. Preheat the oven to 400 degrees.

4. Roll out half the dough between sheets of wax paper, or on a floured board, to fit a nine-inch pie plate.

5. Fit the dough into the pie plate.

6. Arrange the apples in the pie shell. Combine the carrot juice with apple butter, cinnamon and wheat germ and pour over apples. Sprinkle the nuts and raisins over all.

7. Roll out remaining dough to fit top of pie. Place on pie, seal edges and decorate. Make a steam hole. Brush a very light film of tahini over the surface and bake 35 to 45 minutes or until pastry is done.

Yield: Six servings.

FIVE-MINUTE RAW BLUEBERRY PIE

2 pints blueberries, washed and drained
½ cup pitted chopped dates or figs
2 ripe bananas, sliced
½ cup monukka raisins

1. Place the berries in an electric blender. Turn blender to low speed and add dates or figs gradually. Pour into two nine-inch pie plates. Add one banana and one-quarter cup raisins to each pie.

2. Refrigerate for at least three hours and serve as pie.

Yield: Ten servings.

GOLDEN PINEAPPLE PIE

2 cups very finely chopped fresh
pineapple or canned crushed
unsweetened pineapple
1 cup crystallized honey
5 tablespoons arrowroot
2 tablespoons water
1 tablespoon butter
1 cup cottage cheese
1 teaspoon vanilla
½ teaspoon sea salt
2 eggs, lightly beaten
1¼ cups milk
1 unbaked 10-inch pie crust
(see page 342, 343)

1. In a small saucepan, combine the pineapple, one-half cup honey, two tablespoons arrowroot and the water. Bring to a boil, stirring, and cook one minute. Cool.

2. Preheat the oven to 450 degrees.

3. Beat together the butter, cottage cheese, vanilla, salt, eggs, milk, remaining honey and remaining arrowroot until smooth.

4. Pour cooled pineapple mixture into the pie shell. Pour cottage cheese mixture over the pineapple mixture and bake 15 minutes. Lower the oven heat to 325 degrees and bake 45 minutes longer or until set. Cool and chill.

Yield: Six servings.

YOGURT CHEESE PIE

½ cup rolled oats
½ cup pitted dates
2 tablespoons safflower oil
8 ounces soft cream cheese
⅔ cup yogurt (see page 311)
1 teaspoon vanilla
2 tablespoons honey
6 dates, cut up

1. Put the oats and pitted dates through the fine blade of a food grinder. Mix with the oil and press into an eight-inch pie plate to make a pie shell.

2. Beat together the cream cheese, yogurt, vanilla and honey until very smooth. Stir in the cut-up dates and pour into the pie shell. Refrigerate several hours or overnight before serving.

Yield: Six servings.

Note: This is an unbaked pie.

RHUBARB CREAM PIE

Lighthearted pie crust:
- ½ cup sesame oil (or sunflower oil)
- ⅓ cup cold water
- 2 cups whole wheat flour or unbleached white flour
- 1 teaspoon vegetable salt
- Sesame seeds

Filling:
- 1 cup brown sugar
- 3 tablespoons unbleached white flour
- 2½ cups stewed, but not mushy, unsweetened rhubarb
- 2 eggs, separated
- ⅓ cup orange juice
- Grated rind of one orange
- 1 tablespoon butter
- ½ cup honey

1. Preheat the oven to 400 degrees.

2. To prepare crust, mix the sesame oil with the water, quickly add the flour and salt and mix fast with a fork. Form into a ball.

3. Place half of the ball of dough between sheets of wax paper and roll to fit an eight- or nine-inch pie plate. Remove top piece of wax paper and turn dough side down into pie plate. Remove second piece of wax paper and fit pastry into pan. Decorate edges.

4. Sprinkle with one-half tablespoon sesame seeds and bake about 15 minutes or until light golden brown. Cool. Other half of dough can be made into a second pie shell or stored refrigerated for later use.

5. For the filling, mix the sugar and flour together. Add the rhubarb and pour into a saucepan. Heat, stirring, until mixture thickens.

6. Beat the egg yolks lightly. Spoon a little hot mixture onto the lightly beaten egg yolks; mix well. Return to the bulk of the mixture in the pan. Heat, stirring, until mixture thickens slightly. Do not allow to boil.

7. Remove from the heat and add orange juice, rind and butter. Cool the mixture.

8. Pour cooled mixture into cooled pie shell. Beat the egg whites until they are frothy and then very gradually beat in the honey until meringue stands in peaks (five to 10 minutes beating). Pile onto the pie, spreading meringue all over pie. Bake five to seven minutes or until golden.

Yield: Six servings.

PIE-ETTES

Filling:
 1 pound mixed dried fruits
 ⅓ cup orange juice
 ½ cup wheat germ
            or
 1 pound homemade mincemeat
    and ½ cup wheat germ

Pastry:
 3 cups whole wheat pastry flour
 ½ cup soy flour
 1 package (3.2 ounces)
    non-instant dry milk solids, or
    enough non-fat dry milk
    solids for making one quart
    reconstituted milk
 3 teaspoons baking powder
 ½ teaspoon sea salt
 1 cup raw wheat germ
 ¾ cup brown sugar
 5 eggs, lightly beaten
 ½ cup oil
 2 teaspoons vanilla
 Raw sugar

1. If using the mixed fruits and orange juice instead of mincemeat, place fruits and juice in a small saucepan and bring to a boil. Simmer 15 minutes or until tender.

2. Cool and chop very finely. Add the wheat germ to the filling.

3. Preheat the oven to 350 degrees.

4. To prepare pastry, sift together the whole wheat flour, soy flour, milk solids, baking powder and salt. Stir in the wheat germ and brown sugar. Stir in four of the eggs, the oil and vanilla.

5. Divide the dough into quarters and roll out one quarter at a time on a floured board until dough is quite thin. Cut out four-inch circles. Place half of the circles on lightly oiled baking sheet.

6. Place a teaspoon of cooled filling on each circle, top with a second circle and pinch edges to seal. Brush with remaining egg and sprinkle with a little raw sugar. Bake 25 to 35 minutes or until done and golden. Repeat with remaining pieces of dough and filling.

Yield: About two and one-half dozen.

PUMPKIN PIE

Crust:
1½ cups unbleached white flour
½ teaspoon sea salt
½ cup butter
Ice water

Filling:
2 eggs
1¾ cups pumpkin pulp or puree
¾ cup honey
½ teaspoon sea salt
1 teaspoon cinnamon
½ teaspoon ground ginger
⅛ teaspoon ground cloves
1 cup evaporated milk
½ cup skim milk

Topping:
Whipped cream, sweetened
with honey

1. To prepare crust, place the flour and salt in a bowl. Cut in the butter with two knives until mixture resembles coarse oatmeal.

2. With one knife, cut in three tablespoons ice water. Very slowly cut in enough extra ice water until dough hangs together loosely. Turn onto a well-floured board and roll to fit a nine-inch pie plate. Fit into pie plate; decorate edge.

3. Meanwhile, preheat the oven to 425 degrees.

4. Place all the filling ingredients in an electric blender and blend until smooth. Pour into the prepared pie shell and bake 15 minutes. Reduce the oven heat to 350 degrees and bake 45 minutes longer or until pie is set.

5. Serve warm or cold, with whipped cream.

Yield: Six servings.

RAW APPLE CAKE

1¼ cups brown sugar
2 eggs
½ cup oil
1 teaspoon vanilla
3 cups peeled finely diced raw apple (about 5 medium)
1¾ cups whole wheat flour
½ teaspoon sea salt
1 teaspoon baking soda
½ teaspoon cinnamon
½ teaspoon nutmeg

1. Preheat the oven to 350 degrees.

2. Beat together the sugar and eggs until thick and light. Beat in the oil and vanilla. Stir in the apples.

3. Sift the flour with the salt, baking soda, cinnamon and nutmeg and fold into the apple mixture. Pour into an oiled and floured nine-inch square baking pan and bake 45 minutes or until done. Serve warm.

Yield: Nine servings.

WHOLE WHEAT APPLE CAKE

½ cup finely chopped nuts
¾ cup raw sugar
1 teaspoon cinnamon
2 teaspoons wheat germ
1½ cups thin peeled apple slices
½ teaspoon lemon juice
½ cup butter
2 eggs
1¼ cups sifted organic whole wheat flour
1½ teaspoons baking powder
½ teaspoon baking soda
½ cup sour cream
½ teaspoon milk
Whipped cream

1. Preheat the oven to 350 degrees.

2. Combine the nuts, one-quarter cup of the sugar, the cinnamon, wheat germ, apple slices and lemon juice in a small bowl and set aside.

3. Cream the butter and remaining sugar very well. Beat in the eggs, one at a time.

4. Sift together the flour, baking powder and baking soda. Combine the sour cream and the milk. Stir the sifted dry ingredients into the creamed mixture alternately with the sour cream mixture.

5. Pour half the batter into a well-buttered 9-by-5-by-3-inch glass loaf pan, spread the apple mixture over and top with remaining batter. Bake 50 minutes or until done. Serve warm with whipped cream.

Yield: Six servings.

APPLE WHEAT GERM COFFEECAKE

2¼ cups whole wheat pastry flour
¼ cup non-fat dry milk solids
4 teaspoons baking powder
1 teaspoon sea salt
3 teaspoons cinnamon
¾ cup wheat germ
1 cup honey
½ cup peanut oil
4 eggs
1 teaspoon grated orange rind
1 teaspoon vanilla
6 small sweet apples, pared, cored and thinly sliced

1. Preheat the oven to 350 degrees.

2. Sift together the flour, milk solids, baking powder, salt and cinnamon.

3. Combine the wheat germ, honey, peanut oil, eggs, rind and vanilla and stir into the dry ingredients. The batter will be liquid.

4. Place one-third of the batter in an oiled 3-quart baking dish; spread half the apples over the surface.

5. Top with another third of the batter, then the remainder of the apples and the last third of the batter. Bake 45 minutes or until done. Cover with aluminum foil if cake starts to overbrown before it is baked. Cool slightly in pan and serve warm.

Yield: Eight servings.

APPLESAUCE-OATMEAL CAKE

1¼ cups thick sweetened homemade applesauce (see page 316)
¾ cup rolled oats
1 cup raisins
½ cup butter
¾ cup raw sugar
1 egg
1 cup unbleached white flour
¼ cup soy flour
1 tablespoon bone meal
1 tablespoon brewer's yeast
1 tablespoon lecithin
1 tablespoon rose hip powder (optional)
1 teaspoon baking soda
1 teaspoon cinnamon
¼ teaspoon ground cloves

1. Heat the applesauce, oats and raisins to just below boiling. Set aside for 20 minutes.

2. Preheat the oven to 350 degrees.

3. Cream the butter and sugar together until very light and fluffy. Beat in the egg. Sift together the remaining ingredients.

4. Stir dry ingredients into creamed mixture alternately with applesauce mixture. Pour into a well-buttered nine-inch square baking pan and bake 50 to 55 minutes or until done. Cool in the pan.

Yield: Nine servings.

UNLEAVENED HEALTH NUT-HONEY CAKE

2 cups whole wheat flour
½ cup wheat germ
½ cup sunflower seed meal
¼ cup non-fat dry milk solids
3 tablespoons carob powder (optional)
¼ teaspoon cinnamon
⅛ teaspoon nutmeg
⅛ teaspoon allspice
½ cup soft butter
1 cup honey
1 teaspoon vanilla
¼ teaspoon almond extract
2 eggs
1 cup coffee or coffee substitute
¾ cup sunflower seed kernels
1 cup raisins
1 cup golden raisins

1. Preheat the oven to 350 degrees.

2. In a small bowl, combine the whole wheat flour, wheat germ, sunflower seed meal, milk solids, carob powder, cinnamon, nutmeg and allspice.

3. In a large bowl, combine the butter, honey, vanilla and almond extract and beat until well blended. Beat in the eggs.

4. Stir the dry ingredients into the butter mixture alternately with the coffee. Beat mixture two minutes. Add the sunflower seed kernels, raisins and golden raisins. Mix well.

5. Pour mixture into an oiled 9-by-13-by-2-inch baking pan and bake 40 minutes or until done. Cool in the pan.

Yield: Twelve servings.

PUMPKIN CAKE

2 cups honey
1 cup oil
2 cups sieved cooked pumpkin
4 eggs, lightly beaten
3 cups whole wheat flour
2 tablespoons cinnamon
3 teaspoons baking powder
2 teaspoons baking soda
2 teaspoons almond extract
1 teaspoon sea salt
1 cup chopped nuts or seeds
1 cup raisins or chopped figs

1. Preheat the oven to 350 degrees.

2. Mix all the ingredients together in a large bowl. Pour into two well-oiled or buttered nine-inch layer pans or one oiled nine-inch tube cake pan. Bake layers 50 minutes and tube pan one hour and 25 minutes or until done.

Yield: Two layers or one cake; about twelve servings.

MAYONNAISE RAISIN CAKE

1 cup raisins
1 teaspoon baking soda
1 cup hot water
1 cup homemade mayonnaise
   (see page 186)
2 tablespoons carob powder
1 teaspoon vanilla
1 teaspoon cinnamon
½ teaspoon sea salt
½ cup honey
1¾ cups unbleached white flour

1. Preheat the oven to 350 degrees.

2. Mix together the raisins, baking soda and hot water and let stand.

3. Mix together the mayonnaise, carob powder, vanilla, cinnamon, salt and honey. Add the flour and the raisin mixture to the mayonnaise mixture.

4. Pour into an oiled 8½-by-4½-by-2½-inch loaf pan. Bake 30 to 45 minutes or until done. Cool in pan 15 minutes; turn onto rack.

Yield: Eight servings.

SOY NUT COFFEECAKE

2 cups raw sugar
6 eggs, at room temperature
1 teaspoon vanilla
½ teaspoon sea salt
½ cup soy oil
½ cup butter, melted and cooled
2½ cups unbleached white flour
½ cup soy flour (full fat or low fat)
3 teaspoons tartrate baking powder (Royal brand)
½ cup milk
Nut mixture:
½ cup brown sugar
½ cup raw sugar
1 teaspoon cinnamon
⅓ cup wheat germ
½ cup chopped nuts

1. Preheat the oven to 325 degrees.

2. Beat the sugar and eggs together until thick and light. Beat in vanilla and salt.

3. Fold in the soy oil and butter. Sift together the white flour, soy flour and baking powder and fold into batter alternately with the milk.

4. Combine all the ingredients for the nut mixture in a small bowl.

5. Pour half the cake batter into an oiled 10-inch tube cake pan; sprinkle with about three-quarters of the nut mixture. Top with remaining batter and then remaining nut mixture. Bake one and one-quarter hours or until done. Serve slightly warm or cool.

Yield: Twelve servings.

STRAWBERRY SHORTCAKE

2 cups whole wheat pastry flour
1 teaspoon baking powder
2 tablespoons brown sugar
½ teaspoon sea salt
6 tablespoons butter
2 eggs, lightly beaten
⅔ cup milk
1 quart strawberries, sliced
1 cup heavy cream, whipped

1. Preheat the oven to 450 degrees.

2. Sift the flour with the baking powder. Add the sugar and salt and cut in four tablespoons of the butter until the mixture resembles coarse oatmeal. Combine the eggs and milk and stir into the dry ingredients.

3. Mix well. The dough will be soft. Place in a well-buttered, or oiled, nine- or 10-inch layer pan and bake 20 minutes or until done.

4. Remove from the pan, split and butter the cut sides with remaining butter. Cover bottom half with sliced strawberries.

5. Place top half in position, cover with remaining berries and top with whipped cream.

Yield: Eight servings.

CARROT CAKE

1 cup grated raw carrot
1¼ cups whole wheat flour
1 egg
½ cup honey
1 cup melted butter
½ teaspoon cinnamon
1 teaspoon baking soda
2 teaspoons baking powder
¼ cup lemon juice

1. Preheat the oven to 350 degrees.

2. In a large bowl, combine all the ingredients and mix well.

3. Pour into a well-buttered five-cup ring mold. Bake 45 minutes or until done. Let cool in the pan 10 minutes before unmolding. Cool before serving.

Yield: Six servings.

GINGERBREAD I

½ cup safflower oil
½ cup raw sugar
2 eggs
1 cup sorghum or unsulphured molasses
2 teaspoons baking soda
1 teaspoon cinnamon
1 teaspoon ground cloves
1 teaspoon ground ginger
¼ teaspoon sea salt
1½ cups whole wheat flour
½ cup wheat germ
½ cup soy flour
1 cup hot water

1. Preheat the oven to 350 degrees.

2. Beat the oil, sugar and eggs together until very light and thick. Beat in the sorghum or molasses.

3. Sift together the baking soda, cinnamon, cloves, ginger, salt and flour. Stir in the wheat germ and soy flour and add to the beaten egg mixture alternately with the hot water.

4. Turn into an oiled 12-by-8-inch baking pan and bake 30 minutes or until done.

Yield: Eight servings.

GINGERBREAD II

2⅓ cups sifted whole wheat pastry flour
1 teaspoon baking powder
½ teaspoon sea salt
½ teaspoon baking soda
1 teaspoon ground ginger
½ teaspoon cinnamon
½ teaspoon nutmeg
⅓ teaspoon allspice
½ cup soft butter
1 cup brown sugar
2 eggs
½ cup unsulphured molasses
¾ cup hot water

1. Preheat the oven to 350 degrees.

2. Sift together the flour, baking powder and salt.

3. Blend together the baking soda, ginger, cinnamon, nutmeg, allspice and butter. Stir in the sugar. Beat in the eggs. Stir in the molasses and add the hot water alternately with the flour mixture. Pour into well-buttered nine-inch square pan and bake 45 minutes.

Yield: Nine servings.

WONDERFUL OLD-FASHIONED GINGERBREAD

¾ cup unsulphured molasses
½ cup butter
2⅓ cups whole wheat flour and unbleached white flour combined in any proportion
¼ teaspoon sea salt
1 teaspoon baking powder
2 teaspoons cinnamon
2 teaspoons ground ginger
¼ teaspoon ground cloves
1 cup yogurt (see page 311)

1. Preheat the oven to 350 degrees.

2. Heat the molasses and butter in a small pan until the mixture bubbles. Cool.

3. Sift together the flours, salt, baking powder, cinnamon, ginger and cloves.

4. When butter mixture has cooled, stir in the yogurt and add to the dry ingredients. Mix well. Pour into a buttered nine-inch square baking pan and bake 30 to 40 minutes or until done. Cool in the pan.

Yield: Eight servings.

DATE AND NUT CAKE

4 eggs, at room temperature
1 cup raw sugar or brown sugar
½ cup oil
1 cup whole wheat flour
1 teaspoon salt
3 cups chopped dates
3 cups chopped pecans
1 teaspoon vanilla

1. Beat the eggs, sugar and oil together very well.

2. Stir in remaining ingredients until thoroughly blended. Place in an oiled and floured 9-by-5-by-3-inch loaf pan and place in a cold oven. Set the temperature at 300 degrees, light oven and bake two hours or until done.

Yield: Ten servings.

RAW FRUIT "CAKE"

4 cups ground figs
4 cups grated nuts
4 cups chopped dates
4 cups unsweetened shredded fresh coconut

1. On a small six-inch plate or dish, spread a layer of one cup of the figs. Top with layer of one cup nuts, then one cup dates and one cup coconut.

2. Repeat the four layers three more times. Apply light pressure to top of "cake." Cut in small wedges.

Yield: Ten servings.

HOT WATER MOLASSES CAKE

½ cup butter
½ cup raw sugar
½ cup blackstrap molasses
1 egg
⅛ teaspoon sea salt
½ teaspoon cinnamon
1½ cups whole wheat pastry flour
1 teaspoon baking soda
¾ cup hot water
Warm homemade applesauce
(see page 316)

1. Preheat the oven to 325 degrees.

2. Beat the butter, sugar, molasses, egg and salt together. Combine the cinnamon, flour and baking soda.

3. Stir dry ingredients into beaten mixture alternately with hot water. Pour into well-oiled nine-inch square baking pan and bake 30 minutes or until done. Serve slightly warm with applesauce.

Yield: Nine servings.

Note: This is a moist, very tender cake.

QUICK UPSIDE-DOWN CAKE

1 quart home-canned peaches, apples, pineapple or cherries
Honey
2 tablespoons whole wheat flour
2 eggs
½ cup oil
1 teaspoon vanilla
1¾ cups whole wheat pastry flour
2 teaspoons baking powder
½ teaspoon sea salt
¾ cup milk
Whipped cream

1. Preheat the oven to 350 degrees.

2. Drain the fruit, reserve liquid and place fruit in a buttered 9-by-13-by-2-inch baking pan.

3. Measure one and one-quarter to one and one-half cups reserved liquid into a small saucepan. Add honey to sweeten (one-quarter cup, or to taste) and stir in the two tablespoons whole wheat flour. Bring to a boil and simmer one minute. Pour over fruit and set pan in oven.

4. Beat together the eggs, oil, vanilla and one-half cup honey.

5. Sift together three times the pastry flour, baking powder and salt. Add alternately with the milk to the egg mixture. Pour over fruit mixture and bake 35 to 45 minutes or until cake is done (fruit bubbles up all over). Serve warm with whipped cream.

Yield: Ten servings.

CREAMY CHEESEY CAKE

¼ cup wheat germ
1 teaspoon cinnamon
8 eggs, at room temperature
2 pounds (4 cups) cottage cheese
3 tablespoons lemon juice
1 cup yogurt (see page 311)
1 cup honey
¼ cup whole wheat flour

1. Preheat the oven to 350 degrees.

2. Mix together the wheat germ and cinnamon and sprinkle over very well-buttered nine-inch springform pan. Roll pan until inside is evenly coated with mixture. Chill in refrigerator.

3. Beat the eggs until very thick and creamy. Gradually beat in the cottage cheese. Stir in the lemon juice, yogurt, honey and flour. Mix well.

4. Pour into prepared pan and bake one hour. Turn oven off but leave cake in oven one and one-half hours longer (do not open oven door). Chill overnight in refrigerator.

Yield: Ten servings.

MOCK CHEESECAKE

½ cup graham cracker crumbs
½ teaspoon cinnamon
¼ cup melted butter
3 eggs, separated
¼ cup lemon juice
2 cups thick homemade applesauce (see page 316)
1 can sweetened condensed milk

1. Preheat the oven to 350 degrees.

2. Combine the cracker crumbs, cinnamon and butter in a small bowl. Butter an eight-inch springform pan well. Reserving two tablespoons of the crumb mixture, sprinkle remainder over inside of buttered pan.

3. Beat egg yolks and lemon juice until thick. Stir in the applesauce and condensed milk. Beat the egg whites until stiff but not dry and fold into mixture. Pour into prepared pan. Sprinkle with reserved crumbs and bake one hour or until a knife inserted in cake comes out clean.

4. Open oven door, turn oven off and leave cake in oven one hour longer. Chill well.

Yield: Six servings.

ORGANIC CHEESECAKE

1 pound cottage cheese
1 pound soft cream cheese
1½ cups raw sugar
4 eggs
3 tablespoons stoneground
    whole wheat flour
3 tablespoons arrowroot
1½ teaspoons vanilla
2 tablespoons lemon juice
½ cup melted butter, cooled
2 cups sour cream

1. Preheat the oven to 325 degrees.

2. Sieve the cottage cheese and whip, or beat, with the cream cheese for five minutes. Still beating, gradually add the sugar.

3. Beat in the eggs, one at a time. Add flour, arrowroot, vanilla and juice. Mix well.

4. Fold in the butter and sour cream and pour into an oiled nine- to 10-inch springform pan. Bake one hour. Turn heat off and leave cake in the oven one hour longer without opening the oven door.

Yield: Twelve servings.

WHOLE WHEAT SPONGECAKE

12 eggs, separated
1½ cups raw sugar
½ teaspoon sea salt
1½ teaspoons cream of tartar
¼ cup honey
1½ cups whole wheat flour or
    unbleached white flour
1½ teaspoons vanilla
1 teaspoon grated lemon rind

1. Preheat the oven to 300 degrees.

2. Beat the egg whites at highest speed on an electric mixer until soft peaks form. While still beating, gradually add one cup of the sugar, the salt, cream of tartar and honey. Continue to beat until stiff peaks form or until mixture clings to bowl.

3. Beat the egg yolks with same beaters in a second bowl. Gradually add the remaining sugar and beat until thick and light in color.

4. Fold yolk mixture into whites mixture gently but quickly. Fold in the flour, vanilla and lemon rind. Turn into an ungreased nine-inch tube cake pan and bake one hour. Increase oven heat to 350 degrees and bake 15 minutes longer. Invert pan to cool cake. Loosen with spatula.

Yield: Ten servings.

SUNSHINE CAKE

Cake:
  4 eggs, separated
  ½ cup honey
  3 teaspoons vanilla
  1 teaspoon grated lemon rind
  3 teaspoons baking powder
1¼ cups whole wheat pastry flour
  ¼ cup carob powder
  ⅓ cup water

Frosting:
  2 tablespoons soft butter
  ⅔ cup non-fat dry milk solids
  ⅓ cup carob powder
  ¼ cup honey
  ¼ cup heavy cream
  1 teaspoon vanilla

1. Preheat the oven to 325 degrees.

2. To prepare cake, beat the egg yolks until very light and thick. Gradually beat in the honey. Add vanilla and lemon rind.

3. Sift the baking powder with one-half cup of the flour. Combine remaining flour with the carob powder.

4. Fold the carob mixture alternately with the water into the egg yolk mixture. Stir in the baking powder mixture.

5. Beat the egg whites until stiff but not dry and fold into batter. Pour mixture into a buttered nine-inch tube pan and bake 45 minutes or until done. Invert pan and cool cake in pan.

6. To prepare frosting, cream together the butter and milk solids. Stir in the carob powder. Beat in remaining ingredients and use to frost cooled cake.

Yield: Eight servings.

WHOLE WHEAT POUNDCAKE

  1 cup butter
  2 cups brown sugar or raw sugar
  1 teaspoon grated lemon rind
  3 eggs, lightly beaten
2¼ cups sifted whole wheat flour
  ¼ teaspoon baking soda
  ½ teaspoon sea salt
  1 cup yogurt (see page 311)

1. Preheat the oven to 325 degrees.

2. Cream the butter until light. Gradually beat in the sugar. Add remaining ingredients; blend with electric mixer at low speed. Beat three minutes at medium speed, scraping bowl occasionally.

3. Pour batter into well-buttered and floured 10-inch tube cake pan. Bake 65 minutes or until done. Cool in pan for 15 minutes before transferring to a rack.

Yield: Twelve servings.

FIG FILLING

2 cups ground unsulphured figs
½ cup honey
2 tablespoons unsweetened prune juice
1 tablespoon lemon juice
1 tablespoon orange juice

1. Combine all the ingredients in a saucepan. Bring to a boil and simmer, stirring constantly, for 15 minutes. Cool.

2. Use as a filling for yeast or layer cakes.

Yield: About two and one-half cups, enough for two cakes.

UNCOOKED HONEY FROSTING

1 egg white
⅛ teaspoon sea salt
½ cup warm honey
¼ teaspoon almond extract

1. Using a rotary beater, beat the egg white with the salt until peaks form. While still beating, add the honey in a slow constant stream.

2. Add the almond extract and continue to beat until mixture is thick and fluffy.

Yield: Enough to cover a nine-inch layer cake.

EASY BAR COOKIES

1 cup graham cracker crumbs
1 tablespoon melted butter
1 small can (5⅓ ounces) evaporated milk
1½ tablespoons honey
¼ cup wheat germ
¼ cup soy grits
½ cup unsweetened shredded coconut
¼ cup sesame seeds
½ cup chopped nuts

1. Preheat the oven to 350 degrees.

2. Combine all the ingredients in a bowl and mix well. Pat into an oiled eight-inch square baking pan and bake 20 minutes or until done.

3. Cool in the pan and cut into bars while still slightly warm.

Yield: One dozen bars.

APRICOT BAR COOKIES

⅓ cup honey
⅓ cup molasses
½ cup oil
1½ cups steel cut oats
1 cup whole wheat flour
½ cup wheat germ
3 tablespoons soy flour
⅛ teaspoon sea salt
1 cup cut-up unsulphured
   apricots
1 cup raisins
½ cup sunflower seed kernels or
   pumpkin seeds
Orange juice, if necessary

1. Preheat the oven to 375 degrees.

2. Beat together the honey, molasses and oil very well in an electric mixer or electric blender.

3. In a large bowl, combine the oats, whole wheat flour, wheat germ, soy flour and salt. Pour in the honey mixture and stir to moisten dry ingredients.

4. Add apricots, raisins and sunflower seed kernels or pumpkin seeds and mix well. If mixture is very stiff, add a small quantity of orange juice. Press mixture into a well-oiled nine-inch square baking pan. Bake 20 minutes. Cool in the pan. Cut into squares.

Yield: Sixteen squares.

DUTCH BUTTER COOKIES

1 cup butter
¾ cup raw sugar or brown sugar
1 egg, separated
1 teaspoon vanilla
¼ teaspoon sea salt
1½ cups whole wheat pastry flour
1 cup unbleached white flour
½ cup chopped pecans

1. Preheat the oven to 375 degrees.

2. Cream the butter and sugar together very well. Beat in the egg yolk, vanilla and salt.

3. Stir in the whole wheat flour and unbleached white flour. Press the mixture into a well-buttered 15-by-10-by-1-inch jellyroll pan. Sprinkle with the nuts and press them in. Beat the egg white lightly and brush over top.

4. Bake 20 minutes or until well browned and done. Cut into bars or squares while hot. Cool in the pan.

Yield: About five dozen squares.

JELLY CAKES

Dough:
⅔ cup safflower oil
⅓ cup cold water
3 eggs, lightly beaten
3 to 4 cups whole wheat pastry flour

Filling:
4 to 6 tart apples, peeled, cored and sliced
¼ cup plus 2 tablespoons honey
Cinnamon to taste
½ cup jam or marmalade
½ cup raisins

1. Preheat the oven to 350 degrees.

2. To make the dough, combine the oil, water and eggs in a bowl and gradually work in enough of the flour to make a dough that is soft but not sticky. Divide into three balls, cover and let rest while peeling the apples.

3. Oil the bottom of a large baking sheet with ¼- to ½-inch sides.

4. Roll out one ball of dough between sheets of wax paper, or on a lightly floured board, into a ⅛th-inch-thick rectangle. Transfer rolled-out dough to the baking sheet.

5. Cover with the apples, dot with one-quarter cup honey and sprinkle with cinnamon.

6. Roll out the second ball of dough the same size and place over the apples. Spread this layer with jam or marmalade and sprinkle with raisins.

7. Roll out remaining ball of dough and place over jam layer. Drizzle remaining honey over the top and sprinkle with cinnamon. Bake one hour or until pastry is brown and filling bubbly. Cool slightly, cut into squares and serve warm or at room temperature.

Yield: Eighteen squares.

NUT SQUARES

2 eggs, lightly beaten
⅔ cup honey
6 tablespoons whole wheat flour
¼ teaspoon sea salt
1 cup chopped nuts
½ cup sesame seeds

1. Preheat the oven to 350 degrees.

2. Beat the eggs and honey together. Stir in the remaining ingredients and turn into an oiled nine-inch square baking pan. Bake 20 to 25 minutes or until done. Cool in the pan and cut into squares.

Yield: One dozen squares.

PEANUT BUTTER AND BANANA BARS

2 eggs, well beaten
⅓ cup peanut butter
¼ cup molasses
½ cup brown rice flour or rice polishings
½ cup chopped walnuts or peanuts
1 ripe banana, chopped
½ teaspoon cinnamon
¼ teaspoon sea salt

1. Preheat the oven to 350 degrees.

2. Combine all the ingredients and mix well. Turn into a buttered eight-inch square baking pan and bake 15 minutes.

3. Cut into bars while still warm.

Yield: Twelve to eighteen bars.

SCOTCHER SHORTBREAD

3½ cups rolled oats
⅔ cup raw sugar
¼ cup unbleached white flour
¾ cup soft butter
½ teaspoon sea salt
1 teaspoon vanilla

1. Preheat the oven to 325 degrees.

2. Place all the ingredients in a bowl and work together lightly with a wooden spoon or the fingertips. Press into well-buttered 9-by-13-inch baking pan. Bake 30 minutes or until done. Cool 10 minutes. Cut into squares.

Yield: About two dozen squares.

Note: The contributor says that children love this and it isn't too sweet.

NUTRITIOUS CHEWS

3 eggs, well beaten
1 cup raw sugar
1 cup chopped walnuts
1 cup unsweetened shredded
  coconut
1 cup chopped dates
¾ cup whole wheat flour
¼ cup wheat germ

1. Preheat the oven to 350 degrees.
2. Combine all the ingredients and press down into a well-oiled nine-inch square baking pan. Bake 20 minutes or until done. Cut while warm into squares or bars.

Yield: About sixteen squares.

SESAME STRIPS

¾ cup raw sugar
½ cup oil
2 tablespoons non-fat dry milk
  solids
2 eggs
½ teaspoon grated orange rind
1½ teaspoons vanilla
2 tablespoons wheat germ
1¼ cups toasted sesame seeds
¼ cup toasted cashews, coarsely
  chopped
½ cup raisins
3 cups unbleached white flour
  or whole wheat pastry flour,
  approximately

1. Preheat the oven to 300 degrees.
2. Place the sugar, oil and milk solids in a mixing bowl and mix with an electric mixer on medium speed two minutes. Add one egg, the orange rind and vanilla and mix two minutes longer.
3. Stir in the wheat germ, one-quarter cup of the sesame seeds, the cashews and raisins and mix well. Stir in enough flour to make a dough that can be rolled. Shape into a ball. Cover and let dough rest 10 minutes; divide into two.
4. Roll out half of the dough into an approximate 5-by-16-inch strip. Transfer carefully to an oiled baking sheet, using wide spatulas if necessary to prevent breaking. Beat the remaining egg lightly and brush over the dough strip. Sprinkle with half of the remaining sesame seeds.
5. Repeat rolling, brushing and sprinkling with second half of dough. Bake strips 45 minutes or until lightly browned and done.
6. Cut into one-inch strips, on diagonal if you wish, while still hot.

Yield: Thirty-two strips.

CAROB BROWNIES

1 cup raw sugar
⅔ cup peanut oil
2 eggs
½ teaspoon vanilla
½ cup unsifted unbleached white flour
½ cup unsifted full fat soy flour
1 teaspoon baking powder
½ teaspoon sea salt
3 tablespoons carob powder

1. Preheat the oven to 350 degrees.

2. Mix together the raw sugar and the oil. Beat in the eggs and vanilla. Sift together the unbleached flour, soy flour, baking powder, salt and carob powder.

3. Combine the egg mixture with sifted dry ingredients. Mix well. Pour into a well-buttered nine-inch square baking pan and bake about 30 minutes or until done. Cut into squares or bars while still slightly warm.

Yield: Sixteen to twenty squares or bars.

CAROB NUT BROWNIES

½ cup butter
⅓ cup honey
⅓ cup raw sugar or date sugar
1 egg
½ teaspoon salt
1 teaspoon vanilla
1 teaspoon ground coriander (optional)
½ cup carob powder
1 tablespoon oil
⅔ cup whole wheat pastry flour
1 teaspoon baking powder
1 cup chopped nuts

1. Preheat the oven to 350 degrees.

2. Cream the butter with the honey and the sugar until light and fluffy. Beat in the egg, salt, vanilla and coriander. Mix the carob powder with the oil and beat into the butter mixture.

3. Sift flour with baking powder and stir into carob mixture. Stir in the nuts. Spread batter in a nine-inch square pan lined with wax paper. Bake 30 minutes.

4. Cool in the pan and cut into squares while still warm.

Yield: Sixteen brownies.

CAROB AND HONEY BROWNIES

½ cup butter
⅔ cup honey
2 eggs
1 teaspoon vanilla
½ teaspoon sea salt
½ cup carob powder
⅔ cup whole wheat pastry flour
1 teaspoon baking powder
1 cup chopped nuts
3 tablespoons milk

1. Preheat the oven to 350 degrees.

2. Cream the butter with the honey. Beat in the eggs, one at a time. Beat in the vanilla and salt.

3. Sift together the carob powder, flour and baking powder and stir with nuts and milk into batter. Turn into a well-oiled, or buttered nine-inch square baking pan and bake 30 minutes or until done. Cut into squares while still warm.

Yield: Sixteen brownies.

WHEAT GERM SQUARES

4 eggs
2 cups brown sugar
2 tablespoons carob powder
1 tablespoon melted butter
2½ cups wheat germ
1 cup chopped nuts
½ teaspoon sea salt
2 teaspoons vanilla

1. Preheat the oven to 375 degrees.

2. Beat the eggs until stiff. Gradually beat in the sugar until mixture is very thick and light.

3. Dissolve the carob powder in the melted butter and stir into the egg mixture. Stir in the wheat germ, nuts, salt and vanilla. Pour into an oiled 13-by-9-inch baking pan and bake 20 to 30 minutes.

4. Cool in the pan and cut into squares while still slightly warm.

Yield: About two dozen squares.

MOLLIE COOKIES

½ cup butter
1 cup raw sugar
2 eggs
1½ cups whole wheat pastry flour
1 teaspoon baking powder
½ teaspoon sea salt
1 teaspoon vanilla

1. Preheat the oven to 375 degrees.

2. Cream the butter and sugar together until very light and fluffy.

3. Beat in the eggs. Sift together the whole wheat flour, baking powder and salt and stir with the vanilla into the creamed mixture.

4. Drop by teaspoonfuls, at least two inches apart, onto an oiled baking sheet. Bake eight to 12 minutes or until lightly browned and done.

Yield: About four dozen cookies.

CARROT COOKIES

⅓ cup oil
⅓ cup brown sugar
⅓ cup unsulphured molasses
1 egg, lightly beaten
1 cup unbleached white flour
½ teaspoon baking powder
½ teaspoon baking soda
¼ teaspoon nutmeg
¼ cup non-fat dry milk solids
1 teaspoon sea salt
¼ teaspoon cinnamon
1 cup grated carrots
½ cup raisins
1¼ cups quick cooking rolled oats

1. Preheat the oven to 400 degrees.

2. Beat the oil, brown sugar, molasses and egg together until well mixed. Sift together the flour, baking powder, baking soda, nutmeg, milk solids, salt and cinnamon and stir into oil mixture.

3. Add the carrots, raisins and oats and mix well. Drop by teaspoonfuls onto a lightly oiled baking sheet and bake 10 minutes or until lightly browned around the edges. Cool on a rack.

Yield: Three dozen to four dozen cookies.

APPLE COOKIES

½ cup raw sugar
2 eggs
½ cup whole bran or whole
  wheat flour
½ cup wheat germ
½ cup Tiger's milk
⅛ teaspoon sea salt
1 tablespoon brewer's yeast or
  yeast flakes
1 tablespoon lecithin
¼ cup safflower oil
3 small apples, peeled, cored and
  finely diced

1. Preheat the oven to 375 degrees.

2. Place all the ingredients except the apples in a bowl and mix well. Stir in the apples.

3. Drop teaspoonfuls of batter onto an oiled baking sheet. Bake about 15 minutes or until lightly browned and done.

Yield: Eighteen to twenty-four cookies.

APPLE OATMEAL COOKIES

½ cup butter
1 cup brown sugar
2 eggs
1¾ cups whole wheat pastry flour
½ cup rolled oats
½ teaspoon sea salt
2 teaspoons baking powder
½ teaspoon cinnamon
1 cup chopped raisins
1 cup chopped walnuts
1½ cups finely chopped apples

1. Preheat the oven to 350 degrees.

2. Cream the butter with the sugar. Beat in the eggs very well.

3. Combine all remaining ingredients and stir into the creamed mixture. Drop by teaspoonfuls onto oiled baking sheet and bake 12 to 15 minutes or until done. Cool on a rack.

Yield: Three to four dozen cookies.

APPLESAUCE COOKIES

1 cup brown sugar
¾ cup oil
1 cup thick homemade
  applesauce (see page 316)
½ cup chopped nuts
½ teaspoon sea salt
1 teaspoon vanilla
4 cups rolled oats
½ cup chopped dates

1. Preheat the oven to 375 degrees.

2. Beat the brown sugar and oil together until well blended.

3. Add remaining ingredients and mix well. Drop from a teaspoon onto an oiled baking sheet. Bake 25 minutes or until well browned and done. Cool on the sheet.

Yield: About five dozen cookies.

CAROB CHIP COOKIES

½ cup mixed peanut and safflower oils
¾ cup packed dark brown sugar
2 eggs
½ cup non-fat dry milk solids
½ teaspoon sea salt
1 tablespoon vanilla
2 teaspoons baking powder
1½ cups wheat germ flour or whole wheat flour with wheat germ (sold under El Molino and Elam's brand names respectively in health food stores)
1 cup cara-coa nuggets

1. Preheat the oven to 350 degrees.

2. Mix together the oils, sugar, eggs, milk solids, salt and vanilla.

3. Combine the baking powder, flour and cara-coa nuggets. Stir into batter. Drop by teaspoonfuls, two inches apart, onto buttered baking sheet. Bake eight to 10 minutes or until done.

Yield: About four dozen cookies.

CAROB OR CAROB-RAISIN CHIP COOKIES

2½ tablespoons butter
1 cup honey
1 teaspoon vanilla
2 eggs, lightly beaten
3 cups whole wheat flour or unbleached white flour, or 1½ cups whole wheat flour, 1¼ cups unbleached white flour and ¼ cup soy flour
1 teaspoon baking powder
1 bag (10 ounces) cara-coa nuggets, or equivalent amount of carob-covered raisins

1. Preheat the oven to 350 degrees.

2. Melt the butter over low heat. Add honey, vanilla and eggs and mix well. Cool.

3. Combine the flour and baking powder. When honey mixture is cool, gradually add the flour mixture. Fold in the carob chips or carob-coated raisins.

4. Drop by teaspoonfuls, at least two inches apart, onto oiled baking sheet. Bake 15 minutes or until done. Cool on a rack.

Yield: About two dozen cookies.

Note: The contributor says these are delicious eaten on the way to a Stockhausen, Vt., concert.

HONEY COOKIES

⅓ cup melted butter
1 cup honey
2 eggs
½ cup milk
3½ cups unbleached white flour
2 teaspoons baking powder
½ teaspoon baking soda
¼ teaspoon sea salt
1 teaspoon cinnamon
½ teaspoon allspice
1 cup chopped mixed dried fruits such as raisins, dates, apricots and dried apples
½ cup sunflower seed kernels

1. Preheat the oven to 375 degrees.
2. Combine the butter and honey. Stir in the eggs and milk.
3. Sift together the flour, baking powder, baking soda, salt, cinnamon and allspice. Add the fruits and kernels to flour mixture and stir into the honey mixture.
4. Place by teaspoonfuls on an oiled, or buttered, baking sheet.
5. Bake 12 to 15 minutes or until done. Cool on a rack.
Yield: About five dozen cookies.

CASHEW COCONUT COOKIES

1 cup oil
1 cup honey
1 cup soy milk
2 cups unsweetened shredded coconut
⅛ teaspoon sea salt
1 cup raw unsalted cashews, roughly chopped
1 cup whole wheat flour
1 cup full fat soy flour
3 cups rolled oats
4 teaspoons vanilla

1. Preheat the oven to 350 degrees.
2. In a large bowl, combine all the ingredients and mix well.
3. Drop by teaspoonfuls onto oiled baking sheet and bake 10 to 12 minutes. Cool on a rack.
Yield: About five dozen cookies.

MOLASSES DROPS

½ cup butter
⅓ cup raw sugar
1 egg
½ cup blackstrap molasses
¼ cup water
¼ cup non-fat dry milk solids
½ cup wheat germ
1 teaspoon baking powder
¼ teaspoon ground ginger
¼ teaspoon ground cloves
¼ teaspoon allspice
¾ cup chopped dates or raisins
1½ cups unbleached white flour

1. Preheat the oven to 375 degrees.

2. Cream the butter and sugar together until light and fluffy.

3. Beat in the egg, molasses and water. Add remaining ingredients and mix well. Drop by teaspoonfuls onto oiled baking sheet. Bake 10 minutes or until done. Cool on a rack.

Yield: About two dozen cookies.

MOLASSES OATMEAL COOKIES

⅓ cup oil
½ cup molasses
3 tablespoons honey
2 eggs, lightly beaten
½ cup whole wheat flour
½ cup unbleached white flour
1 teaspoon baking powder (optional)
1 teaspoon cinnamon
⅛ teaspoon sea salt
½ teaspoon ground cloves
½ teaspoon ground ginger
½ teaspoon allspice
2 tablespoons brewer's yeast
½ cup wheat germ
2 cups rolled oats
½ cup raisins

1. Preheat the oven to 375 degrees.

2. Beat together the oil, molasses, honey and eggs.

3. Sift together the whole wheat flour, unbleached white flour, baking powder, cinnamon, salt, cloves, ginger and allspice. Stir in the brewer's yeast, wheat germ, rolled oats and raisins.

4. Add oil mixture to dry ingredients and mix well. Drop by teaspoonfuls onto oiled baking sheet and bake eight to 10 minutes or until done. Cool on a rack.

Yield: About four dozen cookies.

OATMEAL CHEWS

⅔ cup sweetened condensed milk
¼ cup non-fat dry milk solids
¼ cup wheat germ
⅛ teaspoon sea salt
2 teaspoons vanilla
⅓ cup steel cut oats
½ cup raisins

1. Combine all the ingredients in a bowl and mix well. Set aside for 30 minutes, stirring occasionally.

2. Preheat the oven to 325 degrees.

3. Drop teaspoonfuls of batter onto baking sheet lined with oiled parchment paper. Bake 15 minutes. Lift cookies from paper while still hot and transfer to rack to cool.

Yield: About two dozen cookies.

OATMEAL DROP COOKIES

1¼ cups raw sugar
½ cup safflower oil
2 eggs
6 tablespoons unsulphured molasses
1¾ cups brown rice flour
1 teaspoon cinnamon
1 teaspoon baking soda
1 teaspoon sea salt
2 cups rolled oats
½ cup chopped nuts
1 cup monukka raisins

1. Preheat the oven to 400 degrees.

2. Cream the sugar with the oil until light and fluffy. Beat in the eggs and then the molasses.

3. Sift the rice flour with the cinnamon, baking soda and salt and stir into the sugar mixture. Stir in the remaining ingredients. Drop by teaspoonfuls onto oiled baking sheet. Bake eight to 10 minutes or until done. Cool on a rack.

Yield: Three dozen cookies.

BIG SUR COCONUT COOKIES

¾ cup butter
¾ cup brown sugar
2 eggs
1 teaspoon vanilla
2 cups whole wheat pastry flour
2 tablespoons milk
½ cup unsweetened shredded coconut
½ cup raisins

1. Preheat the oven to 350 degrees.

2. Cream the butter with the sugar until light and fluffy. Beat in the eggs and the vanilla. Sift the whole wheat flour and stir in with the milk, coconut and raisins.

3. Drop by teaspoonfuls onto an oiled baking sheet and bake eight to 10 minutes or until done.

Yield: About four dozen cookies.

RAISIN COOKIES

1 cup water
2 cups raisins
1 cup soy oil or safflower oil
1½ cups honey
3 eggs
1 teaspoon vanilla
4 cups whole wheat pastry flour
1 teaspoon baking powder
1 teaspoon baking soda
1 teaspoon cinnamon
¼ teaspoon nutmeg
¼ teaspoon allspice
1 teaspoon sea salt
1 cup chopped nuts
1 cup wheat germ, approximately

1. Place water and raisins in a saucepan, simmer five minutes and cool.

2. Preheat the oven to 400 degrees.

3. Mix together the oil, honey, eggs and vanilla. Beat well. Add cooled raisin mixture and remaining ingredients including enough of the wheat germ to give a batter that can be dropped by teaspoonfuls onto oiled and floured baking sheet and maintain shape.

4. Bake 12 to 15 minutes or until done. Cool on a rack.

Yield: About eight dozen cookies.

Note: The contributor says that part of the batter may be frozen for use at a later time.

RAISIN-NUT OAT COOKIES

½ cup raw sugar
1 egg
1 teaspoon safflower oil
¼ teaspoon sea salt
½ cup rolled oats
½ cup unsweetened shredded coconut
½ cup chopped nuts
½ cup raisins
½ teaspoon vanilla

1. Preheat the oven to 375 degrees.

2. Beat the sugar and egg together until light and fluffy. Add remaining ingredients and mix well.

3. Drop by teaspoonfuls, two inches apart, on oiled baking sheet and bake 10 minutes or until tops are golden. Cool on baking sheet several minutes, then carefully remove to a rack.

Yield: About eighteen cookies.

HONEY-SESAME BITES

2 egg whites, at room temperature
¾ cup raw sugar
2 tablespoons honey
1 cup raw wheat germ
½ cup unsweetened shredded coconut
1 tablespoon rice polishings
½ cup toasted sesame seeds
½ teaspoon vanilla

1. Preheat the oven to 325 degrees.

2. Beat the egg whites until soft peaks form. Gradually beat in the sugar and then the honey until mixture is very stiff and holds stiff peaks.

3. Fold in the wheat germ, coconut, rice polishings and sesame seeds. Stir in the vanilla.

4. Drop mixture by the teaspoonful onto a buttered and floured baking sheet. Bake for about 20 minutes or until lightly browned.

Yield: About three dozen.

SESAME SEED CRISPS

½ cup sesame seeds
½ cup raw sugar
½ cup soft butter
1 egg
¾ cup unbleached white flour
¼ teaspoon single-acting baking powder (Royal brand)
¼ teaspoon sea salt
2 tablespoons heavy cream
1 teaspoon vanilla

1. Preheat the oven to 375 degrees.

2. Place the seeds in a dry skillet and toast over medium heat, shaking occasionally, until light golden in color; cool.

3. Cream together the sugar, butter and egg until very light and fluffy. Sift together the flour, baking powder and salt.

4. Stir the sifted dry ingredients, cream, vanilla and seeds into creamed mixture.

5. Place by teaspoonfuls, at least two inches apart, on an oiled baking sheet. Bake 10 to 12 minutes or until lightly browned around the edges and done. Cool on a rack.

Yield: About thirty cookies.

SORGHUM-DATE COOKIES

1 cup butter
⅓ cup sorghum or unsulphured molasses
2 eggs, well beaten
2 cups chopped fresh unsulphured dates
2 cups rolled oats
1¼ cups sifted whole wheat flour
¼ cup full fat soy flour
3 teaspoons single-acting baking powder (Royal brand)
1 teaspoon vegetable salt or sea salt
½ teaspoon cinnamon
½ teaspoon nutmeg
⅔ cup milk
2 cups chopped nuts

1. Preheat the oven to 350 degrees.

2. Cream the butter with the sorghum or molasses until light and fluffy. Beat in the eggs. Stir in the dates and oats.

3. Sift together the whole wheat flour, soy flour, baking powder, salt, cinnamon and nutmeg and add alternately with the milk to the batter.

4. Stir in one cup of the nuts. Drop teaspoons of batter onto ungreased baking sheet. Sprinkle with remaining nuts and bake 15 minutes or until done. Cool on a rack.

Yield: About four dozen cookies.

SOYA COOKIES

¼ cup butter
½ cup raw sugar
¾ cup unbleached white flour
1 teaspoon single-acting baking powder (Royal brand)
1 teaspoon cinnamon
⅛ teaspoon sea salt
1 egg, lightly beaten
½ teaspoon vanilla
¼ cup soy grits
18 walnut halves, approximately

1. Preheat the oven to 375 degrees.

2. Cream the butter and sugar together until light and fluffy.

3. Sift together the flour, baking powder, cinnamon and salt. Mix the egg with the vanilla. Add flour mixture alternately with the egg mixture to the creamed mixture.

4. Stir in the soy granules. Place rounded teaspoonfuls of the mixture on oiled baking sheets, decorate each cookie with a walnut half and bake 12 minutes, or until lightly browned.

Yield: About eighteen cookies.

SUNFLOWER SEED COOKIES

1 cup butter
½ cup raw sugar
¾ cup packed brown sugar
2 eggs, lightly beaten
2 teaspoons vanilla
1⅓ cups unbleached white flour
1 teaspoon sea salt
1 teaspoon baking soda
3 cups old-fashioned rolled oats
¾ cup sunflower seed kernels
½ cup wheat germ

1. Preheat the oven to 375 degrees.

2. Cream the butter together with the raw sugar and brown sugar until light and fluffy. Beat in the eggs and the vanilla.

3. Sift together the flour, salt and baking soda and stir into creamed mixture.

4. Fold in the oats, sunflower seed kernels and wheat germ.

5. Place teaspoonfuls of batter, two inches apart, on ungreased baking sheets. Bake 10 to 12 minutes. Cool on a rack.

Yield: About five dozen cookies.

WHOLE WHEAT FRUIT COOKIES

½ cup molasses or honey
½ cup oil
2 eggs, well beaten
1 teaspoon vanilla
⅛ teaspoon sea salt
2 cups whole wheat flour
½ cup raisins
½ cup chopped nuts
¼ cup chopped dates
¼ cup chopped figs

1. Preheat the oven to 375 degrees.

2. Blend the molasses or honey with the oil. Beat in the eggs and vanilla.

3. Stir in the remaining ingredients and mix well. The batter should be stiff but be soft enough to place by the teaspoonful on an oiled baking sheet. If batter is too thick, add a small quantity of unsweetened fruit juice. If too thin, add a little more flour. This is a necessary precaution as the water absorption of different whole wheat flours varies so much. Place on baking sheets.

4. Flatten the teaspoonfuls of dough with the bottom of a tumbler dipped in water. Bake 12 to 15 minutes or until done.

Yield: About four and one-half dozen cookies.

WHEAT GERM SNICKER-DOODLES

1 cup soft butter
1½ cups brown sugar
2 eggs
1 teaspoon vanilla
½ cup wheat germ
2½ cups whole wheat flour
2 teaspoons baking powder
½ teaspoon salt
½ cup raw sugar
1 teaspoon cinnamon

1. Preheat the oven to 400 degrees.

2. Cream the butter and brown sugar together until light and fluffy. Beat in the eggs, one at a time.

3. Blend in the vanilla and wheat germ.

4. Sift together the flour, baking powder and salt and stir into creamed mixture. Combine the raw sugar and cinnamon in a small bowl.

5. Form the dough into balls the size of a small walnut; roll in the cinnamon-sugar mixture. Place two inches apart on an ungreased baking sheet. Bake eight to 10 minutes.

6. Cool on a rack.

Yield: About six dozen cookies.

COCONUT SHORTBREAD

1 cup butter
½ cup less two tablespoons raw sugar
2 cups unbleached white flour
1 teaspoon vanilla
1 cup unsweetened shredded coconut
⅛ teaspoon sea salt

1. Cream the butter and sugar together very well.

2. Add remaining ingredients and, with a wooden spoon or the fingers, work into a dough. Form into a roll about nine inches long and one inch in diameter. Wrap in wax paper and chill several hours or overnight.

3. Preheat the oven to 350 degrees.

4. Cut the rolls into quarter-inch-thick rounds and place on ungreased baking sheets. Bake 10 minutes or until lightly browned and done.

Yield: About three dozen cookies.

CHESTNUT CREAM-FILLED COOKIES

1 cup dried chestnuts (available in Italian grocery stores)
Water
¼ teaspoon cinnamon
1 teaspoon vanilla
Raw sugar or honey to taste
Wheat germ, if necessary
2 cups whole wheat pastry flour
½ cup soy flour
¾ teaspoon sea salt
6 tablespoons safflower oil
2½ tablespoons ice water, approximately

1. Place chestnuts in a saucepan with water to cover. Let soak several hours. Heat to boiling and simmer 25 minutes or until tender, adding more water if necessary. Drain well and force through a ricer or food mill or whirl in an electric blender.

2. Beat the pureed chestnut with the cinnamon, vanilla and enough sugar or honey to sweeten lightly. If mixture becomes too thin, add wheat germ to make a filling consistency. If too dry, add a little water.

3. Preheat the oven to 375 degrees.

4. Place the whole wheat pastry flour, soy flour and salt in a bowl.

5. Add the oil. With the fingertips or a fork, work the oil through the dry ingredients until evenly moistened. Add only enough ice water to make a dough that leaves the sides of the bowl clean.

6. Divide dough in half and roll out one half to pie-crust thickness between sheets of wax paper or on a floured pastry cloth.

7. Cut into two-inch rounds and place on a baking sheet. Repeat with second half of dough. Bake cookies five to seven minutes or until done. Cool on a rack.

8. When cool, put two cookies together as a sandwich with the chestnut cream as a filling.

Yield: One and one-half dozen to two dozen filled cookies.

WHEELS OF STEEL

½ cup butter
½ cup raw peanut butter
1 cup brown sugar
1 egg
1 teaspoon vanilla
¾ cup whole wheat flour
¼ cup wheat germ
½ cup non-fat dry milk solids
¾ teaspoon sea salt
¼ teaspoon baking powder
¼ teaspoon baking soda
3 tablespoons milk
1 cup quick-cooking rolled oats
1 cup raisins, chopped
3 tablespoons sesame seeds

1. Preheat the oven to 375 degrees.

2. Cream the butter, peanut butter and sugar together until light. Beat in the egg and vanilla.

3. Combine the whole wheat flour, wheat germ, milk solids, salt, baking powder and baking soda. Stir into creamed mixture.

4. Add milk, oats and raisins and mix well. Place a heaping tablespoon of the batter on an oiled baking sheet and spread into a circle about four and one-half inches in diameter. Sprinkle with one teaspoon sesame seeds.

5. Leave ample room for cookies to spread. It may be wise to have only two on one large sheet. Repeat circles with remaining batter and seeds. Bake about 12 minutes or until done. Cool on pan five minutes and then, using a wide spatula, transfer carefully to a rack.

Yield: About nine giant cookies.

TAHINI COOKIES

6 tablespoons tahini (sesame paste)
¼ teaspoon sea salt
¾ cup honey
½ cup sunflower seed kernels
1½ cups rolled oats

1. Preheat the oven to 350 degrees.

2. Stir the tahini, salt and honey together until well blended.

3. Stir in the kernels and oats. Drop by teaspoonfuls onto an oiled baking sheet and bake 10 minutes or until edges are brown. Let cool on baking sheet several minutes, then carefully remove to rack.

Yield: About three dozen cookies.

GINGER COOKIES

½ cup butter
½ cup raw sugar or brown sugar
½ cup molasses
1 egg
½ cup unbleached white flour
1 cup whole wheat flour
¼ cup soy flour
2 tablespoons brewer's yeast
½ cup non-fat dry milk solids
½ teaspoon sea salt
2 teaspoons baking soda
3 teaspoons ground ginger,
  or to taste
1 teaspoon cinnamon
¼ cup wheat germ
Raw sugar

1. Preheat the oven to 350 degrees.

2. Cream the butter and one-half cup sugar together until light and fluffy. Beat in the molasses and egg.

3. Sift together the unbleached white flour, whole wheat flour, soy flour, yeast, milk solids, salt, baking soda, ginger and cinnamon.

4. Stir the sifted dry ingredients into the creamed mixture. Stir in the wheat germ. Mix until ingredients are well blended.

5. Form the dough (it's fairly soft) into balls the size of a walnut. Roll in sugar and place two inches apart on an oiled baking sheet.

6. Bake about 15 minutes or until lightly browned and tops are crackled. Cool on a rack.

Yield: About four dozen cookies.

HOMEMADE GRAHAM CRACKERS

4 cups whole wheat flour
1 cup butter
1 cup raw sugar
1 teaspoon baking soda
1 teaspoon cream of tartar
1 egg, lightly beaten
½ cup hot water, approximately
Unbleached white flour

1. Preheat the oven to 350 degrees.

2. Place the whole wheat flour in a bowl. Cut in the butter until mixture is the consistency of coarse oatmeal. Add the sugar, baking soda, cream of tartar, egg and enough hot water to make a dough that can be rolled like pastry.

3. Roll out the dough to one-eighth- to one-quarter-inch thickness on a floured pastry cloth or board (use unbleached flour for rolling). Cut into three-inch squares. Place on ungreased baking sheet and bake 15 to 20 minutes or until done. Cool on a rack.

Yield: About two dozen crackers.

ITALIAN SESAME COOKIES

¼ cup soft butter
½ cup raw sugar
1 teaspoon vanilla
3 eggs
1¾ cups unbleached white flour
3 teaspoons baking powder
¼ teaspoon sea salt
2 tablespoons wheat germ
2 tablespoons stoneground
  yellow corn meal
½ cup sesame seeds

1. Preheat the oven to 425 degrees.

2. Cream the butter, sugar and vanilla together until very light and fluffy. Beat in two of the eggs very well.

3. Mix together the flour, baking powder, salt, wheat germ and corn meal and stir into the creamed mixture gradually.

4. With the hands, shape mixture into rolls about two inches long and three-quarters inch in diameter. Beat remaining egg, dip cookies in egg and roll in sesame seeds. Place on ungreased baking sheet and bake 12 minutes, or until brown. Cool on a rack.

Yield: About three and one-half dozen cookies.

HONEY NUT BALLS

¼ cup soft sweet butter or soy
  margarine
½ teaspoon kelp
⅓ cup honey
2 cups wheat germ
2 teaspoons almond extract
1 teaspoon vanilla
1 teaspoon cinnamon
⅓ cup chopped pecans

Combine all the ingredients except the pecans and mix well. Form into one-half-inch balls and roll in the pecans. Chill two hours.

Yield: Eighteen to twenty-four cookies.

Note: A whole almond can be placed inside each ball of dough instead of rolling cookies in the pecans.

CONSCIOUSNESS III COOKIES

1 cup butter
¼ cup carob powder
1 teaspoon vanilla
2 eggs
2 tablespoons honey
1 cup almond meal
Unsweetened shredded coconut
1 cup quick cooking oats
½ cup wheat germ
1 cup slivered or sliced almonds

1. Melt the butter in a small saucepan and stir in the carob powder and vanilla.

2. Place the eggs in an electric blender and blend one second. Add the butter mixture while blending and add the honey.

3. In a large bowl, mix together the almond meal, one cup coconut, the oats, wheat germ and almonds. Pour in the butter mixture and mix well. Form into one-inch balls. Roll in coconut.

4. Now, pick your consciousness:
   1. eat the cookies raw
   2. freeze them and serve frozen, or
   3. place them on a lightly oiled baking sheet and bake 10 minutes in a 350-degree oven.

Yield: About forty cookies.

Note: Dry ingredients may be varied with the use of chopped dates, pecans, walnuts, raisins and sunflower seed kernels. The contributor advises the cook to prepare these with love, and share with everybody, for best possible results.

NUTBALLS

⅔ cup honey
⅓ cup unsulphured molasses
¾ cup sunflower seed kernels
¾ cup soy milk powder
¾ cup carob powder
Unsweetened shredded coconut

1. Combine the honey, molasses, sunflower seed kernels, soy milk powder, carob powder and one-quarter cup coconut. Form into balls the size of walnuts. Roll in coconut.

2. Let stand an hour or two to allow flavors to blend. Store in the refrigerator.

Yield: About three dozen cookies.

15
PRESERVES, RELISHES & SPREADS

Beautiful homebaked breads should be lovingly spread with good-tasting,
unadulterated and nutritious fillings such as those given in this chapter.
Picnickers and the lunch box crowd become the center of attention and
envy when they set out something different and they know
it's worth talking about.
A cupboard full of homemade preserves, pickles and relishes gives
a feeling of security. You know they taste good and that
nothing unnecessary has been added.

PLUM CONSERVE

2 thin-skinned Florida oranges,
  seeds removed
3 pounds fresh plums, pitted
  and quartered
3 pounds raw sugar
1 pound raisins
½ pound chopped walnuts

1. Grind the oranges through the fine
blade of a meat grinder.

2. In a heavy saucepan, combine the
oranges, plums, sugar and raisins. Cook,
stirring occasionally, until mixture is very
thick, about one and one-half hours.

3. Stir in the nuts and cook 20 minutes
longer. Pour into hot sterilized jars.
Cover and cool.

Yield: About two quarts.

UNCOOKED JAM FOR THE FREEZER

3 cups crushed fruit (strawberries,
  blueberries, blackberries,
  peaches, apricots)
5 cups raw sugar
1 package powdered pectin
1 cup water

1. Combine the fruit and sugar, stir well
and let stand 20 minutes.

2. Dissolve powdered pectin in the water,
bring to the boiling point and boil one
minute. Add to fruit-and-sugar mixture
and stir two minutes. Let stand 24 hours
and then freeze. The jam can be served
directly from freezer.

Yield: About three pounds.

Note: This is good over homemade
ice cream. If only liquid pectin is available,
follow the directions for uncooked jam in
the liquid pectin brochure and freeze.

MUSHROOM AND ARTICHOKE RELISH

1 cup button mushrooms, or
large mushrooms cut into
quarters
1½ cups 1-inch lengths celery
2 cups peeled and diced
Jerusalem artichokes
½ cup lemon juice
1 teaspoon sugar
Cold water

1. Place the mushrooms and celery in a colander and steam over boiling water five minutes. Turn into a bowl.

2. Place the artichokes in the colander and steam over the boiling water until barely tender, about 12 minutes. Add to the mushroom mixture.

3. Stir in remaining ingredients including enough water to cover vegetables. The relish mixture will keep a week or more in the refrigerator.

Yield: Six servings.

FULL CIRCLE FARM CHUTNEY

3 onions, sliced
2 pounds quince, peeled,
cored and diced
3 pounds apples, peeled,
cored and sliced
1½ pounds raisins
½ teaspoon cayenne pepper
4 cloves garlic, finely chopped
2 quarts cider vinegar
½ pound candied ginger,
chopped
1 teaspoon mace
1 teaspoon cinnamon
1 teaspoon ground cloves
3 tablespoons ground ginger
2 tablespoons paprika
2 ounces sea salt
4 pounds honey

1. Combine all the ingredients in a heavy kettle and bring to a boil.

2. Cook gently, stirring occasionally, for about three hours or until the mixture is quite thick.

3. Pour the hot chutney into hot sterilized jars; seal and cool. Store in a cool, dark, dry place.

Yield: About seven pints.

Note: It is recommended that this chutney be boiled in a well-ventilated kitchen because the mixture emits a strong odor while cooking.

PEPPER RELISH

3 large green peppers
1 small fresh hot chili pepper
Olive oil
Sea salt to taste
Cumin to taste

1. Preheat the oven to 450 degrees.

2. Place the green peppers and hot chili pepper on a shallow pan and bake until browned, about 20 minutes.

3. Using pot holders, transfer the peppers to a bowl of cold water.

4. Skin the peppers, remove stems and seeds and chop peppers finely.

5. Add enough olive oil to give a spreading consistency. Season with salt and cumin. Store in a jar in the refrigerator and serve as a relish or spread.

Yield: About three pints.

HALF-SOUR PICKLED CUCUMBERS

2 pounds small unwaxed pickling cucumbers
½ cup coarse salt
5 cloves garlic, cut into quarters
Water
10 sprigs fresh dill weed
2 hot dried chili peppers

1. Wash the cucumbers very well and cut a one-quarter-inch slice off each end. Mash together the salt and garlic.

2. Pack the cucumbers into two sterilized jars, fitting cucumbers as close together as possible. Fill each jar with water.

3. Pour water off cucumbers into a pan. Add salt-and-garlic mixture to the pan. Bring to a boil.

4. Place five dill sprigs and one hot chili pepper among the cucumbers in each jar. Pour the boiling water over. Cover and let stand at room temperature three to four days. Test one jar by tasting a pickle to see if it is ready. Store in refrigerator.

Yield: Two pints.

RAW REFRIGERATOR RELISH

1 dozen red and green sweet
  peppers, seeded and diced
6 pounds cabbage, shredded
6 medium-size carrots, shredded
6 medium-size onions, sliced
Vegetable salt or kelp to taste
6 cups cider vinegar
3 to 4 cups honey, or to taste
1 tablespoon celery seeds
1 tablespoon mustard seeds

Combine all the ingredients in a large
bowl and mix very well. Ladle into jars and
store in the refrigerator several days before
using.

Yield: About six quarts.

Note: Alternately, the ingredients can be
brought to a boil in a kettle and boiled 20
minutes before being poured into hot
sterilized jars. Cool and store in the
refrigerator.

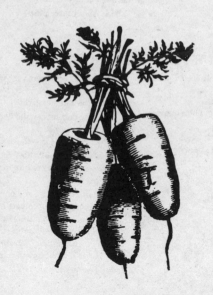

LIVER SPREAD

¾ pound beef liver, pork liver
   or chicken livers
2 tablespoons butter
1 small onion, finely chopped
2 hard-cooked eggs, chopped
Sea salt and freshly ground
   black pepper to taste
1 tablespoon chopped parsley
¼ teaspoon tarragon

1. If the liver is beef or pork, skin and trim it, slice thinly and steam over boiling water 15 minutes.

2. Heat the butter in a heavy skillet and sauté the onion in it until tender. Add the steamed beef or pork liver or uncooked chicken livers and cook quickly until browned and tender. (Chicken livers will still be a little pink in the middle.) Grind in a meat grinder or chop finely.

3. Add remaining ingredients and mix well.

Yield: Enough for four sandwiches

VEGETARIAN CHOPPED LIVER

1 pound fresh string beans
Boiling water
3 tablespoons oil
2 large onions, finely chopped
1 rib celery, chopped
¼ cup chopped walnuts
3 hard-cooked eggs
Sea salt to taste

1. Cook the string beans in the boiling salted water until barely tender. Drain beans and use liquid in soup.

2. Heat the oil in a skillet and sauté the onions in it until tender. Add celery and cook two minutes longer.

3. Grind the beans, onion mixture, walnuts and eggs through the coarse blade of a meat grinder. Season with salt. Serve as sandwich spread or as salad on lettuce leaves.

Yield: Four servings.

AVOCADO SPREAD

½ ripe avocado, mashed
2 teaspoons lemon juice
¼ tomato, skinned and diced
2 tablespoons diced green pepper
2 tablespoons alfalfa or flax seed
   sprouts (see page 195)
Kelp or vegetable salt to taste

Mash the avocado and add remaining ingredients. Mix well but do not beat until smooth because mixture should have some texture.

Yield: Enough for two to three sandwiches.

AVOCADO AND BANANA SPREAD

1 ripe avocado, peeled, pitted
   and mashed
1 tablespoon lemon juice
½ ripe banana, mashed
¼ cup wheat germ
2 tablespoons coarsely
   chopped walnuts

Combine all the ingredients and mix lightly.

Yield: Enough for three sandwiches.

DANDELION SPREAD

1 cup young dandelion leaves
½ cup cottage cheese
¼ cup chopped nuts
Homemade mayonnaise
   (see page 186)

Place dandelion leaves, cheese and nuts in an electric blender and blend until smooth. Mix in enough mayonnaise to make spreading consistency.

Yield: About one and three-quarter cups.

MIXED CHEESE SPREAD

2½ ounces farmer cheese
2 tablespoons ricotta cheese
¼ cup diced mozzarella cheese
1 tablespoon raisins

Place all ingredients in an electric blender and blend until smooth.

Yield: Enough for one sandwich.

CREAM CHEESE OR COTTAGE CHEESE SPREADS

1) 3 ounces cream cheese or cottage cheese, ¼ cup chopped walnuts

2) 3 ounces cream cheese or cottage cheese, 1 tablespoon grated onion, 1 teaspoon chopped green pepper, 1 tablespoon chopped celery, vegetable salt to taste

3) 3 ounces cream cheese or cottage cheese, ¼ cup sliced radishes, ¼ cup chopped peeled seeded cucumber, kelp to taste

4) 3 ounces cream cheese or cottage cheese, ¼ cup chopped walnuts, ¼ cup chopped watercress, ¼ cup grated raw carrot, sea salt to taste

5) 3 ounces cream cheese or cottage cheese, ⅓ cup chopped dates, figs, dried apricots or raisins, 2 teaspoons lemon juice, ¼ cup chopped nuts

Yield: Each of the spreads will fill three sandwiches.

CELERY-NUT FILLING

1 cup finely chopped celery leaves
1 cup pecan meal or very finely ground pecans
Sea salt to taste
Homemade mayonnaise
(see page 186)

Combine the celery leaves, pecan meal or pecans, salt and enough mayonnaise to give a spreading consistency.

Yield: About one and one-half cups.

HOMEMADE PEANUT BUTTER

1 pound shelled and skinned
   unroasted peanuts
¼ cup wheat germ
1 tablespoon sea salt
   (optional)
1 tablespoon tahini
   (sesame paste)

1. Preheat the oven to 300 degrees.

2. Place the peanuts on a well-oiled baking
sheet and bake, stirring several times, 10 to
15 minutes, or until golden.

3. Place all but one-quarter cup of the
peanuts in an electric blender with the
wheat germ, salt and tahini. Blend until
smooth. Chop the reserved nuts roughly
and add to the blended mixture.

Yield: Enough for six sandwiches.

Note: The peanuts can also be ground
without roasting first. Mix the finely
ground nuts with enough tahini to make
a spreading consistency.

PEANUT-BASED SPREADS

1) ½ cup raw peanut butter, ¼
   cup grated carrot, 2
   tablespoons chopped celery

2) ½ cup raw peanut butter, 2
   tablespoons lemon juice, 1
   tablespoon chopped dates or
   figs, 1 tablespoon raisins

3) ½ cup raw peanut butter, 2
   tablespoons chopped
   cashews, 1 tablespoon lime
   juice, 2 tablespoons
   shredded and toasted
   coconut

Yield: Each of the spreads will fill three to
four sandwiches.

THE CHIC PEANUT BUTTER SANDWICH

Unhydrogenated raw peanut
  butter
2 slices homemade rye toast
  or whole wheat toast
Homemade mayonnaise
  (see page 186)
Thin slices of cucumber
  and tomato

Spread peanut butter on one slice toast
and mayonnaise on the other and sandwich
together with cucumber and tomato slices.

Yield: One sandwich.

STRAWBERRY-SESAME SPREAD

¼ cup dried chick-peas
  Water
½ cup tahini (sesame paste)
2 tablespoons tamari (soy sauce)
2 tablespoons toasted sesame
  seeds
¼ cup wheat germ
6 to 8 large strawberries, finely
  chopped
1 to 2 tablespoons sunflower seed
  kernels
Alfalfa sprouts (see page 195)
  or parsley

1. Pick over and wash the chick-peas.
Cover with water and let soak overnight.

2. Cook the soaked chick-peas in a
saucepan until soft and outer husks slip off
easily. Mash the chick-peas roughly. Add
tahini, tamari and one-quarter cup water.

3. Beat mixture while adding the sesame
seeds and wheat germ. Stir in the
strawberries. Spread over whole grain
breads. Sprinkle with sunflower seed
kernels and alfalfa sprouts or parsley.

Yield: Enough for four to six sandwiches.

NUT BUTTER SPREAD

2 cups nuts (cashews, pecans,
  walnuts, almonds)
1 cup sunflower seed kernels
1 cup sesame seeds
Oil
Honey to taste

1. Place the nuts, sunflower seed kernels
and seeds in an electric blender and blend
until fine. Add enough oil to blend them
to a paste. Sweeten with honey.

2. Store in covered jars in the refrigerator.

Yield: About two cups.

SOY MAYONNAISE

½ cup soy flour
1 cup water
½ teaspoon sea salt
½ teaspoon paprika
⅛ teaspoon cayenne pepper
1 teaspoon grated onion
1 cup oil
¼ cup lemon juice

1. Place the soy flour, water, salt, paprika, cayenne and onion in an electric blender. Blend until smooth.

2. With blender on high speed, add the oil, drop by drop to begin with until mixture starts to thicken. As it thickens, add oil a little faster.

3. Add the lemon juice and chill well.

Yield: About two cups.

SOYBEAN SPREAD

½ cup mashed cooked soybeans (see page 157) or soy flour
½ cup raw peanut butter
1 tablespoon brewer's yeast
3 tablespoons chopped scallions or chives
3 tablespoons chopped parsley
2 tablespoons chopped raw peanuts

Mix all the ingredients together until well blended.

Yield: Enough for six sandwiches.

RAISIN COCONUT SPREAD

½ cup monukka raisins
½ cup unsweetened shredded coconut
Yogurt (see page 311)

Place raisins and coconut in an electric blender and blend until smooth. Mix to spreading consistency with yogurt.

Yield: About one-half cup.

BLENDER SPREAD

½ cup sesame seeds
1 teaspoon kelp
½ cup water
1 tablespoon chopped onion
1 tablespoon chopped celery
¼ cup alfalfa sprouts
(see page 195)
½ cup lentil sprouts
(see page 195)
1 tablespoon tahini
(sesame paste)
2 tablespoons lemon juice

Place all the ingredients in an electric blender and blend until smooth.

Yield: Enough for three sandwiches.

SANDWICH RELISH

2 cups homemade mayonnaise
(see page 186) or soy
mayonnaise (see page 394)
¼ cup chopped dill pickle
¼ cup chopped celery
1 tablespoon chopped sweet
red pepper
1 tablespoon chopped parsley
¼ teaspoon basil
¼ teaspoon oregano
¼ teaspoon chervil
¼ cup chopped scallions
1 tablespoon tamari (soy sauce)
2 teaspoons turmeric
2 teaspoons lemon juice

Mix together all the ingredients except the turmeric and lemon juice. Dissolve the turmeric in the lemon juice and add to the mixture. Chill.

Yield: About three cups.

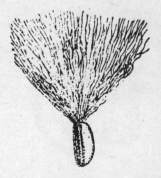

APPLE BUTTER

10 pints apples, peeled
  and sliced
1 quart water
4 cups raw sugar
1 cup brown sugar
1 tablespoon cinnamon
1 teaspoon ground cloves
1 teaspoon ground allspice

1. Combine the apples and water in a large kettle, bring to a boil and simmer, covered, until apples are soft. Pass through a food mill.

2. Combine strained applesauce with remaining ingredients in a clean kettle. Bring to a boil, stirring until sugar is dissolved.

3. Cook gently, uncovered, until mixture becomes quite thick, at least two and one-half hours. Stir often. Pour into hot sterilized jars and seal.

Yield: About two quarts.

HIGHLAND ORCHARD APPLE BUTTER

20 pounds organically grown
  apples, washed and cut up,
  cores and peel included
Water
1 gallon sweet cider boiled in
  open kettle until syrup is
  formed (be careful not to burn)
½ teaspoon sea salt
4 to 5 cups raw sugar
3 or 4 cinnamon sticks

1. Place the apples and a small quantity of water in a large kettle, bring to a boil and cook gently until soft.

2. Preheat the oven to 325 degrees.

3. Pass apple mixture through a food mill and mix with boiled-down cider syrup. Pour into a large flat pan.

4. Bake until sauce is reduced by about half, stirring occasionally. Add salt and sugar, return to oven and cook one and one-half hours longer or until butter is reddish amber color. Add cinnamon sticks during the last half hour of cooking. Ladle into hot sterilized jars; seal.

Yield: About three quarts.

CREAMED APPLE BUTTER

½ apple, sliced and peeled
1 teaspoon honey
½ ounce cream cheese
½ teaspoon raw nut butter
1 walnut, chopped
2 teaspoons raisins, or two
   dates, chopped

1. Place apple slices on broiler pan, brush with honey and broil under preheated broiler, with temperature set at 350 degrees, for 15 minutes or until soft.

2. Mash the broiled apple, the cheese and nut butter together. Add walnut and raisins or dates. Blend until smooth.

Yield: Enough for one sandwich or salad.

FOUR VEGETABLE SPREADS

1) 1 cup shredded cabbage, ¼ cup chopped dried apricots, 2 tablespoons chopped walnuts, mixed together and moistened with homemade mayonnaise (see page 186)

2) 1 cup shredded cabbage, ⅓ cup grated carrot, 1 tablespoon chopped chives, moistened with homemade mayonnaise

3) 1 cup grated carrots, ¼ cup finely chopped celery, ¼ cup finely chopped apple, 2 tablespoons finely chopped green pepper, moistened with homemade mayonnaise

4) 1 cup mashed home-baked navy beans or soybeans, ¼ cup finely chopped celery, 1 tablespoon chopped onion, moistened with homemade mayonnaise

Yield: Each of the spreads will fill about four sandwiches.

16
BABY FOODS

In general, baby foods can be made from meat, poultry, fish, steamed
vegetables and fruits prepared in the normal way except for reduction
in or elimination of the amounts of salt, spices, herbs and other seasonings.
All bones, skin, gristle and fat should be eliminated. The foods can be
chopped in an electric blender or finely shredded with a knife for a
toddler or pureed in an electric blender or food mill
for a baby.
Fruits and vegetables should be cooked without peeling, but after thorough
scrubbing, in the smallest amount of water for the shortest amount of time.
There is no need to add any seasonings. Serve at once
and freeze any extra.
Almost all soups cooked from scratch with a minimum of seasonings for
the rest of the family can be blended or pureed in a food mill
for baby. Seasonings for the family can be added
after baby's portion is removed.

BABY'S TOMATO JUICE

3 to 4 pounds ripe tomatoes
½ teaspoon sea salt (optional)

1. Wash tomatoes well, quarter and cut out white core and stems Place tomatoes in a large kettle and simmer over low heat until soft.

2. Spoon tomatoes into a food mill placed over a bowl and force the juice through. Add salt if desired.

3. The juice can be further strained at this point through several layers of muslin if desired.

4. Heat the juice to boiling and pour hot juice into hot sterilized canning jars to within one inch of top. Cover and set on a rack in a water bath with boiling water extending one inch above the tops of jars. Cover kettle and when water returns to boil, simmer gently 15 minutes. Remove jars, tighten tops and set on two to three thicknesses of cloth. Cool 12 hours. Test for seal.

Yield: About one quart.

VEGETABLE AND FRUIT JUICES

1) equal parts of celery and carrot juice made with a juicer or by blending the vegetables in an electric blender and straining out the pulp

2) washed, unpeeled and uncored apples, prepared as above

3) washed grapes made into juice and mixed with mashed banana

4) equal parts carrot, beet and celery juice sweetened with honey

5) equal parts spinach, carrot and tomato juice

In most cases these strained juices can be tolerated by normal healthy babies three months old.

PUREED GREEN BEANS

¼ pound green beans
½ cup boiling water

Wash the beans well and cut off stem ends. Cut into one-half-inch lengths. Place in a saucepan with the water, cover and cook over medium heat 10 minutes. Puree in a food mill.

Yield: One-third cup.

MASHED CARROT

1 cup thinly sliced well-
scrubbed unpeeled carrot
⅔ cup boiling water
1 tablespoon chopped celery

Place carrot, water and celery in a saucepan and cook, covered, over medium heat for about 10 minutes or until just tender. Strain through a food mill.

Yield: One-third cup.

MASHED CARROT AND POTATO

1 medium-size carrot, scrubbed
but unpeeled, chopped
1 medium-size potato, scrubbed
but unpeeled, chopped
1 cup boiling water
Milk (optional)

Place carrot, potato and water in a heavy saucepan and cook, covered, over medium heat 10 to 12 minutes. Strain through a food mill. If desired, mixture can be thinned with milk.

Yield: Three-quarters cup.

BLENDED SALAD FOR CHILDREN ("GREEN GLOP")

2 tomatoes, skinned
¼ cup orange juice or water
2 ribs celery, quartered
1 Italian-style green pepper, seeded and diced
1 small cucumber, peeled
Romaine, Boston or Bibb lettuce leaves
¼ cup oil
Lemon juice or lime juice to taste
2 tablespoons brewer's yeast

1. Place the tomatoes, orange juice or water, celery, green pepper and cucumber in an electric blender and blend until smooth.

2. Gradually add the lettuce leaves while blending, pushing them down into the mixture with a rib of celery, used like a spatula, until mixture is desired consistency.

3. Blend in the oil slowly and then the juice and yeast. Serve immediately.

Yield: About four servings.

Note: The contributor says her twins have been eating this since they were a few months old and they've never tasted commercial baby foods.

MASHED POTATO WITH SPINACH

1 small to medium-size potato, scrubbed but unpeeled and chopped
½ cup boiling water
1 cup loosely packed well-washed spinach leaves with tough center stems removed
Milk (optional)

Place the potato in a heavy saucepan with the water. Cover and cook six minutes. Add the spinach and cook three to four minutes longer or until potato is tender. Strain through a food mill. Thin with milk if necessary.

Yield: About one-half cup.

BABY'S APPLESAUCE

4 pounds medium-size apples
  (about 12)
½ cup water
½ cup honey (optional)

1. Wash the apples and cut into quarters but do not peel or core. Place apples in a large five-quart kettle.

2. Add water, cover and cook over low heat, stirring occasionally, 20 to 25 minutes or until apples are soft.

3. Spoon apples into a food mill placed over a bowl and force through in batches. (Leave excess liquid in bottom of kettle; use in fruit cup.) Sweeten with honey if desired. Many babies will eat the applesauce without added sweetening.

Yield: About six and one-half cups.

Note: To freeze the applesauce, chill it quickly by setting the bowl in ice. Spoon chilled sauce into washed, rinsed and cooled freezer containers, leaving one-inch air space at the top for expansion. Cover, label and freeze.

SCRAPED APPLE

1 apple, cut in half and core removed

Scrape the side of a spoon across the apple in quick short strokes, feeding the baby a bite at a time as apple is scraped. This is the most convenient, neat baby food for the car and while visiting as well as at home.

BABY BANANA MUSH

½ small ripe banana, mashed
2 tablespoons wheat germ
  Yogurt (see page 311)

Mix together the banana, wheat germ and one-quarter cup yogurt. Adjust consistency with additional yogurt if necessary.

Yield: About one serving.

FRUIT AND YOGURT

¼ cup yogurt (see page 311)
¼ cup non-fat dry milk solids
 1 or 2 walnuts
½ banana or ¼ cup other fresh
  fruit

Combine all the ingredients in an electric blender and blend until smooth and the nuts are fine enough for the child to cope with. The thickness of the mixture can be adjusted by adding more yogurt.

Yield: One serving.

SWEET MIX FOR TODDLERS AND CHILDREN

½ cup finely ground sesame seeds,
  sunflower seed kernels or
  pumpkin seeds
⅔ cup water
 1 tablespoon maple syrup
½ ripe banana, mashed
 1 apple, peeled, cored and
  grated or sliced, depending
  on age of child
Lime juice to taste

1. Place seeds and water in an electric blender and blend until smooth. Add maple syrup and blend again.

2. Pour into a bowl, add the banana, apple and lime juice and serve at once.

Yield: About two servings, depending on the age of the child.

CHILDREN'S NUT BUTTER

Blanched almonds, walnuts,
  cashews or peanuts
Water or grape juice

Grind almonds, walnuts, cashews or peanuts in a Moulinex grinder until a fine powder. Moisten the powder with a little water or grape juice. Serve with a spoon or form into tiny balls for children to eat out-of-hand.

Note: The contributor's children have been raised as vegetarians and the nut butter is one of their main sources of protein. The contributor started giving the children the nut butter when they were around one year old. She purchased unsalted raw nuts from a wholesaler.

17
CANDY

As long as people crave sweetmeat morsels, it is the wise mother and hostess who makes her own. In this way, the sugar content can be controlled and good-tasting tidbits of nutrition included.

MARCIA'S KAⁱKEⁱS

½ orange
⅓ cup oil
⅔ cup honey
 3 cups rolled oats
½ cup wheat germ
¼ cup sesame seeds
½ cup shredded unsweetened
   coconut
 2 tablespoons brown sugar
¾ teaspoon sea salt
½ cup chopped walnuts

1. Remove pulp from the orange rind; freeze the rind. When solidly frozen, grate the rind, including some of the white pith, on the fine side of a grater.

2. Preheat the oven to 350 degrees.

3. In a mixing bowl, combine the oil and half the honey. Add the grated rind, the oats, wheat germ, sesame seeds, coconut, sugar, salt and walnuts. Mix together thoroughly so that all ingredients become coated with the oil-and-honey mixture.

4. Add remaining honey and mix well. Press into a foil-lined nine-inch square baking pan and bake 20 minutes or until brown.

5. Score with not-too-sharp knife into squares. Cool.

6. Break along the score marks. The pieces stay fresh several days but can be frozen if desired.

Yield: About three dozen squares.

SESAME SEED FLATS

 1 cup sesame seeds
 Honey to taste
¼ teaspoon almond extract
½ cup raisins
 18 walnut halves, approximately

1. Place the seeds in an electric blender and blend until they are a smooth mass. Turn onto a board and gradually knead in honey. (The seeds are fairly sweet alone.) Knead in the extract.

2. Work in the raisins and when mixture is a compact ball, pinch off small pieces and shape into flat rounds. Press half a walnut into each candy. Store in a covered container in the refrigerator.

Yield: About eighteen candies.

SESAME SEED BRITTLE

2 cups raw sugar
2 cups sesame seeds
1 teaspoon vanilla

1. Place the sugar in a heavy iron skillet and heat gradually, stirring constantly, until sugar melts and forms a golden syrup. Take care not to burn sugar.

2. Remove from the heat and stir in the seeds and vanilla. Pour mixture onto a buttered cookie sheet, heatproof platter or marble slab. Spread into a thin layer. Cool.

3. When cold, break into small pieces.

Yield: About one pound.

SUNNY SEED CANDY

1 cup raw sugar
1 tablespoon peanut oil
½ cup sesame seeds
½ cup sunflower seed kernels

1. Place the sugar and oil in a small heavy skillet and stir over low heat until sugar melts. This will take about 10 minutes. Do not try to hurry the process or the sugar will burn.

2. Stir in the seeds and sunflower seed kernels and pour mixture onto a buttered heatproof platter or marble slab. Cool. When cold, break into pieces.

Yield: About one pound.

SEED AND NUT BUTTER BALLS

2 tablespoons sunflower seed kernels
2 tablespoons sesame seeds
16 almonds, blanched or unblanched
2 tablespoons tahini (sesame paste)
2½ tablespoons honey
2 teaspoons raw peanut butter
Coconut meal

1. In an electric blender or Moulinex grinder, grind together the sunflower seed kernels, seeds and almonds.

2. Mix seed mixture with the tahini, honey and peanut butter; blend together well. Form into tiny balls and roll in the coconut.

Yield: About eight balls.

SEED CANDY

1 cup honey
2 tablespoons soft butter
½ cup flax seeds ground in a Moulinex grinder
½ cup sunflower seed kernels ground in a Moulinex grinder
1 cup wheat germ
1 cup almonds ground in a Moulinex grinder
1 cup finely shredded unsweetened coconut

Mix the honey and butter together and add remaining ingredients except the coconut. Form into tiny balls, roll in the coconut and store in a covered dish in the refrigerator.

Yield: About one pound.

GRANOLA CANDY

Honey
Shredded unsweetened coconut
Crunchy Granola

Add enough honey and coconut to the Granola to make it stick together. Form into balls. Wrap in wax paper. This is good for lunch box candy.

FUDGIE REMBRANDTS

½ cup blackstrap molasses
¼ cup oil
3 eggs
½ teaspoon kelp
1 teaspoon vanilla
1 teaspoon almond extract
2 teaspoons cinnamon
½ cup carob powder
1 cup soy flour
1 cup broken walnuts

1. Put in an electric blender the molasses, oil, eggs, kelp, vanilla, almond extract, cinnamon and carob powder. Blend until well mixed.

2. Turn mixture into a bowl and add the soy flour (mixture will be very thick). Mix in the nuts. Lightly grease the fingers with butter and push the mixture down into a buttered 9-by-5-by-3-inch loaf pan.

3. Place pan in cold oven. Turn temperature to 350 degrees and light oven. Bake 25 minutes. Let cool 10 minutes, then cut into small squares.

Yield: About three dozen squares.

GOAT'S MILK CAROB FUDGE

1½ cups honey
⅔ cup goat's milk
2 tablespoons butter
⅓ cup carob powder
1 teaspoon vanilla
⅓ cup chopped nuts

1. Place honey, milk, butter and carob powder in a heavy saucepan. Heat, stirring, until mixture is well blended and then cook, without stirring, until it registers 238 degrees on a candy thermometer or forms a soft ball when a drop is placed in cold water.

2. Cool to lukewarm and then beat until mixture loses its shininess. Work in the vanilla and nuts. Pour into a greased pan. When set, cut into squares.

Yield: One dozen squares.

NO-COOK HEALTH FUDGE

½ cup non-fat dry milk solids
½ cup carob powder or peanut butter
1 cup shredded unsweetened coconut
½ cup sunflower seed kernels
½ cup cashews
¼ cup honey
¼ cup water
2 tablespoons brewer's yeast
½ cup sesame seeds

Combine all the ingredients in a large bowl and mix until mixture sticks together. Press into a flat buttered pan. Cut into squares and wrap in wax paper for storing.

Yield: About one and one-quarter pounds.

HONEY POPCORN NUT CRUNCH

½ cup melted butter
½ cup honey
3 quarts popped popcorn
1 cup chopped nuts

1. Preheat the oven to 350 degrees.

2. Blend the butter and honey together and heat gently. Mix the popcorn with the nuts and pour the butter-honey mixture over. Mix well. Spread on a cookie sheet in a thin layer.

3. Bake 10 to 15 minutes or until crisp.

Yield: About three quarts broken nut crunch.

CAROB FUDGE

2 cups raw sugar
6 tablespoons carob powder
2 tablespoons butter
⅔ cup milk
⅛ teaspoon sea salt
1½ teaspoons vanilla

1. Combine the sugar, carob powder, butter, milk and salt in a heavy saucepan. Heat, stirring, until sugar is dissolved. Continue to boil, without stirring, until mixture registers 225 degrees on a candy thermometer or a drop placed in a bowl of cold water forms a soft ball.

2. Add vanilla. Cool to lukewarm. Beat until creamy. Pour into a buttered pan and cool. Cut into squares.

Yield: About one pound.

TURKISH DELIGHT

½ cup boiling water
2 cups raw sugar
2 tablespoons unflavored gelatin
½ cup cold water
½ cup orange juice
¼ cup lemon juice
Raw sugar, powdered in an electric blender or Moulinex grinder

1. Place boiling water and two cups sugar in a heavy pan and heat, stirring until sugar dissolves. Continue to boil, without stirring, until mixture registers 225 degrees on a candy thermometer or spins a thread.

2. Meanwhile, soak the gelatin in the cold water. Add soaked gelatin, orange juice and lemon juice to sugar syrup. Put through a fine sieve. Pour into a chilled pan one inch deep. Let stand until firm.

3. Cut. Coat with powdered raw sugar.

Yield: About one pound.

LOLLIPOPS

1 cup carob powder
1 cup soy grits
1 cup sesame seeds
1 cup unsulphured molasses
1 cup wheat germ
1 cup raw peanut butter
1 cup sunflower seed meal

Mix all ingredients together very well. Form into small balls and insert a stick or toothpick in each.

Yield: About two dozen bite-size lollipops.

PEANUT-BANANA POPS

¼ cup raw nutty peanut butter
(see page 392)
¼ cup non-fat dry milk solids
1 tablespoon honey
⅓ cup light cream
4 peeled and frozen bananas
⅓ cup chopped peanuts

1. Place the peanut butter, milk solids, honey and cream in an electric blender and blend until smooth.

2. Roll the bananas in the peanut mixture or spread it over them. Roll in or sprinkle with peanuts. Freeze.

Yield: Four pops.

CARROT HALVA

3 pounds carrots
(the contributor uses organically grown carrots)
1 quart milk
10 cardamom seeds, ground in a mortar and pestle
2 sticks cinnamon, broken into thirds
8 ounces honey
1 cup sweet butter
½ cup sliced blanched almonds
¼ cup non-dyed shelled pistachios

1. Grate the carrots and place in a saucepan with the milk.

2. Add cardamom, cinnamon and honey and bring to a boil. Boil over low heat, stirring often, until mixture is very thick. Remove cinnamon.

3. Add the butter and simmer mixture about 25 minutes longer. Pour into a buttered pan. Cool to room temperature. Sprinkle with almonds and pistachios.

Yield: About four pounds.

FIG AND ALMOND BARS

1 pound black Mission figs,
stems removed
2 cups almonds, blanched or unblanched
Sesame seeds or unsweetened shredded coconut

Put the figs and almonds through the fine blade of a meat grinder. Roll out on wax paper to about one-half-inch thickness. Cut into bars about one inch by three inches. Press sesame seeds or unsweetened shredded coconut into the surface of the bars. Wrap in wax paper for storing.

Yield: About one and one-half pounds.

OM BARS

1½ pounds black Mission figs, stems removed
1 pound pitted dates
½ pound golden raisins
¼ pound sunflower seed kernels
½ pound shelled walnuts
½ pound shredded unsweetened coconut
2 tablespoons carob powder

1. Mix together the figs, dates, raisins, sunflower seed kernels and half the walnuts. Put the mixture through the medium blade of a meat grinder.

2. Knead the ground mixture on a layer of the coconut and gradually work in the carob powder and coconut. Shape into balls, bars or triangles and decorate with the remaining walnuts.

Yield: About four and one-quarter pounds.

PECAN DELIGHT

1 pound dried figs, stems removed
¾ pound shelled pecans
¼ pound raisins
¼ pound pitted dates

Grind the ingredients through the medium blade of a meat grinder and mix well. Press into a buttered pan and cut into squares.

Yield: About two and one-quarter pounds.

RAISIN NUT TWIGS

¼ cup raisins
⅓ cup apple juice, approximately
¼ cup dates
1 cup almonds ground in a Moulinex grinder
1 cup cashews ground in a Moulinex grinder
Finely grated unsweetened coconut

1. Place the raisins in a small bowl and add apple juice to cover. Let soak overnight.

2. Next day, blend the raisins, juice and dates in an electric blender until well mixed. Add a little more juice if necessary.

3. Mix fruit with the ground nuts and form into sticks two inches long by one-half inch in diameter. Roll in the coconut.

Yield: One dozen twigs.

Note: The contributor says the twigs are good for babies.

INGREDIENT CHART & SOURCES

KEY TO INGREDIENT CHART

* * Available organically grown
* † Sold in health food stores
* ‡ Available from mail-order sources, see list or *The Organic Directory* (Rodale Press)
* 0 Available in some supermarkets (there are natural foods sections in certain supermarkets and specialty stores)
* 1 Agriculture Handbook No. 8, *Composition of Food, Raw, Processed, Prepared*. Published by Agricultural Research Service, United States Department of Agriculture. Sold by Superintendent of Documents, U.S. Gov't. Printing Office, Washington, D.C. 20402 ($2). Figures are for commodities as sold in supermarkets. Some independent testing for nutrient evaluation of organic or natural foods has been done, but there is no single recognized source of results.
* 2 *El Molino Cookbook*, El Molino Mills, Alhambra, California ($1)
* 3 Food Composition Table for Use in Africa, U.S. Dept. HEW, PHS and FAO of U.N. 1968
* 4 Table of the Vitamin Content of Human & Animal Foods, Fixsen & Roscoe, *Nutrition Abstracts & Reviews*, 9 (4):830, 1940
* – No information available

Note: Foods contributing extra amounts of particular nutrients are noted.

INGREDIENTS & SOURCES	FORMS AVAILABLE, WITH MOST DESIRABLE OR RECOMMENDED GIVEN FIRST	SOURCE FOR DETAILED NUTRITION COMPOSITION
* † ‡ **ALFALFA SEEDS**	Untreated	2
* † **ALFALFA SPROUTS**		
† ‡ 0 **ALMOND MEAL** (partially defatted)		
* † ‡ 0 **ALMONDS**	Shelled, unblanched, blanched, fresh and raw	1

INGREDIENTS & SOURCES	FORMS AVAILABLE, WITH MOST DESIRABLE OR RECOMMENDED GIVEN FIRST	SOURCE FOR DETAILED NUTRITION COMPOSITION
• † ‡ 0 APPLES Abandoned orchards		1
• ‡ 0 JERUSALEM ARTICHOKES (knobbly root vegetable) Farm stands		1
† ‡ 0 BAKING POWDER	Rumford, aluminum-free single-acting	
• † ‡ BARLEY	Whole, hulled and not pearled. And Barley flour	3
† ‡ BEANS, ADUKI Oriental stores		1 see red beans
• † ‡ BEANS, MUNG † MUNG BEAN SPROUTS Oriental stores	Green, whole. Split	1
† ‡ BONE MEAL	Ground animal bones	—
0 BRAINS beef, calves', pig's and sheep		1
• † ‡ BRAN, WHOLE	Flakes (layers covering wheat germ which are usually removed in refining)	1
† ‡ BREWER'S YEAST and FLAKES	Debittered and Torula—inactive	1
• † ‡ 0 BUCKWHEAT, WHOLE GRAIN (kasha) and FLOUR		1
† ‡ BULGHUR (cracked wheat) Middle Eastern shops	2 or 3 grades fineness	1
† ‡ 0 BUTTER	Churned from sweet cream, no additives	1
† ‡ CARA-COA NUGGETS	Substitute for chocolate chips	see carob
† ‡ CAROB FLOUR OR POWDER	This is dried fruit of St. John's bread tree and a cocoa-chocolate substitute	1
• † ‡ 0 CASHEW NUTS	Fresh and raw	1
† ‡ 0 CHEESE	Natural and unprocessed From raw milk, no additives From pasteurized milk, no additives	1
† ‡ 0 CHICK-PEAS (garbanzos) Spanish & Italian groceries	Dried, or cooked and canned	1
† ‡ COCONUT	Fresh grated Dried, unsweetened, shredded, no additives	1
• † ‡ CORN MEAL Specialty stores	Whole grain, stoneground, unfumigated	1

INGREDIENTS & SOURCES	FORMS AVAILABLE, WITH MOST DESIRABLE OR RECOMMENDED GIVEN FIRST	SOURCE FOR DETAILED NUTRITION COMPOSITION
* **DANDELION GREENS** Italian produce shops	Picked wild	1
* † ‡ 0 **DATES**	Fresh and dried	1
† ‡ **DULSE** Oriental stores	Dried seaweed	1
* † **EGGS** Farms and farm stands	Fertile. From chickens allowed to roam, scratch and mate and not injected	1
† ‡ 0 **FAMILIA OR SWISS BIRCHERMUESLI**	Imported dry mixed cereal with fruit and nuts	–
* † ‡ 0 **FILBERTS OR HAZELNUTS**	Fresh and raw	1
* † ‡ **FLAX SEEDS, FLAX SEED MEAL**		
† **FLAX SPROUTS**	Sprouts—homegrown, high in vitamin C	2
* † ‡ 0 **FLOUR, WHEAT** Specialty shops	Stoneground whole wheat, unfumigated, no additives. Whole wheat pastry flour Unbleached white	1
* † ‡ **FRUITS, DRIED** Specialty shops	Unsulphured, apples, apricots, peaches, pears, prunes and figs	1 for sulphured
† ‡ 0 **CRUNCHY GRANOLA**	Toasted oat cereal with raisins, nuts, honey, coconut, etc.	–
0 **HEARTS** beef, calves', chicken, pig's, lamb and turkey		1
* † ‡ 0 **HERBS AND HERB SEEDS**	Seeds include fennel, flax and caraway	–
* † ‡ 0 **HONEY**	Raw	1
† ‡ **KELP** Oriental shops	Dried seaweed High in minerals	1
0 **KIDNEYS** beef, calves', pork, lamb	High in protein and B vitamins	1
† **KOMBU** Oriental shops	Dried seaweed	–
* **LAMB'S QUARTERS**	Picked wild, high vitamin A	1
† ‡ **LECITHIN** liquid and granules	Fat emulsifier	
* † ‡ 0 **LENTILS** whole and split	Fairly good source protein	1
* † ‡ 0 **LIVER** beef, calves', chicken, pork, lamb, turkey, goose	Good source protein, vitamin A and B vitamins	1
* † ‡ 0 **MAPLE SYRUP**		1
† ‡ **MILLET**	Hulled, whole grain meal and flour Fairly good source protein	1
† ‡ 0 **MILK, COW'S** Farms	Raw (difficult to get), pasteurized, whole & skim, non-instant low heat, spray processed & instant dry milk solids	1

INGREDIENTS & SOURCES	FORMS AVAILABLE, WITH MOST DESIRABLE OR RECOMMENDED GIVEN FIRST	SOURCE FOR DETAILED NUTRITION COMPOSITION
† MILK, GOAT'S Farms	Fluid, fresh and canned High in iron compared with cow's milk Forms easily digested curd	1
† ‡ O MOLASSES	Unsulphured, blackstrap, Barbados, medium, light High in minerals and B vitamins	1
• † ‡ O OATS rolled, meal or flour	Steel cut	1
† ‡ O OILS for cooking and salad dressings	Includes safflower, sunflower, soy, sesame, corn, peanut, olive, wheat germ, corn germ Cold pressed, no additives	1
• † ‡ O PEANUTS and butter Specialty stores	Fresh and raw Unhydrogenated, no additives	1
• † ‡ O PEAS	Dried whole & split	1
• † ‡ O PECANS Specialty stores	Fresh and raw	1
O PEPPERS, HOT CHILI Spanish & Italian markets	Green and immature Good source of vitamin C	1
• † ‡ O PUMPKIN SEEDS		1
• † ‡ RAISINS Specialty stores	Monukka, untreated & unsulphured Thompson seedless and Smyrna	1
• † ‡ O RICE, BROWN	Unpolished	1
• † ‡ RICE FLOUR, BROWN		
• † ‡ RICE POLISH OR POLISHINGS	Outer covering rice—rich in minerals	1
† ‡ O RICE, WILD		1
• † ‡ ROSE HIPS and ROSE HIP POWDER Scandinavian shops	Fresh, picked wild Dried Good source vitamin C	4
• † ‡ RYE FLOUR	Whole grain, stoneground	1
† ‡ O SEA SALT Specialty stores	Source minerals, iodine	–
• † ‡ SESAME SEEDS and SPROUTS Homegrown sprouts	Unhulled Hulled Sprouts, source vitamin C	seeds 1 sprouts
† ‡ SORGHUM SYRUP	Molasses-like syrup from a cane-like grass	–
• † ‡ SOYBEANS and SPROUTS	Green, immature fresh, canned & frozen Dried yellow mature, and cooked and canned	1 1# dry, raw mature beans contains more protein than 1# Cheddar cheese with similar calories

INGREDIENTS & SOURCES	FORMS AVAILABLE, WITH MOST DESIRABLE OR RECOMMENDED GIVEN FIRST	SOURCE FOR DETAILED NUTRITION COMPOSITION
† SOYBEAN CURD or TOFU Oriental stores	Fresh and canned Homemade from soy milk Good source high quality protein	1
• † ‡ 0 SOY FLOUR	Full fat, high fat, low fat and defatted	1
• † ‡ 0 SOY GRITS	Ground or cracked soybeans with high protein content	1 see dry, raw mature
† SOY MARGARINE or BUTTER Homemade	Finely ground beans or soy oil beaten into soy flour	–
† ‡ SOY MILK AND MILK PRODUCTS		1
† ‡ SOYBEAN PASTE or MISO (barley & bean paste) Oriental stores	Fermented products	1
• † SOYBEAN SPROUTS Homemade or Oriental stores	Good source vitamin C	1
• † ‡ 0 SUNFLOWER SEED KERNELS	Unhulled and hulled Can be sprouted Good source protein	1
• † ‡ SUNFLOWER SEED FLOUR or MEAL	Partially defatted	1
SUGAR	Maple sugar Date sugar Raw (Jaggery) sold in Indian stores Raw and Turbinado Brown	1
0 SWEETBREADS yearlings', calves', lamb	Thymus gland	1
† ‡ TAHINI (sesame paste or butter) Middle Eastern shops	Ground sesame seeds	see sesame seeds
† ‡ TAMARI Oriental stores	Soy sauce made from wheat and soybeans by natural aging—no additives	1
† ‡ VEGETABLE SALT	Powdered dry vegetables or salt flavored with dried vegetables	
• † ‡ 0 WALNUTS Specialty stores	Fresh, raw	1
† ‡ 0 WHEAT GERM	Fresh and raw, good source vitamin E, vitamin B complex, vitamin A Toasted, sweetened	1
• † ‡ WHOLE WHEAT BERRIES and SPROUTS Homemade sprouts		1
† ‡ 0 YEAST	Compressed (baker's), bulk dry active with no preservatives	1

MAIL ORDER SOURCES FOR NATURAL & ORGANIC FOODS

(for more sources see THE ORGANIC DIRECTORY, Rodale Press)

GENERAL SUPPLIERS

Deer Valley Farm Guilford, N.Y. 13780
Erewhon Trading Corp. 8003 Beverly Blvd., Los Angeles, Calif. 90048
General Nutrition Corp. New Englewood Mall, Denver, Colo. 80200
Jaffe Bros. P.O. Box 636, Valley Center, Calif. 92082
Natural Sales Comp. P.O. Box 25, Pittsburgh, Pa. 15230
Shiloh Farms Sulphur Springs, Ark. 72768
Walnut Acres Penns Creek, Pa. 17862

SPECIALTIES

Arrowhead Mills Box 866, Hereford, Tex. 79045 Grains
Cartwright Groves Box 331, Carrizo Springs, Tex. 78834 Citrus
Diamond Dairy Goat Farm P.O. Box 133, North Prairie, Wis. 53153 Goat products
Golden Acres Orchard Box 70, Front Royal, Rte. 2, Va. 22630 Apples
Jefferson Organic Orchards Rte. 1, Box 224, Mission, Tex. 78572 Fruits
Hazel Hills Nursery Rte. 1, River Falls, Wis. 54022 Nuts
Lang Apiaries Gasport, N.Y. 14067 Honey
Lee Anderson's Covalda Date Co. P.O. Box 908, Coachella, Calif. 92236
    Citrus, dates, date products, pecans
Lee's Fruit Co. Box 450, Leesburg, Fla. 32748 Citrus fruit, sweet potatoes
Lyman Apiaries Greenwich, N.Y. 12834 Honey
Mease's Natural Foods Inc. Schoeneck, Pa. 17574 Whole grain breads
Nightingale Organic Grove & Nursery Rte. 1, Box 847, Punta Gorda, Fla. 33950
    Citrus and pineapple
Organic Farms and Mission Rte. 1, Henning, Minn. 56551
    Spring wheat, beef, turkey, potatoes, alfalfa and clover
Organic Food Research Farms Rte. 3, Box 304, Dayton, OH. 37321
    Apples, pears, grapes, rose hips, nuts
Pine Hills Herb Farm P.O. Box 307, Roswell, Ga. 30075 Herb plants & dried
Plimmers Enterprises P.O. Box 701, Alpine, Tex. 79830
    Pecans, sunflower seeds, herbs, apples, radishes
Rolling Ledge Maple Orchard Enosburg Falls, Vt. 05450 Maple products
Thousand Island Apiaries Clayton, N.Y. 13624 Honey
Vita-Green Farms P.O. Box 878, Vista, Calif. 92083 Jerusalem artichokes
Wolf's Neck Farms Freeport, Me. 04082 Meats

BIBLIOGRAPHY

1. COOKBOOKS
General:

CHURCH, RUTH ELLEN, *Mary Meade's Country Cookbook*. Chicago: Rand McNally, 1964

HUNTER, BEATRICE TRUM, *The Natural Foods Cookbook*. New York: Simon & Schuster, 1961 (Paperback: Pyramid and Simon & Schuster)

KRAFT, KEN and PAT, *The Home Garden Cookbook*. New York: Doubleday, 1970

LEVITT, ELEANOR, *The Wonderful World of Natural Food Cookery*. New York: Hearthside Press, 1971

ROMBAUER, IRMA S. and BECKER, MARION R., *Joy of Cooking*. Indianapolis: Bobbs-Merrill, 1931

ROSS, SHIRLEY, *The Interior Ecology Cookbook*. San Francisco: Straight Arrow Books, 1970

SUTTON, NANCY, *Adventures in Cooking with Health Foods*. New York: Frederick Fell, 1969

TEICHNER, MIKE and OLGA, *The Gourmet Health Foods Cookbook*. New York: Paperback Library, 1969 (Paperback)

TOMS, AGNES, *Eat, Drink and Be Healthy*. Old Greenwich, Conn.: Devin-Adair, 1963 (Paperback: Pyramid)

Breads & Grains:

BRAUE, JOHN RAHN, *Uncle John's Original Bread Book*. Jericho, New York: Exposition Press, 1965 (Paperback: Pyramid)

BROWN, EDWARD ESPE, *The Tassajara Bread Book*. Berkeley, Calif.: Shambala Publishing, 1970 (Paperback)

CASELLA, DOLORES, *The World of Breads*. New York: David White, 1966

EL MOLINO KITCHENS, *El Molino Best Tested Recipes*. Alhambra, Calif.: El Molino Kitchens, 1953 (Paperback)

ORTON, MILDRED ELLEN, *Cooking with Whole Grains*. New York: Farrar, Straus & Giroux, 1951 (Paperback: Farrar, Straus & Giroux)

RICHARDS, HAZEL, *Make a Treat with Wheat*. Salt Lake City: Family Press, 1968 (Paperback)

ROBERTS, ADA LOU, *The New Book of Favorite Breads from Rose Lane Farm*. New York: Hearthside Press, 1970 (Paperback)

ROSENVALL, V., MILLER, M. and FLACK, D., *Wheat for Man Why and How*. Salt Lake City: Bookcraft, 1966 (Paperback)

STANDARD, STELLA, *Our Daily Bread*. New York: Funk & Wagnalls, 1970

STANDARD, STELLA, *Whole Grain Cookery*. New York: Paperback Library, 1972 (Paperback)

Dairy:

HAZELTON, NIKA, *Eggs!* New York: Simon & Schuster, 1969

HELLER, JANE, ed. from Dutch of Ben J. Kuyper, *World's 50 Best Cheese Dish Recipes*. New York: Herder & Herder, 1971 (Paperback)

MARSHALL, M. E., *The Delectable Egg*. New York: Trident Press, 1968 (Paperback: Pocket Books)

SMETINOFF, OLGA, *The Yogurt Cookbook*. New York: Frederick Fell, 1966 (Paperback)

Salads:

DAHNKE, MARYE, *Marye Dahnke's Salad Book*. New York: Pocket Books, 1954 (Paperback)

MARTON, BERYL M., *The Complete Book of Salads*. New York: Random House, 1969

TRUAX, CAROL, *The Art of Salad Making*. New York: Doubleday, 1968

Vegetables:

BENNETT, VICTOR, *The Complete Bean Cookbook*. Englewood Cliffs, N.J.: Prentice-Hall, 1967

BERG, SALLY and LUCIAN, *The Vegetarian Gourmet*. New York: Herder & Herder, 1971

FARM JOURNAL FOOD EDITORS, *America's Best Vegetable Recipes*. New York: Doubleday, 1970

FITZGERALD, PEGEEN, and SMITH, MARGARET, *Meatless Cooking: Pegeen's Vegetarian Recipes*. Englewood Cliffs, N.J.: Prentice-Hall, 1968

HEINDEL, *New Age Vegetarian Cookbook*. Oceanside, Calif.: Rosicrucian Fellowship, 1968

HELLER, JANE, ed. from German of Elisabeth Anzlinger, *World's 50 Best Vegetarian Recipes*. New York: Herder & Herder, 1971 (Paperback)

HOOKER, ALAN, *New Age Gourmet Cookery*. San Francisco: 101 Productions, 1970 (Paperback)

LIGHT, LUISE, *In Praise of Vegetables*. New York: Scribners, 1966

MEHTA, K. R., *Vegetarian Delights*. Jericho, New York: Exposition Press, 1966

RICHMOND, SONYA, *International Vegetarian Cookery*. New York: Arco, 1965 (Paperback)

VAN GRUNDY JONES, DOROTHEA, *The Soybean Cookbook*. Old Greenwich, Conn.: Devin-Adair, 1963 (Paperback: Arc Books)

WALDO, MYRA, *The Complete Book of Vegetable Cookery*. New York: Bantam Books, 1962 (Paperback)

WALKER, JANET, *Vegetarian Cookery*. Hollywood: Wilshire Book Co., 1970

WASON, BETTY, *The Art of Vegetarian Cookery*. New York: Ace Books, 1970 (Paperback)

WIENER, JOAN, *Victory Through Vegetables*. New York: Holt, Rinehart & Winston, 1971 (Paperback: Holt Paperback)

Other Specialties:

ATWOOD, MARY S., *A Taste of India*. Boston: Houghton Mifflin, 1969

BERGLUND, BERNDT and BOLSBY, CLARE E., *The Edible Wild*. New York: Scribners, 1971

CHEN, JOYCE, *Joyce Chen Cook Book*. Philadelphia: Lippincott, 1963

CHU, GRACE, *Pleasures of Chinese Cooking*. New York: Simon & Schuster, 1962

ELLIS, ELEANOR, *Northern Cookbook*. Ottawa: Indian Affairs & Northern Development, Canadian Government, Queen's Printer, 1967

GAYLORD, ISABELLA, *Cooking with an Accent: The Herb Grower's Book*. Newton Centre, Mass.: Charles Branford, 1963

HODGSON, MOIRA, *The Quick & Easy Raw Food Cookbook*. New York: Grosset & Dunlap, 1971

HUNTER, KATHLEEN, *Health Foods and Herbs*. New York: Arc Books, 1963 (Paperback)

KIMBALL, YEFFE, and ANDERSON, JEAN, *The Art of American Indian Cooking*. New York: Doubleday, 1965 (Paperback: Avon)

LIN, HSIANG JU and TSUIFENG, *Chinese Gastronomy*. New York: Hastings House, 1969

MILLER, AMY BESS and FULLER, PERSIS, *The Best of Shaker Cooking*. New York: Macmillan, 1970

2. COOKBOOKS WITH HISTORY, FOLKLORE, OR OTHER INFORMATION

ANGLER, BRADFORD, *Free-for-the-Eating Wild Foods*. Harrisburg, Pa.: Stackpole Books, 1966

ANGLER, BRADFORD, *More Free-for-the-Eating Wild Foods*. Harrisburg, Pa.: Stackpole Books, 1969

BERQUIST, EDNA SMITH, *High Maples Farm Cookbook*. New York: Macmillan, 1971

GIBBONS, EUELL, *Stalking the Blue-Eyed Scallop*. New York: David McKay, 1964 (Paperback: David McKay)

GIBBONS, EUELL, *Stalking the Good Life*. New York: David McKay, 1971

GIBBONS, EUELL, *Stalking the Healthful Herbs*. New York: David McKay, 1966 (Paperback: David McKay)

GIBBONS, EUELL, *Stalking the Wild Asparagus*. New York: David McKay, 1962 (Paperback: David McKay)

HAWKES, ALEX D., *A World of Vegetable Cookery*. New York: Simon & Schuster, 1968

HERITEAU, JACQUELINE, *How to Grow & Cook It Book of Vegetables, Herbs, Fruits and Nuts*. New York: Hawthorn Books, 1970

JONES, MUSKIE, *Muskie Jones's Northwoods Cookbook*. Toronto: Algonquin Publishing, 1965 (Paperback)

TILLONA, FRANCESCA and STROWBRIDGE, CYNTHIA, *A Feast of Flowers*. New York: Funk & Wagnalls, 1969

3. COOKBOOKS WITH HEALTH THEORIES OR CLAIMS AND/OR PHILOSOPHIES

ABEHSERA, MICHEL, *Zen Macrobiotic Cooking*. New York: University Books, 1968 (Paperback)

BIRCHER, RUTH, *Eating Your Way to Health*. London: Faber & Faber, 1961

BRAGG, PAUL C., *Four Generation Health Food Cookbook & Menus*. Burbank, Calif.: Health Science, 1966 (Paperback)

CAYCE, EDGAR, *Edgar Cayce on Diet and Health*. New York: Paperback Library, 1969 (Paperback)

DAVIS, ADELLE, *Let's Cook It Right*. New York: Harcourt, Brace, Jovanovich, Inc., 1947 (Paperback: New American Library)

ELWOOD, CATHARYN, *Feel Like a Million*. New York: Pocket Books, 1971 (Paperback)

FATHMAN, GEORGE and DORIS, *Live Foods*. Show Low, Ariz.: Sun Haven Enterprises, 1967 (Paperback)

HAUSER, GAYELORD, *The Gayelord Hauser Cookbook*. New York: Capricorn Books, 1963 (Paperback)

HITTLEMAN, RICHARD, *Yoga Natural Foods Cookbook*. New York: Bantam Books, 1970 (Paperback)

KEYS, MARGARET and ANCEL, *The Benevolent Bean.* New York: Doubleday, 1967

KINDERLEHRER, JANE, *Confessions of a Sneaky Organic Cook.* Emmaus, Pa.: Rodale Press, 1971

KORDEL, LELORD, *Cook Right—Live Longer.* New York: G. P. Putnam's Sons, 1966 (Paperback: Award Books)

LAPPÉ, FRANCES MOORE, *Diet for a Small Planet.* New York: Ballantine, 1971 (Paperback)

LOEWENFELD, CLAIRE and BACK, PHILIPPA, *Herbs, Health & Cookery.* New York: Hawthorn Books, 1967 (Paperback: Award Books)

MILLER, MARJORIE, *Introduction to Health Foods.* Los Angeles: Nash Quality Paperback, 1971 (Paperback)

TOBE, JOHN, *"No-Cook" Book.* St. Catherine's, Ontario: Provoker Press, 1969

TONSLEY, CECIL, *Honey for Health.* New York: Award Books, 1970 (Paperback)

VITHALDAS, YOGI and ROBERTS, SUSAN, *The Yogi Cookbook.* New York: Crown Publishers, 1968 (Paperback: Pyramid)

WADE, CARLSON, *Carlson Wade's Health Food Recipes for Gourmet Cooking.* New York: Arc Books, Inc., 1969 (Paperback)

WALKER, N. W., *Diet and Salad Suggestions.* Phoenix: Norwalk Press, 1952 (Paperback)

WALKER, N. W., *Raw Vegetable Juices.* Phoenix: Norwalk Press, 1953 (Paperback)

WARMBRAND, MAX, *Eat Well to Keep Well.* New York: Pyramid, 1970 (Paperback)

(All by different contributors), *The "About" Series,* Nos. 1 through 38 on Diet. London: Thorsons Ltd., 1950-1970 (Paperback)

4. NUTRITION BOOKS

Composition of Foods, Agricultural Handbook No. 8. Washington, D.C.: Government Printing Office, 1963

FLECK, HENRIETTA C. and MUNVES, ELIZABETH, *Introduction to Nutrition.* New York: Macmillan, 1962

FOOD & NUTRITION BOARD, *Recommended Dietary Allowances.* Washington, D.C.: National Academy of Sciences, 1968 (Paperback)

LEVERTON, RUTH, *Food Becomes You.* Ames, Iowa: Iowa State University Press, 1965 (Paperback: Doubleday)

THE NUTRITION FOUNDATION, *Food: A Key to Better Health.* New York: The Nutrition Foundation, 1970 (Paperback)

STARE, FREDERICK J., M.D., *Eating for Good Health.* New York: Doubleday, 1964 (Paperback: Cornerstone Library)

5. CONSUMERISM AND ENVIRONMENTALISM BOOKS

BAY LAUREL, ALICIA, *Living on the Earth.* New York: Random House, 1971 (Paperback: Vintage)

BENARDE, MELVIN A., *The Chemicals We Eat.* New York: American Heritage Press, 1971

BICKNELL, FRANK, M.D., *Chemicals in Your Food.* London: Emerson Books, Inc., 1961

CARSON, RACHEL, *Silent Spring.* Boston: Houghton Mifflin, 1962 (Paperback: Fawcett)

GARRISON, OMAR V., *The Dictocrats Attack on Health Food and Vitamins.* New York: Arc Books, 1970 (Paperback)

GRAHAM, FRANK, *Since Silent Spring.* Boston: Houghton Mifflin, 1970

HARMER, RUTH MULVEY, *Unfit for Human Consumption.* Englewood Cliffs, N.J.: Prentice-Hall, 1971

HOWARD, SIR ALBERT, *The Soil and Health.* Old Greenwich, Conn.: Devin-Adair, 1947

HUNTER, BEATRICE TRUM, *Consumer Beware.* New York: Simon & Schuster, 1971

MARGOLIUS, SIDNEY, *The Great American Food Hoax.* New York: Walker & Co., 1971

RIENOW, ROBERT and LEONA TRAIN, *Moment in the Sun.* New York: Dial, 1967 (Paperback: Ballantine)

TRAGER, JAMES, *The Enriched, Fortified, Concentrated, Country-Fresh, Lip-Smacking, Finger-Licking, International, Unexpurgated Foodbook.* New York: Grossman, 1970

TURNER, JAMES S. (Ralph Nader Study Group), *The Chemical Feast, the Report on the Food and Drug Administration.* New York: Grossman, 1970 (Paperback)

WILEY, FARIDA A., ed., *John Burroughs' America.* Old Greenwich, Conn.: Devin-Adair, 1951

6. HEALTH THEORY BOOKS

AIROLA, PAAVO O., *Health Secrets from Europe.* New York: Arc Books, 1971 (Paperback)

BIELER, HENRY, M.D., *Food Is Your Best Medicine.* New York: Random House, 1966

BRAGG, PAUL C., *Healthful Eating Without Confusion.* Burbank, Calif.: Health Science, 1971 (Paperback)

CLARK, LINDA, *Get Well Naturally*. Old Greenwich, Conn.: Devin-Adair, 1968 (Paperback: Arc Books)

CLARK, LINDA, *Secrets of Health and Beauty*. Old Greenwich, Conn.: Devin-Adair, 1969 (Paperback: Pyramid)

CLARK, LINDA, *Stay Young Longer*. New York: Pyramid, 1968 (Paperback)

DAVIS, ADELLE, *Let's Eat Right to Keep Fit*. New York: Harcourt, Brace, Jovanovich, Inc., 1954 (Paperback: New American Library)

DAVIS, ADELLE, *Let's Get Well*. New York: Harcourt, Brace, Jovanovich, Inc., 1965

DAVIS, ADELLE, *Let's Have Healthy Children*. New York: Harcourt, Brace, Jovanovich, Inc., 1951

HAUSER, GAYELORD, *Look Younger, Live Longer*. New York: Fawcett Crest Book, 1951 (Paperback)

MARSH, EDWARD E., *How to be Healthy with Natural Foods*. New York: Arc Books, 1967 (Paperback)

NEWMAN, LAURA, *Make Your Juicer Your Drug Store*. New York: Beneficial Books, 1970 (Paperback)

ROSE, IAN F., *Faith, Love and Seaweed*. New York: Award Books, 1969 (Paperback)

WAERLAND, EBBA, *Rebuilding Health*. New York: Arc Books, 1968 (Paperback)

WEINER, JOAN, *Get Your Health Together*. New York: Lancer Books, 1971 (Paperback)

7. DICTIONARIES AND DIRECTORIES

BALFOUR, MICHAEL, ed., *The Health Food Guide* (covers U.K.). London: Garnstone Press, 1970 (Paperback)

DE SOLA, RALPH and DOROTHY, *A Dictionary of Cooking*. New York: Hawthorn Books, 1969

RODALE, J. I. and Staff, *Encyclopedia of Organic Gardening*. Emmaus, Pa.: Rodale Books, 1959

RODALE, J. I. and Staff, *The Organic Directory*. Emmaus, Pa.: Rodale Books, 1971 (Paperback)

SKRECZKO, LYNNE, *The Natural Guide to Health Food Stores and Restaurants in and Around New York*. New York: Ballantine Books, 1971 (Paperback)

8. MISCELLANEOUS BOOKS

HARRIS, BEN CHARLES, *Eat the Weeds*. Barre, Mass.: Barre Publishers, 1971 (Paperback)

HUNTER, BEATRICE TRUM, *Gardening Without Poisons*. Boston: Houghton Mifflin, 1964 (Paperback: Berkley Medallion Books)

KAYSING, BILL, *The Ex-Urbanite's Complete and Illustrated Easy-Does-It First Time Farmer's Guide*. San Francisco: Straight Arrow Books, 1971

MEDSGER, OLIVER PERRY, *Edible Wild Plants*. New York: Macmillan, 1966

OGDEN, SAMUEL, *Step-by-Step to Organic Vegetable Growing*. New York: David McKay, 1971

Staff of Organic Gardening and Farming, *The Organic Way to Plant Protection*. New York: World Publishing Co., 1969

RODALE, J. I. and Staff, *How to Grow Vegetables and Fruits by the Organic Method*. Emmaus, Pa.: Rodale Books, 1961

ROLLINS, R. L., FERNALD, M. L. and KINSEY, A. C., *Edible Wild Plants of Eastern North America*. New York: Harper & Row, 1958

STOUT, RUTH, *Gardening Without Work*. Old Greenwich, Conn.: Devin Adair, 1961

9. PERIODICALS

Environment. Committee for Environmental Information, 438 N. Skinker Blvd., St. Louis, Mo. 63130

Fitness for Living Magazine. Rodale Press, 33 East Minor Street, Emmaus, Pa. 18049

Health for All. Gateway House, Bedford Park, Croydon CR 9 2AT, Surrey, England

Health From Herbs. 14 Dransfield Road, Sheffield S10, 5Rn, England

Herald of Health. Paragon Publications, Mount Ayr, Iowa 50854

Let's Live Magazine. 444 North Larchmont Blvd., Los Angeles, Calif. 90004

Natural Food and Farming. Natural Food Association, Box 210, Atlanta, Tex. 75551

Natural Life Styles. 53 Main Street, New Paltz, N.Y. 12561

The Order of the Universe. Box 203, Prudential Center Station, Boston, Mass. 02199

Organic Gardening and Farming. Rodale Press, 33 East Minor Street, Emmaus, Pa. 18049

Organic Gardening Guide to Organic Living. Rodale Press, 33 East Minor Street, Emmaus, Pa. 18049

Prevention. Rodale Press, 33 East Minor Street, Emmaus, Pa. 18049

INDEX